Magic by the Bay

Magic by the Bay

How the Oakland Athletics
and San Francisco Giants
captured the baseball world

JOHN SHEA
JOHN HICKEY

with illustrations by
THOM ROSS

North Atlantic Books
Berkeley, California

To Zdena for her love and support, and Jan for his inspiration.
With love to Mom, Terry, Mike, Dan and Frank.
In memory of Dad.

— John Shea

In memory of Jim Hickey.

— John Hickey

Magic By the Bay
How the Oakland Athletics and San Francisco Giants
captured the baseball world

Copyright © 1990 by John Shea and John Hickey

ISBN 1-55643-086-8

Published by North Atlantic Books
2800 Woolsey Street
Berkeley, California 94705

Cover photographs by Martin Klimek (below), Chuck Porteous (above)
Back cover photograph by Scott Henry
Cover and book design by Paula Morrison
Production by Lori Pelton
Edited by Rob Krier, Terry Shea, Jon Stein

Magic by the Bay is sponsored by the Society for the Study of Native
Arts and Sciences, a nonprofit educational corporation whose goals are to
develop an ecological and crosscultural perspective linking various scien-
tific, social, and artistic fields; to nurture a holistic view of arts, sciences,
humanities, and healing; and to publish and distribute literature on the
relationship of mind, body, and nature.

Library of Congress Cataloging-in-Publication Data
Shea, John, 1958–
  Magic by the bay : how the Oakland Athletics and the San Francisco
Giants captured the baseball world / by John Shea and John Hickey.
    p.   cm.
  ISBN 1-55643-086-8 : $12.95
  1. San Francisco Giants (Baseball team) 2. Oakland Athletics
(Baseball team) 3. World series (Baseball) I. Hickey, John, 1950-.
II. Title.
GV875.S34S34   1990
796.357'646—dc20
                                                    90–31854
                                                    CIP

Table of Contents

Acknowledgments

The authors wish to thank Jay Silverberg, Mark Whittington, Peter Horvitz, Lori Pelton, John Brown, Ed Padgett, Scott Henry, Frankie Frost, Martin Klimek, Robert Tong, Marian Little-Utley, Beth Renneisen, Larry Stone, Barry Locke, Dino Vournas, Jay Clapper, Barry Bloom, Kirk Kenney, Jeff Frank, Marie Linvill, Bob Stanley, Duffy Jennings, Matt Fischer, Robin Carr, Dirk Smith, Jay Alves, Kathy Jacobson, Eric Kubota, Mickey Morabito and, of course, managers Tony La Russa and Roger Craig and their players.

FOREWORD
Roger Craig

In the 40 years I've been in baseball, I've had more satisfaction in 1989 than in any other year. People thought we couldn't win. They predicted we'd finish fourth or fifth, but I had a feeling the season could be special. I'm not the kind of guy to say "I told you so," and I never told that to anyone all season. But looking back at everything that happened, we just had an unreal year. Even though we lost four in a row in the World Series, it almost feels as if we won it all because we did have such a good year.

I remember the first day of spring training. Al Rosen and I usually go to Arizona early to play golf and set up spring training. We had been criticized for not going out and getting an outfielder or someone who could hit the long ball, but we both thought Kevin Mitchell was on the verge of becoming a star. People were talking trades — Scott Garrelts and Mitchell for Danny Tartabull — and all kinds of things, but we didn't want to do anything. Kevin's first day of batting practice in spring training was absolutely wonderful. He looked great. We thought he'd have a great year. It wouldn't have taken a genius to figure that out. Kevin hit two home runs on Opening Day and never stopped.

Judging pitchers in spring training is almost a waste of time, and we weren't about to make judgments on guys like Rick Reuschel and Don Robinson. But besides Mitchell, the biggest plus of the year was making Garrelts a starter back in spring training. I had made him a starter in 1986, but he would have rather been the bullpen closer. Out of necessity, I eventually put him back in the bullpen, but I knew deep down in my heart that he could be a better starter. When he did make the change in the spring, he became a pitcher instead of just a thrower. And he went on to have a great year.

There were many key moments during the regular season: The

mid-season Steve Bedrosian acquisition made a big difference, Dave Dravecky's comeback was an inspiration to everybody, and the final days of the season when the San Diego Padres were hot made us a better team. Jack Clark and the Padres played like heck in the last month — we were good, but they were great — but we managed to stay in first place. In fact, one of our greatest accomplishments was staying in first place for 111 straight days.

Through it all, our fans have been fabulous. I remember after we lost the playoffs in 1987, they met us at the airport and were very supportive and emotional. I remember the chant, "Can't wait 'til '88." We didn't do it in '88, but we sure did in '89. My fan mail has been unreal. There's been so much, I still haven't read it all. And everyone has been positive when looking back at the season.

It's hard to believe that Don Zimmer and I were talking late in spring training about how things didn't look so good for either of us. It seemed we were losing in the ninth inning to Oakland every day, but I think I felt better about the Giants than he felt about the Cubs. We were picked to finish fourth or fifth, and he was picked to finish fifth or sixth. It's funny how we both won our divisions and met each other in the National League playoffs.

In the World Series, baseball had to take a back seat to the earthquake. It probably had an effect on us. The toughest part was the long delay and the constant working out. It was difficult to keep players motivated, but I thought we were ready to play when the games resumed. We just didn't play that well. The A's are a great team, and give them credit. But we feel very good about what happened. Finishing second out of 26 teams is quite a feat.

Bob Lurie has gone all out. He gave us beautiful rings. I've been in six World Series and won four of them, but this is the most beautiful ring I've ever received. It's just another reminder of the success we enjoyed in 1989.

It's a year people will think back on as the year of the earthquake, but I won't think of it that way. I'll think of 1989 as a great year for the San Francisco Giants.

FOREWORD
Tony La Russa

On that night in Candlestick Park when the last out meant the world championship, my first reaction was crystal clear: a group hug with the coaches and trainers in the dugout. But afterward, it was a blur. It was tough to focus on anything except a growing sense of satisfaction. I remember the first two hours as a series of interviews and congratulations among players and members of our organization, which included our families, a welcome part of the clubhouse celebration.

Once there was quiet, I wanted to understand why the satisfaction of winning the world championship was felt so strongly. In time, I realized that there were many pieces to winning and that each added something special. What these pieces are and how they came together make for a great story, a story of a talented team with personality and character that was able to win with power and finesse. Each day, I understand it better and enjoy it more.

It all started with the commitment at the ownership level and carried through to the player development system. Looking back, I'm especially proud of how everyone in the organization from day one made the commitment to win the world championship. That resolve to win was tested time after time. There was the adversity of the first-half injuries. Had we backed off, any or all of them could have overwhelmed us. But the team and the organization toughed it out, made the adjustments necessary and kept competing.

In terms of adjustments, one of the best examples was our front office's response to our offense becoming vulnerable in mid-season. Sandy Alderson made a trade for Rickey Henderson that not only added a key player, but reaffirmed the organization's commitment to compete. The final example of our commitment was the team's reaction to the tragic interruption in the World Series caused by the earthquake. During the delay, everywhere I looked, the team's message was clear — whenever and wherever we would resume, the A's would be ready.

As a matter of fact, we had been ready to compete virtually every day for two years. We won a total of 109 games in 1988 and 107 in 1989. The entire organization has contributed to those 216 wins. But the majority of the credit should go to our players. They have taken their outstanding talent, established respect and closeness among themselves and matched it with a desire to play baseball with 100 percent effort and execution. Especially in this championship season, our players should be recognized for how often and how deep they had to reach to succeed.

The players deserve special credit for repeating successful seasons. In 1988, they reached almost total success. In 1989, they dealt with that success without losing effectiveness and, in fact, they achieved even more.

After losing to the Dodgers in 1988, we felt we understood what they had done right and what we had done wrong. But because we lost, we had to live with criticism that our success had been easy, that the Dodgers had a "book" on us, exposing our weaknesses and our inability to handle the pressure.

I suffered in relative silence. But among ourselves, we knew we had handled the pressure of being the 1988 pre-season favorite and then playing as a front-runner all season against tough competition, especially Boston in the playoffs. But the difference between knowing and showing was enough to set up our 1989 season.

That's why the world championship has extra significance. Our team answered the remaining questions. We first had to win a tight division race against very good competition. Next there were the tense and hotly contested playoffs. And finally there was the World Series success against a Giants team we knew well and respected. That generates a lot of warm memories.

In the end, there was no "book" on the A's. It's the same book for all of us. You take your best shot and let the numbers take care of themselves. Even now, the feeling of satisfaction helps. It drives us to take our best shot at winning and experience this satisfaction all over again.

Tony La Russa

Introduction

Incredible. Spectacular. Remarkable. Phenomenal.

All of the above, and more.

It was also magical.

The 1989 baseball season was one for the ages. Especially in the San Francisco Bay Area, where the two major-league teams found themselves pitted against each other in the 86th World Series.

Although each had previously appeared in the World Series, never before had the Oakland Athletics and San Francisco Giants gone all the way simultaneously. The 1989 season was different altogether, in several ways.

On the national level, the baseball spectrum encompassed a huge variety of scenes. From Jim Abbott's arrival to Mike Schmidt's departure. From Nolan Ryan's 5,000th strikeout to Pete Rose's lifetime banishment. From A. Bartlett Giamatti's arrival as commissioner to A. Bartlett Giamatti's sad and untimely death.

In the Bay Area, there were highs.

Kevin Mitchell's 47 home runs. Will Clark's .333 batting average. Scott Garrelts' league-leading 2.28 ERA. Dave Stewart's 21 wins. Carney Lansford's .336 batting average. Rickey Henderson's 52 steals.

And, of course, Dave Dravecky's comeback.

But there were lows.

Most notably, Dave Dravecky's comeback.

Dravecky played out a fantastic story that went beyond the game of baseball. It dealt with life and its rewards. It dealt with life and its pitfalls. More than anyone, Dravecky typified the season. His actions drew a variety of emotions. He brought people together, made them laugh and made them cry.

In the post-season, feelings were sky high as the Bay Area hosted its very own World Series. Some called it Bay's Ball. Some called it the BART Series after the Bay Area Rapid Transit system that links the two cities. Others called it the Bay Bridge Series. The latter name, a reference to the quickest route between San Francisco and Oakland, took on another meaning midway through the series when a devastating 7.1 earthquake shook Northern California and left the bridge impassable.

The quake hit October 17, postponing Game Three and leaving the World Series in doubt. Baseball was only an afterthought as the Bay Area put itself back together.

It was an unprecedented climax to an already eventful season. On their parallel paths, the Giants and A's attracted interest on a national level. In the Bay Area, loyalties were divided. On one hand, the A's outdrew the Giants for the second consecutive season. On the other hand, a Marin Independent Journal poll of residents in six Bay Area counties revealed 55 percent of the people favored the Giants and 45 percent were loyal to the A's.

By the end of September, both teams were winners. The A's had won their second straight division championship. The Giants had won their second in three years. Then came the playoffs, the final step to an A's-Giants World Series. With the A's ousting the Toronto Blue Jays in five games and the Giants beating the Chicago Cubs just as quickly, 1989 belonged to the Bay Area. The world's two best baseball teams were but a bay apart.

On to the World Series. This was history in the making. The first two games were played in Oakland, and the A's had a surprisingly easy time winning both of them. After a day off, the series moved to San Francisco for the first World Series game at Candlestick Park in 27 years. It was a lovely day. Willie Mays was set to throw out the first pitch. The Gatlin Brothers were tuning up to sing the National Anthem. More than 60,000 fans were settling into their seats. Millions more were switching on their TV sets at home.

The national telecast came on at 5 p.m., West Coast time. The third game of the World Series was just a half-hour from its scheduled first pitch — Don Robinson to Rickey Henderson. ABC-TV was opening its telecast by showing replays of Game Two. Dave Parker was chugging into second base, beating Candy Maldonado's throw for a fourth-inning double. The image is all too clear.

Then the earth rocked. And then it moved. Players, coaches and fans alike tried to stay still, and time stood still with them. The people watching their TVs could notice only unsteady camera work. Finally, after a long moment, announcer Al Michaels let the world know the story.

"... I think we're having an earth ..."

THE BEGINNINGS

How the Giants and A's prepared for the season

The Oakland A's and San Francisco Giants couldn't have been more different entering the spring of 1989. True, they both played baseball, and they both played it in the Bay Area. But their agendas were light years apart. Oakland manager Tony La Russa's job was to keep the A's from resting on their laurels. San Francisco manager Roger Craig's job was to get the Giants some laurels on which to rest.

Predicting an A's-Giants World Series before the season was almost laughable. The A's were the defending American League champions, acknowledged by many as the best team in baseball after 104 regular-season wins in 1988 and a four-game sweep of Boston in the playoffs before stumbling against Los Angeles in the World Series. The Giants were ne'er-do-wells in 1988. After winning the National League West in 1987, San Francisco won barely more games than it lost in 1988 and finished fourth.

The A's, some said, were a dynasty in the making. As for the Giants, well, who knew what to make of the Giants? There was considerable talent dressed out in orange and black, but considerable holes existed, too.

In one area, at least, the A's and Giants were alike. Both clubs opened the spring of 1989 with rosters substantially identical to the ones that had become so familiar in the Bay Area in '88. And while there was talk of a Bay Area World Series — every year there's that talk, at least in the Bay Area — the best chance for one metropolitan area to host a World Series seemed to be 3,000 miles away, where the Mets and Yankees were the talk of the town as everconfident New Yorkers speculated on the chances of viewing a Subway Series. But then, north of the border, speculation raged about the likelihood of a first All-Canadian World Series, with the Montreal Expos and Toronto Blue Jays looking to be two of the strongest teams in baseball. And the eyes of Texas were squarely focused on the possibility of a first Lone Star shootout, with the revamped Texas Rangers and the durable Houston Astros figuring to be in the chase all the way.

Even while the National Football League's San Francisco 49ers were dominating newspaper headlines with their drive to the Super Bowl, the A's and Giants were making enough noise in the winter to keep baseball from being relegated to the back page. Oakland signed free-agent pitcher Mike Moore in December. The Giants were shut out in the free-agent market, but general manager Al Rosen engineered a post-winter meetings trade that brought in outfielder Tracy Jones from Montreal in exchange for Mike Aldrete. Six weeks later, San Francisco added the veteran expertise of catcher Terry Kennedy, sending Bob Melvin to Baltimore to swing the deal. And word came from the Dominican Republic that Giants shortstop Jose Uribe spent three days in a San Cristobal jail before a charge against him of rape broke down for lack of evidence.

Whenever there was a dull day, chances were good that another Jose, Oakland's Jose Canseco, would be making headlines. For instance, Canseco got married to Esther Haddad — twice. In front of a Miami justice of the peace in early November, the outfielder and the former Miss Miami exchanged vows. About a month later, they re-enacted the wedding for family and friends.

Canseco, who would be starting only his fourth major-league season in 1989, already had proven to be one of a special breed. Like Reggie Jackson, George Brett or Pete Rose, Canseco had the innate knack of being able to dominate the sports pages — occasionally, even the news and business pages — 12 months a year. Everything he does — and, frequently, everything he doesn't do — is news. And so it was in the winter of 1988-89. He was stopped by Florida's highway patrol and ticketed for going 125 mph in his new Jaguar. He protested he wasn't doing 125 at all. "It was more like 140," he said. At least he was being honest. And Canseco's off-season would prove to last longer than most when, for the third straight year, he was the last of the A's to report to spring training at Scottsdale Community College.

While monitoring Canseco's tumultuous off-season appeared to be a full-time job, Oakland general manager Sandy Alderson and La Russa somehow found the time to set their strategy for the 1989 season. The A's were fortunate in that they hadn't lost any key players to free agency. They avoided that by signing center fielder Dave Henderson to a three-year contract. That done and with their roster virtually intact, they could address preparing for a season that others were already proclaiming as jinxed. Such proclamations weren't to be taken personally. But the reality is, there exists a de facto "no-repeat" rule in baseball. No team had made repeat trips to the World Series since the 1977-78 Yankees and Dodgers. Sometimes injuries would hold teams back. Sometimes complacency would. Frequently, though, the shackle was the fact that a pennant winner became a marked team, a team that every other took special pride in beating. Not every team can go to the World Series. But that doesn't mean that every team can't beat up on a World Series team.

And not every team that goes to the World Series wins. Even heavily favored teams can lose in a short, pressure-packed series where every hit and every out is magnified a hundredfold. Oakland did. The A's went into the 1988 World Series against Los Angeles as clearly the best team in baseball. But after the Dodgers pulled off one of the great World Series upsets by beating the A's in five games, Oakland was left without its final prize. Despite the outcome, it was tough to declare the Dodgers a superior team, man-for-man. Orel Hershiser had a career year and Kirk Gibson never lost his flair for the dramatic, but it was hard to see a lineup full of Mickey Hatchers, Franklin Stubbses and John Shelbys — even with the 1989 addition of Eddie Murray — working that kind of magic two years running.

Oakland, on the other hand, had lost its bid for the world title, and La Russa was fully prepared to use that loss as ammunition the following year. He entered the spring with only one significant player gone from the '88 team, that being Don Baylor. Oakland had made no attempt to re-sign Baylor, a deteriorating player who had already done his duty in Oakland. Baylor had been added to the 1988 roster as a designated hitter and steadying influence in the clubhouse. He didn't hit much, but he provided a reasoned voice, a voice of a winner — he'd been in the World Series with Boston in 1986 and with Minnesota in 1987. Perhaps his influence was most heavily felt with first baseman Mark McGwire.

Once a popular target of brushback pitches, the calm McGwire would seldom challenge pitchers throwing high and tight at his shoulders or even at his head. When hit, he'd drop his bat and trot to first base. Boston's Wes Gardner hit McGwire in the head in '87, and California's Kirk McCaskill did it in the first month of '88. The difference in the two beanings was that Baylor witnessed the second. Baylor, who was livid that anyone would throw at the A's meal ticket, was even more upset that McGwire didn't respond to the challenge. Baylor took McGwire aside and chewed him out. React, Baylor said. Respond. Be tough. Send a message. Several weeks later, when New York's Neil Allen came in high and tight, the 6-foot-5, 230-pound McGwire charged the mound, tackling Allen as both benches cleared. The word got out, and McGwire saw few pitches of that genre again.

Baylor had done his job, and that was one of the reasons the A's liked him. But there were drawbacks, such as his .220 overall average and .083 pinch-hitting average. But the clincher that blew his chances of returning in 1989 came on the eve of the 1988 World Series when Baylor took that leadership role too far. Understand that La Russa prefers a tight ship and rarely says anything that opponents can post in their clubhouse as a motivational tool. He especially doesn't want his players badmouthing the opponent. But Baylor did, ripping former A's reliever Jay Howell, who had been traded to the Dodgers.

After the Dodgers won the National League pennant, Howell asked if the Dodgers should apologize to Baylor, who had publicly wished for an A's-New York Mets World Series. Baylor read Howell's comment and popped off himself, suggesting Howell wasn't good enough to pitch for the A's. Baylor also said he wanted Howell to pitch against Oakland so the heavily favored A's could get a piece of him. Howell did pitch, and the A's did rock him. McGwire's home run in the ninth inning of Game Three gave the A's their first victory. But it turned out to be their last victory, as the Dodgers won the final two games. In Game Four, Howell got even when he induced McGwire to pop up with the bases loaded in the seventh, and he retired Canseco and Dave Parker in the ninth for the save.

La Russa obviously wasn't pleased with the result of his first World Series, and he was fuming over Baylor's untimely remarks. Shortly after the series, the A's announced Baylor was excluded from their future plans.

The A's didn't want to go into 1989 unchanged. After all, they fell three wins shy of baseball's ultimate achievement. Not willing to part with the talent and chemistry already on the payroll, they tried the free-agent market. Although the A's posted the league's lowest ERA in '88, Alderson subscribed to the theory that you can never have enough pitching. So Alderson set his sights on free-agent pitcher Mike Moore, late of the Seattle Mariners. Moore was a career 66-96 pitcher — just 18-34 the previous two seasons — but almost every club in baseball wanted the man with a fastball that Boston third baseman Wade Boggs compared favorably to Nolan Ryan's.

Moore, who in 1981 had been the first right-handed pitcher ever drafted as the nation's number one pick, spent his November days in the Phoenix suburb of Ahwatukee indulging himself in his passions for playing golf and working out. Then he'd come home to a library's worth of message slips from managers and general managers. "It was like college recruiting all over again," Moore said. "Everyone wanted to make their pitch." And no one pitched harder than Alderson, who gathered together his shock troops in late November and stormed Moore's Bastille. La Russa, pitching coach Dave Duncan and scout Ron Schueler went to Ahwatukee and pleaded the A's case.

Because Moore had played 6½ seasons for a Seattle team that never had a winning season, the A's didn't have to play hardball.

With just one winning season to his credit, Moore was ready to make the move to a winner. A week before the winter meetings in Atlanta, the A's signed Moore to a three-year, $3.95 million contract. Alderson drew some initial abuse for the move as critics pointed out that this newcomer who had never won a game for the A's was now Oakland's best-paid pitcher. Alderson readily admitted the inequity of the situation, especially regarding two-time 20-game winner Dave Stewart. But less than two weeks later, his strategy was borne out as the market for free-agent pitchers, particularly Bruce Hurst, went through the roof. It was seen then that Alderson had gotten a bargain price. Of course, that's all relative because Alderson later admitted the A's wouldn't have gone much higher to get Moore. But the Mariners, who offered Moore a three-year, $3.85-million deal, were never in contention, and St. Louis didn't want to commit to more than two years at $2.3 million. "The question is how you can pay somebody who hasn't won consistently that much money," Alderson admitted. "The answer for us is that he's never had the opportunity to pitch on the kind of club we have."

It was only after signing Moore that Alderson set out in pursuit of some help for the Oakland offense. Luis Polonia, the designated leadoff man, was a fiery singles hitter who could run. But he never walked much — if there is one statistic to which Alderson is wedded, it is on-base percentage — leaving the A's without a true leadoff hitter. In fact, for about half of the 1988 season, third baseman Carney Lansford led off simply because he was the only man among the bashers whom La Russa felt comfortable with in the position. So began Alderson's pursuit of Rickey Henderson. Henderson, an Oakland native and a star for five years with the A's before being traded to the Yankees, was wearing thin in a New York lineup that was growing older without getting better. The Yankees acquired him in 1984 and thought baseball's premier leadoff hitter would be the final piece to the puzzle. But the Yankees' propensity for trying to get by with pitching that is either too old or too awful ruined their chances. Still, Alderson was rebuffed repeatedly by the Yankees in his attempt to swing a deal for Henderson at the winter meetings. He never lost the Yankees' number, however, and months later he would still be at it, attempting to hammer out a deal that would solidify the Oakland offense.

Even without Henderson, the A's were the consensus pick to

win the West in 1989. But it was clear from the outset that the A's weren't going to take any chances in their drive to get back to the World Series and get it right this time. There was the dumping of Baylor that made Parker the full-time designated hitter. There was the signing of Moore. And then there was the pressure from La Russa, who attempted from the first day of spring training to combat any feeling of over-confidence that 1988's 104-win season had produced. Toward that end, La Russa invited friends and acquaintances with special knowledge about success to address the team from time to time during the spring. There was nationally syndicated political author George Will, who was writing a book about baseball in which La Russa was one of four central characters. There was Reggie Jackson, who'd retired after spending the 1987 season with the A's, to lend "Mr. October's" perspective. And there was Doug Williams, who'd quarterbacked the Washington Redskins into the Super Bowl and himself had been named Super Bowl MVP. "Every one of those men has a unique perspective that I think can help us," La Russa said. "These guys have been at the top. They know what it takes."

Unlike the year before, when they sported eight new faces — one third of the roster — the A's knew not only who they were but how good they could be during the spring of 1989. But clearly, this was not going to be a breeze. Reacting to the pressure applied when the A's added Moore to their arsenal, the rest of the West beefed up. Kansas City added Bob Boone to shore up a chronically weak catching corps. California added left-handed rookie Jim Abbott and right-handed veteran Bert Blyleven to its starting rotation. And the Rangers made the boldest moves of all, adding second baseman Julio Franco and first baseman Rafael Palmeiro in winter-meeting trades and signing free-agent pitcher Nolan Ryan, who was in quest of his 5,000th career strikeout. "If we want to be competitive (with Oakland), we have to be bold," Texas general manager Tom Grieve said.

If there was one factor telling against an Oakland repeat, it was history. Although Oakland was the logical favorite, repeating was still a tall order. The 1988 A's might have been considered the best team in baseball, but picking them to win the division again in 1989 was challenging history. Dynasties are things of the past, thanks largely to free agency, which does two drastic things to star players on star teams: It moves them to other teams, and it provides financial security. The spinoff of financial security is often complacency, and there's nothing worse in baseball than a complacent multimillionaire. If football teams don't repeat because of parity, baseball teams don't repeat because of complacency. Babe Ruth would laugh at the notion that titles aren't won in consecutive years because other teams are shooting for the champs. Soon after the Babe joined the Yankees in 1920, New York began its fabulous string of 33 pennants and 22 World Series over 60 years. The winning ended in 1982, when the Yankees finally joined the modern era and stopped repeating. The no-repeat syndrome has run rampant through the majors, as seemingly invincible teams flop in only one year. The '84 Tigers and '86 Mets were the decade's best hopes for winning consecutive World Series titles, but the '85 Tigers and '87 Mets ended up just like the '88 Twins. They couldn't even repeat in their own divisions.

The A's set out to change recent history, and La Russa used the five-game loss to the Dodgers the previous October as incentive. La Russa knew all too well about the repeat syndrome. His '83 White Sox won their division by 20 games. His '84 White Sox finished 14 games under .500. "I have to stress that last year was last year," La Russa said. "You can't expect the memory to carry you. We could use it to gain confidence, but this is a different year. The biggest thing for me is to present the challenge of repeating."

The Giants had no intention of repeating their '88 finish. They'd just as soon forget all about finishing fourth and think more about their division-winning season of '87. But prognosticators opt for the what-have-you-done-for-me-lately theory. And because the Giants were coming off a sorry ending to '88 and made only two significant winter move (some said both were insignificant) by trading Aldrete and Melvin for Jones and Kennedy, fourth place was expected once again.

The big cheeses of the National League West were supposed to be San Diego and Cincinnati. The Padres were the division's best team in the second half of 1988 and added Jack Clark and Bruce Hurst. The Reds, perennially the most talented team in the division but a victim of four straight second-place finishes, also expected big things despite a few whispers around Plant City, Florida, that manager Pete Rose might have been linked in some way or another to gambling.

Easily the most intriguing division entry was San Diego, seeking its first championship since the Garvey-Nettles-Gossage era of 1984. The Padres had the talent and the confidence. "We're going to win it," San Diego's Tony Gwynn said. Added Jack Clark, a Giant in a lesser era: "Everybody looks like they want to win some of that playoff money." Roger Craig, who got his first managing gig with the Padres, knew about the hype as much as anybody. Craig had built a stupendous log cabin on his 40 acres in the tiny northern San Diego County village of Warner Springs, and he kept track of all the Padres' winter news through the local papers. According to Craig's translation of the writings, which didn't blend well with his morning coffee, the Padres had all but clinched the National League pennant.

"They can do no wrong down here," Craig said before leaving for spring training. "I'm not going to knock their ballclub. I respect (manager) Jack McKeon. But we've got a 162-game season. They've finished strong the past two years, but let's see what they can do in a full season."

Strong words from Roger, but it was a clear indication that he believed his Giants shouldn't be overlooked by those prognosticators. But by examining the Giants on paper — and paper is all there is before Opening Day — it was difficult to imagine the Giants finishing any better than second.

The huge concerns with right fielder Candy Maldonado (would he continue to sink?) and third baseman Matt Williams (would he ever reach his potential?) were bad enough, but the pitching staff posed another disturbing and much larger problem. It was obvious the demise of the '88 club was caused by an epidemic of pitching injuries, and the pitchers' status didn't seem too improved entering 1989. Dave Dravecky developed a cancerous tumor in his left arm that put his odds of pitching again at no better than 1 in 10, and Mike Krukow underwent rotator-cuff surgery for the second time and wasn't expected to recover by the opener. That left Rick Reuschel, Kelly Downs, Don Robinson and Atlee Hammaker to form the rotation. And that foursome definitely lacked permanence. The 39-year-old Reuschel had a long history of arm problems; Downs missed part of '88 with a shoulder injury; Robinson hadn't started a full season since 1980; and Hammaker still wasn't at the stellar form he had reached before the '83 All-Star Game. The early favorite as fifth starter was Terry Mulholland, who had missed much of the previous season with a broken forearm. Even relievers Mike LaCoss and Joe Price were coming off operations.

To add insult to injury, Scott Garrelts was penciled in for another season as the bullpen closer. Craig made it known over the winter that Garrelts would be his "pet project," and the manager was prepared to convert Garrelts into another Dennis Eckersley, using him only in save situations. Garrelts always had been one of the game's best relievers while warming up in the bullpen, but for some reason he lost his stuff on the way to the mound.

Three-fourths of the infield and two-thirds of the outfield were already in place. The Giants' lineup would be set if only Williams could complement Will Clark, Robby Thompson and Jose Uribe. And if only Maldonado could play with Brett Butler and Kevin Mitchell. The other department in question, catching, didn't seem promising, either, thanks to Kirt Manwaring, an untested and passive big-leaguer of just 40 games, and Terry Kennedy, who came over from Baltimore in a catcher-for-catcher deal involving Bob Melvin. The trade didn't seem beneficial on the surface at first — Melvin, 28, hit .234 with eight homers and 27 RBIs, and Kennedy, 32, hit .228 with three and 16 — but general manager Al Rosen was playing a hunch that a return to the National League and a reunion with his father, Giants executive Bob Kennedy, might give him a lift.

With only a couple of cosmetic changes, the Giants were all too similar to the club that finished 11½ games behind the Dodgers in '88. Although he desperately tried, Rosen had struck out in his efforts to obtain any marquee players. He K'd with Dale Murphy and Joe Carter. He whiffed with Nolan Ryan. And he even went down swinging with his astonishing proposal to land Don Mattingly for Clark. Giants fans, whether they liked it or not, were forced to accept their team as is.

And "as is" meant putting up with some pretty weighty off-field news on one of the incumbent players. While the A's brass was forced to answer for Canseco, the Giants had their own riddle in Jose Uribe. Deserving or not, the Jose brothers brought batches of terrible public relations to their clubs.

The charge against Uribe was threatening a woman with a gun and raping her, and Uribe spent three days in jail in San Cristobal, Dominican Republic. The case was dropped because of insufficient evidence. Despite the closed case, several conflicting stories went unresolved. First of all, Dominican newspapers reported that the woman was a 20-year-old named Elisa Altagracia Moreno. But when Uribe arrived at spring training, he said the woman was a longtime neighbor named Judy and that she was 19 years old. Even though Uribe called the woman a friend, he was unable to recall her last name.

In Arizona, Uribe met with the media to discuss the episode in length. It was the second time in eight months Uribe was asked to divulge his inner feelings following a traumatic personal experience. Midway through the '88 season, Uribe's wife died of heart failure while giving birth to the couple's third child, a boy named Enrique. After Sara Uribe's death, Jose was placed on the disabled list for "emotional stress." The Giants told him he could take as much time as he needed, but he insisted on returning after missing only 15 games.

It's simple to understand that Uribe's problems dwarfed Canseco's. But while Uribe is a lesser-known public figure in this country — he's an all-field, no-hit shortstop who struggles with the English language — Canseco demands attention from fans and non-fans alike, and this off-season was definitely no exception.

Typically, baseball emerges from its annual winter dormancy slowly, but Canseco rocketed out of the gate ahead of the pack, got an early jump on the headlines and remained near the front page throughout the spring. His off-field season started on a rural, southern Florida road early in February, just after he'd signed a new one-year contract for $1.6 million. But even before signing the contract, the man who is arguably the nation's best-known Miamian had a new toy, courtesy of his appearance in the '88 World Series. Canseco, after a grand slam in his second at-bat in Game One, went hitless the rest of the series. Although the A's lost, it was still worthwhile financially, because each player on the losing team received nearly $100,000, which was enough to cover Canseco's 1989 candy-apple red Jaguar XJS V12.

A toy like that was just the thing to set baseball's first 40-homer, 40-steals man apart from the crowd. It did, and the Florida Highway Patrol was one of the first to notice. Early in the morning of February 10, Canseco tried to see just what his new bauble could do. A wholly natural reaction perhaps. After all, he wasn't doing anything many other Americans wouldn't do on their way to maturity. On the other hand, many of them can't afford a car that doesn't break a sweat until the speedometer reaches triple figures.

Canseco was spotted by the highway patrol, chased and pulled over, after which he was cited for reckless driving and traveling at 125 mph. That, as he freely admitted, was only because the patrol's speed gun didn't register anything higher.

It already had been a momentous off-season for Canseco. He'd missed a mid-February card show to which he'd committed in Rochester, New York, forcing the promoters to reimburse ticketholders. Canseco said he missed his flight from Miami to Rochester because his associate David Valdes was asleep when Federal Express attempted to deliver the tickets. (Remember Valdes' name; it always seems to crop up when Jose's in trouble. Jose calls him his cousin, although he's no blood relative, just a chum since school days.) A Rochester radio station jumped on Canseco with both feet, inviting fans to get their revenge by sending Canseco a life-sized Jose Canseco "Slam-O-Gram." The promoters, Jim Kelly and Kevin Boden, sued Canseco over his non-appearance, and Canseco filed a countersuit for defamation of character, claiming he didn't receive his airline tickets on time. The matter wasn't settled until an out-of-court compromise was reached after the season, with Canseco agreeing to appear in another show promoted by the two men. Canseco also skipped an important awards dinner in Baltimore, which was to honor him as baseball's top home-run hitter. Both incidents cost him dearly in goodwill with the public, which wanted to see him badly enough to pay for the privilege.

The saga continued as Canseco arrived on a brisk February morning — late — to the A's spring training camp. La Russa arranged to have the club's daily morning meeting interrupted by a man in a mask, and the interloper breezed into the room, went immediately to Canseco and frisked him. The players and coaches broke up at the gag. Even Canseco, who hadn't lost the ability to laugh at himself after his tumultuous off-season, broke into a smile. La Russa said in his best Bogart deadpan, "We didn't find a gun." They didn't at the time. But it wouldn't be too long before Canseco and handguns were in the spotlight in a much less humorous context.

Canseco's name was linked to firearms even before he began his show-stopping, headline-making, late-night appearances on highway patrol radar guns across America. In January, he and Valdes were in a hurry to board a plane in Detroit's Metropolitan Airport when Valdes set off alarms while going through the security gate. Valdes was apprehended for carrying a handgun in a briefcase that also contained a great deal of the money Canseco had earned for signing autographs over the weekend at a Detroit-area baseball card show. Ballplayers frequently get paid in cash for such signings, so the money was nothing extraordinary. But the gun was. Valdes was arrested, and Canseco was questioned before being released. As always, Canseco had an explanation.

"I have a license to carry a gun, and my cousin has a license to carry a gun," Canseco said. "When you are doing shows in places like New York, sometimes you need to carry a gun because you often carry a lot of cash. He put the gun in his briefcase and forgot to put it back in his suitcase. When it happened, he said, 'Oh my God, I forgot.' "

La Russa, who had never taken much of a liking to the Valdes influence in the on-going Canseco saga, sought throughout the spring to separate Canseco from his longtime companion. Canseco had used Valdes' name as an excuse once in 1988 when he reported 90 minutes late to a night game. It seemed that Valdes, Canseco and some companions were shopping at the Tanforan Shopping Center south of San Francisco that afternoon. They lost track of time, realized it was getting late and then tried to rush. Valdes, driving Canseco's car, was stopped for speeding. Canseco was fined by La Russa, who wasn't crazy about the excuse his star presented. The manager resigned himself to the knowledge that he couldn't control how Canseco spent his time away from the park or with whom that time was spent. But Valdes was banned from the A's spring training workout facilities at Scottsdale Community College and Phoenix Municipal Stadium. If Valdes wanted to see Canseco in an Oakland uniform, the best he could hope for from La Russa would be to buy a ticket. "I've got just the spot for David Valdes," the manager said the day Canseco reported to camp. He then pointed to the top of the mountains that ring Phoenix's Valley of the Sun. "That's as close as he's getting to our workouts."

It didn't help Canseco's rapidly deteriorating public image that late spring training also would see it revealed that Valdes had been in possession of steroids back in January in Detroit. The banned drug was discovered in Valdes' briefcase when he was arrested for carrying the loaded handgun through the security system at the airport. This was the third time Canseco's name had been linked to steroids. Late in the 1988 season, Washington Post columnist Thomas Boswell said on national television that Canseco's use of steroids was well-known, although he didn't support that claim. Canseco and agent Dennis Gilbert said they considered suing Boswell but opted not to. Then during the spring of 1989, Margo Adams, the mistress of Boston's Wade Boggs who did a series of tell-all articles for Penthouse magazine, said Boggs told her Canseco used steroids.

While two steroids charges could be dismissed easily, the third, with Valdes carrying them as the two men traveled together, could not. Canseco said the slightly built Valdes had a prescription for the steroids to combat a physical problem. And he railed at being portrayed in the media as a man with Ben Johnson disease, a man who had bulked up to his current 6-foot-4, 240 pounds by using the banned muscle builders. "Do steroids give you coordination?" Canseco asked. "No way. Nowadays, players are going to the weight room. Look at superstars like Bo Jackson. He's the best athlete I've ever seen. Why should I say he takes steroids? That's way out of line. Why would I try to take away from his athletic ability? But that's what people are trying to do to me — to take way from all the hard work I put in. There are no short cuts."

For all of his off-field problems, Canseco's off-season was far from an entirely miserable experience. He bought a house on a small island near Miami. When his twin brother was married in November, Jose gave his old house to Ozzie Canseco — an A's minor-league prospect — as a wedding present. And Ozzie, of course, wasn't the only newlywed in the family. When Jose married Esther Haddad, his girlfriend of one year, in November, he won a $10,000 bet from teammate Dave Stewart. One day in the spring of 1988 while the rest of their teammates were involved in an exhibition game, Stewart and Canseco were in the locker room discussing the meaning of life and other questions of the day when Canseco mentioned that he was going to be married after the 1988 season. The pitcher, who'd seen Canseco introduce other young women as his fiancee before this, wasn't buying. "There's no way," Stewart said at the time. "You won't do it." And when Canseco continued to insist otherwise, Stewart said he was so sure Canseco would back out, he'd pay for the wedding if it occurred before the end of the calendar year. Canseco's eyes lit up, and when he attempted to pin Stewart down, the bet was whittled down to a more moderate $10,000 — "It'll be a really big wedding," Canseco said. Stewart, who at the time was in the middle of renegotiating his contract, predicted that if he had to pay, "it'll come out of my Cy Young incentive clause money."

As it happened, Stewart could have saved himself a couple of big bucks if he hadn't made the switch to the flat $10,000. Operating on the spur of the moment, Haddad and Canseco were married in front of a Miami justice of the peace in early November. There would be a bigger wedding for family and friends later, but the deed had been done, with pocket change. The bet was the subject of frequent clubhouse banter for the whole of the 1989 season. Stewart said he put the check in the mail and never got it back. Canseco said he never received it. Stewart said he had sent one check and his obligation was complete; Jose wasn't getting another. For the rest of the year, whenever one of the men wanted to agitate the other, the disputed $10,000 would be among the first harpoons thrown.

The $10,000 controversy was mild compared with the $75,000 controversy — that Technicolor nightmare on four wheels. Time and again, the Jaguar would accompany Canseco as he sped into headlines across the nation. In an early April benefit in which Canseco was saluted at a Bay Area roast, La Russa nodded from the podium and said, only half-jokingly, "We're here to honor speed and power. It's strange that a red Jaguar would get that much attention." It seems the Jag got Canseco everywhere fast, except for spring training. In fact, ever since winning the Rookie of the Year Award in 1986, Canseco hadn't found a way to make it to the park on time, and even a car capable of 150 mph wouldn't do it this time around. Teammates Stan Javier and Luis Polonia also were late, but through no fault of their own. The U.S. Government didn't get their work visas to them in their native Dominican Republic. As for Canseco, well . . .

In 1987, Canseco reported late over a contract dispute. That raised no eyebrows. In baseball, it happens all the time. But in 1988, Canseco scheduled a baseball card show for the weekend the A's were to report, and he infuriated the Oakland front office by putting the card show ahead of the requested reporting date. When he finally did arrive, he did so the last possible day before being subject to fines. In 1989, though, he was just late. There were no conflicts with the February 22 reporting date, but there was also no Canseco until 24 hours later. Ironically, Canseco said when he arrived that he was looking to keep a low profile after his high-visibility winter. It wasn't to be.

While returning from dinner on the night of March 2, Canseco, who had shipped the Jaguar to Arizona from Florida, was pulled over by Phoenix police officer Barry Kissell near the Doubletree Hotel that the A's use as their spring training headquarters. It was one of the more memorable pull-overs in Phoenix history. For starters, Canseco received a ticket for running a red light. He also was cited for not carrying a driver's license, for having license plates that were not registered to the car — it turned out they belonged to Esther's white Corvette — and for not carrying proof of insurance. One pull-over, four citations. For a time, the A's brass attempted to brush off the incident. But by this time, Canseco had become a sore spot with management. Faced with having to respond to the media at every Canseco transgression, both La Russa and Alderson met with Canseco the following day, both men attempting to urge Canseco to moderate his public behavior. Alderson admitted he couldn't find any fault with the police, either in Florida or Phoenix, for paying special attention to the one-of-a-kind Jaguar. "Driving a car like that is an open invitation to every law-enforcement officer in the Western Hemisphere," he told Oakland Tribune reporter Kit Stier. "The only place that car wouldn't get stopped is Colombia."

Another minor but telling incident pitted Canseco against Reggie Jackson. Jackson was Canseco's teammate in 1987 and a man Canseco deemed his spiritual father, at least as far as baseball goes. At one point in the 1987 season, Canseco, then a second-year player, asked Jackson if he could wear his number, 44, after Reggie retired. Jackson, who would soon quit the game after putting in a Hall-of-Fame career, was pleased no end by the thought and agreed. But Canseco, afraid number 44 would be retired by the club, stuck with his own 33. One of Jackson's stay-close-to-baseball jobs — he fell short in his goals to land a front office job with the A's or buy a piece of a major-league team — was as an occasional sportscaster for the ESPN television network. Jackson and the network had arranged to interview Canseco early in the spring for a feature to be aired on ESPN, but Canseco never showed.

Canseco's off-season extended far beyond the off-season of his teammates because of a wrist injury that kept him out through the All-Star break. While the rest of the A's were busy playing baseball, Canseco was living life on the disabled list. And in the fast lane, still. The world by now had realized that taking Canseco away from the ballpark only spelled trouble, and the Jag was to have yet another moment of infamy. But this time, the car played second fiddle to a 9mm handgun.

Early in the season, Jose and Esther left their East Bay home and drove the Jaguar to the University of California-San Francisco's Laurel Heights campus for special testing on the left wrist, testing that couldn't be done at San Francisco Children's Hospital, the home base for Oakland team doctors Allan Pont and Rick Bost. The trip to UCSF was uneventful, and the report by the examining doctors was positive. A Magnetic Resonance Imaging test revealed that the earlier diagnosis of strained ligament damage was incorrect. Instead, it was discovered that Canseco had a stress fracture of the hamate bone in his left wrist, a virtual duplicate of an injury that had struck down his brother, Ozzie, early in the A's spring training camp. Jose was given clearance to join Ozzie and begin an injury rehabilitation assignment at Double-A Huntsville to test the strength of the wrist.

The Cansecos were flush with the good news of his eminent return to baseball when they walked out of the hospital. Minutes later, all those good feelings were forgotten when Jose was arrested while getting into his car. While the Cansecos were in the hospital, the flashy Jag apparently had drawn many spectators, one of whom reported to police that a gun was lying on the floor. University police responded, ran a check on the license plate — by this time it was correctly in place — and waited for Canseco to appear. Then they made the arrest after finding a loaded 9mm semiautomatic pistol. Canseco was released several hours later after a tearful Esther posted bail. Under California law, it is a felony to take a weapon onto any University of California campus. Canseco was charged with the felony and also with the misdemeanor offense of having a loaded firearm in a vehicle.

The arraignment in San Francisco Municipal Court was straight out of the Marx Brothers. A court bailiff and a sheriff's deputy were among those who asked him for autographs. A group of fans cheered him as he entered the courtroom. And even Municipal Judge David Garcia didn't get too worked up over the severity of the charges filed against the celebrity in his midst. The judge elicited considerable laughter from his crowded courtroom when he

indicated that Canseco should have no trouble making the June 8
date set for his preliminary hearing despite the fact that, "I understand he occasionally is out of this jurisdiction for business reasons. I have heard he's even been seen as far away as Toronto."
Through lawyer Michael Stepanian, Canseco entered a not-guilty
plea to both charges before leaving the courtroom to more ap-
plause.

Away from the courtroom, Canseco again defended his right —
his need — to carry a gun. He said he'd gotten in the habit of carrying the pistol after getting "more than one" threatening telephone
call and after being harassed while driving the Jaguar on Bay Area
streets. However, he had not reported any threatening calls either
to the police or to the A's before the gun furor erupted. He pleaded
ignorance of the law in taking the gun onto the UC campus but
refused to put on a false show of remorse for having the gun or for
having it in clear view. He reminded everyone that he's from Miami, where, he claimed, it's advantageous to have the gun on display instead of hidden.

The A's were suddenly in the midst of a personal arms debate.
Even La Russa said, "I think there is a significant amount of people
in the public eye who carry guns. Politicians carry guns." Glenn
Hubbard, a 10-year veteran but not a player to catch the public eye
like Canseco, said he often felt uneasy for his family. "When I
drove out to spring training this year with my wife and kids, I was
carrying a gun," Hubbard said. "You are always a target. So much
can happen. You don't ever want to even think about using it, but
it's there if you need it." Dave Parker took it one step further — or
six. Parker said he owns a half-dozen handguns after first purchasing one during his final couple of seasons with the Pittsburgh Pirates. "I carried one in a shoulder holster the last couple of years I
was there." he said. "It was because of the animosity, most of it
created by the press. I got death threats. My mail box was blown
up. My house was broken into. I felt like my life was threatened."
Parker said he never had cause to use any of his guns, but "if a
situation ever came up where I needed a gun, I'd rather be caught
with it than without it. I'm sympathetic to Jose."

Canseco, a 1982 15th-round draft choice for whom so much
had happened so fast, continued to have problems even after the
gun incident was shoved into the background by the passage of
time. The California Egg Commission, concerned about negative

publicity, dropped him as their $25,000-per-year spokesman. "We're not condemning him until he's proven guilty," the commission's president said. "But baseball is supposed to be a family-oriented sport. When we're spending the money that we are, someone like that just doesn't portray the image that we want to portray. He's not the All-American ballplayer." Or the All-American Express player, either. Canseco saw a potentially lucrative American Express sponsorship end after one lavish magazine advertisement. And it was reported that his off-field saga might have cost him a spot in a new national ad campaign for an underwear company.

In the long run, financially speaking and relatively speaking, the lost endorsements couldn't have hurt him too much because he had just signed that $1.6 million guaranteed contract for the 1989 season. But even his contract stirred controversy. Having played three full seasons in the big leagues, Canseco was eligible to test his worth in arbitration. The A's wanted to pay him $1.3 million, and Canseco asked for $1.64 million. Considering the amount of money other fourth-year players were receiving, Canseco's actual contract surprised a lot of baseball people. When Canseco signed for $300,000 more than the A's offered and only $40,000 less than his own request, there was distaste among general managers and owners in other big-league cities. They argued that the $1.6 million would surely heighten the salary structure and set a nasty trend for players entering the arbitration field for the first time.

But what these baseball people failed to acknowledge was that Mr. 40-40 was coming off a season unlike any in major-league history. Had the A's agreed to go to arbitration, they probably would have lost. So in the long run, they saved 40 grand by signing Canseco early. It doesn't sound like much in relative terms, but 40 grand can get a heck of a lot of bats and balls.

Both Bay Area teams worked out on their own for a couple of weeks before opening the exhibition season, the A's settling into modern Phoenix Municipal Stadium and the Giants neighboring at crusty but cozy Scottsdale Stadium. As is the case in every preseason, Cactus League records and statistics are downplayed because, after all, come Opening Day every team is 0-0 and every pitcher's ERA is 0.00. But there was something prophetic about the spring of '89. The A's and Giants were to meet a record nine times, which equates to roughly one-third of the entire Cactus League schedule. In the end, they would grow tired of playing each other, although it wasn't quite as wearing on the A's as it was for the poor Giants. In nine tries against their interleague rivals, the Giants won once. A winning percentage of .111 does not earn championships. But at least the Giants could take refuge in the fact that this was only an exhibition season. But still, as it was transpiring, the Giants had to be wondering what the heck was going on. The A's beat San Francisco in Phoenix, in Scottsdale, in New Orleans, in Oakland, even in San Francisco. Nine games over 23 days, and the Giants managed only one victory — and they needed 11 innings and a Kevin Mitchell cycle to do so. If this were softball, where games last only seven innings, the Giants would have been in good shape, but the A's scored a total of 30 runs in their final at-bats and devastated what was supposed to be a reasonably decent bullpen.

In the midst of the beatings, Roger Craig blurted out a statement that no one really took seriously. "I don't think they're any better than we are. . . . We'll turn it around in the World Series." Yeah, right, Roger. And Mitchell will hit 47 home runs.

The spring series started innocently enough on a sunny Saturday afternoon in Phoenix. In one of only two games not decided in the winning team's final at-bat, the A's won a routine 6-2 decision. But a telling sign that this would be no ordinary series came in the eighth inning when Craig issued an intentional walk to Parker. A few eyebrows were raised at Municipal Stadium when Craig set up the double-play situation by walking the designated hitter, but it showed just how much the Giants wanted to beat the defending American League champions. The strategy backfired when Billy Beane followed with a run-scoring single. Craig later defended his move, and La Russa later defended Craig by suggesting the competitive juices were beginning to flow. "The fact that we play them nine times this spring will prepare us even more for Opening Day."

After playing the Giants so often, the A's would be more than ready for Opening Day; they were ready to open the playoffs. The messy spring series began getting out of hand in Game Two, the most memorable and remarkable of the nine. The final score was 20-7, which wasn't unusual on the surface considering many spring training pitchers aren't good enough to reach the majors. But this game was decidedly irregular. After all, the A's trailed 7-6 in the ninth before exploding for a couple of touchdowns — and extra points. The amazing 14-run inning featured 19 batters, 10 hits and five walks. Doug Jennings was the only player in the A's lineup without a hit, but he walked in the inning, was hit by a pitch, drove in a run and scored twice.

The fact that the game was a laugher, in more ways than one, was not the issue concerning the Giants. The real question was their bullpen, notably closer Scott Garrelts. It was Garrelts who was summoned to pitch the ninth, to close the door on the A's, to prove his worth in a game the Giants dearly wanted to win. But it was Garrelts who suffered his worst outing in his worst spring. He was knocked around for six runs, four hits and two walks, all without registering an out. When Craig asked catcher Terry Kennedy how Garrelts was throwing, Kennedy said, "I don't know. I didn't catch very many."

A few days later, Garrelts pledged not to talk with the media for the entire season because he believed repeatedly dissecting his bad performances only proved distracting. The day before his vow of silence, he granted what he swore would be his final interview. "I can see where they're concerned," he said. "If I'm the manager, I'd be concerned. The way I've thrown the last couple of outings, I should be on somebody's mind."

Lugging the liveliest arm in the organization but not having yet shown the mental makeup of an effective reliever, Garrelts appeared destined for another disappointing season, one similar to his '88 season when he blew 11 saves. Something evidently was missing from his repertoire, and it wasn't his fastball, which traveled well into the 90s. Maybe he just lacked a gimmick that all successful closers seem to have. He didn't show his emotion by raising his fist, a la Dennis Eckersley. He didn't show his emotion by growling at the batter, a la Goose Gossage. And he didn't show his emotion by prancing around the mound, a la Al Hrabosky. No, Garrelts walked out to the mound, pitched, then walked off the mound, always emotionless. And, too often, he left with bad results.

Craig became so fed up with Garrelts' inability as a short reliever that he did something that seemed to make little sense at the time. He made Garrelts a starter. Some punishment. Most relievers go an entire career praying for a chance to start, and here was Garrelts driving away with a Cadillac job only because he was inadequate in the bullpen. But after what he'd seen, Craig argued, "I'd be crazy to put him in the ninth inning Opening Day with a one-run lead." Garrelts' bullpen days were apparently behind him, and he was hoping to leave his 15.00 ERA down in the bullpen as well.

Then a funny, almost miraculous, thing happened in Garrelts' first start. He experienced some crazy metamorphosis and promptly retired the first and only nine Milwaukee Brewers he faced, five on strikeouts. The three perfect innings even drew cheers from the fans, who had followed San Francisco's spring saga and had booed Garrelts at every opportunity. Garrelts found a sudden comfort with starting every fifth day, and it was clear his relief days were nearing an end.

With Garrelts gone from the pen, the Giants had to rely on their next-best potential closer, in this case Mike "Buffy" LaCoss. But LaCoss was no better than Garrelts, as he proved in Game Three against the A's. This, in its own way, was even uglier. Instead of simply losing a one-run lead, the Giants blew a five-run lead, and the A's scored seven times in the ninth to win 9-7. LaCoss yielded six runs, four hits and two walks without retiring a batter — a line identical to Garrelts' in the previous A's game. Despite LaCoss' bad outing, the Giants had no intention of giving Garrelts his old job back, and little relief appeared in sight.

The A's-Giants rivalry was quickly becoming one-sided. The A's were winning too frequently, and the Giants were becoming classified as just another team. "It's important to beat them," La Russa said. "But it's also important to beat Milwaukee." In fairness, the Giants-A's competition had never really matched the intensity of the Mets and Yankees or the Cubs and White Sox, other geographic rivals. La Russa, a former White Sox skipper who lived through the annual north versus south battles of Chicago, was constantly hassled by Sox fans who told him beating the Cubs in the exhibition games was more important than doing well in the regular season. But no A's fan had ever told La Russa practice games with the Giants would make or break a season. There was certainly no pressure on the A's now, considering how the teams had fared in 1988. While the A's were paying relatively little attention to the Giants, the Giants tried everything and anything to stop the A's. In Game One, Craig intentionally walked Parker. In Game Three, he used all his regulars the full nine innings. Nothing worked. Everything failed.

Before Game Three, Craig stressed the importance of beating the A's, especially with Giants owner Bob Lurie sitting in the second row at Scottsdale Stadium. Lurie never did enjoy losing even a spring game, and he assuredly wanted to beat the A's and his old golfing pal and fellow San Franciscan Walter Haas, Oakland's majority owner. By the ninth inning, however, Lurie's seat was empty. He either had too much faith in his bullpen, or he'd forgotten what happened the last time these teams played. Lurie learned later that the A's had added another blemish to the Giants' spring. Mitchell put an end to the losing skid when he singled, doubled, tripled and homered in a 6-4 11-inning win in Game Four, but victory wasn't assured until after the Giants' relievers had blown yet another ninth-inning lead. The game was noteworthy for another reason. Canseco took two swings then took himself out after reinjuring his tender left wrist. It was his final spring game.

Later in March, the series resumed in another state and another time zone — but with similar results — when the A's and Giants reunited in New Orleans for Games Five and Six. Louisiana officials were planning, although probably in vain, to lure an existing team or an expansion franchise to the Cajun Country, and they hoped a successful two-game exhibition would make a statement to major-league baseball. But baseball and New Orleans may never mix, especially if the city's sluggish economy isn't revitalized. Some folks can barely afford a home-cooked plate of shrimp creole and blackened catfish, let alone $10 tickets to watch a baseball game in the Superdome.

Another worry — if you call this a worry — is the town's festive atmosphere. Running a team in New Orleans could be a manager's nightmare. There's nothing like a night in the French Quarter preceding a day game to throw a player out of whack. The Giants arrived in New Orleans a day before the A's, meaning the players could enjoy a night on the town. Craig refused to impose a bed check, but he considered pulling an old trick he learned from Casey Stengel. Stengel would give a baseball to the elevator man at the hotel and tell him to ask each player coming in after midnight for his autograph. In the morning, Stengel would look at the ball and know which players had come in late. Fortunately for Craig, some Giants were unfamiliar with New Orleans. "Bourbon Street?" asked James Steels, a non-roster player bidding for a spot on the big club. "What's Bourbon Street?"

La Russa knew all about Bourbon Street. He was an original Pel, as in Pelican, as in New Orleans Pelicans, a Triple-A club in the American Association. Back in 1977, La Russa was winding down his playing career in the first and only year of the Pelicans' existence. It wasn't much of a season for Tony, except for Opening Day when he became the first Pel to hit a home run. For his efforts, a local clothes manufacturer gave him a free suit. La Russa still owns that suit, but it's been many an Opening Day since he fit inside it. Some good did come out of that final season, though, as La Russa got a chance to manage for several days late in the season, and the next year he was handed his own team, the White Sox's Double-A affiliate in Knoxville. Late the following season, he was managing in Comiskey Park.

No one in the traveling party, not even La Russa, knew more about New Orleans than Will Clark. Born, raised and still living in New Orleans in the off-season, Clark was a 13-year-old kid knocking balls around city parks when the Pels were big. Twelve years later, Clark was a featured and honored visitor making his first appearance in Louisiana since his All-America days at Mississippi State. The games' promoters took full advantage of that fact and used Clark in ad space in exchange for 400 tickets for his relatives and friends. Will used them all and could have used more.

Clark and his teammates got a kick out of their off-day workout in the Superdome, which boasts 9.7 acres of roof (really) but only 318 feet of chalk between the plate and left-field fence. The power alleys were only 358 feet, meaning little power was required to knock one out of this windless yard. Garrelts was the first Giant to take his batting practice hacks and, not coincidentally, he was the first to go deep, even adding a couple of upper-deck shots. Mitchell later belted four straight over the short porch. It all made onlookers wonder what the A's bashers would do in this tiny ballpark when they arrived for the game the next day.

Despite the threat that the close fences would make the exhibitions a mockery, only two home runs were hit in the two games, thanks only to Dave Henderson and Mark McGwire. Meanwhile, two key factors indicated this city was not quite ready for a baseball team. The first? The pianist from Busch Stadium was called in to work the games and repeatedly played that irritating beer jingle. The second? Fans did the wave. By the way, the A's won both times, once in the ninth inning. LaCoss, doing the same things that caused Garrelts to lose his role as bullpen stopper, allowed all three runs in the ninth and took the 4-3 loss. LaCoss actually entered in the eighth, replacing Craig Lefferts with two outs and Carney Lansford due to hit. Roger Craig, who agreed with the Bay Area's

Channel 2 to hook up a microphone so his comments could be aired live back home, told Lefferts (and the viewing audience), "I know you can get him out, but I want to see what Buff can do in this spot." What Buff did in that spot was go on to blow a two-run lead.

Before the teams went north to their respective Bay Area communities, each manager tried, although it was a struggle, to put the A's dominance in perspective. Craig: "I don't think they're any better than we are." La Russa: "Things that happen in this game, don't try to explain them." As for LaCoss and his spring ERA that had ballooned to 10.65, he was saying, "They're just lucky right now. Everything they do is going right for them."

And the trend continued over Games Seven, Eight and Nine at the eighth-annual Bay Bridge Series. The Giants had won five of the first seven Bay Bridge clashes and hoped that history was on their side, but they would continue to realize that 1989 was a unique season altogether. The A's swept the Oakland games and won the finale in Candlestick Park, and two of the three wins were pulled off in their last at-bat.

As LaCoss was getting hit hard (this is a not recording) in the first Oakland game, reports of the Giants' interest in veteran reliever Goose Gossage were surfacing. Gossage would be an interesting acquisition because the Giants could sign him for a bargain price. They'd need to pay only the big-league minimum of $68,000, with the Cubs obliged to dish out the rest of his $1.2 million salary. Goose had been released by the Cubs earlier in the spring after walking 13 batters in 11 innings, but the Giants' bullpen was certainly sorry enough for them to consider a 37-year-old pitcher who could still throw in the low 90s. Despite the talk, however, no action was taken before Opening Day, and the Giants had no other choice but to employ a closer-by-committee system with LaCoss, Lefferts and rookie Jeff Brantley alternating in late innings.

Brantley had cracked the roster by virtue of his right arm. The Giants were overstocked with lefties and needed one more right-hander to round out the bullpen, and Brantley was the best among the competition. A teammate of Will Clark's at Mississippi State, Brantley was built like a fireplug, with a fiery personality to match. Despite his youth, he wasn't willing to back down to established veterans, as proven during a clash with Carney Lansford in the Bay Bridge Series. Immediately after Dave Henderson's home run gave the A's the lead for good, Brantley threw a warning pitch at Lansford that grazed the third baseman, prompting Lansford to drop his bat and head for the mound. Both benches emptied onto the field, but order was restored before any physical damage was inflicted.

"Regardless of who it is, you get tired of one team kicking your butt day in and day out," explained Brantley. "They've beaten us (eight) times in spring training, and even though it's only exhibition, it gets old after a while."

Thankfully for the Giants, the gloom finally ended with Ed Jurak's throwing error that led to two runs in the ninth inning of Game Nine. Final final: A's 6, Giants 4. Jurak, by no means a great defensive player, was another newcomer to the Giants' roster. He made the club as a non-roster man because of his success at the plate during the spring, but his off-field fame surely overshadowed anything he accomplished between the lines. After all, if it weren't for Ed Jurak, Wade Boggs might own an unsullied reputation. Jurak had the distinction of introducing Boggs to Margo Adams at an Anaheim nightclub. Margo became Wade's road mistress from 1984 to 1987 and revealed Ed's connection in the April '89 issue of Penthouse in an article entitled "Designated Swinger." As Margo freely explained (perhaps not totally free; Penthouse paid her $100,000), Ed met Margo and her girlfriend at the nightclub. The three decided to leave together. Ed asked if he could bring one of his Boston teammates along. Margo pointed to Wade. And life at Fenway hasn't been the same since.

The Giants broke camp with three non-rostermen, Brantley, Steels and Jurak. All three were long shots in February, but they all enjoyed exceptional springs and were rewarded for their work. Jurak, 31, and Steels, 27, hit .326 and .344, respectively. Were they happy to return to the majors? Combined, Jurak and Steels had played 809 Triple-A games. Yeah, they were happy. Only nine pitchers made the final cut, but that was only because Mike Krukow was due to return from the disabled list by late April. The roster was set, although it was hard to see this as a contending team. The new people included Jones, Kennedy, Brantley, Steels and Jurak.

The A's, feeding off eight straight spring wins, were fully prepared to begin the season at home against Seattle. And the Giants, losers in five of their last six, were to load up the charter and fly to San Diego to meet the division's real contenders. The A's and Gi-

ants were done playing each other for the rest of the year unless, of course, they met again in October. A Bay Area World Series?
Get real.

THE DISTRACTIONS
How the Giants and A's overcame early obstacles

Hello April. Hello trouble. The first month of the 1989 season gave little indication that the last month would come down to a Bay Area World Series.

Oakland's Tony La Russa and San Francisco's Roger Craig would have been better off in April had they been able to tag "M.D." after their names. Forget that both the A's and Giants camped near the top of their respective divisions for the entire month. Forget, too, that players such as Oakland's Dave Stewart and Mike Moore and San Francisco's Kevin Mitchell and Will Clark opened 1989 at the peak of their games. The fact was, both clubs were hit hard by injuries. In Oakland, the Bash Brothers be-

29

came the M*A*S*H brothers when Jose Canseco missed the entire month and Mark McGwire missed over half of it, unable to do much more than sign autographs for the kids. Across the bay, it was clear the Giants weren't going to win the arms race, not with starting pitchers Dave Dravecky and Mike Krukow opening up on the disabled list. Canseco and McGwire had the gift of youth, so the outlook for getting both bashers up and swinging again was good. But the Giants had to wonder about the future of the incapacitated, not-so-young Dravecky, 33, and Krukow, 37.

The agonies of April didn't stop with a reading of the disabled list. In Oakland, there were offensive problems, key among them the painfully slow start of designated hitter Dave Parker, the A's only left-handed bat with major potential for malice. In San Francisco, offense wasn't a big problem — the exception being third baseman Matt Williams, who like Parker seemed overmatched every time he picked up a bat. And even with Clark and Mitchell ripping out hits, outscoring the other guys was difficult for the Giants, thanks to a bullpen that wasn't too adept at holding leads.

Nevertheless, the two teams set the tone for the season by overcoming adversity in a big way in April. The A's finished the month with 18 wins, thereby keeping pace in the American League West, which boasted no fewer than four fast-starting teams. Texas, California, Kansas City and Oakland each played .600 or better for the month. And while the Giants were able to play only .500 at 12-12, they finished April just two games out of first in the slower-starting National League West.

Although the Giants had many concerns — key injuries, inconsistent relief pitching, a lack of production from the bottom half of the lineup — probably the biggest disappointment was Williams, the so-called third baseman of the future who could have built up plenty of frequent-flyer mileage with all the times the Giants sent him back to Triple-A Phoenix.

The Matt Williams story began the day the Giants obtained the University of Nevada-Las Vegas shortstop in the first round of the 1986 draft, and it had been a roller-coaster ride ever since — although this particular roller coaster took more dips than soars. Williams had spent most of his professional career trying to return to the place everyone thought he belonged — the major leagues, the only leagues that counted. But Williams' inability to connect with major-league pitches, specifically off-speed pitches, led to all those repeat trips back to Phoenix. Yet the Giants repeatedly stood in his corner, hoping he'd mature into a legitimate major-leaguer. The president of Williams' fan club from day one was Al Rosen, who made Williams his initial pick in his first Giants draft following his appointment as general manager. Rosen, himself an MVP third baseman for the '53 Indians, noticed Williams' quick hands and powerful swing and guessed his future would be at third base.

Williams made brief minor-league stops in Rookie League Everett, Single-A Clinton and finally Phoenix. And only one year after his All-American junior season at Las Vegas, Williams found himself up with the Giants and in the midst of the 1987 pennant race. Because of injuries to infielders, Williams played often and started at shortstop in a four-game series against Atlanta in which the Giants set a major-league record with 15 double plays. But his bat never matched his glove as pitchers continued to get away with a curveball-only allotment to him. Williams had two stints with the Giants in '87 and hit only .188 in 84 games. He had two more stints in '88, with similarly bad results — .205 in 52 games. But Rosen stuck with Williams, despite several attractive offers from other clubs willing to surrender top-line pitching for his services. When John Tudor was a hot item in the summer of '88, the Cardinals were willing to trade the left-hander for Williams and minor-leaguers Tony Perezchica and Trevor Wilson. But Rosen told the Cards to take a hike, and Tudor went to Los Angeles for Pedro Guerrero and helped to wrap up a division championship for the Dodgers. The Giants closed out the season with Williams at third base and finished fourth.

The 1989 season was advertised as being new and improved because Williams, for the first time, was named the Opening Day third baseman even before spring training. Rosen suggested that Williams spend the off-season with new club fitness expert Mackie Shilstone, and when the boss makes a suggestion, a 23-year-old should consider it an order. Williams did. He spent the winter working with Shilstone in New Orleans, rooming with Will Clark at Clark's family's home. Shilstone made Williams replace his steady diet of Coca-Cola and Snickers bars for fruit juice and granola. As Shilstone forced Williams to run and eat his way into shape, Clark was working on the kid's mental game. Too many times in his brief big-league tenure, Williams would strike out, throw his helmet and lose all confidence for the rest of the day. He was a perfect example of why players shouldn't take the game home with them. Williams would go 0-for-4, turn the clubhouse upside down and carry those mental scars with him the next day, only to go 0-for-4 again. Pretty soon, after a few more oh-fers, he'd be 0-for-20.

Clark, only a year older than Williams, learned much earlier in his career to forget about the bad days and visualize the good ones, and he emphasized such discipline to Williams in nightly fireside chats. And when it came time to hit, these guys hit and hit and hit. How much? Oh, about 10,800 hacks worth. Six days a week, they took 200 swings in the morning and, if they added a second round, an additional 100 to 200 in the afternoon. An average of 300 swings a day six days a week for six weeks amounts to 10,800 hacks. With positive reports on Williams from Clark and Shilstone, the Giants were feeling good when Williams reported to camp. Craig predicted Williams would "stumble across" 25 to 30 homers. Even Williams felt good, saying, "I could drive in as many runs as anyone on this team."

But a funny thing happened on Williams' way to San Diego for the season opener. He forgot to take his hitting shoes and ended Opening Day with another 0-for-4 (three strikeouts). Soon he was 0-for-14, then 1-for-24, then sitting on the bench and watching Ed Jurak man the hot corner. Williams' problem wasn't hitting fastballs. He could even hit Orel Hershiser's fastball, no big deal. The problem was Hershiser and the rest of the pitchers were still refusing to throw him fastballs. The report on Williams was quite simple. Don't let him beat you with the gas. Feed him a steady diet of junk and he'll miss big-time. The strategy continued to work, and Williams found himself hitting only .130 through the season's first month.

On May 1, after the Giants lost to the Cubs in 12 innings to fall behind by 2½ games, their largest deficit to date, assistant general manager Ralph Nelson made it official and announced the Giants were giving up on Williams once again. The latest Matt Williams Experiment was over after only 21 games because the youngster had made it clear he still couldn't tackle big-league pitching. The Giants had no other choice but to send him back down to Phoenix. Williams, just 23, already had a career's worth of transactions and was about to board his fifth flight back to Triple-A. "How am I supposed to feel?" snapped Williams after being asked his initial reaction. Following a long moment of silence, Williams apologized and quietly said, "I feel like I'm going to work my rear off and get back here." At the time, it wasn't guaranteed that Williams would ever return to the majors. After all, he had failed in each of his three short big-league tries, hitting .188, .205 and .130 for a dreadful career mark of .187. Would another demotion help? "I have no idea," Williams said. "I don't know if one year would help me or not. Or three years or five years." The only thing Williams knew for sure was that after all his winter work, he still wasn't ready for the bigs in April 1989. It hurt even more knowing a .152 hitter would be taking his place on the big club's roster. The Giants called up an unknown, an all-field, no-hit prospect named Greg Litton (10 hits, 20 strikeouts at Triple-A Phoenix), and told Ernest Riles he'd be the every-day third baseman.

Williams was on his way to the minors with an order for his coaches to-be: "Lay off me." Matt Williams of the '80s was turning into the Dave Kingman of the '70s. Another power hitter who tried to fit in at third base but struck out too much, Kingman was given an overdose of advice from coaches and teammates and never quite gelled with the Giants. Williams was headed in that direction, so Rosen told Phoenix manager Gordie MacKenzie to let the kid play every game without a trace of instruction. The brass sent him off and only hoped he would one day board a flight — a one-way flight this time — from Phoenix to San Francisco.

The Giants' bid to straighten out Williams was soon overshadowed by the fact that they had to first straighten out themselves. The Williams demotion was one of several moves the Giants made in the wake of a recent slump. Left-hander Joe Price, whose highlight was five innings of one-hit relief in Game Five of the '87 playoffs, was a victim of the southpaw-laden organization. Price was released, his roster spot was taken by James Steels, who did some time earlier in the month. Veteran pitcher Mike Krukow had already come off the disabled list and was willing to give his right arm another try. And Craig replaced troubled right fielder Candy Maldonado with Tracy Jones, in effect replacing a .228 hitter with a .043 hitter. Craig was forced to briefly spell injured second baseman Robby Thompson with Ed Jurak. It wasn't the lineup the club foresaw when spring camp broke, but Craig and Rosen did what they're known to do during down times — make changes.

The A's parallel to Matt Williams was Dave Parker, who was also expected to drive in a lot of runs but, like Williams, suffered a terrible first month. The 37-year-old Parker opened the season on a mission and with fire in his eyes, perceiving himself historically as the victim of off-field injustices.

When he reported to the A's in 1988, Parker came to camp angry over statements made by Pete Rose, his former manager in Cincinnati. At the end of the '87 season, Reds owner Marge Schott fired general manager Bill Bergesch and replaced him with Murray Cook. It was Cook who told Parker of many of Rose's feelings, which were later confirmed to the slugger by Schott.

"Cook asked me about negative leadership," Parker said. "I said, 'What are you talking about?' He said he heard from Marge Schott that Pete couldn't handle me anymore. Marge Schott said that Pete had come in and said he was mad I took a day off. She said he was constantly complaining about me. It was a total shock to her. She knew we were friends. It was all a mystery to me. . . . I only played in 370-some straight games before I took a day off over there. I only hit more home runs than anyone over a four-year period. I only drove in more runs over a four-year period. And I had the highest batting average over a four-year period. I rest my case. How much more leadership do you need?"

Said Rose: "You don't appoint a team leader or elect one. It comes from your peers. I thought we needed one because of all the young players. If Dave interprets that as being a negative influence, then there's nothing I can do."

With the A's, there was never a mention of Parker being a negative influence. In fact, it was just the opposite. Few men took greater pride in their positive, up-tempo influence in the clubhouse than Parker, who considered Rose's statements as fighting words. He was aghast — and hurt. In the course of the 1988 season, Oakland found nothing to support Rose's opinion. A loud and distinctive voice in the clubhouse, pleasantly abusive to his teammates and usually very cooperative with the media, Parker found a new, comfortable home. More of the same could have been expected for 1989, but come spring training, Parker's anger found a new direction — his own players' union.

Hanging over his head throughout the 1988 season was the fact that Parker's first team, the Pittsburgh Pirates, filed a suit against him to negate the $5.3 million they owed him in deferred salary through the year 2007. Parker said the Major League Baseball Players Association deserted him, leading him to agree to an out-of-court settlement after the 1988 season. In the suit, the Pirates claimed Parker's admitted drug use — he said he voluntarily gave up cocaine in 1982 — was a breach of the contract he signed in 1979 that made him baseball's first $1 million-per-season player. As part of the settlement, neither side was allowed to talk about terms of the final financial settlement to the media. That didn't stop Parker from addressing the case's emotional impact, saying it "was part of a modern-day lynching. The players' association chose not to support me. (It was) an injustice to me. The commissioner's office turned its back, too. We discovered that hundreds and hundreds of players in baseball had some drug relationship, and yet they chose (to sue) only me. I thought it was on the borderline of being a racist thing as well because (the Pirates) had no reason to do what they did."

Pirates President Carl F. Barger took exception, denying that it was a "personal vendetta." After the settlement, Barger said, "We don't feel that we should (have had to) pay him the money. (The suit) went forward on the basis of principles and economics."

"I've been maligned my whole career," Parker said. "After being maligned as a player and having my character run down, it means a lot to me to go out and show everybody that, through it all, I'm still on top of my game. I want them to be able to say, 'He went through hell, but look at him; he's still producing.' "

Only he wasn't, at least not in April. There was little evidence to support any claim of life in Parker's bat. He drove in four runs in the second game of the season and had two homers in his first five games, but then the well went dry. He was hitting .306 on April 16 but would get just three hits the rest of the month. By the close of April, La Russa was repeatedly being asked by the media what could be done. La Russa, who had learned well the lessons of patience that come with managing two different American League West champions, got tired of the questions, but his answers seldom varied. Parker would come around; he was sure of it. "We have to have Dave Parker hitting and driving in runs for us," La Russa said. "He's done it all his career. He's not going to stop now. He'll be all right." Parker finished the month hitting only .196.

At least Parker was in the lineup every day. Because of injuries, too many of the A's couldn't make that claim in the early going.

On April 3, La Russa reclined uneasily in the swivel chair behind his office desk in the cold, concrete, bunker-like complex that serves as Oakland's clubhouse. Ever since the World Series loss to the Dodgers in October, La Russa had been thinking about his next task — filling in the lineup card for Opening Day in 1989. Now that it was here, however, he was at something of a loss as to how he should proceed. The loss was his MVP right fielder, Jose Canseco. In a spring game against the Angels, Canseco struck out, missing badly in his first career appearance against rookie Jim Abbott. Canseco came out of the game complaining of a sore wrist, which was initially diagnosed as ligament damage. Canseco came back, felt pain again, and again sat on the sidelines. As the spring wore on, it became clear that the early diagnosis was incorrect and that Canseco would be out longer than the 10 days or two weeks first anticipated. Two weeks became three, then four, but the wrist didn't respond to treatment.

As the season began, the A's were still scrambling to find out the exact problem with The Wrist That Wouldn't Heal. At the time, there was hope in the Oakland camp that Canseco would miss no more than the first two or three weeks of the season. When it was finally determined that Canseco had a chipped hamate bone in his left wrist that might require surgery, doctors hoped that rest would strengthen the wrist, that surgery wouldn't be necessary and that Canseco could be back in the lineup by the middle of May. "I think being a 30-30 man (30 home runs, 30 stolen bases) would still be possible if I get back by then," Canseco said. He began his injury rehabilitation assignment in early May for the A's Double-A farm team in Huntsville, the spot where Canseco found his game in 1985 and where he climbed to stardom with a Southern League MVP season. That year, he had a .318 batting average, 25 homers and 80 RBIs in just 58 games. Two games into the comeback attempt, however, the wrist failed, and surgery to remove the chipped bone that had sapped the power from Canseco's swing became necessary.

Tony La Russa had no way of knowing on Opening Day that his scramble to replace the right fielder would cover 88 days and wouldn't be over until after the All-Star break. "We'll miss Jose, there's no denying that," La Russa said as he printed Stan Javier's name into his April 3 lineup card. "But at the same time, we're not a one-man team, either. We've got some other guys who can play." At times, it would seem like an endless supply of "other guys." In

all, seven men made one or more starts in right before Canseco returned. Among the field entries in this handicap race were Dave
Parker; a spring free-agent signee, Billy Beane; a rookie who was
expected to be the A's second baseman in the 1990s, Lance Blankenship; a catcher, Terry Steinbach; and a second baseman, Tony
Phillips.

Javier, a part-time player for three seasons and the son of former Cardinals second baseman Julian Javier, was the Opening Day
starter, but La Russa quickly turned to another Dominican switch-
hitter, rookie Felix Jose, to fill in. Where Javier was perhaps the
A's best defensive outfielder, his offense was too limited. In his first
three seasons with the A's, Javier hit just .230 with only four
homers. When set against those numbers, Jose, a potential star-of-
the-future — he hit .317 with 83 RBIs for Triple-A Tacoma in 1988
— was an obvious choice for La Russa. During spring training, Jose
hit .329 and was third on the team with 17 RBIs, and his relentless
offensive showing would have earned him roster spot consideration
even if Canseco were healthy. La Russa rushed him into the lineup,
hopeful that he could bring a modicum of life to right field in the
star's absence.

After starting four of the A's first seven games, Jose was still
having trouble settling in when potential disaster struck the A's
again. Mark McGwire, the '87 Rookie of the Year, joined Canseco
on the disabled list. McGwire injured a disc in his back while on
defense in the first road game of the year in Anaheim April 10. Two
days later, after it had become apparent that McGwire needed
more than a little time to recoup, he went on the 15-day disabled
list. Now La Russa's troubles were to begin in earnest. If the A's
were vulnerable with Canseco out, they seemed very fragile with
both of their bashers sidelined. What was worse, doctors compared
McGwire's disc trouble with that suffered before the season by
Yankees outfielder Dave Winfield, who wasn't expected back before the All-Star break. If the same was true for McGwire, Oakland
could well find itself out of the race in no time.

To fill in while La Russa scratched for answers, Oakland recalled Billy Beane, a veteran utility man who'd bounced around for
six years after turning down a scholarship from Stanford to sign
with the Mets in 1980. La Russa's troubles weren't helped when
middle reliever Gene Nelson, who'd already missed nearly a week's
worth of action, was placed on the disabled list three days later

with injured ribs. Felix Jose, who had just four hits and two RBIs as Jose Canseco's replacement, was returned to the minor leagues for more seasoning. La Russa's dabbling in right field decreased markedly after that, as Stan Javier became the starter the bulk of the time until Canseco's return.

In McGwire's absence, La Russa started third baseman Carney Lansford, Terry Steinbach and even the much-traveled Beane at first base while attempting to glue the pieces of the Oakland offense back together. It was a formula he would use time and again, and it gave evidence that something special was happening in Oakland: Even while McGwire was out on the disabled list for 15 days, missing 14 games, the A's went 10-4.

With the new-look Rangers off to the best start in franchise history (14-4), and with Canseco out and Dave Parker slumping, the A's could have found themselves facing a five- or six-game deficit when McGwire returned from the disabled list with a week left in April. Instead, when he returned to add stability to the number four spot in the batting order, the A's were just a half game out of first place. It helped to have a pitching staff that had led the league in ERA the year before, then add a guy of Mike Moore's stature. Dave Stewart won his first six games, but Moore's success wasn't far behind. Moore, after being battered badly in his first start, allowed just two earned runs in his next four starts, winning three. Oakland pitching dominated when the offense wasn't up to the task. Still, for all of the success that the A's enjoyed in April, stronger tests were to come their way as they learned their first month was an indication that the season would not be as injury-free as 1988.

On May 18, Walter Weiss came across second base to take a throw from Mike Gallego, starting a double play that helped starter Storm Davis get out of a first-inning jam against the Yankees. Weiss didn't help the A's again for 10 weeks. The prognosis was for a two-week stay on the disabled list, and everything was going according to plan. But when the A's visited Boston at the end of the month and Weiss was less than a week away from returning, the unthinkable happened: a freak accident. Weiss had fallen asleep in his hotel room while waiting for a friend to call. The ringing phone roused him, and as he stood up to walk across the room to answer it, his knee gave out. He was in agonizing pain. Instead of being a week away, now the shortstop would be absent for more than one-third of the season.

Lance Blankenship, who had already been called up and sent down once, was Weiss' replacement on the roster. He also had his story of intense pain. In the spring, Blankenship had left Oakland's workout sessions to return home to Concord, a 30-minute drive from Oakland, to visit his father, who was dying of cancer. As long as he was on the roster, Blankenship could stay close to his father. But when Mark McGwire returned on April 26, the A's sent Blankenship to Triple-A Tacoma — technicality sent him, that is. While the A's needed his spot on the roster, they weren't without compassion. They gave Blankenship permission to remain in Concord with his family. His father died less than a week later.

Another man looking for his bearings in 1989 was second baseman Glenn Hubbard, who had joined the A's as a free agent in 1988 and played in a World Series for the first time. Other than that, however, his time with the A's had been bittersweet, as his injuries and the continued emergence of Mike Gallego and Tony Phillips shoved him into a secondary role. In spring training of 1988, Hubbard was hit in the head by a pitch from Cubs rookie reliever Jeff Hirsch. He suffered multiple fractures around his left eye and spent a month on the disabled list. Throughout the year, he had trouble with his legs and missed the playoffs with hamstring problems before being reinstated for the World Series. Hubbard was to be the starting second baseman in '89, but he missed 11 days in April with leg troubles. He blew out his hamstring later in the season, virtually ending his career with the A's.

The Weiss and Hubbard mishaps were but a couple of rough waves in what would prove to be a string of miserable injuries for the A's in 1989. Bob Welch, a 17-game winner in 1988, became a casualty in mid-June when he pulled a groin muscle in a start in Kansas City. To replace Welch, the A's activated Matt Young, who had been part of the '87 trade that brought Welch to the A's. Young himself was coming back from elbow problems that first struck in 1987. Storm Davis, a 16-game winner in 1988 but struggling with a 3-3 record and 6.14 ERA produced in part by a spate of injuries, went on the 21-day disabled list in mid-May because of problems with his left hamstring, right shoulder and right knee.

Also in May, a devastating injury hit Dennis Eckersley, who entered a game in Yankee Stadium in quest of his 15th save, but who left in agony. With a runner on first base, Eckersley pitched to

Don Slaught out of the stretch, which requires more arm energy than while pitching from the windup. On his second pitch to Slaught, he felt a sudden pain in his right shoulder. La Russa made several steps toward the mound, then thought better of it. Eckersley went on to strike out Slaught, but La Russa and trainer Barry Weinberg, troubled by what they had seen, raced to the mound. Eckersley threw one practice pitch, then was led off the field and was taken to the trainer's room.

Eckersley was examined two days later by a long-time friend, Red Sox team physician Dr. Arthur Pappas. The hope was that Eckersley had suffered only a slight strain. It was several weeks before he was diagnosed as having pulled a muscle around the right rotator cuff. If there was one player the A's couldn't do without, Eckersley was the player. When he was first placed on the disabled list, the A's had hoped only 15 days would be needed for him to recover. But when the shoulder injury was diagnosed as a rotator cuff problem, it was clear that Oakland would have to do without Eck for a long time.

Eckersley, trying hard to live down the home run he allowed to Kirk Gibson that cost the A's Game One of the World Series, was a masterful reliever in April. Only a sacrifice fly by the White Sox's Ivan Calderon on April 16 kept Eckersley from being perfect. And Eck even won that game with 1⅔ innings of hitless relief when Walter Weiss delivered a game-winning single. The A's pitching was so dominant in the early stages of the season — three shutouts and two or fewer runs 11 times — that they lost only twice in April when they scored at least four runs. And they were 11-1 in games decided by one or two runs.

Still, Eckersley would find this a tough month personally. He missed the April 14 game in Chicago because he had to testify as a character witness in the trial of his brother, Wallace, who was being tried on charges of attempted first-degree murder, first-degree kidnapping and aggravated robbery after the 1987 abduction of a 58-year-old Colorado Springs woman. Dennis and Wallace Eckersley hadn't been close in recent years, but the strain of the trial on the Eckersley family was enormous. During the winter, Dennis had "dropped the A-bomb," as he liked to call it, telling Sports Illustrated's Peter Gammons that he had kicked alcoholism with a stint in a detox center after the 1986 season. He admitted to himself that his career was faltering in part because of his dependency on alcohol. He went public, he said, because the news would have come out in his brother's trial, anyway.

Wallace Eckersley, at 36 two years older than Dennis, admitted during his trial that he was an alcoholic and a "transient bum." On April 24, the jury returned a guilty verdict, and on July 11 Wallace Eckersley was sentenced to 48 years in Colorado State Prison. Dennis tried to be philosophical about the verdict and sentencing, saying, "We all had a feeling this was coming. It wasn't exactly a surprise." And he expressed less concern for his own piece of mind than for that of his mother, Bernice. Through it all, it was Dennis Eckersley's obligation to put all his personal concerns behind him to remain at the top of his game, and he did that, saving 14 games in his first 15 opportunities before the rotator cuff injury sidelined him in May.

With all the setbacks that hit the A's star players in the season's first month, it was time for the lesser lights in the Oakland offense to shine. With the Bash Brothers out of commission, the "Gnat Pack" took over. It was Tony Phillips who gave the new-look A's an identity of their own when he described the club as "a bunch of gnats" after Stan Javier saved the day on April 18 with a game-winning, bases-loaded double against Seattle. "Without the big guys in there, we can still get the job done," Phillips said. "It's just that we're not going to do it with the three-run homer."

It was a great month for the Gnat Pack. On April 5, Walter Weiss turned in the first two-homer game of his professional career. It was such a rare feat that he recalled a time in Little League when he also hit two homers in a game. He even remembered the pitcher. "Yeah, actually I do. It was a kid who lived right down the street from me." On April 22, Mike Gallego, who hit .442 with six doubles during the month, tripled and stole home in a four-run fifth inning that beat Bert Blyleven and the Angels 4-3. On April 24, Luis Polonia delivered a pinch-hit double with the A's losing by a run in the ninth inning. Javier walked, and one out later Phillips doubled both men in, beating Toronto relief ace Tom Henke 5-4. On April 25, Billy Beane, just up from the minors and with only two steals in his big-league career, stole two bases and scored the winning run in a 3-2 win over the Blue Jays.

Luis Polonia was in the midst of a wretched slump earlier in the month when he stole a page from the movie "Major League" by setting up a shrine to "Joe Vu, Slump Breaker" on his locker. Joe

Vu, the voodoo idol that was the obsession of one of the characters in the movie, came through. Polonia went on to contribute significantly in the month. On April 29, his eighth-inning triple gave the A's a 3-2 win over Detroit.

The offense provided by the Gnat Pack held up until — and beyond — Mark McGwire's return April 26. Was Oakland happy to get the big guy back? Carney Lansford, who'd seen much of the playing time at first base in McGwire's absence, said "I'm going to bring some flowers, put them on my first-base glove and bury it. I belong at third base. Mac belongs at first base." For his part, McGwire said, "I was going crazy. I had to do something, so I was building some cabinets with my brother for my new house." McGwire proved to be a better man swinging lumber than hammering it. After debuting with a 0-for-4 effort against Baltimore in Oakland on April 26, he hit a couple of homers the next night. "Just like that, I'm seeing better pitches as soon as Mac comes back into the lineup," Dave Henderson said.

One of the few A's not bitten by the injury bug was Mike Moore, who left the hardships of Seattle and quickly emerged as one of the best pitchers in the American League. When the A's went out on a limb to sign the free agent, they drew more than a few inquisitive stares. Three years? $3.9 million? He was 30 games under .500 for his career. The Mariners wanted him back. But they didn't want him enough to pay more than $1 million a year for three years, and they weren't going to pay big money for a pitcher whose last two seasons had been 9-19 and 9-15. Moore had had exactly one winning season in 6½ tries, and that had come back when McGwire was still playing for the U.S. Olympic team. George Orwell aside, 1984 was a long time removed.

Those statistics were, at best, difficult to interpret, but the men who had to make a living trying to hit against Moore could read between the lines. Like Boston's Wade Boggs, who downplayed the return of Nolan Ryan to the American League, by saying, "What's the big deal? Ryan doesn't throw any harder than Mike Moore." Or how about this, from Minnesota third baseman Gary Gaetti, who knew full well that Moore had a career losing record (5-6) against the Twins: "When he was with Seattle, either we beat him because they didn't have anybody to bring in (in relief), or they brought somebody else in and we beat him." That's not the way Dick Williams remembered it. Williams, whose job as

Mariners' manager depended in great measure on Moore's success, said Moore couldn't win the big one.

Coming to Oakland was Moore's chance to prove his old skipper wrong. In his first start of the season, Moore looked anything but a winner. He walked seven and allowed nine hits in 5⅔ innings against the White Sox. Had he done that in the Kingdome, Moore might have been booed out of the park. In Oakland, where fans took an occasional loss in stride after seeing their boys win 104 games the year before, they were patient. But not much patience was required. Moore won three of his next four starts, three times allowing no earned runs.

If his success was typical of the A's of the late 1980s, Moore himself was not. Although he could be jovial enough around his teammates, he created a quiet, reserved persona for himself during his Seattle years, and he brought that with him to an Oakland clubhouse that, thanks to the agitating ways of Dave Parker, Dave Henderson and Tony Phillips, frequently bordered on the boisterous. Moore had his share of laughs, but his utter lack of emotion in the performance of his duties was unusual. Except to the expert eye, it was all but impossible to tell from Moore's demeanor whether he'd won a game or gotten knocked out of the box in the second inning.

Matt Young and Ken Phelps knew Moore from his Seattle days and had some of the best insights into the suddenly dominating pitcher. "He's not average in any sense of the word," Young said. "He's got this little smile on his face. When he loses, the most you'll get out of him is a roll of the eyes, or a "geez, I stunk today.' " Added Phelps, "Easy-going Mike Moore out of Eakly, Oklahoma. That's the way he's always been. I guess there were a lot of guys (in Seattle) who were upset that he didn't show more emotion, and certain managers like to see that in a player." A's pitching coach Dave Duncan, who had coached Moore in Seattle for one year and had lobbied hard to have A's general manager Sandy Alderson pursue Moore in the winter, said, "He doesn't get excited like we think of excited."

At the press conference announcing his signing, Moore said that he didn't want to be the A's stopper or the man on the spot. He'd leave that to Dave Stewart. "I just want to do my job and contribute." Privately, some of the A's executives were taken aback. "When you sign a guy to all that money ($3.95 million for three years), you'd like to have him come in and say, 'I'm going to come in and make the difference,' " said one teammate. "You'd like to have him march in and say, 'I'm going to win 20.' " But the A's were to learn that simply wasn't Moore's style — at least the big talk wasn't. Winning 20? Well, he'd give that a shot.

The only time Moore came off as excited was when he talked golf. If baseball was his livelihood, golf was his passion. The A's had a group of golfing fiends — Welch, Eckersley, Parker, Nelson, Javier and McGwire — who quickly found in the spring that Moore wasn't to be trifled with, or bet against, on the golf course. Even during the season, Moore pursued his second game when his first gave him the time. In Seattle, he'd gotten into the habit after occasional day games of putting a golf ball on the turf near home plate and driving it into the outfield seats. He brought that practice with him to Oakland and would draw a crowd of teammates when, two hours after a game, he'd tee up in an empty Coliseum and drive ball after ball into the left-field bleachers.

In the always-losing situation with which he'd been saddled in Seattle, perhaps Moore needed golf as an outlet. In Oakland however, there wasn't quite the need. "Winning's a lot of fun," Moore said. "I had never played on a losing team until I signed with Seattle, so it's good to be back on a winning team. It makes all the difference in the world to be in this atmosphere."

Across the bay, it was no laughing matter that the Giants, who had suffered perhaps their worst year ever in terms of injuries in 1988, seemed destined to duplicate the feat in '89. Dave Dravecky was making slight progress in his battle with cancer, but nobody truly believed he would ever pitch again. Mike Krukow's bid to come back from rotator-cuff surgery was put off all month as he set records for most innings pitched — in simulated games. Other stricken Giants were Robby Thompson and Chris Speier, and practically everyone on the pitching staff wondered if he would be able to avoid time on the disabled list.

The Giants' season opener featured one constant from spring training (Kevin Mitchell) and one change (Mike LaCoss). Mitchell brought his sizzling bat from the Cactus League and LaCoss provided rare relief, as the Giants beat San Diego 5-3. Mitchell hit a home run, and LaCoss earned a save on behalf of Rick Reuschel, who won on Opening Day for the first time in 17 years. It was La-Coss' first save since his Kansas City Royals days of 1985, and the

Giants thought they had found a closer. But it proved to be a false hope.

In their home opener April 10 against the world champion Dodgers, the Giants surrendered five runs in the ninth and lost 7-4. Atlee Hammaker and LaCoss were roughed up in the ninth, La-Coss coughing up a grand slam to Dodgers newcomer Eddie Murray, who upped his slams lead among active players to 15. On April 23, Hammaker ruined Will Clark's first five-hit game when he walked home the winning run with two outs in the bottom of the 10th, dealing four straight balls to .196-hitting Jeff Hamilton and furnishing the Dodgers with a 7-6 win. Seemingly intent on proving their spring training debacle was no fluke, the bullpen continued to blow late-game leads throughout April.

There were other ways the Giants lost games in the first month. Like the 16-inning game April 7 in Cincinnati. In the 11th inning, Mitchell's fly ball allowed Speier to tag from third base and cross the plate to give the Giants a 4-3 lead. But Pete Rose noticed Speier had left the bag early and appealed with the umpiring crew. The umpires agreed with Rose and called Speier out. Five innings later, the Reds would score for real and win for real. It was tough to blame the bullpen for that loss, but the relievers could be blamed for many others.

The Giants' brass realized they would never contend in the West without an imposing closer, one who could save a game instead of waste a game. The only good news to come out of the pen was Craig Lefferts' streak of retiring 29 consecutive batters, 12 shy of the major-league record held by former Giant Jim Barr in 1972. But Lefferts was better suited for the set-up role, although in this case there was no one he could set up for. No one on the current staff seemed capable, and there was little hope for getting immediate help from a trade. April traditionally is an off month for trades because general managers tend to let the dust settle in hopes of finding out if they can win with their given lot. For example, Philadelphia's Steve Bedrosian may have been available in the off-season, but he was labeled untouchable once the season started. The fact that the lowly Phils turned in a surprisingly good 11-12 start convinced general manager Lee Thomas that his club could contend, and he didn't want to mess with the chemistry, including former Cy Young winner Bedrosian.

The Giants' only alternative became scouring the free-agent

wire, where Goose Gossage, among others, awaited new employ-
ment. Talk of acquiring the Goose had stalled late in spring training when Roger Craig and Al Rosen decided Gossage wasn't the
answer. But come April, the bullpen-depleted Giants came to sense
they had no better alternative than to resume conversations with
the runner-up in career saves (302, 39 shy of Rollie Fingers) who
was well beyond his prime. Gossage, 37, was already financially secure and was still picking up paychecks from the Cubs, with whom
he had signed a guaranteed $1.25 million deal. In addition, on the
basis of a five-year deal he signed with the Padres back in '84, Gossage would be paid through the year 2016. But the old reliever figured he could catch Fingers' save record, and that pushed him into
working for a living instead of sitting in his easy chair waiting for
his twice-monthly checks. At the time, the Giants were desperate
and probably would have talked with Hoyt Wilhelm if the knuckle-
baller had wanted to come out of retirement.

The Giants, who would be required to pay only the big-league
minimum salary of $68,000 for Gossage's services should they de-
cide to sign him, invited him to work out before a game at Candlestick, so Goose flew north from San Diego to give the Giants a gan-
der. Gossage threw 40 pitches and was clocked as high as 94 mph,
several miles per hour slower than his best blazer of the late '70s
and early '80s. But knowing he could no longer get by solely with
his fastball, Gossage had added a slider to his repertoire, and Craig
was willing to teach him the split-fingered fastball.

This was indeed a different Goose from the one who saved 27
games for the champion Yankees in 1978 and 25 for the champion
Padres in 1984. And he didn't get a glowing recommendation from
his previous manager, Chicago's Don Zimmer, who happened to be
one of Craig's closest friends. Zimmer had often pitched Gossage in
blowouts, and Gossage frequently had responded by getting blown
out himself. He was never one willing to settle for mop-up work; his
personality was that of a closer. When Zimmer released him after
an unsuccessful spring training (13 walks, 11 innings), Gossage
complained that Zim hadn't given him enough work. Zimmer said,
"You look at his ERA, and it looks good. But he walked 13. That's
not Goose's bag." Goose said, "It's kind of a weak excuse."

Despite the friction that had existed between his new pitcher
and his old friend, Craig needed a reliever, and fast. He had made
16 pitching changes in the Giants' first seven games, and his 59-

year-old legs were taking a beating just getting him to the mound three and four times a day. As a result, three days after Gossage's 40-pitch workout, the Goose was signed and in a Giants uniform. He admitted he was rusty and agreed to initially work as a set-up man, but at least it was the major leagues again. His first day, he pranced around the clubhouse, saying, "I feel like a spring Goose."

A few days later, in his first outing as a Giant, Gossage was assigned to mop up a non-pressured 7-2 loss to Atlanta and threw two scoreless innings. Despite the Giants' new addition, Craig continued to employ his bullpen-by-committee system and called on anyone — sometimes everyone — to work a given game or situation.

One memorable Monday evening at Candlestick, the delighted manager finally was able to give his weary and wary pen a day off, thanks to newly appointed starter Scott Garrelts. Garrelts, coming off a dreadful spring in relief, beat the Padres by throwing his first complete game in three years and his first shutout in six years. And the moon wasn't even full. Garrelts' stunning performance excited Candlestick's first-ever Family Night crowd. Al Rosen had conjured up the idea of Family Night — parents and children sitting in a no-beer zone in the football bleachers in right field — after an infamous July 1988 double-header against the Dodgers that lasted past midnight. Giants-Dodgers games in Candlestick have a long history of being played in front of rowdy, sometimes drunken crowds, and, given the length of the double-header, this crowd was both.

In the wake of several arrests at Candlestick, National League umpires pushed the Giants for some sort of crowd control. The Giants' immediate reaction was to set up police barriers to prevent fans in the left-field bleachers from jumping onto the turf in pursuit of home runs. This had long been a colorful tradition at Candlestick, generations of kids chasing down bouncing balls in the open area behind the left-field fence. But the shenanigans had gotten out of hand that wild night in '88 when thugs nearly brought down the fence. So the barriers remained, and the '89 season brought the inception of Family Night. The right-field bleachers were roped off, and the rules were clear. No booze, no cigarettes, no cussing and no bad times. It was heaven to some parents, although some folks in left field likened it to hell. Still, there were no casualties on that first Family Night except for the San Diego lineup, which was victimized by Garrelts' superlative return to the starting rotation.

Garrelts' performance gave the Giants their seventh win in nine games. The offensive spark during the tear was Kevin Mitchell. The cleanup hitter won Player of the Week honors with three homers and 13 RBIs, prompting Roger Craig to suggest that Mitchell's stroke was so smooth, he'd do well against a ball shot out of a bazooka. Mitchell homered in both of the season's first two games and added his third April 13 off Fernando Valenzuela to push the Giants into first place, where they remained for nearly three weeks. Mitchell went on to hit six home runs in April, practically a career month for the fourth-year major-leaguer who never hit more than 22 in a season. But, amazingly, it would prove to be the least productive month of the season for the home-run czar to-be.

Will Clark was also hot in April, going 12-for-30 in his first seven games and closing the month at .375. His quick start prompted his manager to make a statement that wasn't too believable at the time. "I think he could lead the league in hitting," Craig said. To which Clark responded, "It's nice Roger would say that. Anything's possible as long as you keep your concentration."

As for Scott Garrelts, he made it known that his self-imposed vow of silence that began during his dog days of spring was over. For the first time in a month, Garrelts would let the public know just how he felt. "I'm feeling good now," he revealed. So was his manager. "I've told the players that there isn't a club in this league any better than them," Craig said. "Getting the (bleep) kicked out of us by the A's (in the spring) might have been the best thing that ever happened to us."

The Padres bowed to Garrelts but won the next two games of that series, thanks to one Jack Anthony Clark. The series marked Jack Clark's Candlestick debut in a Padres uniform. He had come this way in St. Louis garb before jumping to the American League for a brief stay with the Yankees, but San Francisco fans knew him best for the decade he put in with the Giants. They recalled Clark as having one of the most feared swings in the game, but they also recalled Jack ripping the Giants' organization, the ballpark and the fans. San Francisco was a second-division team during most of Clark's time; the Giants finished fourth three times, fifth twice and last once during his tenure. It was after the last-place '84 season that Clark was shipped to St. Louis for four players, three of whom

(David Green, Gary Rajsich and Dave LaPoint) lasted in San Francisco one season or less. Only a fellow named Jose Gonzalez had any longevity with the Giants — in body only, not in name. Gonzalez figured there were too many Jose Gonzalezes in the game, so he decided to change his name and became known to the baseball world as Jose Uribe. In the words of Hank Greenwald, the Giants' witty announcer, Gonzales truly was the player to be named later.

By 1985, the blockbuster trade had evolved into a straight Clark-for-Uribe swap, which was fine for the Cardinals because Uribe was a minor-league shortstop who had no future in St. Louis as long as the wizard of Oz, Ozzie Smith, called Busch Stadium home. The Cards were yet another team that had to keep from laughing while consummating a deal with the Giants, a club that had a history of dumping players with plenty of good years left. There was George Foster. Garry Maddox. Gary Matthews. Bobby Bonds. Dave Kingman. Gaylord Perry. Even Orlando Cepeda. All were let go with the Giants getting very little in exchange, and by 1985, Jack Clark's name was added to the list. In defense of the Giants, they had never won with Clark, and Clark had an occasionally unsettling influence in the clubhouse. Nevertheless, Clark left the Giants and helped the Cardinals make it to two World Series in three years. His most memorable moment came in the '85 playoffs on what many consider Dodgers manager Tommy Lasorda's biggest blunder. When Lasorda refused to have Tom Niedenfuer walk Clark with two outs in the ninth inning of Game Six, Clark, by far the most dangerous man in the St. Louis lineup, hit a series-winning three-run homer.

Again in '87, Clark was in the playoffs, although he was injured and the Cardinals had to beat the Giants without him. Which they did. The Cards fell to the Twins in the World Series that year, and over the winter Clark signed a free-agent deal with the Yankees. But he quickly realized he had no love for the American League or its umpires, so he requested a trade back to California and the National League. That meant either Los Angeles or San Diego; San Francisco was not a consideration. Yankees owner George Steinbrenner granted his wish, and Clark began the 1989 season hitting behind the league's best hitter, Tony Gwynn. With the additions of pitchers Bruce Hurst and Walt Terrell, the Padres were favorites to win the West, so the mid-April Padres-Giants series at Candlestick drew crowds interested in seeing the new kids on the block.

The series turned into the Jack Clark Show, with the fans booing his every appearance, reminiscent of his final days as a Giant. But Clark's swing hadn't disappeared — he cranked a wicked line drive into the left-field bleachers to beat the Giants in the second game 4-2. The fans booed his entire jaunt around the bases. "I kind of had the last laugh," Clark said. "I could look back there and say, 'Are you enjoying yourself in the cold?' "

The series capper featured Clark in a different light. When teammate Benito Santiago took a called third strike in the eighth, Clark argued the call and gestured at umpire Bob Davidson from the dugout, which earned Clark an immediate ejection. That's all Clark needed to storm out to the plate and engage in a wild Billy Martin-type argument with all of Billy's tactics. Clark kicked dirt, first on the plate, then on Davidson. "I'd like to bury them both," said Clark, referring to both the plate and the umpire. Clark didn't retreat despite being held back by manager Jack McKeon and several teammates. While going after Davidson, Clark pushed crew chief Doug Harvey. As Pete Rose, who was suspended in '88 after shoving ump Dave Pallone, can attest, baseball has a strict hands-off policy concerning umpires. However, Clark never drew a suspension because Harvey claimed the push was unintentional and Clark was just being Clark. "Typical Jack Clark ejection," Harvey said. "He never gets ejected and just leaves." Clark, who had driven in the eventual game-winning run with a bases-loaded walk, ultimately did leave, slowly making the long walk to the clubhouse door in the right-field corner, the fans continuing to boo through the duration of his journey.

Surprisingly, Clark was a cool customer after the game, but another Jack was blowing his top in the manager's office. McKeon wasn't as upset with Jack Clark's ejection as he was with the writers who covered the game. Accustomed to the media entering his office immediately after games, McKeon was irked when the media approached Clark first and lit into the writers when they finally arrived in his office. A few words have been changed to protect the innocent, but here is the essence of the exchange:

"I'll be here in my office after the (bleeping) game. If you don't want to come in, then (bleep) you. That's it. We won't have any more of that (bleep). You want to hear about the (bleeping) game, fine. If you want to hear about a negative (bleeping) guy who goes

0-for-2 and gets thrown out of the (bleeping) game, and if you want to (bleep) the other guys, I'll tell the other guys to (bleep) you guys and don't bother to talk about the game."

Bill Plaschke, who covered the Padres for the Los Angeles Times, immediately retaliated. "Who had the game-winning RBI? Didn't Jack walk with the bases loaded? We're doing our job. Come on." To which McKeon responded, "Is that your (bleeping) job? Did you ask Clark about the game-winning RBI?"

"Yeah."

"Ah, (bleep)."

"We're doing our job so everybody in San Diego can know what happened."

"And I'm doing my job, but I'm not going to wait all (bleeping) day. Do you understand that?"

"We're not making you wait all day. You could have left."

"You're (bleeping) right. The next time, the door will be barred for a while. I'll let you guys cool off. I wish to (bleep) that I kept you guys out for 15 or 20 minutes. Next time, I will. None of you guys intimidate me. None of you. I don't give a (bleep) what you write. You don't intimidate me. Next question."

Barry Bloom of the San Diego Tribune pointed out that "no one has seen anybody in the National League shovel dirt over a plate and bury a plate." McKeon responded, "You never saw it before? That's the same thing Billy Martin did (in the American League)."

"What I'm saying," said Bloom, "is if Clark gets thrown out of the game, it's nothing. What turns that into a big story is the antics that went on. He tried to push Doug Harvey."

"That's got nothing to do with the (bleeping) game. You guys are preoccupied with Clark getting kicked out of the (bleeping) ballgame. That's the big story? Run it. I don't want to talk about Clark. That's history. We won the (bleeping) ballgame. Jack Clark comes over here. A lot of money. Hell, yeah. Big deal. he's been kicked out probably more than anybody on this team. . . . Anybody got anything else to say? If not, I'm done." With that, McKeon took a puff from his cigar and called it a day, satisfied with winning two of three from the Giants, even if his battle with the media was only a draw.

The Giants began the San Diego series five games above .500, but after Scott Garrelts' shutout win, San Francisco lost six of nine games. The Giants were slumping, and a 3-1 loss at St. Louis on April 26 knocked them out of first place and started a string of three straight losses. San Francisco finished out the month losing four of its last five to end round one on a discouraging note. The top of the lineup carried the team while the bottom just enjoyed the ride. Aside from Matt Williams' .130 average, Jose Uribe hit .229, Candy Maldonado .222, Tracy Jones .071 and Kirt Manwaring .205. They were a .500 team at the end of the month, and Al Rosen, not one to wait for fate to change by itself, stepped in and tried to make a difference on his own. Just one month into the season, Rosen demoted Williams, ending yet another unsuccessful experiment and posting notice that the Giants, just like those guys across the bay, weren't willing to settle for second best.

THE SUPERSTARS
How Kevin Mitchell and Jose Canseco rose to stardom

There are rules. Then there are rules for Kevin Mitchell and Jose Canseco. There are traditional ballplayers. Then there are ballplayers such as Kevin Mitchell and Jose Canseco. There are guys who grow up collecting baseball cards and dreaming of playing in the major leagues. Who want nothing more than to stand in the outfield, spit tobacco and scratch themselves. Who think baseball is the only way of life. Who would bend over backwards for anyone who could grant that dream. Who would do anything their bosses say. Who would follow every order. Who would show up on time. Who would show up, period.

Then there are Kevin Mitchell and Jose Canseco.

If lesser athletes did the things these guys did, they'd be out of the game. How would the A's react if Lance Blankenship showed up late to spring training three years in a row? What would the Giants do if Kirt Manwaring missed a mandatory workout? Certainly more than issue a slap on the wrist, which is all Mitchell and Canseco received. But who's to argue with the A's or Giants if they look the other way when these beat-of-a-different-drummer guys start to strut? It seems the Yankees didn't hand down too many penalties for the off-the-field shenanigans of one George Herman Ruth. The way the Babe saw it, when you're making more than the president of the United States — and having a better year — you can do anything you please. Just don't hurt anybody. The Yankees looked the other way and just let him hit, much like the Giants and A's have done with Mitchell and Canseco.

In a game where conformity is often required, or at least requested, Mitchell and Canseco are different. They're one of a kind, maybe two of a kind. Their class, their breed, their look are unprecedented and, to be sure, uncopied. Canseco was the best player in the American League in 1988, and Mitchell was turning into the National League's premier talent in '89. During their moments in the limelight, both were trying to accomplish something never done before, Canseco with his 40-40 vision and Mitchell with his eye on the single-season home-run record. Yet at the same time, neither realized the impact of his pursuit. When Canseco made his 40-40 prediction in the spring of 1988, he had no idea no one had ever reached that plateau. And in 1989 when Mitchell was on target to challenge the home-run record, he insisted he had never heard of Roger Maris, whose 61 home runs in 1961 stood as the all-time mark for a single season.

When Canseco set his goals for the '88 season at hitting 40 home runs and stealing 40 bases, he became a marked man — the "40-40 man." Most people thought this cocksure 24-year-old was just plain crazy. This kid actually thought he had the talent to pull off something nobody else could do, not Willie Mays, not Mickey Mantle, not Roberto Clemente, not Bobby Bonds.

"Is that right?" he asked.

That's right, Jose.

"I said I'd try for it, because I knew I had the ability to do it. I figured five or six players must have done it. But after I said it, people looked at me as if I were crazy. If I had known at the time that no one had done it, I wouldn't have said anything."

When Mitchell came within 10 feet of hitting four home runs on May 3, 1989, against Pittsburgh — he hit two over the fence and two up against the fence in a 5-3 loss — he didn't realize he had flirted with the single-game record that was shared by his pal Willie Mays.

"Is that right?" he asked.

That's right, Mitch.

"I wish I had known that. I could have had something to tell Willie about."

This is a story about two superstars who weren't ever supposed to become superstars, if they became ballplayers at all. Neither was a big baseball fan as a kid, and no big-league team thought they carried much potential to crack the majors. Canseco wasn't drafted until the 15th round, and Mitchell wasn't drafted at all, yet they eventually became the hitting sensations of their respective leagues. By May 1989, Canseco and Mitchell were at opposite ends of the baseball spectrum. Mitchell increased his season home-run total to 15, and Giants fans loved him. While Mitchell was wreaking havoc with his bat, Canseco's homer total, because he was still sidelined with his wrist injury, stood at ground zero. Yet he continued to headline the news because . . . well, because of his nature.

Although probably the best, these were easily the most controversial figures on their teams. They're the bad boys of baseball, and they got away with it because they're very good. Both followed unusual paths from their earlier, unsure baseball days and overcame unsavory labels — warranted or not — to reach the game's elite level. Canseco was said to be weak and skinny. Mitchell was said to have a bad attitude. Both were raw and inexperienced. But something happened along the way. Jose and Mitch were touched by that undefinable spark which turns ordinary mortals into superheroes.

In a clubhouse where double-breasted suits and thin briefcases are the norm, Mitchell struts around in leather pants and belt pouches, wild sunglasses and headsets and gobs of gold all over his body — three gold neck chains, a gold earring and even a gold tooth. The golden left front tooth, which has become his trademark, was inserted in 1984, following a tough day in the Mexican League. As Mitchell tells the story, he was replacing a Mexican national in the lineup during a winter game in Tijuana when a thug from the stands heaved a huge metal screw his way, cutting his mouth and knocking the tooth out of place. Mitchell said he started running after the thug but got hung up on a fence. He caught his leg on barbed wire threaded through the fence, gouging a long furrow in his calf, which still bears the scar of that encounter. Mitchell returned to the United States and replaced his front tooth with a gold one, which he flashes with every grin. The story is vintage Mitchell.

While Canseco's story starts on the baseball fields of Miami, Mitchell's begins on the streets of San Diego. Most of Mitchell's tales, some documented but many conflicting, stem from his troubled background and turbulent days in San Diego's uneasy southeast neighborhoods. He was a street kid, a fighter who ran with gangs and fought for the slightest reasons. He packed a gun. He claims he would wallop somebody simply for walking in his path, usually flooring the poor soul with one punch. He shows off his multitude of scars as proof of his imperfect childhood. His most noticeable scar stretches across his back as a result of a deep knife wound. He also has scars from gunshot wounds in his right thigh, right wrist and back.

It was easy to see why baseball was considered an afterthought to his first loves, fighting and football — and football only because of the fighting. Mitchell thought baseball was boring and didn't play much organized ball as a kid, but he was clearly a special athlete. He never pursued a baseball career, but one autumn day in 1980, baseball came calling on him. Mitchell and some buddies were messing around on a local field when Mets scout Dean Jongewaard noticed a short, bulky kid swatting balls all over the yard. It wasn't long before Jongewaard convinced the undrafted 18-year-old to give the professional game a try. Mitchell reported to Kingsport in the Appalachian League the next spring and hit .335 in 62 games.

But the game wasn't always so easy. Mitchell found himself arguing with managers and brawling with heralded prospect Darryl Strawberry, and he decided to quit several times. But an old friend kept popping up in Mitchell's down times to set him straight.

Josie Whitfield would always urge Mitchell to stick with baseball, Mitchell would refuse to put up an argument, and so the conversation would quickly end. Mitchell had never argued with his grandmother in the past and wasn't about to start over something silly like his livelihood. Mitchell advanced from Kingsport to Lynchburg to Jackson and finally Tidewater, the Mets' top farm team, before getting his first crack at the majors in September 1984. He got into seven games and managed three hits — one off Steve Carlton before the left-hander took the plunge into mediocrity and sadly tried to convince every general manager in North America he could still pitch. Mitchell played all of the next season in Triple-A, not just because he needed to work on his game but because he needed to work on his attitude. As Mets hitting coach Bill Robinson said about Mitchell's brief big-league experience, "He had a terrible attitude."

If Whitfield pushed Mitchell in the minors, it was Robinson who kept him straight in the majors, using a sort of a reverse psychology to keep him in line. "I sat him in front of me and told him how much I disliked him," Robinson said. "I jumped all over him. I told him about life. I told him that baseball doesn't owe him a damn thing. If he didn't change, he'd be out of the game." Mitchell respected Robinson as if he were his father, an analogy Mitchell would often use later, and he eventually did change after a time. Instead of a mean guy who frightened his teammates, he became a pleasant man who made people feel comfortable in his presence. His on-field presence also improved, and he surprised a lot of people when he survived the final cuts in the spring of '86 and broke camp with the Mets.

As a rookie in New York, Mitchell was a utility man who played six positions and batted primarily against left-handers. He was a little-known ballplayer, but the media nonetheless found him a fascinating figure. As an athlete in New York, he would have been the subject of countless interviews anyway, but his murky background made him an even more desirable topic. The media soon realized he was a warm yet intriguing person and couldn't believe how a former gang member could be such an easy-going human being. But they would learn later that all of those interviews and all those stories weren't always on the level.

One of Mitchell's favorite stories is about the time he played for San Diego's Clairemont High School in a championship football game at San Diego Jack Murphy Stadium. Supposedly, he was a big star at Clairemont and later graduated from the school. But a check of the school records indicates both stories were exaggerated. Mitchell didn't play in a championship football game at all, and

Clairemont never played in the stadium during Mitchell's high school years. Clairemont's only visit to the stadium was December 1981, one month before Mitchell's 20th birthday and 13 months after he signed with the Mets. In December 1981, Mitchell was awaiting his second year in the minor leagues. Marc Appleman, then at the Los Angeles Times, reported Mitchell had actually attended at least three San Diego area high schools, and Clairemont's registrar's office revealed Mitchell attended the school for only one month, September to October 1978. The Mets apparently were unaware of Mitchell's high school history, and their media guide mentioned that he "graduated from Clairemont." After the Padres traded for Mitchell, they changed his bio wording from "graduated" to "attended."

Another discrepancy involved Mitchell's relationship with his mother and grandmother. Where the name Josie Whitfield enters practically all of Mitchell's interviews — "she raised me" — his mother says grandma Josie was a latecomer in Mitchell's life. "I was very depressed about articles written saying that his grandmother raised him. That wasn't true," said Alma Mitchell, saying she separated from Kevin's father, Earl, when she was 19 and Kevin barely 2. "It is a hurting situation. Raising (the family) by myself was hard. All the tribulations, and then someone else gets the credit. I can't go to lunch or dinner without someone saying that his grandmother raised him. I'm very depressed about it. I cry for three weeks when I read some of those things. . . . Nobody else was ever around. People only started being around after Kevin signed a professional contract. Kevin did not go to his grandmother's until then. I had no help from her. It bothers me to see a lie go forth." Mitchell's grandmother disagrees with his mother, saying, "When his mom wouldn't let him have his way, he'd run here. I have more patience with him than with my own children. Kevin has always stuck by me."

The contradictions and inaccuracies follow Mitchell wherever he goes. Although no one denied that Mitchell's 16-year-old stepbrother, Donald, was killed in a 1984 gang-related incident, the extent of Mitchell's involvement in gangs has been disputed. Stephen Schryver, the Mets' minor-league director, questioned the validity of some of Mitchell's stories. "Kevin tells the stories about the gangs to which he belonged. Sometimes I think he embellishes things." Even Josie Whitfield can't quite believe her grandson was a gang member. "There was all that talk about Kevin and gangs," she said. "This is the part I didn't know about. It's kind of shocking. When Kevin was around me, he always showed respect for me. I never saw that side of his attitude. He said, 'That's how smart I was.' I said I could never tell that you had a bad attitude. Maybe it's different when a bunch of men get together."

But Alma Mitchell will all but confirm Kevin hung with the wrong crowd. "Kevin got in a lot of things. He was a busy boy. Everybody in town knew Kevin got in trouble."

That might or might not have been the reason the Mets traded Mitchell after his successful rookie season, curious considering his big contribution in Game Six of the World Series. Mitchell delivered a pinch single and scored the tying run in the 10th inning of a 6-5 victory, and the Mets went on to beat the Red Sox in seven games. But soon after the celebration, in December, Mitchell was traded to the Padres. Mitchell had considered the Mets his family and was shocked for months that they would abandon him, even though the trade sent him back home. Perhaps out of protest, or maybe affection, he wore a Mets T-shirt under his Padres game jersey. But the Mets had their reasons for the trade, and acquiring Kevin McReynolds might not have been the only one. Reports out of New York described Mitchell as a negative influence on Darryl Strawberry and Dwight Gooden, the latter checking into a drug rehabilitation center the following spring. Mitchell has always claimed he's clean and doesn't drink or take drugs.

Shortly after the trade, Terry Kennedy predicted Mitchell wouldn't last two years in San Diego. The Padres had dealt Kennedy to Baltimore the same winter they acquired Mitchell, and the two had never been teammates. It's easy to imagine why Mitchell didn't appreciate the complimentary fortune-telling. "The thing Kennedy said, he's talking about attitude, the way I approach people, the way I talk to people," Mitchell said. "I never had a reputation like that. He doesn't even know me. He never talked to me in my life. He never even said 'hi' when he was catching and I came to bat."

There would soon be plenty of time for greetings and small talk, as Kennedy would join Mitchell with the Giants two years later. But looking back at Kennedy's prediction, it was obvious he knew something about Mitchell, who didn't last two years in San Diego, not even one. He was supposed to be the starting third baseman, but that status didn't last long. He hit only .245 and had a falling out with Larry Bowa, the rookie manager whose vociferous manner alienated many of his players.

As a San Diegan, Mitchell was back home, commuting to work only a few minutes from his old stomping grounds while residing at his grandmother's house in a poorer section of town. Bowa knew all about the outside influences that seemed to be bringing down Mitchell's game, but Mitchell wasn't willing to change his habits or friends. Mitchell's old acquaintances visited at all hours of the day and night. It got so bad that he began parking his car behind his house to make it appear he wasn't home. When his friends caught on and came to the door, his grandmother wouldn't let them in. "He needs his sleep," Whitfield would say. But even when his friends weren't around, Mitchell didn't always get his sleep. If he went 0-for-4 that day, his grandmother would keep him up and let him know about it, preaching to him on the finer points of hitting. "I had to listen," Mitchell said. "If I didn't, she'd bawl me out just like Larry Bowa."

Despite the pep talks, Mitchell wasn't the same player who hit .277 with the Mets, and it became evident that the distractions at home were affecting his game. The Padres preferred that Mitchell stay away from his old buddies, but Mitchell wasn't about to forget his past and move to upper class La Jolla or Del Mar. He was already upset that Marcus Allen refused to return to the same San Diego streets after hitting the big time in the National Football League. "I don't want to go big-headed like Marcus," Mitchell said.

Mitchell, like Canseco, has a habit of not adhering to the team schedule. And, like Canseco, he always offers an excuse. Following his winter trade from New York to San Diego, he was the only no-show at the Padres' first spring training workout. Where several of his new teammates who reside in San Diego were able to safely cross the snow-topped mountains to Yuma in time, Mitchell said he was stopped by the California Highway Patrol because he didn't have proper snow tires on his Cadillac. He was forced to return to San Diego and hunt down his cousin, who eventually chauffeured him in his four-wheel-drive vehicle. Once in camp, Mitchell blew off an entire workout for a dental appointment in San Diego, although he later said he didn't see any dentist. He was fined.

Then there was the time in Montreal when he almost caused the cancellation of the team's chartered flight. Twenty minutes before the airport's curfew, Mitchell was detained at customs trying to beat a $150 duty on $2,000 of newly purchased suits hidden in his carry-on bag. Mitchell told the customs agents he had purchased the suits a year earlier, but the agents uncovered a current local receipt from his bag. Traveling secretary Doc Mattei bailed out Mitchell and paid the $150 out of his own pocket.

Mitchell always denied that his ties to his old neighborhood caused his game to suffer, and he tried to reason that his new full-time role of hitting against both left-handers and righties was the big problem. He also blamed Bowa for not giving him more support. "It got to the point where I was scared the ball would be hit to me or I'd strike out with men on base," he said. "Larry Bowa was always screaming from the dugout. If you made a mistake, he'd yell at you. Grandma even said I looked uncomfortable on the field."

Mitchell had been demoted to platoon status by the time he was included as a throw-in in the seven-player blockbuster trade on the Fourth of July, 1987. The Padres had seen enough of him after only three months and shipped him to San Francisco, 500 miles from his hometown. The Padres didn't mind seeing Mitchell go, even if it meant he'd be replaced at third base by Chris Brown. "I felt like hell," said Mitchell, recalling his teary-eyed night following the trade. But even he realized he wasn't fitting in with the Padres. "The Padres didn't like my style. Fast truck, loud music, the way I dress." He didn't realize this at the time, but the trade turned out to be for Mitchell's good.

Under Davey Johnson, Larry Bowa and Roger Craig, Mitchell took an uneasy roller-coaster ride that finally began leveling out in San Francisco. Craig immediately informed him that he would be the everyday third baseman, and Mitchell responded with an impressive second half. The Giants had secured needed pitching in Dave Dravecky and Craig Lefferts, but it was Mitchell who became the biggest surprise in the package. He slugged two home runs off Chicago's Les Lancaster in his first game — as the number two hitter. He'd broken the 62-game homerless slump he'd had with the Padres and remained hot in 1987 throughout his 69-game joy ride in San Francisco, improving all his offensive statistics (.245 average to .306, seven homers to 15, 26 RBIs to 44 and zero steals to nine) and proving to be one of the reasons for the Giants' first division championship in 16 years.

Craig, who had never managed a championship team, was especially pleased, saying, "I can't believe that two good organizations with a lot of good baseball men would trade him. This guy has had a bad rap some place." Not some place; each place. In New York, it was the drug rumors and the relationship with Strawberry and Gooden. In San Diego, it was the threat of trouble knocking on his front door. But in San Francisco, Craig did what neither Johnson nor Bowa could — he kept Mitchell in the lineup and happy. It took some getting used to, but Mitchell eventually settled in to his new surroundings and had few complaints. He was even happy with his condominium, a residence unlike any of his previous homes. The glamorous Foster City unit off San Francisco Bay had all the modern conveniences, even a pond with, as Mitchell so eloquently put it, "ducks and stuff."

Away from his hometown, Mitchell developed into a fine all-around ballplayer. His batting average slipped to .251 in 1988, but he hit 19 home runs and had a career-high 80 RBIs while turning in a fair job at third base. It was all coming together for a guy who battled nagging injuries all year, but the Giants could do no better than fourth place. If they were to improve or even contend in '89, Mitchell would have to put up bigger numbers, especially if he were to be the new cleanup hitter.

It was obvious the Giants had lacked a legitimate number four hitter. In '87, when their 205 home runs were the club's most in 40 years, they had power guys throughout the lineup, with six players hitting at least 15 homers. But beginning with Chili Davis' (24 homers) 1988 departure to the Angels, three of those players would soon be gone. In '88, Candy Maldonado had a miserable year, his home-run total dropping from 20 to 12. Bob Brenly's fell from 18 to five, Will Clark's from 35 to 29, Mitchell's from 22 to 19 and Jeffrey Leonard's from 19 to 10 (only two with the Giants). It was evident that season's juiced-up baseballs significantly helped the Giants' numbers, but it was also becoming obvious that some of these players had already seen their best days and some changes would have to come. First, there was Chili's move to the Angels. Then Leonard, despite his playoff MVP trophy, was shipped to Milwaukee in a controversial trade for utility infielder Ernest Riles. And after Brenly couldn't secure a contract with the Giants, he went to Canada to play for the Blue Jays. With only Clark, Mitchell and Maldonado still around by the spring of '89, the Giants were still uncertain who would hit fourth behind Clark. Al Rosen was unable to land a quality cleanup hitter — no Dale Murphy, but Tracy Jones; no Joe Carter, but Terry Kennedy — so Craig was forced to choose between Maldonado and Mitchell.

Craig had already given Candy about seven million chances to redeem himself in '88, but Maldonado did his best to waste each and every opportunity. Craig figured Maldonado would return to his old form (85 RBIs in both '86 and '87), but the native of Puerto Rico showed no traces of his past and hit .255 with only 68 RBIs. The Giants could ill afford having a cleanup hitter put up those numbers for another season, but Craig showed why he's a swell guy — or maybe just a slow learner — when he gave Maldonado yet another chance in the spring of 1989. At one point in February, Craig even announced that Maldonado was the favorite to hit fourth. But once the Cactus League games began, it was clear who was Craig's cleanup hitter, and the situation was long confirmed by the end of the exhibition season. Mitchell had hit .455 with seven homers and 21 RBIs. "I got tired of seeing Will walk last year," Mitchell said. "I want to make it so pitchers don't want to pitch to either of us."

The Giants needed Mitchell to have a great year. Every other team in the division enjoyed attractive three-four combinations, especially San Diego with Tony Gwynn and newcomer Jack Clark. The Dodgers had Kirk Gibson and Eddie Murray, the Reds Eric Davis and Kal Daniels, the Astros Glenn Davis and Kevin Bass and the Braves Gerald Perry and Dale Murphy. The Giants, on the other hand, were coming off a season of Will Clark and Ernest Riles. The opposition could afford to pitch Clark carefully, and the sorry cleanup situation was the main reason for Clark's league-leading 100 walks — he didn't walk a hundred times just because he has a good eye.

But Mitchell had never proven over an entire season that this job was for him. In '88, he hit 19 homers but only one after August 12 because of a myriad of injuries (knee, back, finger), and post-season surgery in his right knee made the solid-bodied man appear somewhat fragile. Mitchell hadn't been on the disabled list since 1985, but he always seemed to be in the trainer's room for one reason or another.

No one knew if Mitchell's spring was a fluke. Remember Randy Elliot? He was the Giants outfielder in the '70s who had great springs but fell apart in the summers, hitting a career .215 in only

114 games. The Giants of '89 had no other choice available and inserted Mitchell into the cleanup slot and asked if he'd mind not breaking any bones. Mitchell obliged and promptly posted a .292 average in April, which nicely accompanied his six home runs and baseball-leading 25 RBIs. It was evident Clark wasn't going to defend his crown as the league leader in bases on balls.

Instead of slowing or even keeping the same pace in May, Mitchell went even wilder, blasting nine more home runs and driving in 23 runs. Clark was also on fire, thanks in part to Mitchell, who discouraged pitchers from working around him much. Clark was leading the league in hitting through May with a .362 average, 38 points ahead of runner-up Lonnie Smith. His 10 home runs and 42 RBIs prompted people to think Triple Crown, but he'd need to pass Mr. Mitchell first, no small chore. "I've never seen a guy go through what Mitch is going through," Clark said. "You see it for a week. But not for a two-month stretch."

Why the sudden change? Ask Mitchell and he'd give a different answer every time. He would say he was better because all that off-season Wiffle ball made it easier to hit curveballs. Or because all that off-season softball made him develop a nice upper cut. Or because his new contact lenses allowed him to see the ball easier. Or because the 50-pound logs he carried up and down his street built his strength. Or because his girlfriend brought peace and harmony to his life. Or because his move from third base to left field made it easier to concentrate on offense. Or because the advice he received from Willie Mays and Dusty Baker provided a newfound confidence.

It didn't really matter why he was so improved as much as it mattered he just was improved. And the improvement carried over to his defense. Sometimes an erratic third baseman, Mitchell was becoming a solid left fielder in only his first year on the beat. In the season's second month, Mitchell had already made the defensive play of the year when he barehanded — barehanded! — a fly ball by Ozzie Smith in the left-field corner at Busch Stadium. As Mitchell chased the fly, he wanted to make sure he had room to make the catch so he took a quick glance at the wall behind the Giants' bullpen. However, he soon discovered he had overrun the ball and his only alternative was to reach back with his non-glove hand. As soon as he stretched out his arm, the ball landed smack in the middle of his palm, and Mitchell shocked everyone in attendance by not dropping the thing. Call it instinct or reflex, but be sure to call it an all-time highlighter. It has already been replayed a few thousand times, but Mitchell seemed to be one of the least impressed, insisting a full week later that he hadn't yet seen a single replay.

Mays was perhaps most instrumental in Mitchell's smooth transition from third base to left field, and he also stamped his imprint on Mitchell's swing. In fact, Mitchell's swing is very similar to Mays', although Willie claims, "I didn't teach him that." It was still clear Mitchell wasn't swinging the bat as he had in previous seasons. His '89 swing was the classic power swing, the one that ends with a distinct upper cut. His home runs aren't mistakes. They're supposed-to-bes. "Just like Willie," said Mitchell, who uses an enormous amount of strength bursting through the strike zone, his quick and explosive bat significantly increasing the wind-chill factor with every follow-through.

"When Mitchell was playing in New York, I told the Mets he could hit," Mays said. "But back then, he had a right-field swing. The reason was he was part time and a platoon player. San Diego was similar. He really didn't have a chance to play. But when he got to San Francisco, he played every day. And his swing really improved. He became a home-run hitter."

Mitchell is the same height as Mays (5-foot-11) but much bigger, built like a tree stump with thick branches as arms and legs. Mays had natural strength throughout his body; Mitchell's is concentrated. "It's in his legs. His legs and his butt," Dusty Baker said. "When he goes bad, he's not going through with his legs and butt." This was not a time in which Mitchell would go bad. He and power partner Clark were becoming the most explosive local tandem since Mays and McCovey and the most explosive national combo since Maris and Mantle. A Giants find-a-nickname promotion resulted in the catchy "Pacific Sock Exchange," but Mitchell preferred the label of "M&M Boys," the same tag given to Mays-McCovey and Maris-Mantle. How could the "M&M Boys" define Clark and Mitchell? "The Milkman and Chocolate Milk," chuckled Mitch.

Over and over, Mitchell would give an example of why he's different from the rest. One of the most telling examples came the day he told a few reporters that he uses mentholated jelly to fight colds. The reporters didn't take the comment as a big deal until Mitchell explained how he used the stuff. "I eat it," he said. Of course, nobody believed Mitchell. This was just another of his sto-

ries. But Mitch was willing to back up his statement. He walked
into the trainer's room and returned with a jar of Vicks VapoRub.
He removed the lid, dipped his finger and stuck the goo down his
throat. A message on the label warns, "Do not swallow or place in
nostrils," but Mitchell said he swallows the ointment regularly.

There is only one Kevin Mitchell.

Mitchell apparently had found a new home with the Giants,
and his accomplishments in April and May hinted that this might
be a magical season. It was as if all the negatives in his past had
been forgotten, or at least were easier to overlook. It appeared
nothing or nobody could distract him any longer. "All that's back
in the past right now," Mitchell told Barry Bloom of the San Diego
Tribune. "You grow up, you have to watch your back; that's all. I
did a lot of fights. But, you know, it's all over with. It ain't like that
no more, anyway. People, they don't want to fight no more. They
use something else. They used to straight off fight. Now it's, like,
let's get it over with. It's scary, scary stuff. It's everywhere. It's a lot
of drug-related stuff. It's so hot everywhere that people keep mo-
vin'. They think police are following them. I got friends now that I
don't know what they're doin'. They're not workin', but still they
got nice things. How do they do it? I don't even want to know. I
don't want to ask questions. You just deal with it. You don't want
to lose your friends. You don't want to lose the respect of your
friends, but you don't want to have problems with what they're doing, either. You see, people talk. All they do is talk about you.
They're jealous. I don't care what people say about me. I know
what I'm doin'. My family knows what I'm doin'. As long as I go out
there and play my game, they can talk all they want. It doesn't
matter."

"We all have our ways, but there's a lot of good in him," said
grandma Josie. "He's a rugged guy who's always been able to protect himself. Maybe that's why they say those things about him."

They say other things about Canseco, who overcame an undistinguished amateur career to enjoy great success in the major
leagues. A 15th-round pick out of Miami's Coral Park High School
in 1982, Canseco was just another outfielder slugging it out in the
low minor leagues for his first three seasons. The A's saw enough
from Canseco's .276 average and 15 home runs at Single-A Modes-
to to kick him up to Double-A Huntsville for the '85 season. That's
where the Canseco legend started.

Canseco attained semi-divine status in Alabama by the time

the season was half over. By hitting .318, slamming 25 homers and driving in 80 runs in just 58 games, he was promoted to Triple-A Tacoma by June. For the Tigers, he hit .348, punched 11 more homers and drove in 47 runs in 60 games. That was good enough for enrollment with the big club, which was struggling to wind up a lackluster season. Canseco became an instant regular, hit .302 in 29 games, adding five home runs and 13 RBIs. His cumulative season — 41 home runs and 130 RBIs — was such that despite playing only a minor role for the big club, Canseco's name made the cover of Oakland's 1986 media guide: "Introducing Jose Canseco as The Natural." Just like that, he was the new Roy Hobbs.

Hobbs was the fictional baseball hero created by Bernard Malamud in his book "The Natural" and brought to life on film by Robert Redford, but he actually had very little in common with Canseco. Hobbs was left-handed, Canseco right-handed. Hobbs was all but over the hill when he got his chance in the big leagues with the New York Knights; Canseco was just 21 when he first faced — and beat — big-league pitching. Hobbs was from the vast wheat fields of mid-America. Canseco, born in Cuba and brought with his twin brother, Ozzie, to the United States before his first birthday, was raised amid the glitz and glitter of southern Florida. But both were strong-armed outfielders who had pitched in high school. And both had sweet and "Natural" swings that could send baseballs soaring out of any park in the land, save perhaps Yellowstone.

Canseco was such an overwhelming presence in the A's 1986 spring training camp in Phoenix that then-manager Jackie Moore broke with tradition and let the rookie hit last in batting practice, calling him his "fireworks show." His pre-game long-ball exhibitions were such that both his own teammates and the opposition would stop what they were doing just to watch the kid drive the ball clear out of the Valley of the Sun. Once the season began, the same ground rules applied. In late April, he hit a ball 450 feet for a home run. It wasn't remarkable until you realized he was a right-handed batter hitting the ball the opposite way, to right field. "He hits the ball where I hit them," said left-handed slugger Reggie Jackson, then of the Angels. "And he's right-handed. That's scary."

Once off to a good start, Canseco went on a reign of terror. Despite some obvious drawbacks — he struck out 175 times, setting a rookie record, and had one 0-for-40 streak — he was a runaway winner in the Rookie of the Year balloting over considerably above-average competition that included Seattle's Danny Tartabull and California's Wally Joyner. In August, Canseco admitted that if the award came down to a popularity contest, Joyner would win. Instead, it came down to numbers, and Canseco's were 33 home runs and 117 RBIs, one RBI shy of the Oakland club record.

It was obvious from that first bit of success that Canseco and fame might not be entirely compatible. He didn't develop many close friends on the 1986 team. That club was stocked mostly with veterans, and Canseco spent a good deal of time listening to the sage advice of the club's top home-run hitter, Dave Kingman, baseball's ultimate pariah. There were those who thought Kingman's influence would be deadly. But even here, Canseco went his own way, thought his own thoughts and listened to almost no one. He certainly didn't listen much to hitting coach Bob Watson, who said, "I've hit behind Cesar Cedeno, Jim Rice, Fred Lynn, Reggie Jackson and Dale Murphy. But Canseco's in a class by himself." Watson believed that Jose could operate at peak efficiency if he would only find one comfortable batting stance and stick with it. Instead, Canseco changed stances with almost every at-bat — feet spread wide one time, narrow and flexed the next, up tight in the batter's box the third and off the plate the fourth. Watson came to call it the "Canseco Dance," and although he did his best to get Canseco to change, he never succeeded. Indeed, by 1987 Watson had been made the A's bench coach, with third base coach Jim Lefebvre adding the title of hitting coach to his repertoire. The fact that Watson couldn't see eye-to-eye with Canseco probably was one of the factors that led to his repositioning. A year later, he left the A's to join the Houston Astros as assistant general manager.

By the time he reached Huntsville, Canseco had become addicted to lifting weights. By spending six days a week in the weight room in the off-season and lifting about every other day during the season, he built himself into one of the most impressive physical specimens baseball has ever known. Detroit manager Sparky Anderson took one look at Canseco during his rookie year and uttered a now-classic malaprop. "That Canseco's built like a Greek goddess." Canseco's body was certainly all the rage in the Coliseum, where a faithful cadre of 13-to 18-year-old girls liked to sit and watch and scream for their hero. Canseco, a left fielder his first two years and a right fielder after that, ate it up, flexing his muscles, waving to the crowd and talking with his loyal band of followers.

But there was a dark downside to his physical prowess, and a debate surfaced over how Canseco grew from a skinny boy into a huge man — that is, if he ever was a skinny boy at all. Even if he always had been big, some people argued that nobody could have built a body like that without help — anabolic steroids to be specific. While rumors circulated, nothing came of it until the Washington Post's Thomas Boswell said on national television that Canseco had indeed used steroids. Boswell had no conclusive proof — baseball does not test for steroids — but he did point to what he claimed was the vast physical disparity between Jose and his twin brother, Ozzie, as circumstantial evidence. While it was clear that Jose had the more imposing body of the two, it also was clear the difference in size wasn't significant. At 6-foot-4, 240 pounds, Jose had about a half-inch and 10 pounds on his twin. Ozzie, a pitcher when he signed with the Yankees, didn't lift weights until he was signed by the A's and converted to an outfielder in mid-1986.

And if Canseco bristled, some of those who had known him as a youth in Miami were incredulous. Sal Pirrotta, who coached both Cansecos at Coral Park High in Miami, wouldn't hear of tales of the weak, skinny Jose Canseco who played for him in 1981 and 1982. Pirrotta told the story of the school extending the top of the left-field fence by 20 feet because the people living across the street were complaining that baseballs were breaking their windows. "Jose hit most of them," Pirrotta said.

Similar outcries were heard from Camilio Pasqual, a long-time major-league pitcher and a Miami resident who had taken a job as an A's scout in 1982. Pasqual was the man who insisted the club sign this big kid nobody else wanted. He met Canseco when Jose played on one of his son's teams, and he said the first thing he noticed was Canseco's size. "Skinny? Canseco was never skinny," Pasqual said. "He was 6-3 and 190 pounds at 17 years old. Canseco always swung a big bat." Pasqual urged A's scouting director Dick Wiencek to draft the kid, and Pasqual was getting nervous when the A's had made their ninth and 10th picks and hadn't included Canseco. During the draft, Pasqual screamed at Wiencek, "Dick, you draft him, and I'll pay the money myself to sign him. I'll be his agent." Finally, the A's chose Canseco in round 15. "I couldn't believe another team didn't have him by then," Pasqual said. "Canseco is the first player I ever signed. I'll never have another one so good. Players like him come every 100 years."

Canseco, though, tells another story of his youth. "I wasn't always this big. I was skinny, slow and weak. I worked my way up to
this. It's not like I go home and lay on my butt and eat Latin food
and gain weight. I'm always active. I have respect for my body. I
take care of myself. You don't just wake up one morning and look
like this. It doesn't just happen."

Canseco's fabulous rookie season was followed by a solid sophomore season in which he hiked his batting average 17 points to
.257, hit 31 homers and drove in 113 RBIs. If anything, Canseco
seemed to enjoy the season more. One reason was the A's were winning as many as they were losing. After Jackie Moore was fired in
June 1986, Tony La Russa, himself fired by the White Sox in June,
came to the A's as the new manager in July. La Russa, a motivator,
an intellectual and something of a firebrand, turned the A's into a
different team. They won 11 more than they lost the rest of the way
to finish 10 games under .500 at 76-86. By 1987, the A's had added a
second rookie whiz, first baseman Mark McGwire, and the veteran
bat of designated hitter Reggie Jackson. With Reggie and McGwire
flanking him, Canseco was no longer alone in the Oakland lineup.
If his power numbers were not much better than those of 1986, he
took comfort in the fact the A's were in contention for much of the
year, in first place as late as the first week in September, playing
.500 ball and finishing just four games out of first.

All that merely set the stage for the greater glory to come in
1988. Canseco had made his 40-40 prediction in the spring, and it
was too late to turn back and change his mind. On the face of it, the
proposition was nothing short of ridiculous. For one thing, Canseco
was just in his third year, and as good as his first two years had
been, he'd never hit more than 33 homers. And stolen bases? The
guy had exactly 15 steals in each of his first two seasons. Rickey
Henderson, he was not. At least, not yet. But he'd shown a glimmer. Six of his 15 steals in 1987 were steals of third base, as opponents, intimidated by Canseco's power, forgot about his speed, ignoring him as a base-stealing threat.

Canseco was ready to be turned loose, although La Russa
didn't exactly give him free rein. Instead, the manager picked Canseco's spots, only with ever-increasing frequency as it became obvious that the A's had a new, unexpected weapon at their disposal.
By May 20, not only did Canseco have 10 homers, but he'd already

equaled his previous best with his 15th steal. By this time, La Russa was coming to trust Canseco's instincts as a base runner and began to turn off the red light. As that happened, the steals began to mount up. La Russa insisted on just two things, a high percentage of success and running only to help the A's win — no cheapie steals in the ninth inning of 9-2 games. A player on a good run such as Canseco's will frequently take off like a shot and slow down toward the end of the season as the league's pitchers catch up. But Canseco, despite having his legs battered by trying to maneuver his 240 pounds into soft slides that by their very nature were as abrasive as sand paper, didn't fall into the trap. He stole successfully on 10 of his first 13 attempts and on 10 of his last 13.

A prodigy had been born in Oakland. And something else, too — a style. By chance, Canseco and McGwire managed to give the A's their own identity with a home-run celebration called the Bash. Toward the end of the '87 season, the Oakland behemoths were sitting side-by-side on the A's bench after one of McGwire's prodigious home runs when they began, as dedicated body builders will do, to compare forearms. They then rammed those gigantic pieces of beef into each other in a test of strength. A simple act in itself, almost an afterthought. But they were to sculpt it into something else, a ritual greeting at home plate after home runs that would come to define the A's of the late 1980s. The style and the substance of the unique, and occasionally painful, ritual was a vast departure from the Dodger-spawned high-fives that had been the rage in baseball over the last decade. By the end of spring training in 1988, the entire Oakland team was in on it, and identities were born. The A's were the Bashers, and Canseco and McGwire were the Bash Brothers. One of the classic Bay Area collector's items from the 1988 season is the Bash Brothers poster, Canseco and McGwire giving their best Blues Brothers look in front of — ironically, it would turn out for Canseco — a police car.

As off-the-wall as his stolen bases were, it was still his seemingly limitless power that continued to define Canseco as a baseball player. And it was the home-run that defined the A's as a team. Early in August, Canseco hit his 100th homer. Baseball had never seen a player reach 100 homers so quickly, in fewer than three full seasons. For Oakland, however, it would turn out to be routine. A year later, McGwire became the second man to reach 100 in that short span of time as the A's became synonymous with the home run. It was a curious thing, too, because Oakland's home park, the Coliseum, had long been considered a graveyard for power hitters. Other than Reggie Jackson hitting 47 in 1969, a year given over to hitters because of expansion, the Coliseum had never been host to a 40-homer season.

There was no expansion in 1988, but the bats of Canseco and McGwire — and Dave Parker and Dave Henderson — were too much for any ballpark to bottle up for long. Canseco took batting practice before the 1988 All-Star Game in Cincinnati's Riverfront Stadium, then promptly labeled the park that had hosted the last 50-homer season in major-league history — George Foster's 52 in 1977 — "a joke. The ball just shoots out of here." By contrast, Canseco, and to a lesser extent McGwire, Parker and Henderson, missed no opportunity to run down the Coliseum as a hitter's ballpark. After going over the wall in Arlington Stadium in a game against the Rangers, Canseco intimated that playing in a home-run hitter's park such as Riverfront would be the baseball equivalent of going to the Land of Oz. When he hit five homers in a four-game series in Seattle in the last three days of July, he used the media to warn Oakland management that the degree of difficulty posed by the Oakland Coliseum should be taken into consideration come contract time. Canseco used Chicago right fielder Andre Dawson, the 1987 National League MVP, as an example. "He was handicapped by the park he played in when he was in Montreal," Canseco said, pointing out that Dawson had a career high of just 32 homers while hanging his shingle at spacious Olympic Stadium before going to Chicago as a free agent and hitting 49 in 1987 in cozy Wrigley Field. "Then he was compensated."

Sandy Alderson had heard all of that before, but he was steamed to hear contract talk in the middle of the season. Later, he mellowed — or at least masked his anger — by saying, "Instead of paying Jose more money, maybe we'll just move (the Coliseum) fences in."

Come the '88 playoffs, Canseco put on a grand display as the A's swept Boston, winning the first two in Fenway Park before returning to Oakland to clinch the franchise's first trip to the World Series in 15 years. In Game One, he launched a home run to help beat Bruce Hurst 2-1. The A's were down 2-0 the next night when Canseco came up in the seventh with a man on and launched a moon shot over the Green Monster. The A's went on to score another run in the inning and, after Rich Gedman's homer tied it, Oakland eventually won on Walter Weiss' ninth-inning, two-out RBI single. After going hitless in Game Three, Canseco came back to hit his third homer of the series in the first inning of Game Four, pushing the A's into a lead they would never lose. He also doubled, singled, stole a base and scored another run as the A's made it into the World Series on the strength of a 4-1 victory over Hurst. Although reliever Dennis Eckersley earned playoff MVP honors by saving all four of the games, Canseco had etched his name deeper into the national consciousness.

The World Series seemed destined to bring more of the same Canseco's way as the A's faced Los Angeles, a team that had none of the A's credentials but had surprised the more potent New York Mets in the National League playoffs. After being hit by a pitch in the first inning of Game One, Canseco came up with the bases loaded and two out in the second. Facing ex-Oakland farmhand Tim Belcher, Canseco lined the first grand slam of his career out to the deepest part of Dodger Stadium, in the process erasing a 2-0 Los Angeles lead. But the A's were not to score again that night against the Dodgers' bullpen, and Eckersley, one out from putting away a 4-3 win in the ninth, walked Mike Davis and saw limping pinch hitter Kirk Gibson sew a piece of special World Series lore by lining a game-winning home run over Canseco's head into the right-field stands.

Canseco wouldn't get a hit the rest of the series. His slump and the increasingly aggressive Dodgers pitching spearheaded by Orel Hershiser took the A's out of their pattern except for McGwire's game-winning, ninth-inning home run off Jay Howell for a 2-1 win in Game Three. After the five-game loss, Canseco echoed the feelings of his teammates when he said, "We're young enough and good enough to be back here again."

In May 1989, things weren't as bright in Oakland as they were in May 1988, and Canseco's presence on the disabled list was just one of the many reasons. Weiss wasn't hitting much, and he was making errors at shortstop the likes of which the A's hadn't seen in his exceptional 1988 rookie season. Leadoff man and left fielder Luis Polonia was similarly slump-ridden. Starters Curt Young and Storm Davis owned sky-high ERAs. Catcher Ron Hassey, too, was off to his typically slow start. And the A's were hitting into double plays at a prodigious rate.

     With Canseco on the shelf, La Russa used Dave Parker as his
number three hitter for much of the first half of the season. That
left a vacancy at the cleanup spot. In the early days of May,
McGwire claimed it as his own. On May 2, he gave the A's one of
their most dramatic wins of the season. The Blue Jays scored four
runs in the first inning when Rance Mulliniks crushed a grand
slam off Bob Welch. The A's had chipped away after that, but Oakland still faced a 5-4 deficit entering the ninth inning. Duane Ward
blew away the first two hitters in the ninth, striking out Stan Javier and Weiss. But singles by Polonia and Henderson breathed life
into the Oakland bench. Parker, who had singled in each of his
previous two at-bats, was next. As the first man to face Blue Jays
relief ace Tom Henke, he worked his way on with a walk. Henke
had little reason for concern. Left-handers such as Parker had long
been his Achilles' heel, but the right-hander with the mean fastball
and vicious slider had made a career out of dousing the bats of big
swingers such as the right-handed McGwire. In fact, McGwire was
a particular patsy, having struck out in all six meetings between the
two. But this time, McGwire launched a towering left-field grand
slam, the last homer an Oakland hitter would ever get in Exhibition Stadium, with the Blue Jays due to take up tenancy in the
SkyDome in a month's time. McGwire, who had homered twice in a
rout of Baltimore on April 27, would bring a streak of five homers
in nine games to a close on May 7 in Detroit.
     The grand slam was the most memorable of the five and
brought a breath-taking end to a night of high drama as the A's
scored an 8-5 victory that was significant in a couple of ways. First,
it moved Oakland past Texas and atop the American League West
for the first time since the first week of the season, a position the
A's would hold, with the exception of one day, until the Fourth of
July holiday. In addition, it heightened the A's-Jays rivalry that
would last through the end of the season.
     The game was loaded with heated events, most involving Jays'
left fielder George Bell. With two outs in the ninth, Gene Nelson
replaced Rick Honeycutt to pitch to Bell, who was a perfect mirror
to reflect the sense of frustration Toronto was feeling. Not only
was manager Jimy Williams in trouble — he would be fired and
replaced by Cito Gaston within a month — but the Jays were about
to fall to six games under .500. For his part in the evening's festivi-
ties, Bell waved at a couple of A's hits as they streaked by him en

route to the left-field fence, fueling a three-run rally in the seventh inning that gave McGwire the chance to win it in the ninth. Then, because he jogged to first base on his own hit in the seventh, he was unable to advance to second when Henderson bobbled the ball in center field. The crowd booed him mercilessly. Bell was determined to get that base back, but he was thrown out stealing by Hassey. In fact, Bell moved all-out only once all night, and that was to charge the mound after being hit in the chest by a Nelson pitch as he leaned over the plate. He missed with a haymaker, but he succeeded in triggering a benches-clearing brawl. "I can understand Bell's frustration," an agitated La Russa said. "But I will swear on my children that all Gene was trying to do was to get him out." Nelson, for his part, wasn't nearly as understanding. "Bell's a mound-chaser," he said. "One time in the minor leagues, he got hit with the bases loaded by one of our pitchers in a tie game and did it. Later, we learned that if he did it again, his teammates had decided he wouldn't get any backing from them. He charged the mound again, and no one helped him."

One of the reasons for the A's successful 16-10 month was Parker, who enjoyed a turnaround from his .196 April, when more than a few sportwriters had written him off. But Parker repeatedly pronounced that his slow start was just that — a start. Through it all, Parker's clubhouse presence, his needling, his braggadocio, his raucous voice was helping the club when his bat wasn't. Throughout April, Parker had taken gobs of extra batting practice. He'd all but blinded himself watching video tapes of him swinging — a sorry sight given his sub-.200 batting average. He spent hours with La Russa and hitting coach Merv Rettenmund. If his sense of humor was intact, it was clear that nothing else was. On May 1, the A's flew from Oakland to Toronto to begin an eight-game road trip through the American League East. Parker, searching for answers, begged off. La Russa granted Parker's request to get away from it all for a day, and Parker flew home to Cincinnati to visit his wife, Kellye, and the couple's two children, Danielle and David II.

Parker arrived at 6:15 a.m., and little time passed before he was summoned for a game of catch by David. So father and son, like so many fathers and sons before them, headed out to the back yard to toss around the baseball. It was during that brief stopover that Kellye assumed the role of batting coach. She told her husband, "Relax. You've hit, and you're always going to hit." It wasn't anything he hadn't heard before, but it definitely made sense. Although he didn't pick up a bat the entire time off, something had happened when he got to Toronto the next afternoon. Suddenly, Parker found he could pick up the flight of the ball as it left the pitcher's hand. "Sometimes, that's just what you need. I hadn't seen my kids since spring training. And seeing them, I was able to get the slump off my mind. They are what's important to me."

In an effort to keep the flavor of home with him, Parker brought Kellye and the kids to Detroit the following weekend. He had two hits and scored two runs in a 5-4 victory over the Tigers in a game that was to be the turning point in his season. Parker went hitless in just three of his final 20 games in May. In the process, he hit six home runs, drove in 18 runs and had hitting streaks of 10 and five games.

While the A's concluded May 34-18 and in a tie with the Angels for first place, the Giants held a narrow one-game edge over Cincinnati with a 29-22 record. The Giants moved back into first place briefly during their first of two five-game win streaks in the month, the first culminating with Rick Reuschel's 200th career victory, a 2-1 decision at Montreal on May 12. The win came four days before Reuschel's 40th birthday, providing hope for middle-aged, overweight men everywhere. It gave the Giants a 3-0 start on an 11-game road trip that proved to be very important and successful. Although they completed the trip at 7-4, all four losses could have been avoided, and an 11-0 trip wasn't far from reality. After suffering two tough one-run losses at Montreal, they flew to Philadelphia and dropped one of the trip's two demoralizing, extra-inning losses. After Clark and Mitchell homered back-to-back off Steve Bedrosian to end an 11-inning scoring drought, Philly's Bob Dernier hit a three-run homer to beat the Giants 3-2 — a three-run, inside-the-park homer, that is. The Giants came back to beat the Phils two straight. Then in the opener at Shea, with two outs in the 10th, Craig Lefferts and Goose Gossage walked two batters apiece — Gossage on nine pitches — to force home the deciding run of a 3-2 loss. But the uncrushed Giants surfaced the next two days to beat the Mets twice. Each time after a tough loss in extra innings, the Giants came back to easily win the series' next two games.

As the Giants headed for home, Craig said, "I think the players have discovered that they could win this thing." And a couple of newcomers to the '89 roster who had played in previous World Series weren't about to argue. Terry Kennedy ('84, Padres) said, "You know you have a good team, so you just try to stay close and avoid the blowouts because you know you have the ability to come back and win." And Ken Oberkfell, who had been acquired from Pittsburgh on May 10, said, "We weren't picked that year ('82, Cardinals), but everything fell into place. That's what you need. This is a tough, well-balanced division. But in the nine days I've been here, I've seen a lot of character."

But, like the A's, there were problems. In the spring, Craig said over and over that the season would rest on four players, but the so-called keys to the season did nothing but open jobs for other players. When the season began, Mike LaCoss was the bullpen closer, Kirt Manwaring the catcher, Matt Williams the third baseman and Candy Maldonado the right fielder, but none of the four did as much as the Giants had hoped. LaCoss was demoted to middle relief, Williams was in Phoenix, Manwaring played less than Kennedy and Maldonado fell to third-string status behind Tracy Jones and Donell Nixon. Maldonado was especially disappointing. If the Giants were desperate for a number four hitter in '88, their need was even more apparent for a number five hitter in '89. Someone was finally protecting Clark, but now no one was protecting Mitchell, and this time it would be Mitchell, not Clark, whose name would be among the league's walk leaders. And Maldonado was to blame in both cases, Candy already blowing his chance to hit fourth and looking even worse hitting fifth. "I see what Will was talking about last year, about being unprotected," Mitchell said. "I don't want to walk. I want to hit." But Maldonado was making life difficult. By mid-May, he was slumping worse than ever, to the tune of 0-for-13 and 3-for-36. He had no homers for the season and only nine RBIs. "I'm very honest," Craig said. "I don't know what I'll do with Candy. I saw this guy drive in 85 runs (in both '86 and '87) when he didn't even play much. What happened?"

The same question could be asked of LaCoss. By May 11, he had walked 16 batters in 22⅔ innings compared with Craig Lefferts' two walks in 25⅓ innings. In one unforgettable May 5 evening, LaCoss walked three batters, made an error and allowed two runs — all in one-third of an inning. Afterward, he said relieving might not be his forte and had planned to ask Craig for a return to the rotation. When Craig got wind of the story, he screamed, "I'll make those decisions, not him. He's been (bleeping) hurt in the neck and toe. And he's got to pitch better than he pitched tonight, I guarantee you (bleeping) that. That's bull."

LaCoss' problems weren't centered solely on the field in the month of May. On the evening of May 11, outside a popular Montreal restaurant four blocks from the Giants' hotel, LaCoss and a teammate were approached by several young men. Words were exchanged, a scuffle ensued and punches were thrown. LaCoss found himself with a black eye, and he sported a shiner the rest of the two-week road trip. His bruised right eye was readily visible during his May 14 pitching stint that was televised back to the Bay Area, but LaCoss never spoke publicly about the melee until Henry Schulman of the Oakland Tribune chronicled the incident the next day. Although Schulman reported that LaCoss hadn't provoked a fight, LaCoss confronted Schulman and warned him that he "picked the wrong guy to mess with."

Another reliever of note in May was Gossage, who secured his first save as a Giant May 2 against the Cubs, the team that had released him only five weeks earlier. It was evident that there was still bad blood between Goose and Cubs manager Don Zimmer, who had let him go. After Goose saved the 4-0 victory, he was asked if he had talked to Zimmer since his release. "I said 'hi,' " he said. Asked more about the conversation, he said, "I said 'hi.' " Zimmer was more vocal when pressed about Gossage's performance. "I know what you want me to say," he began. "Everyone wants me to say something bad about Goose Gossage. Six out of seven people (in this room) want me to say something bad about Goose Gossage. Here's a guy who's been one of the greatest (bleeping) pitchers ever in baseball, and I'll say something bad about him? I was a .230 hitter. You think I'm going to say something bad about Goose Gossage? I'm too (bleeping) smart. I'm not saying anything about Goose Gossage."

If nothing else, Clark and Mitchell continued their hot hitting. After the deadly three-four combination took New York's Bob Ojeda deep back-to-back on May 20, Ojeda said, "They seem to feed off each other. You can't pitch around them. That combination back-to-back is tough."

Good hitting will beat good pitching; and vice versa. It's baseball's version of "what comes first? the chicken or the egg." By the end of May, a merger was the only way the Giants and A's could have had both parts of the equation. The A's needed hitters who were slump-proof and not on the disabled list. The Giants needed pitchers who could simply pitch. Sheer grit wouldn't keep them at the top of their divisions indefinitely. And so in June, both went shopping to beef up their rosters.

THE ACQUISITIONS
How Rickey Henderson and
Steve Bedrosian filled the gaps

The A's have always tried to upstage the Giants, and they've often been successful. The Giants frequently do things first, but the A's just as frequently do things better. The Giants arrived in San Francisco in 1958 and took five years to get to the World Series. The A's came along in 1968 and also found themselves in the World Series five seasons later. And six seasons later. And seven seasons later. It was a staggering performance — three straight world titles.

The anything-you-can-do-I-can-do-better trend has evolved into a tradition. In 1986, the Giants introduced a slick first baseman named Will Clark. The kid from New Orleans turned into the finest rookie to hit Candlestick since the early '70s, when Gary

Matthews and John Montefusco won Rookie of the Year honors.
The following year, it was the A's turn. They unveiled their own
rookie first baseman, Mark McGwire, and all he did was hit an unprecedented 49 home runs in his first season. Well, not quite all; he
also won the Rookie of the Year title, just as A's outfielder Jose
Canseco did a year earlier and A's shortstop Walter Weiss did a
year later.

There's more. In 1987, the Giants captured the hearts of the
Bay Area by winning a division championship. A year later, it was
the A's turn. They not only won the division but the American
League pennant as well.

That brings us to June 1989. The A's and Giants each were
having dreams of playing in the World Series, but nightmares kept
interrupting. The Giants were still without a reliable bullpen closer; the A's were still without a reliable leadoff hitter. The Giants
had tried everyone but Kevin Mitchell as their door-slammer and
had been forced to rely mostly on Craig Lefferts, a left-hander
whose abilities could be better used in a set-up role. The A's had
experimented with a slew of leadoff men but kept coming back to
Luis Polonia, a little lefty as occasionally inconsistent and erratic
at the plate as he was in left field.

Enter Al Rosen and Sandy Alderson, a couple of general managers who despised imperfection and were willing to try everything
in their power to eliminate their teams' bad dreams. Rosen, in Giants tradition, acted first and dealt for a marquee bullpen closer,
Philadelphia's Steve Bedrosian. Then Alderson, not to be outdone
and following the A's tradition, required only three days to respond
to Rosen's big move. Alderson obtained an even bigger star, prodi-
gal son Rickey Henderson, who had left the A's back in 1985 for the
glitz, glory and greenbacks of the New York Yankees.

The A's and Giants had eliminated their biggest weaknesses,
but huge prices were required to pull off such enormous transactions. Each team doled out three young players, but Rosen and Alderson had gambled that their chances to win immediately would
be much better with Bedrosian and Henderson and were more than
willing to sacrifice some youth for a quick fix. With possible apolo-
gies to the '90s, the future was now for both clubs.

The A's, like the Giants with Bedrosian, had tried to woo
Rickey to the Bay Area long before the third month of the '89 season. In fact, even after Oakland's 104-win regular season in '88,

Alderson saw room for improvement, particularly in left and at the leadoff position. Polonia hit .287 as a rookie and .292 in '88 and had proven he could hit for an average, but he'd never mastered the fine art of taking pitches and working his way on base with a walk. With Carney Lansford, Dave Henderson, Jose Canseco, Dave Parker and Mark McGwire stretching through the heart of the order, the A's primary need in a leadoff hitter was someone who could get on base with exceptional frequency, setting up the big bats to follow. Somebody just like Rickey Henderson. At the '88 winter meetings, Alderson went to the Yankees looking to work a deal. No dice. Henderson was untouchable, the Yankees said. Alderson backed off, but all was not well with Henderson in New York in '89. Shortly after reporting to camp, he told reporters that the '88 Yankees had been crippled by excessive alcohol consumption. "I saw too many people getting drunk," Henderson said. "How can you perform the next day? Liquor does not leave you overnight. You have to know when to party and when not to party."

Henderson quickly became the least popular player in the Yankees' spring training camp. Relief ace Dave Righetti, who was not one of those named by Henderson, was clearly the most upset by those statements. He was a close friend of pitchers Bob Shirley, Tim Stoddard and Neil Allen, all named by Henderson and all no longer with the team. "He drinks along with everyone else," Righetti said of Henderson. "People in glass houses shouldn't throw rocks. He doesn't understand the ramifications. It's going to affect family lives. Right now, we're all labeled alcoholics. I don't like to be labeled like that." Yankees manager Dallas Green refused to intervene, but several days later Henderson and Righetti met to clear the air. Still, it was a tough year for the Yankees in general — Green was replaced midway through the season — and Henderson in particular. In the middle of June, he was hitting under .250, a career low.

As for the A's, they had played just about as well as they could for as long as they could without Canseco, but it was becoming increasingly obvious that the Oakland offense was running on fumes. In a seven-game stretch from June 12 to 18, Oakland was held to two runs or fewer five times. "We need some fuel for the engine," Tony La Russa said. "We're fighting it." It was in June that Alderson went back to the Yankees' brass to inquire about Henderson. His wasn't the first call Syd Thrift, the Yankees' vice president, had received. In fact, Henderson had already turned down one trade that would have brought him back to the Bay Area. Using Henderson's agent, Richie Bry, as an intermediary, the Giants asked Henderson if he would consider coming to San Francisco. There was a catch, though; in fact, a couple of them. The Giants already had Kevin Mitchell in left field, so would Rickey be interested in moving to right field? And how would he feel about hitting fifth? The Giants were searching high and low for somebody with some pop to hit behind Will Clark and Kevin Mitchell. Matt Williams was still struggling to regain his stroke in the minor leagues. Roger Craig had shuffled bodies in and out of the number five spot in an effort to buy some protection in the lineup for Mitchell, but nothing was working — although Mitchell seemed to be getting along just fine without any support.

"I'm not saying that I couldn't bat fifth, but I think I'm best as a leadoff hitter," Henderson said. "At least at this stage of my career. And if I'm going to start a new position and move somewhere else in the lineup, I think it would make sense to do it starting in spring training. That way, I'd get used to it and wouldn't have to be learning while we're playing games that count."

Although Henderson later spoke freely of the proposed trade, Al Rosen said the Giants were "never close to a deal. We knew the Yankees wanted to make a deal for him, but I didn't think we could satisfy them." But rumors, unconfirmed by Rosen, had the Giants willing to give up Scott Garrelts as part of a Henderson deal. No matter. Henderson, whose contract included the option to veto any trade, turned down the proposal. "It would have been interesting," he said. "But I hadn't played much in right. I had never played in the National League and didn't know the pitchers, and I would rather lead off, if it's up to me."

That philosophy played right into Alderson's hand. With pitching to trade and a combination left fielder/leadoff hitter to throw into the bargain, Alderson made another call to the Thrift shop. The Yankees were in the middle of the pack in the American League East, a half dozen games off the pace and going nowhere. There were those in the New York organization who thought Henderson's legs were gone, that his best years as a player had passed. Why not get what they could for him and pass on trying to sign him to a new contract? The Yankees were negotiating with Bry to give Henderson a new three-year deal worth about $2.6 million a year.

Many in the organization looked at Henderson's poor batting average and thought such a signing was a risk. So, despite the fact that Henderson was willing to stay — Yankees general manager Bob Quinn said the contract would have been finalized by the All-Star break — Thrift got what he could from Alderson and agreed to the deal. The Yankees acquired two much-needed pitchers in left-hander Greg Cadaret and right-hander Eric Plunk, and Polonia. In return, Henderson went "to the only other place besides New York that I ever wanted to play."

The deal was arranged on June 20, and on the morning of June 21, with the A's holding a two-game lead in the American League West, the transaction was announced in Oakland amid great fanfare. Henderson would not join the A's until the next day, but the A's players were ecstatic. "I'm really excited," third baseman Carney Lansford said. Lansford was one of just three members of the team who was around during Henderson's first tour of duty with the A's, the others being Curt Young and Tony Phillips. "I think that this is the perfect situation for him. We have different personnel now. Rickey is going to be really pumped to be on this team. He'll be coming home. We'll welcome him."

And so they did, even Dennis Eckersley, who'd had an on-going feud with Henderson since the outfielder first broke in with the A's. Eckersley objected to the flashiness of Henderson's game, labeling him a "hot dog" and exulting every time he struck Henderson out. Henderson countered by saying that Eckersley threw a spitter. But now they were to be teammates and integral parts of the same team. Eckersley couldn't afford not to have a second opinion.

"It's never been like I've never talked to him on the field or never said hello," Eckersley said in explaining his position. "I'm glad to see that we got him. We're trying to win games here, and a player like Rickey can really help us. The thing is, he's just sort of an irritating batter to face. He's flashy but frustrating for a pitcher to face because he has such a small strike zone." Henderson proved Eckersley correct in the duration of the season, as all of his offensive numbers immediately began to rise.

If anyone had earned the right to share in the magic of the '89 season, it was Henderson, who knew firsthand the difficulties the A's endured earlier in the decade. But Henderson's experiences in Oakland predate his time with the A's. He likes to tell the story of trying to make the baseball team at Oakland Technical High School as a sophomore in the spring of 1974. The coach didn't know much about the muscular kid with the wide grin and flying feet, so he sent him to another field to join the rest of the sophomores in the junior varsity tryouts. Henderson couldn't believe it, and he wasn't going to do it, no matter what the coach said. Instead of leaving the varsity field, Henderson walked into the outfield with the rest of the varsity players and waited. Near the tryout's end, the coach called the players in and asked if everyone had hit. Henderson, still hanging out, said he had not. His defiance and grit paid off when he was given a chance for a few swings. "Rickey was knocking the ball all over the place," recalls Fred Atkins, Henderson's best buddy at the time and another candidate for the varsity. "The coach put him on the team right there." Henderson wound up starting for Tech in the outfield and was named to the first-team All-Oakland Athletic League.

Bobbie Henderson likes to tell the story of her youngest son before she moved the family from Pine Bluffs, Arkansas, to Oakland. Pine Bluffs was rural, and Bobbie Henderson's pre-school-aged son picked up a strange habit. "We were living with my mother at the time," she said. "My mother raised chickens, and Rickey loved to run after them. He would always be running. He was chubby, really fat, when he was real young. But he's always been fast. He's always been a runner, ever since chasing those chickens."

Those two vignettes comprise the Rickey Henderson story, boiled down to its essence. His is the story of a player who knows his own worth, who isn't afraid of that knowledge and who won't let himself be judged by another person's opinion. It is the story of a player blessed with exceptional speed and athletic instincts, an athlete designed for success. Those stories were repeated time and again after Henderson signed his first pro contract with the A's in 1976. By June 1979, he'd spent 3½ seasons in the A's minor-league system, never batting under .300. He was hitting .309 for Ogden, Utah, in June 1979 when he was recalled from Triple-A to join the A's, the joke of the American League.

It hadn't always been so. Club owner Charlie Finley had moved the team from Kansas City to Oakland before the 1968 season, and within four seasons the A's were American League West champions. Finley, acting as his own general manager for the most part, had put together the best pitching staff in the league, anchored by home-grown starters Catfish Hunter, Vida Blue, Chuck Dobson and Blue Moon Odom and an organization-bred relief ace, Rollie Fingers. The A's system also provided seven of the eight everyday players, including outfielders Reggie Jackson, Joe Rudi and Rick Monday, infielders Sal Bando, Dick Green and Bert Campaneris and catcher Dave Duncan. Finley, with his minor-league system suddenly evaporating, turned to trades to beef up the club as it went on to win division title after division title. Newcomers such as Ken Holtzman, Billy North, Ray Fosse, Deron Johnson and Billy Williams would flow into Oakland, joining home products Gene Tenace and Claudell Washington as the A's won five straight division titles from '71 to '75. From '72 through '74, they were the absolute kings of baseball, winning three straight world championships.

The bountiful success of Finley's teams couldn't counteract the acerbic manner of the owner, who ruled the club like an autocrat from his insurance company offices outside Chicago. Players resented his off-hand manner and his habit of laying out as little money as possible in salaries. Finley claimed he always made money in Oakland, but it wasn't shown by the turnstile count. Their dominant play on the field certainly wasn't reflected in Oakland's attendance figures. Only twice in those five years did the A's draw as many as one million fans, and both times they reached that mark only in the final homestand of the year. Finley suffered the indignity of putting a winning team on the field, only to find that his style of promotion didn't have mass appeal in the East Bay. The Giants, fielding mostly inferior teams, consistently outdrew the A's.

Finley constantly cut corners to save money — at one time his entire office staff, headed by his cousin Carl, consisted of seven people. In 1974, however, he cut one corner too many by not making a required payment of $50,000 to Catfish Hunter. Hunter and his attorney claimed that Finley's failure to pay dissolved the contract, and by the time Finley was ready to cough up the money, Hunter could sniff the scent of freedom. The pitcher refused the owner's gesture while waiting for a ruling from arbitrator Peter Seitz, an attorney employed by the owners. Seitz's ruling freed the four-time 20-game winner, and Hunter auctioned his services to the highest bidder, eventually signing with the Yankees after a spirited bidding war.

Hunter's was an isolated case, brought about by Finley's own negligence. But one year later, pitchers Andy Messersmith, a 19-game winner for the Dodgers, and Dave McNally, now in Montreal and near the end of a long career, brought a more far-reaching case in front of arbitrator Seitz. For decades, the standard contract gave management the right to renew a player's contract for one year after it expired. Owners traditionally renewed contracts year after year on the strength of that clause. The pitchers argued, and Seitz agreed, that the clause was not indefinite but allowed clubs to bond players to them for just one "option year," after which players who had not signed contracts would be declared free agents.

The owners, furious, fired Seitz and sued to have his ruling invalidated, but their damage-control procedure was too little. Seitz was gone, but the courts refused to overturn his ruling and players who didn't sign a contract in 1976 would be free to move elsewhere for 1977. Jackson, who made noises that he was going elsewhere, was traded to Baltimore for a swift young prospect named Don Baylor before the 1976 season, a loss that probably cost the A's another division title. They finished 2½ games behind up-and-coming Kansas City, the Royals winning the title in Oakland in the final week of the season when left-handed starter Larry Gura shut out Oakland.

That was the last time the A's were close to the top in the 1970s. Bando moved to Milwaukee to start the 1977 season. Campaneris took off for Texas. Baylor and Rudi both headed to the Angels. Fingers and Tenace found homes in San Diego. There could be no replacing losses of that caliber, and the A's fell fast. They lost 98 games in '77 and 93 more in '78. By '79, when Henderson arrived, the A's were clearly the worst team in baseball. Rickey's arrival had given the A's a bit of a spark — he hit .274 and stole 33 bases — but the A's were big losers on the field, going 54-108. It was the franchise's worst record since 1915-16, when club owner Connie Mack, not unlike Finley in being tight with a buck, offset his own financial difficulties by selling his star players. The '77 A's were also big losers at the gate, drawing an embarrassingly low 306,763, including just 653 for an early-season game against Seattle.

That '79 team that Rickey joined wasn't without some talent. Tony Armas was a solid right fielder, and Dwayne Murphy, like Henderson a rookie, was coming of age in center. There were starting pitchers of promise, too, including Rick Langford, Mike Norris,

Steve McCatty and Matt Keough. The following year, Finley started the new decade with a new manager, Billy Martin, a local favorite from nearby Berkeley. Martin, in between his periodic assignments for Yankees owner George Steinbrenner, was exactly the short-term answer the A's needed. He had pitching coach Art Fowler teach the starters a dry spitter, then pitched his starters until their arms gave out. With the four exceptional starters and an outfield setting baseball on its ear, the A's were born again.

And if the pitchers were the heart of the Oakland resurgence, then Henderson was its soul. He talked glibly in the spring of 1980 about stealing 100 bases, something that had been accomplished just twice in baseball history, never in the American League. He took a lot of verbal abuse, this kid who didn't even have one full big-league season under his belt. But the same kid who stood his ground in the outfield at Oakland Tech in 1975 held firm here, too. Martin gave him a license to steal, and Henderson let fly at virtually every opportunity. He got his 100. And with it, the 21-year-old hit .303 with nine home runs and 53 RBIs and walked 117 times, almost overnight winning acknowledgment as baseball's best lead-off hitter.

As Henderson blossomed, the A's rose with him. From dead last in 1979, Oakland soared to finish second — a distant second at 14 games out — behind eventual league champion Kansas City.

It was a significant year off the field, too. In the middle of the season, Finley, who had been trying to sell the team for most of the second half of the decade, finally succeeded when he sold out to Walter A. Haas Jr., his son, Wally, and son-in-law Roy Eisenhardt. The Haas family was the power behind San Francisco-based Levi Strauss, the maker of the world's best-known jeans, and they weren't used to backing second-place finishers.

Still, a winning record was something Oakland hadn't enjoyed in three seasons. And on the surface, at least, the A's fans had no reason to expect any better in 1980. But they got it. And after the Finley-to-Haas transaction over the winter, the new owners debuted at the top in 1981. Oakland blasted free from the pack with an 11-0 start, then rocketed to 18-1, with the outfielders and starting pitchers carrying the bulk of the load. Even while the A's were coasting back to earth, the longest players' strike in baseball history cut 53 games out of the Oakland season. Consequently, the A's were awarded a first-half championship after the strike had run its course. Despite a lackluster second half, the A's beat second-half champ Kansas City in the divisional playoffs before they were swept by the Yankees in the best-of-five playoffs.

Henderson hit .319 and stole 56 bases in the regular season, but his year ended ignominiously when he and Murphy were injured and had to leave the final game against the Yankees. The Yankees had won the first two games in New York, and left-hander Dave Righetti pitched seven dominating innings and pushed them into the World Series with a 4-0 victory. That game in the Coliseum was notable for one other event. The A's cheerleader, Krazy George Henderson, got fans in the jam-packed Coliseum to stand up in rotation, section by section, in what was perhaps the first-ever fan "wave" at a sporting event. It was refreshing at the time, but the wave would become a bothersome ritual by the middle of the decade, by which time neither of the Hendersons, Rickey or Krazy George, would be with the A's. And by which time the A's would no longer be on top in the American League West.

In the winter between the '81 and '82 seasons, Henderson was on the banquet circuit when he ran into Lou Brock, the all-time stolen-base champion who by this time was three years out of baseball and three years closer to the Hall of Fame. Brock, who was elected to Cooperstown in '85, suggested the two get together for dinner. Henderson jumped at the chance to chat with one of his idols and flew from the Bay Area to St. Louis, where Brock was a successful businessman. In 1974, Brock had shattered the major-league record for stolen bases in one season with 118. It was a marvelous record of one man's endurance and testimony to his ability to play with pain. (He had a history of playing even when he was hurt.) It was a record that Brock said he thought might go down in history alongside Joe DiMaggio's 56-game hitting streak of 1941. Brock, the single-season and career (938) thefts leader, and the up-and-coming Henderson talked for hours about the philosophies and techniques of stealing bases and reading pitchers' moves. By the end of that evening, Brock was convinced that he eventually would hand both of his stolen-base crowns over to Henderson, should the kid remain healthy.

"The amazing thing about Rickey I found out that night was that he was able to grasp at 23 what it took (Maury) Wills and myself so much longer to understand," Brock said. It was Wills' record of 104 steals that Brock had broken in 1974. "We were 28 or

29 before we could put it all together. And he had it already."

Henderson sought the record immediately. After stealing 22 bases in April, he picked up the pace and swiped 27 in 28 games in May. The quest was on. The head-first slides that were a Henderson trademark took a terrible toll on his body, but as long as Martin let him run free, Henderson never looked back. And as his numbers soared, so did his attention from the media. And Lou Brock.

"There probably aren't that many guys who understand what Rickey is going through — Joe DiMaggio, Maury Wills, guys like that," Brock said at the time. "Guys who have cut new ground are the ones who best understand the significance of what he's done and the motivation that has gotten Rickey this far. It's like riding the front end of a tornado, because disaster sits right behind you. What you are dealing with is something very, very scary. You have to realize that you have already reached base, which is the main objective of the game in the first place. Then, suddenly, you risk that, and all eyes are upon you. If you slip or slide, if you think about the possible pitfalls, then those pitfalls will get you. The plain truth is, for all of his talent, Rickey is where he is because he has mastered the fear of failure."

Brock compared Henderson with Willie Wilson, the Kansas City center fielder who had stolen 162 total bases in 1979 and 1980 but whose numbers had fallen off dramatically in 1981 and 1982. "In Wilson, you have a guy who is the best base stealer in baseball, a better pure stealer than Rickey," Brock said. "And he's not running because he's afraid to run. He's the only guy who can walk out on the field and everybody has to take notice, even more than with Rickey. But Wilson doesn't have what Henderson has. His will to win is not as strong as Henderson's."

While Henderson was running, the A's were fading. The tinkering that Martin and Fowler had done to get the pitching staff up and running in 1980-81 was showing its ill effects. Sore arms abounded. After winning 34 games in the previous 1½ seasons, Norris succumbed to a sore shoulder and won just seven games. McCatty, second in the 1981 Cy Young Award chase with a 14-7 record and 2.32 ERA, also had shoulder problems and won just six games. Langford and Keough both pitched with some pain but for the most part stayed in the rotation. However, neither was as effective as in the previous two seasons, Langford going 11-16 and tacking more than a full point to his ERA (4.21) and Keough adding more than two points to his, finishing with a terrible 5.72 ERA and an 11-18 record.

Without dependable pitching and saddled with an undistinguished infield, the A's quickly folded up the tent. By May 20, they were under .500 to stay. A team that was supposed to contend for the title, Oakland found itself 10 games under .500 by June 20 and was a dozen back at the All-Star break. When the club opened the post-All-Star schedule by losing five straight and eight of 10, they were finished. Except for the ever-flying feet of Henderson.

Despite the decrepit team the A's were fielding, Oakland fans continued to turn out in droves to watch Henderson's pursuit of Brock. Eventually, the club drew a franchise record 1.735 million fans despite finishing 68-94 and 25 games out of first place. By the end of July, Henderson had 99 steals, and the eclipse of Brock's record was all but guaranteed. As his steals soared and the record books beckoned ever closer, however, the rest of Henderson's game went into remission. He was in quest of a third straight .300 season, and a .337 July pumped his average to .287. But in the heat of chasing Brock, he hit just .216 after August 1, and his average dived to a career low of .267. Still, that tended to be overlooked in the glitter of a record-setting season. On August 26, in the first game of a series in Milwaukee, Henderson tied Brock's record. The next night, he stole four bases to blow it away. Perhaps the single most enduring memory of that season is Henderson standing at second base in County Stadium on August 26, holding second base over his head. A smiling Brock in coat and tie was standing next to the new champ after Henderson's 119th theft made him baseball's single-season Man of Steal. Henderson would finish with 130 and the the thought that he, too, might have a record that would stand up next to DiMaggio's.

Henderson's batting slump lasted well into the next year, and when he was hitting just .258 midway through the 1983 season, there was talk that the pounding his body had taken during the course of 1982 had permanently scarred his batting stroke. But he enjoyed a second-half renaissance, hitting .327 after the break to bring his batting average up to a respectable .292. He hit .293 in '84 and added a then-career-high 16 homers as well, but the A's continued to lose, finishing in fourth place both seasons, well under .500. Some of his teammates grumbled that he was too self-centered. The A's went so far as to import aging second baseman Joe Morgan for the 1984 season. It was thought Morgan, a two-time Most Valuable Player and like Henderson an Oakland native, could guide the suddenly erratic Henderson, but Henderson, who figured he knew what he was doing, paid only lip service to Morgan's advice. Well before the end of the season, Morgan had stopped offering the advice.

As he looked at the A's before the 1985 season, Sandy Alderson didn't like what he was seeing. A lawyer and professional colleague of Eisenhardt, Alderson had joined the team shortly after the Haas family bought it from Charlie Finley. He began as the team's legal counsel but was groomed for more important duties. His legal duties dwindled as he got more into the baseball administration arm of the organization. After the 1984 season, Alderson, by this time an organization vice-president, became the team's general manager and was now in charge of trades. He didn't have carte blanche — clearance for major deals or free-agent signings still went to the owners — but his bosses respected the ex-Marine officer's keen mind and rapidly burgeoning store of baseball knowledge, and the vast majority of his recommendations were implemented.

Alderson's first trade gave evidence of the calculated daring he would show in helping to rebuild the A's. At the '84 winter meetings, he sent Henderson and minor-league pitcher Bert Bradley to the Yankees in a deal that brought the A's a relief ace, Jay Howell, in addition to three young pitchers — Tim Birtsas, Eric Plunk and Jose Rijo — and an young outfielder, Stan Javier. By making the deal, the A's were admitting that Henderson, as talented as he was, couldn't make the A's a winner by himself. Oakland needed pitching and depth, and Alderson was hoping he'd taken the first steps in that direction. In addition, at the time of the trade, Henderson was one year from free agency. Had Oakland retained him for the 1985 season, there would have been no guarantee they'd be able to afford to re-sign him, and they stood to lose him with virtually no compensation.

The newcomers would help. But the A's were stuck in limbo until the farm system began spewing forth Rookies of the Year with regularity — Canseco in '86, McGwire in '87 and Weiss in '88. Meanwhile, Henderson was the latest in a series of big-name offensive players imported by owner George Steinbrenner in an effort to return the Yankees to the World Series. Henderson was supposed to be able to do it all, and so he did. Despite missing the first three weeks of the '85 season with a sprained ankle, Henderson emerged in pinstripes on April 22 and went on to put together his best all-around season, hitting .314 with 24 home runs, 146 runs scored, 72 RBIs, 99 walks and 80 stolen bases. But with Steinbrenner playing his usual managerial games — Yogi Berra was that year's mid-season exile, replaced by Henderson's old Oakland skipper, Billy Martin, who took over just three weeks into the season — New York finished second. The Yankees finished two games behind the young Toronto Blue Jays and could have given Henderson his first chance at a World Series had they not collapsed in September. New York, which had trailed virtually the entire season, hosted the Jays in a four-game series in Yankee Stadium, but New York couldn't cash in. After winning the first game to close to within 1½ games of first, the Yankees not only lost the last three games of the series but went on to lose eight straight, taking themselves out of the race.

It was more of the same in '86. Henderson wasn't as good, his average falling to a career-low .263. But he again led the league in runs scored with 130 and set personal bests with 28 homers, 31 doubles and 74 RBIs. Still, the Yankees finished second, 5½ games back of Boston, thanks to a lame pitching staff on which only Dennis Rasmussen (18-6) could win as many as 10 games. In those days, the Yankees without Rickey were no contender, as they proved in 1987. Henderson went down with a blown right hamstring that twice put him on the disabled list and cost him more than 50 games. Talk began then in New York that Henderson wasn't tough, that he was spending too much time on the sidelines. But, he explained patiently, "My legs are my game. If I can't run, what can I do?" Leg injuries haunted him throughout 1988 as well, but he managed to steal 93 bases, his best since his days in Oakland, for a fifth-place team still desperate for pitching. He also hit .305 but didn't hit a homer in the final 2½ months of the season.

Then came the slow start in '89 and his return to the A's, making for a festive week in the Bay Area. Suddenly, Alderson and Rosen were celebrated as the toasts of their respective towns. Steve Bedrosian was already a Giant, filling a gap even bigger than the one awaiting Rickey. The popular thought was the A's still had a good chance to win the pennant without Rickey, but the Giants had virtually no shot at all of winning a pennant without Bedrosian. As June approached, the Giants were 0-6 in extra innings, 2-8 when tied after eight innings and 8-13 in one-run games. While the Giants' closest pursuer most of the season, the Reds, boasted of lefty-righty combo John Franco and Rob Dibble, all the Giants mustered in the pen was unreliability. Roger Craig looked at Franco and Dibble, and he saw a 7-2 record and 18 saves. He saw the Reds 11-3 in one-run games, and he saw a 6-1 record in extra innings. Then he looked in his own bullpen and saw five guys with their heads down.

On June 9, Ernie Camacho was brought up from the Giants' Triple-A club in Phoenix and given a chance to win a job that Garrelts, Mike LaCoss, Craig Lefferts and Goose Gossage could not. Camacho was a 33-year-old closer who still had a fastball that traveled in the mid 90s. But getting people out proved to be a problem. At Cleveland, manager Pat Corrales had become irritated when Camacho threw off-speed pitches, so much so that Corrales would stand on the top dugout step and scream at Camacho to throw strictly fastballs. Camacho was at a distinct disadvantage because opposing hitters could overhear Corrales' orders. While working in Phoenix, Camacho learned to be comfortable with his curveball and split-fingered fastball, and the Giants were impressed with his 0.34 ERA and 30 strikeouts in 26⅔ innings. But Camacho lasted only four games in San Francisco, the Giants shipping him back to Phoenix on the basis of his 6.75 ERA.

With the Giants running out of options, the trade rumors again surfaced. There was talk the Giants would acquire save whiz Tom Henke from the Blue Jays, with Matt Williams, Candy Maldonado, Atlee Hammaker and a player to be named going to Toronto for Henke and George Bell. There was the story that left-hander Al Leiter would accompany Rickey Henderson to San Francisco for a similar assortment of players, including Scott Garrelts, but Rickey shot that down, of course. The Giants were even seeking Seattle starter Mark Langston, and pitchers Dennis Cook and Terry Mulholland were mentioned as trade bait.

Mulholland and Cook were constantly mentioned in the rumor mill because they were young, left-handed and apparently expendable. The Giants had more left-handed pitching prospects than any team in the majors and were willing to cough up some of their jewels for the right price. The list of lefties was lengthy — Cook, Mullholland, Trevor Wilson, Mike Remlinger and Eric Gunderson. Roger Samuels, another lefty, had been traded to Pittsburgh in May for Ken Oberkfell, and the Giants were so deep in lefties they could afford to release veteran Keith Comstock shortly before

Opening Day, despite Comstock's spring ERA of 1.23. Upon receiving his pink slip, Comstock said, "They almost want a monopoly on
left-handers. They want plenty of insurance policies in Triple-A.
That's not how I want to go out." And Cook, while at Phoenix earlier in the season, said the Firebirds' pitching staff was as good as
the Giants' but had no place to go and were "rotting" in the minors.

Of the left-handers remaining in the organization, Mulholland
and Cook were furthest advanced. Mulholland started 10 games in
'86, tossed his first big-league complete game in his first start of '88
and was ticketed as a possible fifth starter for '89. Cook arrived
later and threw a two-hitter against the eventual world champion
Dodgers late in the '88 season. But neither pitcher made the final
'89 cuts, and their stay in the Pacific Coast League didn't last long
because of injuries and inadequacies on the big club. As soon as
they were pitching again in the majors, their names were tossed
about by general managers across both leagues, and it was clear
Candlestick wouldn't be their home much longer.

As it became more and more obvious that another live arm was
needed in the bullpen, Rosen concluded that that arm might well
belong to Bedrosian, a right-hander with a Cy Young Award already in his trophy case. Rosen had discussed possible deals with
Philadelphia general manager Lee Thomas before the season, but
the Phils' relatively successful 11-12 April stalled any talks. By
mid-June, two weeks after Mike Schmidt's retirement, the Phils
were where they should have been all along — last place (22-41) —
and Thomas was now willing to dump big-salaried veterans for
younger and cheaper prospects. An outright youth movement took
hold in Philadelphia, with Bedrosian having handed his closing
role over to Jeff Parrett. Bedrosian had had only one save since the
Giants' trip through Philly a month earlier, but the Giants were
figuring that Bedrosian couldn't be at his best unless he was used a
lot. And in San Francisco, Roger Craig would be forced to use him a
lot.

On June 17, a day after the Giants' second straight one-run
loss (Eric Davis' two-run, ninth-inning homer beat Gossage), Rosen confirmed a report out of New York that he had been pushing
for a Bedrosian trade, but he denied Mets broadcaster Tim
McCarver's claim over WWOR-TV that the Phils would receive
three pitchers among a choice of four — Mulholland, Cook, Wilson
and Remlinger. "They'd run me out of town," Rosen said. The

Phils needed starting pitching, and they also wanted someone to replace Schmidt at third base, so Rosen thought for exactly two seconds about his bullpen's 7-13 record and agreed to let go of Mulholland, Cook and minor-league third baseman Charlie Hayes. Because Mulholland hadn't proved himself to any great degree and because the Giants' future included Matt Williams at third base, the toughest player to give up was Cook, who had pitched his best game of the season the same day Rosen was confirming the Bedrosian reports. On June 17, Cook pitched a nationally televised six-hitter to beat the Reds 8-1, pushing the Giants into sole possession of first place. But on June 18, Cook became an ex-Giant, packaged with Mulholland and Hayes for the 31-year-old Bedrosian and a player to be named (minor-league infielder Bruce Parker). On the same day, the Phils dealt Juan Samuel to the Mets for Len Dykstra and Roger McDowell.

Bedrosian came to the Giants at a steep price, costing $1.2 million more than the combined salaries of the Philadelphia-bound threesome. But aside from the implications of his club-high three-year $1.45 million contract, San Francisco had lost the services of three more young players. That was a significant loss considering that those weren't the first young players to go. Rosen had already swapped other pitchers in their 20s — Mark Davis, Mark Grant, Jeff Robinson — for established, high-priced veterans in their 30s, but those late 1987 moves were obviously worth the risk because they brought to the Giants Rick Reuschel, Dave Dravecky and Craig Lefferts, all contributing big-time to the '87 title drive.

The Bedrosian trade pushed the average age of the pitching staff to nearly 33, but Rosen was clearly more concerned with the short run than the long run, and he realized the World Series was a distinct possibility, more so with a legitimate bullpen closer. When reminded that most of the staff might not be around in six or seven years, Rosen snapped, "Neither will I." He added, "I can't see tomorrow, let alone six or seven years from now."

If nothing else, the Giants had acquired tons of bullpen experience, the type of experience that's invaluable in a pennant race. How much is tons? Try 666. That was the total number of career saves by the Giants' pitching staff. Add Bedrosian's 144 to Gossage's 305 to Don Robinson's 56 to Garrelts' 48 to Lefferts' 47 to Camacho's 45 to the four other pitchers' combined 21, and the total is 666.

On his flight from Philadelphia to San Francisco, Bedrosian read a few sports sections and noticed one article that outlined how the Giants had made a steal of a deal and would soon become the second coming of the '27 Yankees, or something of that nature. "It said, 'We got Bedrosian. We're going to the World Series,' " Bedrosian said. "But I remember when Lance Parrish came to the Phils and everyone said, 'We're going to the World Series.' It didn't happen. It's not that easy." No, but it's nice to imagine such things if the next five hours will be spent at 30,000 feet, and that's just what Bedrosian did on his cross-country journey. In fact, somewhere over the Rockies — for all Bedrosian knew — he guessed that June 19, 1989, his first day in a Giants uniform, would be a very special day, perhaps the first of a very special season. Ken Oberkfell met Bedrosian at the airport and noticed his former teammate ('85 Braves) was almost in a different world. "I could tell he was pretty psyched up," Oberkfell said. "He's an emotional guy anyway. He's a little like Will Clark as far as getting mad when he makes a mistake. He hates to lose. But I told him that he's going to like it here." The newest Giant nodded in agreement.

Bedrosian arrived at Candlestick Park with his crimson Phillies bag and the well-groomed beard he had sported for most of the decade. He was quickly informed that club policy prohibits any facial hair other than moustaches. The rule seemed antiquated for the late 1980s, an era of buzz cuts and streaked hair, but the Rosen-Craig regime said no beards. So the players wore no beards. Just happy to be away from Philadelphia and not about to stir up any sudden controversy, Bedrosian followed the guidelines and just before game time shaved it all off except for a few strands above his upper lip. "My kids aren't going to recognize me," he frowned.

Feeling quite cold around the cheeks, Bedrosian walked out to the right-field bullpen to secure a good seat for the Giants-Astros game. He sat for 2½ hours and watched Robinson cough up a pair of solo homers to Glenn Davis and Bob Knepper. Bedrosian was asked to warm up a couple of times but didn't know he'd pitch for sure until a pinch hitter replaced Don Robinson in the lineup. Robinson had pitched eight innings, and the Giants were leading 3-2. Bedrosian's introduction led to a standing ovation from the 21,000 fans, who were tired of watching their team falter in late innings. His first batter, Rafael Ramirez, smacked a check-swing single through the middle. But just as Roger Craig was thinking, "Here we go again," Bedrosian began to get outs, thanks to a fastball clocked at 95 mph. A sacrifice bunt, a ground out and a line drive to short center led to Bedrosian's first save as a Giant, only 34 hours after he learned of the trade.

Bedrosian ran off the field, making sure he shook a hand belonging to each of his teammates. After enduring three straight losing seasons in Philly, Bedrosian was finally back with winners. "It's a dream. It really is. The whole thing. The fan reaction. A first-place team. The importance of my role. Even our pre-game pitchers' meeting was exciting. The adrenaline was flowing, boy." Afterward, Bedrosian placed a souvenir next to his shaving cream and razor. It was the game ball. "I don't keep them all, but I'll keep the big ones. . . . I'll keep the World Series balls this year."

Bedrosian had never been on a World Series team, his best club being the '82 Braves. Atlanta won the Western Division that year but fell to St. Louis in the playoffs. With the Braves, Bedrosian combined with submarine pitcher Gene Garber to form perhaps the best one-two punch in the game. The Braves placed second the next two seasons but fell to fifth in '85, the year Bedrosian moved from the bullpen to the starting rotation. Despite a 1.71 ERA as a reliever in '84, Bedrosian became a starter and promptly fashioned an ugly 7-15 record to earn a trade to Philly that winter. The Phils were smart enough to place him back in the pen, and Bedrosian responded with 29 saves, reinforcing opinion that he's better finishing games than starting them.

Bedrosian, like all good relievers, often pitches best in pressure situations. The strength of a reliever can be determined by how late in a close game he's used. According to this theory, the better the reliever, the later he'll take the mound. With that in mind, it's simple to understand why the closer is the most important man in the bullpen and why stoppers such as Dennis Eckersley and Mark Davis get so many Cy Young Award votes. The early relievers are usually the mop-up guys, and mop-up guys have a different role altogether. No mop-up pitcher will ever win a Cy Young.

Closers make their money facing Jose Canseco or Kevin Mitchell in the ninth inning with runners in scoring position and the game on the line. Mop-up men make their money — and a whole lot less — as often as not by facing the bottom of the order in a game that's already a blowout. One of the reasons Cubs' manager Don Zimmer couldn't warm up to Goose Gossage was that Gossage didn't want to pitch unless the situation meant something. Zimmer often asked Gossage to pitch in garbage time, and Gossage usually responded to those situations with trashy performances.

But the closer role has its pitfalls, and the pressure isn't always so easy to handle. Robinson, acquired by the Giants in '87 to work out of the bullpen, moved into the rotation in late '88 because of injuries to the starters. Once he became comfortable with the once-every-five-days gig, the last thing he wanted was to return to his old relief job. The acquisition of Bedrosian assured Robinson he wouldn't return to the pen, certainly not as the closer. "It's the hardest job in baseball," Robinson said. "You've got to do it every day. If you mess up once, the media and fans jump on you. No one realizes you pitch 70 times a year and get up to throw hard in the bullpen another 30 times. And each time you come in, you'll probably face their best hitter. You're expected to throw 90 mph and face a guy hitting .330 with runners on second and third and no outs. You're told, 'Go get 'em out.' If you don't do it, everyone remembers you. The fans only remember the last part of the game. The next day in the paper, you'll read all about it. . . . I'm happy to get rid of that role."

All relief pitchers fail, but the successful ones are better at forgetting their failures. If they anguish for days over blowing a save, chances are very good they'll blow their next opportunity. Although all relievers claim they forget the bad games, nobody truly does. The successful ones simply do a better job trying to forget. Bedrosian had been around a lot of years, had enjoyed a lot of successes and had agonized over a lot of failures. But in the summer of '89, he learned more than ever how to put his job in perspective. Bedrosian was a good friend of fellow reliever Donnie Moore, the two coming up together in the Braves' organization. Moore, just 35 years old, shot and killed himself after shooting and critically wounding his estranged wife a month after his release from Kansas City. Afterward, Moore's agent, David Pinter, said his client still had been bothered by his performance with the Angels in the 1986 playoffs, when Dave Henderson, then with Boston, homered off Moore to ignite the Red Sox to a dramatic comeback. "I don't know if that had a lot to do with it, that one pitch, but I've always thought and I still do think that baseball's not that important, not as far as that goes," Bedrosian said. "It's amazing, though, how one game like that could prey on your mind for a while. I've learned from that. I've learned not to let things upset you, as hard as it may seem. You've got your priorities. You've got God and your family and then baseball."

Bedrosian was one of the majors' most accomplished relievers when he joined the Giants in June, only two years removed from his best season. As the Giants were winning the West in '87, Bedrosian's Phillies were placing fourth in the East — despite a banner season by Bedrosian, who became only the third National League reliever ever to win the Cy Young Award. Bedrosian rang up 40 saves, posting his 30th on July 31, reaching that level quicker than anyone in big-league history. That record would be broken by Eckersley on July 22, 1988. But Bedrosian's '88 season wasn't wonderful. He came down with mysterious chest pains after only one inning of spring training, beginning the season on the disabled list. Initial X-rays showed a strained muscle in his rib cage, but more tests a few days later indicated he was suffering from pneumonia and pleurisy. He reported to Triple-A Maine and didn't return to the Phils until late May, but he quickly proved he hadn't lost his stuff and saved 28 games, fourth in the league. Through nearly three months of '89, Bedrosian was given only nine save opportunities by the Phillies and saved just six, making it easy to understand why he was so excited about moving to San Francisco.

Bedrosian began his Giants career splendidly, saving five games in his first week (6⅓ innings, no runs, one hit) and hinting to everyone that he'd do more good than harm, which is basically all his teammates wanted to know. Bedrosian arrived amid a season-best, seven-game winning streak and saved four of the wins and helped his new club maintain first place for the rest of June. But just as he was beginning to fit in with his new teammates, he was having doubts about obeying the club's clean-shaven policy. He had pitched most of his career, including his best years, with a face full of hair and felt somewhat out of place when unable to hide behind his trademark. He wasn't alone. Bruce Sutter in his heyday wore a beard to intimidate batters. In Gossage's prime, he had bushy hair everywhere. Hitters couldn't deal with his fastball anyway, and Goose fashioned a grubby look to make his presence even more distracting. Ditto with Al Hrabowsky. Bedrosian, on the other hand, probably owned the most well-kept beard in the majors. He was Donnie Osmond in whiskers. After the shave, he was just Donnie Osmond. "Maybe it's even a mask for me," Bedrosian said.

"I like to fool and joke around, and I don't feel I've been able to do that much."

The Giants' front office might worry about Bedrosian's facial hair, but they had few worries whenever Bedrosian took the mound in those first days — except for Craig Biggio's three-run homer that beat him June 27 in Houston. With Bedrosian leading the relief charge, the Giants finished their best month of the season by going 18-10 in June and making fans forget about the club's traditional June Swoon, a midseason jinx that often turned contending Giants into pretending Giants.

To be sure, Kevin Mitchell knew nothing at all about the June Swoon. Mitchell experienced a phenomenal home-run derby in June, even topping April and May, hitting 10 more long balls and pushing his season total to 25. But opponents continued to try to pitch around Mitchell, and Mitchell was among the league's leaders in walks and intentional walks. That trend got so predictable — his 13 intentional walks by June 11 put him on pace to set a record for right-handers — that Roger Craig considered switching Mitchell with Will Clark in the lineup so Clark could protect Mitchell. But all that would have done was force opponents to pitch around Clark and, fortunately, Roger never made the switch.

The first game of June gave a clear indication that Mitchell wasn't about to relax and call it a season after only two months. His second double-quadruple (two swings, eight bases) of the season pushed the Giants past Atlanta 7-6 to give Rick Reuschel his 10th victory, most in the majors. Mitchell and Reuschel had been helping each other all season, and this game was no exception. Reuschel lent Mitchell his massive-barreled bats, and Mitchell acknowledged the gesture by hitting a pair of home runs for Big Daddy. Mitchell hit another home run the following night and another the next to amass four in the three-game Atlanta series, equaling his 1988 season output of 19 — in the season's 53rd game. But that was only the beginning, as Mitchell pounded seven home runs in the month's first nine games, thanks chiefly to the wonderful series in Atlanta and an even more memorable double-header in Cincinnati in which he went deep three times in 18 innings.

If breaking Roger Maris' record was only a dream before early June, it was quickly turning into a realistic goal. Bay Area newspapers continued to run charts on how Mitchell stacked up with the greatest single-season swatters in history, and with 22 homers in 57 games, he measured right up there with the greatest. In fact, he was better. When Babe Ruth set the single-season record of 60 back in 1927, he hit his 22nd homer in his 60th game. And when Maris broke Ruth's record in 1961, he hit his 22nd in game 58.

The amazing thing about all of this Roger Maris talk was that Mitchell was on the record pace without the benefit of a bona fide number five hitter. When Maris hit 61 in '61, he had tons of help. He hit third in front of cleanup man Mickey Mantle and number five Moose Skowron. Mantle hit 54 homers and Skowron 28. Mitchell had Will Clark in front of him but absolutely nobody behind him. With the lack of a power threat on deck, opposing pitchers attempted to pitch around Mitchell, refusing to let him see a hittable pitch. But this wasn't always the case, because at the same time Mitchell was learning how to consistently go deep, he was discovering how to be selective with the pitches. And even with Candy Maldonado on deck, few pitchers wanted to intentionally walk Mitchell every time up. Mitchell would eventually get a strike, and he usually made someone pay.

For all the hoopla that accompanied Mitchell's multiple-home run days in early June, no single ball measured up with his monstrous upper-deck shot June 25 in San Diego. Facing Eric Show on a typically sunny Sunday afternoon in Jack Murphy Stadium, Mitchell became one of the few players to hit a ball into the stadium's upper regions. The list features some pretty heavy swingers, including Nate Colbert, Dick Allen, Johnny Bench and Dave Kingman. Show threw a 2-1 sinker, and Mitchell hit a second-deck riser, shaking the section's seventh row. It might have traveled 500 feet. Despite the club's longest clout of the season, the Giants still lost 10-7 to snap their winning streak at seven.

As Mitchell continued to glide, Maldonado was still in his slide, and Candy's trade value was diminishing by the month. Rosen shopped Maldonado, but there were no takers. Craig is one of the few managers in baseball with enough faith and patience to stick with a slumping player for such a long period of time, but the manager was sure Maldonado would break out some day. "He's all messed up," Craig said. "It's sad, because you keep playing him and playing him. I've tried everything." Well, not everything. The last resort would have been for the Giants to rid themselves of the man mired in a two-year slump. Maldonado's contract was to end after the '89 season, and because a return in '90 didn't seem likely, a mid-season trade could benefit everyone involved and give Maldonado a new lease on life, similar to the one he received in '85. Maldonado had been rotting on the Dodgers' bench when they traded him to the Giants, and he immediately prospered. But the what-have-you-done-for-me-lately question came in 1989, and Maldonado had no answer. "This whole season has kind of been the worst," Maldonado said. "You let that madness get to you, and then you let yourself go."

Craig had been frustrated with Maldonado for a long time, but it reached the boiling point on June 7 in Cincinnati after Craig made a double switch and pulled both his pitcher and Maldonado. Candy took the news hard and walked off the field. He didn't run or even jog. He just walked, slowly, which drives managers and general managers crazy, and, yes, Craig and Rosen were fuming. Craig later pulled Maldonado aside and let him have it, warning him that he'd lose his job the next time it happened.

Because they were uncomfortable with Maldonado, Tracy Jones or Donell Nixon in a starting role, the Giants were desperate for a right fielder, which triggered a less significant June trade. On June 16, the Giants sent Jones to Detroit for Pat Sheridan. Jones, hitless in his first 21 at-bats, was the latest in a long line of players to use Candlestick Park as an excuse for their inability to perform. Jones followed in the tradition of Bobby Murcer, Johnnie LeMaster and Jack Clark when he said, "It's terrible. The worst place in baseball to play." Jones asked Rosen for a trade after only 38 at-bats. He was hitting .186 at his sendoff, and it's better left unsaid where his average would have been without a four-hit, seven-RBI evening against the Padres in mid-June.

Ironically, Jones had been acquired over the winter for popular (among the Giants' female fans, at least) outfielder Mike Aldrete in a classic trade that hurt both teams. But the Giants could only wish they had Aldrete back to play permanently in right field. Although Aldrete had never proven himself as a starter and was struggling with the Expos, he surely would have been better than anyone the Giants had used out there. Sheridan took over where Jones left off and went hitless in his first 10 at-bats. And Jones, who hadn't homered all season, cranked an upper deck shot in Detroit during his first game as a Tiger. Maybe there was some truth to one of his final statements as a Giant. "Some of the other Giants would hit a lot better somewhere else."

Despite the problems with Jones, Maldonado and then Sheridan, the Giants enjoyed their best June since 1966 and in it their best homestand (10-2) since the same year. Through it all, Matt Williams was not missed, and the successful platoon of Ernest Riles and Greg Litton at third base allowed the Giants to keep Williams in Phoenix. "It doesn't seem necessary to mess up the nucleus and chemistry of the team," said Riles, also speaking for Litton. Still, Craig promised he would bring up Williams before September and even left his uniform jersey in his locker stall, an unusual gesture for a guy who had been sent down to the minors. But there was a slight change in his jersey, thanks to recent arrival Ken Oberkfell, who took Williams' number 10 and left him number 9, the number he'd wear when returning to the big club. But the promotion didn't seem as if it would come soon despite Williams' improvement in Phoenix (.291, 14 homers, 33 RBIs) and the fact he no longer seemed clueless whenever a pitch broke.

June was the Giants' best month to date, but it was the A's worst, and they barely maintained first place in late June. The trade for Rickey Henderson had come about as the A's were experiencing offensive shortages throughout the lineup. Dave Henderson struggled through the month, hitting just .198 without a home run. Stan Javier, although he did become the only Canseco replacement in right field to hit a home run, hit just .241 for the month. Mark McGwire drove in 19 runs, but his .247 average was the beginning of a long dry spell. Terry Steinbach, after hitting .344 through the first two months of the season, hit just .258 in June and drove in just five runs. There were some bright spots, though. Dave Parker, who'd hit .309 in May after ending a long April drought, enjoyed his best month of the year by hitting .318 and driving in 14 runs.

As much of a difference as Henderson's arrival would make, the pitching depth would prove to be the main reason Oakland didn't collapse with Dennis Eckersley on the disabled list. As it was, the A's had their only losing month, 13-14. Two factors mitigated the struggle. One was that the Angels went 12-14, the net result being that the A's moved from a first-place tie at the month's start into a half-game lead by its end. The other factor was the bullpen's new dynamic duo — Rick Honeycutt and Todd Burns. Eckersley they weren't, but the veteran left-hander and the second-year right-hander took their games up a notch as they split time in the closer's role. Burns, used to appearing in middle relief and setup, responded to his shorter role — he averaged fewer than 1⅓ innings per appearance for the month — with a brilliant 1.94 ERA and a couple of saves. Honeycutt was more successful still, saving five games and posting a 1.32 ERA in nine games. During the 40 games that Eckersley missed, starting in the last week of May and extending through the All-Star break, Honeycutt was thrust into 10 save situations. He wound up a perfect 10-for-10.

It was, to say the least, a curious position for the 35-year-old lefty. Originally, he'd been picked up from the Dodgers as an addition to the starting rotation just before the trading deadline in 1987. He'd been a starter for the bulk of his career, beginning in Seattle and extending to Texas and Los Angeles. The Dodgers acquired Honeycutt in 1983 for a promising right-hander named Dave Stewart. At the time of the trade, Honeycutt was 14-8 with a league-leading 2.42 ERA for Texas. He never reached that level of excellence with the Dodgers, hampered throughout his stay by injuries. Then '87 was a disaster. Honeycutt found himself exiled to the far reaches of Tommy Lasorda's bullpen, saddled with a 2-12 record and a 4.59 ERA. He was traded to the A's and was scarcely better, going 1-4 with a 5.32 ERA. But that was the last the world was to see of Rick Honeycutt, starting pitcher. Honeycutt, the reliever, opened to rave reviews in '88 with Oakland, following the same course — long relief at first, then some middle relief work, mixing in an occasional stint as a short man — that had vaulted Eckersley back to the top. In the '88 post-season, Honeycutt won Game One of the playoffs and didn't allow a hit or run in three short appearances, all of which were closed out by Eckersley. And while the World Series brought glory to none of the A's, Honeycutt was again a marvel, allowing no baserunners in 3⅓ innings over three games and picking up the A's only victory.

Honeycutt shined in his new role, earning three saves in four games after Eckersley went down on May 27. He contributed to three A's wins early in the month, but his June didn't officially begin until the 14th when he came in with the tying run on third base in one of Oakland's typically sticky situations in Kansas City. Royals Stadium hadn't been kind at all to Oakland in 1988. The Royals had been the only team in the league with a winning record against the A's. And Oakland had lost the first two games of the first series in Kansas City this time around, allowing the second-place Royals to creep to within 1½ games of first place. With the

A's leading 2-1 in the third game, Honeycutt faced left-hander Jim Eisenreich, who had won the series' first game with an 11th-inning single. Honeycutt jumped ahead in the count with two quick strikes and got Eisenreich to ground out to shortstop Mike Gallego, preserving the lead and eventually nailing down a win that kicked the A's lead in the West back to a more comfortable 2½ games. Honeycutt pitched in six more games the rest of the month, saving five and allowing just one run in 10⅓ innings.

"Honey allowed us to be in a position where we didn't have to think about rushing Eck back," La Russa said. "The lift he gave us those six or seven weeks was as big a boost as we got from anybody all year." For his part, Honeycutt said, "I'm not Eck. But I feel more comfortable in the role every time I'm out there. You need more than just good stuff in that role. After doing it for a month, I can better appreciate what Dennis does. It's a test of nerves as much as it's a test of pitching." And Honeycutt was one nervy guy.

Oakland opened June in a first-place tie with California in the West and won four of six games, including three shutouts in four games with Bob Welch and Mike Moore each winning for the seventh time and Dave Stewart winning his 10th. Storm Davis and Moore won back-to-back 5-1 decisions in Texas as the A's opened up their biggest lead of the season to that point, three games. That was little more than a mirage, however, as losses in six of the next eight games kept Oakland from expanding its lead. Rickey Henderson's arrival didn't immediately alter the situation, either. After two wins, including one on the day the deal was announced, the A's lost back-to-back games at home to Toronto. Oakland came back to earn a split of that four-game series, Stewart pitching a complete game and Davis following with a strong seven-inning effort. Those wins were followed by Oakland's standard difficulties in the Metrodome where the Minnesota Twins became the first team in '89 to sweep the A's in a series. After an off-day, Welch returned from the disabled list and combined with Gene Nelson and Honeycutt for a 5-0 win in a series opener in Cleveland, good enough to give the A's a one-half game lead in the West as the month came to a close.

THE ALL-STARS
How the A's and Giants ruled the Mid-Season Classic

Dave Stewart and Rick Reuschel, once overlooked and released, had blossomed into the envy of every other pitcher in baseball by July. Stewart and Reuschel had experienced their share of door-slammings, but in a few short years both had given new meaning to the word "perseverance." A short time earlier, they were all but forgotten ballplayers. But in July 1989, they were the starting pitchers in the All-Star Game.

Reuschel missed the entire 1982 season and practically all of '83 with a torn rotator cuff, and he was released by both the Yankees and Cubs. Stewart also bounced around, from the Dodgers to the Rangers to the Phillies. In May 1986, thanks to his alarming

6.57 ERA in relief, Stewart was let go by the Phils. These veteran pitchers easily could have called it quits, and many other men would have done so in their positions, but they did themselves — as well as the game — a big favor by sticking it out.

Nobody seemed to have any faith in these has-beens until the Pirates agreed to give Reuschel a minor-league contract and the A's decided to insert Stewart into their starting rotation. Wise choices, both. Reuschel spent only a month in the minors and began winning immediately after his promotion, earning another 68 victories through the '89 All-Star break, including 36 since his trade to the Giants in late '87. Stewart became a starter when Tony La Russa took over as the A's manager in July 1986, and he hadn't missed a turn since, managing 63 wins through the '89 break and setting the pace for his third straight 20-win season.

The '89 season was developing into a career year for both pitchers. Reuschel won 11 games by June 6, earlier than any Giant pitcher in San Francisco history. And Stewart, by the break, had posted more wins than he had at the break in both '87 and '88, each a 20-win season.

Reuschel fashioned a 12-3 record and 2.12 ERA in the first half, and Stewart was 13-4 and 3.30. Their reward for persevering through troubled times and rising to the top of their profession in the first half came on July 11, the day of the All-Star Game in Anaheim. They faced off as the starting pitchers, Reuschel representing the National League and Stewart the American. If this were to be a truly magical season in the Bay Area, it was only fitting for the All-Star Game to pit Reuschel against Stewart.

But other than resurrected careers, they had nothing in common. One's a rock-hard 32-year-old who relies on an assortment of heat; the other's a baby-soft 40-year-old who relies on a collection of junk. The differences abound.

Stewart is a product of Oakland's ghettos who came to baseball right out of high school; Reuschel grew up in rural Illinois and attended college before turning pro.

Stewart is a gregarious and talkative type who's always available to the media; Reuschel is an introspective and subdued person who prefers to duck the press.

Stewart, 6-foot-2 and 200 pounds, is sculpted like Apollo; Reuschel, 6-3 and 230, more closely resembles Joe in the Friday night bowling league.

Stewart takes the field looking as intense as a drill instructor; Reuschel calmly walks out to the mound with a laid-back exterior.

Stewart throws heat; Reuschel has more junk than Fred Sanford.

Stewart's nickname is "Smoke"; Reuschel's is "Big Daddy."

The differences between the two men are many, but cradled around their opposite tendencies is one similarity — a burning desire to win. But even that shows up in different ways. Where Reuschel rarely completes a game and is satisfied with just six innings, Stewart wants nothing more than to pitch all nine. Stewart never asks to come out of a game. Ever. In fact, even when it's clear he doesn't have his best stuff, he doesn't want to leave. Whenever La Russa goes out to the mound to take the game ball, Stewart gives his manager his patented death stare — the meanest frown imaginable, capped by two glaring eyes focused in what La Russa admits is a most unnerving manner — before retreating to the showers. But that's OK with La Russa, who was willing to take Stewart over any other pitcher in the game from '87 through '89.

For the previous two seasons, the easiest call La Russa had to make came every fifth day when he scribbled Stewart's name on his lineup card. Stewart's arrival in Oakland predated that of La Russa by some six weeks, but — spiritually, at least — the pitcher and his manager arrived on the scene at the same time. When La Russa took over as the A's manager on July 7, 1986, for a nationally televised game in Boston, he inherited a club that was 21 games under .500. The A's had been swept up in a month-long torrent of miserable performances that had gotten the previous boss, Jackie Moore, sacked. After winning on June 3 to stay within two games of first-place Texas, the A's crumbled and lost nine straight. In a 30-game stretch under Moore and interim manager Jeff Newman, Oakland lost 25 times to fall as many as 15 games off the pace.

Then came La Russa. The one-time A's middle infielder was free after having been fired by Chicago earlier in the season in the disastrous — for the White Sox, at least — reign of flamboyant general manager Ken "Hawk" Harrelson, who supervised the dismantling of a Chicago team that had won 99 games and the American League West under La Russa in 1983. Harrelson and La Russa clashed repeatedly while the White Sox took a dive, and the manager was bounced in an ugly scene in mid-June. La Russa, who hadn't had a summer free of baseball, promised his wife, Elaine,

and daughters, Bianca and Devon, that they'd use the free time to
take an unprecedented summer vacation. But before the La Russas
could get their Chicago apartment cleared out and ship their be-
longings back to their home in Sarasota, Florida, the A's came calling. While Moore was still at the helm in Oakland, Bay Area and
Chicago newspapers were abuzz with rumors that the A's were in
full pursuit of La Russa.

When the A's did come courting in the presence of co-owners
Wally Haas and Roy Eisenhardt and general manager Sandy Alderson, La Russa found himself torn. "I had always told my wife
that they were building something special in Oakland, that it would
be a great place to be a manager," he said. Balancing the equation
was the vacation promised to Bianca and Devon. "You don't break
promises you make to your children." And you don't get many
chances to manage your dream team, either. In a series of long family meetings, the negotiated settlement included a brief 10-day vacation, during which time the A's would be managed by bullpen
coach Jeff Newman. Only after that would La Russa take up his
new duties.

If studious La Russa, who holds a law degree from Florida
State University, was Oakland's smart and savvy Butch Cassidy,
then Stewart was his Sundance Kid — cool, steady and just the
man to put an end to the nonsense that had occurred under the
previous regime. Stewart hadn't been much of a factor in the A's
disastrous plunge. For that matter, he hadn't been much of a factor
in baseball for anyone for quite a while. When he signed with the
A's on May 23 after getting his release from the Phillies, Stewart
hadn't won a game in almost two years. Used almost exclusively as
a reliever by Moore, Stewart had been little more than a mop-up
man — although given the A's losing ways, the mop-up pitchers of
that time were getting more work than most of the starters. Moore
told Stewart he had other pitchers he wanted to see. That was true
enough. The A's went through 20 other pitchers in 1986, and guys
named Dave Van Ohlen and Doug Bair and Fernando Arroyo kept
cutting into Stewart's time.

The new manager looked for a way to start fresh, and Stewart,
winless in all of 1985 and half of 1986, was as fresh as he could be.
All Stewart had to do was battle Boston's Roger Clemens in Fenway Park, where he and the Red Sox were almost invincible. Stewart took the ball and pitched six innings in the A's 6-4 win, and La

Russa had found the piece of granite around which he would build his new club. Oakland lost its next four games in succession, but when Stewart popped up again on day five, he beat Blue Jays ace Jimmy Key in Toronto. Stewart had found a home.

Stewart grew up on the streets and playgrounds of Oakland, which had long been a hotbed of baseball. Frank Robinson came from Oakland. So did Joe Morgan. Growing up, Stewart, who lived within walking distance of the Oakland Coliseum, hung around with a group of hot-shot athletes, Rickey Henderson, Gary Pettis, Lloyd Moseby and East Bay prep basketball legend Northern "Doc" Shavers. Stewart was a catcher, Pettis a shortstop, Moseby a first baseman. Only the outfielder, Henderson, played the same position he'd wind up playing in the major leagues. When Stewart wasn't playing baseball — and football and basketball — for St. Elizabeth High School, he frequently was to be found at the Oakland Boys Club not far from his home on Havenscourt Boulevard, doing what he could to stay out of trouble on some of the meanest streets in Oakland.

One way to avoid the temptations of the street was to hustle on down to the Coliseum, hop a fence and watch a game. Stewart took a particular liking to the right-field corner where Reggie Jackson's "Reggie's Regiment" used to gather. He mustered up enough courage to introduce himself to Jackson, and before long the A's star right fielder hired the lithe young schoolboy to guard whichever of his already voluminous collection of classic cars Jackson had driven to the Coliseum that day. But for as much as he liked baseball, Stewart was planning on pursuing a career in football after receiving upward of 30 scholarship offers as a linebacker. He was weighing his final alternatives — USC or the University of California — when the Dodgers stunned him by selecting him in the 16th round of the June 1975 draft. Three years later, he was pitching in the big leagues, although it was just one game. Learning his craft took time, and it wasn't until 1981 that he was ready for a return to the show.

In Stewart's first two seasons, he found success first as a reliever, then as a starter. In 1983, again as a reliever, he had five wins, eight saves and a 2.96 ERA when he was traded to the Texas Rangers for Rick Honeycutt. He learned about the trade while listening to the radio on his way to the ballpark. "That hurt," he said. "I expected more class than that from the Dodgers." Stewart was an immediate smash in Texas, winning five of his eight starts and posting a 2.14 ERA. But there were more hurts to follow. A year later, he was 7-14 as a starter and began to hear boos. That off-season, he was back in Los Angeles when things really got ugly. He was arrested in his parked truck with a prostitute, both being charged with lewd behavior in public. It wasn't until later that he found out the "woman" in question, who went by the name Lucille, was actually a transvestite. The charge against Stewart was later reduced to solicitation, a misdemeanor.

Less than 48 hours later after his arrest, the community-minded Stewart was supposed to be given the Rangers' Good Guy Award, as voted on by the Dallas-area media. Almost anybody else would have shunned the spotlight after that kind of negative head-line-raising incident. Stewart, who'd committed himself to going, never wavered. He apologized to the crowd for what had happened in Los Angeles and, as a finale, said, "I guess good guys make mistakes, too." He got a standing ovation from a crowd of 600.

Being a good guy couldn't save Stewart a year later, though, as he went 0-6 for the Rangers before being traded to Philadelphia. He didn't do much in four games that year for the Phillies, and in 1986, his Philadelphia career came to an abrupt end after just eight games and 12 innings. After his release, he called around. Nobody wanted him until the A's, desperate beyond belief for anyone with a live arm, signed him and shipped him off to Triple-A Tacoma. One three-inning relief appearance was all it took to earn him a trip back to the major leagues, but he had to wait until La Russa's arrival before bona fide major-league opportunity came knocking.

"I was a little surprised, stunned really, when Tony and Dunc (pitching coach Dave Duncan) came to me and told me I'd start that first game," Stewart said. His career record at the time was 30-35, and veteran starter Rick Langford, who'd won 19 games for Oakland in 1980, was available to start, as was rookie Bill Mooney-ham. "They told me they'd like to see if I could get us off in the right direction," Stewart said. Roger Clemens notwithstanding, Stewart did just that. That accomplished, he went on to finish the year with a 9-5 record. Oakland management was so impressed with his stuff, his dedication and his desire to pitch in his home-town that the A's broke with habit and offered Stewart the club's first two-year contract since the early '80s. In response, the right-hander went 20-13 in 1987, then in '88 improved to 21-12, including winning his first eight starts, to lead the A's to the division championship.

Almost from the start, Stewart was a great fan favorite in Oakland and not just because the A's were winning more than two of his every three starts. Driven to give something back to the community that had nurtured him, Stewart became the hub of much of the civic-minded A's community service. He could be found shooting pool with kids down at the same Boys Club where he'd hung out 15 years earlier. "There were people there to help me get rid of the bad habits I had when I was younger," he said. "That makes it something I want to do in return." He led a drive to help his old high school, St. Elizabeth, a Catholic school, raise enough money to reinstate football as a sport after it had been slashed under a series of budget cuts. He worked with the Volunteers of America. He sponsored reading programs for kids' athletic teams. And, having been the first athlete to join the "Just Say No" anti-drug program — he personally paid to have a billboard with those three words erected in a prominent spot near Arlington Stadium when he was with the Rangers — he continued his anti-drug work. By 1988, he'd founded KidsCorp, a non-profit organization dedicated to developing year-round sports and educational programs for young people throughout the Bay Area. With Stewart leading the way, corporate sponsors help pay the expenses.

Of course, the fact that he did win with such consistency made Stewart's story that much more remarkable. The morning after his big win over Clemens, Duncan, who had followed La Russa to the A's from Chicago, analyzed the starter's performance. Stewart's reputation was that of a gun-slinger, a pitcher who relied almost exclusively on a 90 mph-plus fastball. But Duncan saw that the right-hander was throwing an occasional off-speed pitch which the Red Sox were never able to hit, so he inquired. Stewart explained that the pitch was a split-fingered fastball (otherwise known as a forkball), something both the Rangers and Phillies told him not to throw. Duncan, however, wasn't about to turn his nose up at a pitch that darted through the strike zone so elusively. The next day, he and Stewart went out to the bullpen in Boston's Fenway Park and worked on mastering the grip and the technique of the forkball. "It was a very fortunate situation," Duncan said. "Everything I suggested to him worked. Right away, Stew was throwing the forkball like he'd been throwing it five or six years. I can't say that Stew wouldn't have become a winning pitcher without the forkball, but I can say that it is what made him a 20-game winner."

Through all of Stewart's successes and failures, he remained a sportswriter's dream, always willing to say what was on his mind. On the other hand, if every ballplayer were like Reuschel, writers could rent out space in their notebooks. Rick is a man of few words, except when he's a man of fewer words, and he'll often try his darnedest to avoid addressing the media. Where Stewart is willing to talk even after his worst games, Reuschel prefers to keep tight-lipped after even after his best games, his silence reaching almost comic proportions. One of his typical bits comes whenever someone feeds him a generic question. "Did you feel pretty good out there today, Rick?" To which Reuschel will answer no but nod yes.

One of the memorable Reuschel sequences came in 1988 during an otherwise dull spring training. The Giants were coming off a division championship, and there were few exceptional stories in camp. One was Reuschel's shoulder, which had been bothering him since he'd reported. The fact that the aging pitcher had been knocked around for five runs and five hits in two innings of his spring debut made the story even more newsworthy. After the game, the media sought out Reuschel, who had tried his best to slip away unnoticed. While the Giants' players and coaches headed for the team bus at Compadre Stadium in Chandler, Arizona, the Brewers' spring training camp, Reuschel took off in the opposite direction. He threaded his way through the flow of departing fans and made a beeline for the locker room up a steep hill through the stands. The reporters were right behind him. When Reuschel arrived in the locker room, he looked over his shoulder and noticed the crowd of reporters. He didn't seem too thrilled.

With no way out of it, he gave an interview that filled about two lines in each of the writer's notebooks.

"Did you have any problems with the shoulder."

"No."

"Have you been feeling OK throwing on the side?"

"Yeah."

"Have you ever had any similar soreness in other springs?"

"All 18 of them."

"Were you able to throw any pitch you wanted?"

"Yeah."

"Have you felt steady progress since the beginning of spring training?"

"Probably."

"So you're not concerned?"

"Nope."

End of interview. All answers were uttered in a let's-get-this-over-with tone. All were vintage Reuschel. He once said his most memorable game was his first one. When asked what was so memorable about it, he said, "I don't remember. That was an awfully long time ago."

Reuschel masks his emotions as well as anyone who has ever played the game; some would even argue he has no emotions. But there was one time a teammate made a nice play behind him to end a game, and Reuschel responded by jumping off the mound and raising a fist. Confronted afterward about this unusual burst of emotion, Reuschel denied all charges. "That wasn't me," he said. Another classic tale came early in the '88 season after Reuschel beat the Cubs and improved his record to 5-1. Giants manager Roger Craig was asked about his pitcher's chances of making the All-Star team, and Craig said the chances were slim because Reuschel would be married on All-Star Tuesday. But when Reuschel was asked about the wedding plans, he said, "That's news to me." For the record, Rick did marry Barbara Thompson on All-Star Tuesday. No writers were known to be in attendance.

Reuschel is a private and mysterious individual who doesn't feed on publicity as do most of his peers and wants no part of sharing his personal life. When the Giants asked him to be the subject of a cover story for a game program in 1988, he refused. But he didn't have such veto power when Sports Illustrated came calling. Despite Reuschel's opposition, the magazine featured him on the cover of its July 10, 1989, edition. Reuschel would obviously never pose for the cover, so SI ran an action shot from the Giants' July 1 game with the Cubs. Meanwhile, Kevin Mitchell, who loves looking at pictures of himself — two huge newspaper photos hung from his locker all season — was elated when he was informed he would appear on the June 26, 1989, cover of SI. He even spent several hours posing for the SI photographer. But he was snubbed for Curtis Strange after Strange dramatically shot 15 birdies in a row to win his second consecutive U.S. Open in Rochester, New York. While Mitchell was bummed because he didn't make the cover, Reuschel was bummed because he did.

Every spring, USA Today asks major-leaguers a host of silly questions, then each day in the sports section runs a picture of one of the players next to his answer. One of the most common questions is, what would the player do if he were baseball commissioner for a day. Most beat reporters know Reuschel well enough to stay away from him with this kind of a question. But when a reporter asked Matt Williams in spring training about the commissioner bit, Reuschel overheard the question from his seat at the lunch table clear across the clubhouse. Then he responded on his own, shouting, "I would never let reporters in the clubhouse. You don't belong in here. A clubhouse is for players only." It was a very Reuschel-like response, but the manner of its delivery — shouting across a room — was very un-Reuschel-like. It just goes to show that he will speak if the subject is to his liking, and the subject of trashing reporters is definitely dear to his heart.

Reuschel, although an avid reader, isn't often caught with a sports section in hand. He says fans don't need to know the insights of a ballplayer and that fans don't care what athletes say. "I don't think that matters to them one bit," he once said. "If you screw up big-time, they don't need to read about it. They know. But if you do your job and what you're supposed to do, they know that already, too." Incidentally, in the same conversation, Reuschel said he had forgotten something in the clubhouse and tried to sneak away, but the group of reporters knew a Reuschel interview was rare, so they surrounded him and wouldn't let him go. Reuschel stayed to answer a couple of more questions.

"Do you still live around Chicago in the off-season?"

"I can't remember."

"Do you try not to think about your next game?"

"Actually, I was doing pretty good at that until five minutes ago."

"When was the last time you were actually nervous before a start?"

"When was my last start?"

"Saturday."

"Last Saturday."

Thanks again, Rick.

About the only time all season Reuschel revealed a trace of his inner self came when he was asked about Fred Martin, one of his minor-league pitching coaches who died of bone cancer in 1979 during Reuschel's eighth year in the big leagues. Martin is known most for developing the split-fingered fastball, a pitch generally linked to Roger Craig. But Craig's success has been in teaching the pitch; he didn't invent it. That distinction goes to Martin, who Reuschel said had more influence on his career than anyone else. "He was the best. He'd do anything for you. He took care of all his pitchers. He'd never call you into his office or into the outfield. He'd have you over for dinner. He was different than a lot of coaches I had. He was able to teach X number of different ways. Some, all they teach is the way they were taught. He'd watch one or two games, and he'd know." In an interview with Barry Locke of The Daily Review in Hayward, Reuschel recalled the day Martin died. "It was a tough day for us but probably a good day for Fred. The cancer ate him up. I remember the day he died. It was the same day that John Wayne died. Both my heroes. I very seldom think of him in a pitching sense anymore. When I think of him now, it's more of times off the field and our friendship."

When the conversation turned to his own accomplishments, Reuschel backed off, as usual. Even after Reuschel won his 199th career game in early May 1989, he wouldn't chat about the big 200. The day before he tried for 200, he must have known he would be pursued by reporters, so he hid out. When he finally was uncovered, he wouldn't comment on the prospect. Only after beating the Expos 2-1 on May 12 to become the 86th pitcher to reach 200 wins did he finally discuss the matter. Asked if he'd treasure the moment when he gets older, Reuschel said, "You'll have to ask me when I get older." Asked when that might be, he said, "I don't know. What's old?" Surely not Reuschel, who won his 200th four days before his 40th birthday. For most athletes, 40 is old. For Big Daddy, 40 is peaking.

As a middle-aged baseball player, Reuschel competed in '89 with kids close to half his age. And more often than not, the competition was one-sided, with Reuschel coming out ahead. With his unconventional display of off-speed yet precise pitches, Reuschel managed a first-half winning streak of nine games and was on pace to better his 19-win season of 1988 and reach 20 for the second time in his career. But Reuschel's overall game goes far beyond just pitching. Aside from being a two-time Gold Glove Award winner, he's the best bunting pitcher on the team and possesses the quickest pickoff move to first base. On July 1, he even tried stealing a base. He was thrown out, but that sight alone was worth the price of admission. The entire package made the Giants look very smart for signing him to a contract extension during spring training. It put Reuschel under contract through 1990 for an extra $1 million (including signing bonus and excluding incentive bonuses), which turned out to be a steal of a deal considering he could have tested the lucrative free-agent waters after the season.

Although Reuschel pitched into the seventh, eighth and even ninth inning several times, he had only one complete game through the '89 All-Star break — a 3-2 loss to the Cubs. If he felt secure enough with his lead, Reuschel would tell Craig he wanted out of the game. And he always offered his standard line: "Complete games and shutouts are for the younger guys." On May 18 in Chicago, Reuschel pitched perfect ball for 6⅔ innings before Tommy Herr's two-out, seventh-inning single ruined Reuschel's bid for perfection. That left Reuschel working on his first career one-hitter, but in true Reuschel form he asked to be relieved before entering the ninth with a 6-0 lead. "It was getting past my bedtime," he said.

Because of the early starting times for All-Star Games, Reuschel had no problem attending the 60th All-Star Game in Anaheim. Tommy Lasorda, the National League manager because his Dodgers had won the pennant in '88, chose Reuschel to start for his side. La Russa, the opposing manager on the basis of the A's winning the American League pennant, had an easier decision when he picked Stewart. The starting pitchers, unlike position players, are chosen by the All-Star managers, with the help of league presidents, leaving the fans to vote for the remaining starters.

There was little debate over which pitchers had the credentials to start. Stewart was clearly the most dominating American League pitcher in the first half, and he definitely deserved the starting nod over a field that included Texas' 42-year-old Nolan Ryan, the sentimental favorite who was making his return to Anaheim Stadium where he had enjoyed some of his finest seasons while with the Angels. Although Reuschel might not have had a huge edge over Houston's Mike Scott (14-5), Scott was unable to perform after pulling a hamstring two days before the game. But Scott, who appeared in uniform in Anaheim, noted that Reuschel was more deserving. "Wins and losses don't mean everything." And Lasorda said he was leaning toward Reuschel, anyway.

None of the other All-Stars were prepared to complain about the All-Bay Area pitching matchup. Said Kansas City pitcher Mark Gubicza, "Having two guys like these start this game is a real boost for all of us. It is a monument to perseverance and dedication on the part of both guys. It shows what you can do to turn things around when you're down." Added St. Louis shortstop Ozzie Smith, "Those two always have been something special. They are fighters, real competitors. They make each at-bat a real challenge. It was that kind of determination that helped them get back to the top."

Although Stewart said the starting assignment was even more special because he'd be facing Reuschel, Reuschel wouldn't admit there was anything special about the two former residents of Lonesome Street suddenly commanding the attention of the baseball world.

"I've always enjoyed watching Rick's career and rooted for him when he was making his comeback," Stewart said. "He's always been the kind of pitcher I can learn from. He takes a nice, positive attitude out to the mound every time he pitches. He knows his strengths and knows what he wants to do and pitches accordingly. He's a textbook."

Said Reuschel, the first Giants pitcher to start an All-Star Game since Vida Blue in 1978, "I don't know that it makes any difference that we've both come back from being released to be here today. But at the same time, it's everybody's dream to be here, whether you've been let go by a team or not. I've come back; Stewart's come back. But I'd be just as happy about pitching in this game if it were Joe Blow pitching for the other side."

The Stewart-Reuschel matchup was a fitting one, but there was all kinds of controversy over the fans' selections. Voting for Jose Canseco and Mike Schmidt was brought into question. Schmidt would have been a likely choice in just about any other of his 17 big-league seasons, but it just so happened that the Philadelphia third baseman had retired from the game 45 days before the Anaheim showdown. The retirement still didn't prevent him from receiving the most votes among National League third basemen. Because Schmidt was an inactive player and therefore ineligible to play, the Mets' Howard Johnson was named the starter.

Then there was Canseco, whose knack to go where no man has gone before carried over into the All-Star hoopla. Canseco's longest non-season was close to coming to an end. He had been recovering from the surgery to remove the fragmented portion of the hamate bone in his left wrist, tuning up his game in Alabama with Double-A Huntsville, and there was a chance he would be activated for the final few games before the All-Star break. Through all of his injuries and his troubles with the law, Canseco somehow never lost the support of the common fan. Although he hadn't played a game in the major leagues all season, Canseco was the third-leading vote-getter among American League outfielders, behind Kansas City's Bo Jackson and Minnesota's Kirby Puckett. As Canseco said about the fans, "They are the ones who vote for who they want to see in the game — their favorites — and obviously I'm one of their favorites."

With a week to go before the game, Canseco said he was not only willing to play; now he was also able to play. The A's, in the person of La Russa, had a different view, and he let out his feelings in a rare public criticism of one of his players. The manager believed, in essence, that if Canseco was so ready, why wasn't he playing in Oakland? The fact that Canseco was still in Huntsville led La Russa and A's general manager Sandy Alderson to believe that Canseco wasn't quite a ready-for-prime-time player. Nothing short of a trip to Lourdes was going to get him in the All-Star Game.

Just one week before the game, Alderson said the chances of Canseco playing in Anaheim were slim. "He's done nothing to this point to indicate that he's ready," Alderson said. La Russa was looking for a replacement for Canseco, but at the same time Canseco was disputing his boss' judgment by saying, "I don't think it's in Tony's jurisdiction to decide whether or not I play in the All-Star Game." But on the same day that La Russa signed a three-year contract extension, he officially announced that Canseco wouldn't be on the All-Star roster. In his place, he selected up-and-coming Texas slugger Ruben Sierra to start. As a compromise, it was decided that Canseco would take part in the traditional All-Star Monday workout and be announced to the Anaheim Stadium crowd during the pre-game introductions, but it didn't quite work that way. Once he learned he wouldn't play, Canseco simply didn't show up.

San Francisco's Will Clark proved to be the most popular player in both leagues among the voters. Fans punched out the little box next to his name 1,833,329 times, and he became the first

Giant ever to win the Top Vote-Getter trophy. Clark came off as unmistakably thrilled to receive the award, knowing he was in the same category as Hank Aaron, Johnny Bench and Reggie Jackson, all leading vote-getters of past years.

Kevin Mitchell finished second to Clark in the balloting, only 19,000 votes behind. Although Candlestick isn't known as a ballot-stuffing ballpark, the two Giants easily received more votes than the Darryl Strawberrys or Kirk Gibsons or other players from media capitals. Ozzie Smith, who had led both leagues in votes for two straight seasons, could manage only third this time. Mitchell's reaction to being named to his first All-Star Game was, well, typical Mitchell. "It's a great honor to go to the All-Star Game," he said. "It's like being invited to the Willie Wonka Chocolate Factory."

The only two A's assured of being in Anaheim, Terry Steinbach and Mark McGwire, were a little surprised to find they had the fan base that would send them there, although both also had been voted to the team in 1988. Steinbach had been hitting just .217 at the time of the '88 All-Star break and spent much of the 48 hours leading up to the game having to defend his right to be in Cincinnati with the rest of the All-Stars. He knew that the inquisition was coming, and that knowledge alone helped him through some tough times with the media. They'd overlooked his big rookie year — .286 and 16 homers, good enough to be Rookie of the Year in many seasons but overshadowed this time by McGwire. All the media saw was .217. Until game time, that is, when Steinbach saw a couple of pitches he could handle. He hit a solo home run and a warning-track sacrifice fly off Dwight Gooden to lift the American League to a 2-1 win, at the same time earning Most Valuable Player honors.

Steinbach had no explanation for his '89 success at the ballot box, but with his history in the '88 game and a .322 batting average at the time of the '89 break, at least he didn't have to explain his presence this time around. But unlike 1988, 1989 saw no shortage of first-class American League catching candidates. Ex-Athletic Mickey Tettleton, the man forced out of Oakland by Steinbach's emergence, had 20 home runs for Baltimore. And two long-time catching stars were having big years, Lance Parrish in California and Bob Boone in Kansas City. But Steinbach had the numbers — both at the plate and in the ballot box — to get the nod.

McGwire's numbers at the break leaned to the downside — a

.244 batting average, 17 homers and 58 RBIs. Nothing horrible, but not Cooperstown material, either. And there was no shortage of candidates at first base for the American League, not with Fred McGriff of the Blue Jays having a banner year and Don Mattingly, after a poor start, putting on his usual strong mid-summer surge for the Yankees. McGwire, for his part, voted for McGriff, who would wind up fifth in the balloting. "I saw how many votes I was ahead by (400,000), and I just shook my head," McGwire said. "I'm not having a bad year except that my average is a little low, but this kind of popularity is amazing to me. When I look at guys like Mattingly and McGriff and see just what great players they are, and then look to see that fans are voting for me, it just sort of blows me away."

La Russa was faced with a dilemma. He had precious little room for his own players on the roster because all 14 teams must be represented with at least one All-Star. Aside from starting position players McGwire and Steinbach, La Russa had an easy choice in Stewart. But La Russa also had to consider Mike Moore, who turned up the heat on his boss by winning his 10th game on July 1 and lowering his ERA to a sparkling 2.35, just .05 off the league lead. "He's got great numbers, anyone can see that," La Russa said. "And I believe that you've got to spread things around, try for equal representation."

Moore wasn't La Russa's only problem. Lansford ended June hitting .340. And what of A's pitcher Bob Welch, who entered the month with a 9-4 record and would have two starts left before La Russa and American League President Bobby Brown had to finalize their decisions? How many of his own players could La Russa bring along and still satisfy the dictates of his conscience? "I don't know," he said. "That may be the toughest question I have." He wound up picking Moore and leaving off Welch and Lansford.

No selection process will ever satisfy everyone. The fans used to get mad at the players when the players voted; now the players get mad at the fans when the fans vote; and everyone likely would get mad at the managers if the managers could vote. So as imperfect as the fan vote is, it's the one that's been in business since 1970, and it's the one baseball has learned to live with. Lansford, who finished 388,000 votes behind Boston's Wade Boggs, led the league in hitting much of the season but was in the unfortunate predicament of playing third base, a position boasting several deserving All-Stars, such as Minnesota's Gary Gaetti and Toronto's Kelly Gruber. And the fact the All-Star roster would be stocked full of A's already also lessened Lansford's chances of being picked as a reserve, even though La Russa was doing the picking, and even though Lansford had made the '88 team despite a worse overall first half.

Lansford, who had made just one previous All-Star team, wasn't necessarily upset that he would be overlooked for the '89 event. A proponent of the players voting, Lansford was more upset at who was elected and how. "With few exceptions, you're not seeing the players having the best years," he said. "That's not right. I don't care what the fans say. It's not right. For a player to work his rear off and then Jose Canseco gets voted into the All-Star Game, that's what infuriates players. That makes me sick." Lansford also suggested that allowing the fans to vote is "a joke. It always has been since I've been in the league, and it always will be." A good indication that Lansford knew his fate long before the All-Star rosters were set came when he made vacation plans weeks earlier.

Other Bay Area candidates didn't make the All-Star cut, but none were as displeased as Canseco or Lansford. San Francisco's Brett Butler and Robby Thompson, the lesser-known pair at the top of the Giants' lineup, were shunned by Lasorda despite stats worthy of All Star consideration. Thompson seemed to have an especially good chance to crack the roster as the reserve second baseman behind Ryne Sandberg of the Cubs. He was tops in the National League in runs scored and triples, and was among the leaders in slugging percentage and on-base percentage. He was just as able on defense, getting in on the most double plays among second basemen and committing the fewest errors — he didn't commit an error until his 51st game. And most of all, Thompson was healthy, virtually free of the pain in his troubled back that had pushed him from the lineup several times in recent years. The bad back even caused Thompson to miss the 1988 All-Star Game. He turned down an offer from Whitey Herzog to be the backup second baseman. In '89, Thompson was ready and willing to go to the All-Star Game if summoned. The only problem, however, was that Lasorda didn't choose Thompson. He picked a Dodger, Willie Randolph.

Butler, as he does every year, faced stiff competition with a healthy dose of power-hitting outfielders grabbing much of the All-Star recognition. Butler was hitting .294, but the little center fielder had just three home runs, not good enough for such a power-dominated extravaganza. But the lack of an invitation was nothing new for Butler, who never has been much of an award-winner. He'd never been an All-Star, and he'd never won a Gold Glove despite leading American League outfielders in fielding percentage in 1985, when he played for the Indians.

The day Lasorda completed his All-Star selections, the Giants were in Pittsburgh during a six-game road trip. Neither Thompson nor Butler publicly complained about Lasorda's decisions, but each registered a silent protest by hitting a home run to help beat the Pirates. Thompson homered in the eighth inning to tie the game at 1-1, and Butler homered in the 10th inning to win the game 2-1. "We got a lot of motivation from Tommy Lasorda," Roger Craig said. "I didn't have to motivate them today."

La Russa had the inauspicious duty of facing Lasorda, 3-0 as an All-Star manager. And Tommy was laying it on pretty heavy on All-Star Monday in Anaheim, predicting he would soon be 4-0 and that his club would walk all over Stewart, whose only manager in his three seasons as a Dodger was Lasorda. "I know we're going to beat his butt," Lasorda said in his typical half-serious way. Stewart didn't take the shot personally, saying, "Listening to Tommy makes me want to go out and pitch right now." Stewart had to wait another day, but he should have enjoyed a good night's sleep knowing the lineup La Russa had posted.

Leading off was Bo Jackson. With that alone, Stewart should have caught some good Z's, but there was more where that came from. Wade Boggs hit second and Kirby Puckett third, followed by Harold Baines, Julio Franco, Cal Ripken, Ruben Sierra, McGwire and Steinbach. Bo first? And McGwire eighth? That kind of lineup can take a pitcher's breath away. Back in June, A's pitching coach Dave Duncan had suggested hitting Bo first, and La Russa liked the idea. McGwire had never hit lower than seventh in his short career with the A's, but then again he never hit in a lineup with Bo leading off. Bo had 21 homers and 59 RBIs at the break, and he still had three months of baseball before he had to start preparing for football, his other job.

The National League's lineup might not have been as power-ful, but no manager would have turned it down. Just the fact that Clark was hitting third and Mitchell fourth made the thing intriguing. Then toss in Tony Gwynn second, and there's no better 2-3-4 combination in the business. Ozzie Smith hit first, Eric Davis fifth, Howard Johnson sixth, followed by Pedro Guerrero, then Ryne Sandberg and Benito Santiago.

The big news in Anaheim was Mitchell, who had already hit 31 home runs with 81 RBIs before the break. But the hundreds of questions — most of which were repeated — didn't seem to faze him. Informed that Roger Maris, as he was closing in on 61 home runs in 1961, noticed hair loss by the day, Mitch said, "It's not falling out. In fact, my hair's growing." There was a subtle irony in the fact that one of the Giants' greatest needs in spring training was a cleanup hitter, and here in Anaheim the cleanup hitter for the National League All-Stars was a Giant. "I just hope I can get a 1-2-3 inning in the first so I won't have to face Mitchell," Stewart said, saying nothing National League pitchers hadn't been feeling for three months.

Incidentally, Lasorda named a captain. It was Reuschel. "That's news to me," Big Daddy said as only Big Daddy could. "I don't want to be captain."

Ronald Reagan, a sportscaster before moving to Hollywood and eventually the White House, called the first inning for NBC-TV. But beforehand, he visited each team's locker room and shook hands with the players and coaches. Asked what he told the troops, Reagan said, "What could I tell them?" McGwire shook Reagan's hand, but he wasn't too impressed; he would have preferred to meet someone else, such as Oliver North. No kidding. "I think he (North) is an interesting person," McGwire said. "It's like Mission Impossible. Who really is Ollie North? I'd like to meet him, but I don't think he'd ever tell me what went on. I already have his autograph, on a ball a reporter from Kansas City got for me." As for Reagan? "I already have Ronnie's autograph. He signed a ball for all of the '84 Olympic players."

Once the pre-game hoopla had ended and Dutch Reagan and half of the U.S. Secret Service had settled into the press box, the 60th All-Star Game was finally ready to commence, but the term "All-Star" could very well have been changed to One-Star on this evening. It didn't take long for Jackson to demonstrate why many consider him the best athlete on the field. In a stadium not far from where he carries footballs for the Raiders, Bo hit Reuschel's second pitch of the game deep to center field, 448 feet, to be precise. And he added a single, two RBIs, a stolen base and a splendid running catch. Not to mention an MVP trophy. Final: Bo 5, National League 3. "He doesn't even spend a lot of time on this game. That's the scary part," Gwynn said. "He runs like the wind, has a cannon arm and has power like you haven't seen. I'm a believer."

After watching Bo's show, Mitchell — with a body type not far removed from Bo's — said he wouldn't mind playing both sports, either. Football was Mitchell's favorite as a kid, and he always envisioned himself as an NFL defensive back because that's where "you can take your aggressions out." Mitchell later admitted he wanted to copy Bo's All-Star feats and tried to hit a home run in each at-bat, but he fell well short of Bo despite his two hits.

McGwire and Steinbach each had a hit, and Mike Moore threw a scoreless inning, but Reuschel, Stewart and Clark had had better days. Reuschel's line: one inning, two runs, three hits. Stewart's line: one inning, two runs, three hits, two walks. Clark's line: 0-for-2 with a strikeout against Nolan Ryan, a pitcher Clark had clearly manhandled in Ryan's years as an Astro.

In the winning manager's office, La Russa refused to accept any credit for his unique lineup or crafty pitching moves. He requested the praise go to anyone in the clubhouse but himself, and he was almost embarrassed to accept any congratulatory handshakes. He kept saying All-Star Games belong to the players, not the managers. But how about that wacky batting order, featuring leadoff man Jackson? "A no-brainer," said Mr. Modest. And the constant pitching changes in the eighth inning, all of which worked perfectly? "Stevie Wonder moves." Modesty aside, La Russa became the first American League manager to orchestrate a second straight All-Star Game win since 1958 and, perhaps more importantly, the first American League manager ever to beat Lasorda.

As the Giants and A's returned to work after the break to resume their regularly scheduled programming, questions mounted regarding their second-half destinies. The A's concerns were especially serious, dealing with the health of Canseco, Dennis Eckersley and Walter Weiss, all of whom were on the disabled list during the All-Star break. Probably the biggest question for Giants followers was whether Mitchell could keep up his unprecedented power pace, for he, too, was battling a few pains.

Mitchell, after hitting six homers in April, nine in May and 10 in June, blasted eight more in July and, typically, did most of his damage early in the month. He had six homers in the first seven games — three over two nights in St. Louis — and entered the break with a magnificent total of 31. His July power barrage began on the 2nd when he broke a 1-for-18 slump at a very important time. In one of the many games Roger Craig labeled the "biggest of the year," the Giants escaped what could have easily been their third straight loss and fifth in six games. The Giants were trailing Chicago 3-1 with four outs to go when Mitchell launched an opposite-field, wind-aided home run into the right-field football bleachers to highlight a rally that gave the Giants a 4-3 win. It wasn't Mitch's most convincing blow of the season, but it might have been his most important. A loss would have kept the Giants' lead over Houston at one game entering a week-long road trip, but the Candlestick wind surfaced at just the right time to send Mitchell's ball into the jet stream. "Anything in the air is an adventure here," said Rick Sutcliffe, who served the home-run pitch.

Candlestick has long been known as the windiest park in the league, and that includes Wrigley Field, but this particular Sunday afternoon prompted the opinion that the Candlestick sun might also be the worst. It's easy to discover the crazy wind conditions by watching the flags atop the center-field flag poles, one waving west and the other east. Determining the difficulty of the sun conditions is not as easy, as Clark will testify. The same day the wind carried Mitchell's ball over the fence, Clark engaged in a fierce battle with the sun every time a Cub hit a popup near first base. "I shook my head. I had no idea how I caught them," he said. "This is the worst sun field in the league for first basemen." Clark wasn't complaining, of course, because Craig and Al Rosen have always prohibited any public criticisms of Candlestick Park. Tracy Jones complained. And was traded, like Jack Clark and Johnnie Lemaster before him. But not too many people complain about success, and the Giants were successful at Candlestick Park in 1989, posting a league-best 28-14 home mark at the All-Star break, not to mention a league-best 51-36 overall record.

Although a late-July slump caused Mitchell to lose significant ground in his chase of Roger Maris, he was still on target to become the first major-leaguer to hit 50 home runs since George Foster's 52 in 1977. At the All-Star break, he was on pace to hit 58 homers and drive in 152 runs, and he was certainly the main reason the Giants entered the break leading the league in runs scored, 389 to runner-up Montreal's 374. The Giants' three-four pool of Clark and Mitchell had combined for 41 home runs and 136 RBIs, putting them on pace to challenge the Giants' all-time power tandems. In 1961, Willie Mays and Orlando Cepeda combined for 86 homers and 265 RBIs, and they collected 84 homers and 255 RBIs in '62.

But as Mitchell was having his fun down in Disney Town, the Giants were concerned with their slugger's health. His left knee — not the knee that had been arthroscopically repaired the previous winter — had been inflamed for much of the first half, and it was expected to be aggravated the rest of the season. Mitchell was even considering taking a three-day hiatus at the All-Star break. "Inactivity is the key," trainer Mark Letendre said, although they were not the words Craig wanted to hear. So Mitchell continued taking his daily doses of anti-inflammatory pills and chose to play despite all the hurts. But Mitchell soon suffered another injury, an inflamed lower back which prompted discomfort in his ribs. Letendre was again called into duty and administered a cortisone shot. Mitchell returned after missing four straight starts, but not without more pain. "My spinal cord is kind of crooked right now," he said.

Mitchell's production slowed somewhat in the immediate aftermath of the All-Star Game. He homered in his second game back, but he went deep just once more in July. But as had been the case all season, if one of the big boys took a few days off, the other would pick up the slack. Clark enjoyed his fourth straight .300-hitting month, adding a .307 July to his .375 April, .351 May and .303 June. Immediately after leaving Anaheim, he knocked in the winning run in the 13th inning of a 3-2 victory over the Pirates. And two days later, he got even with an old nemesis, thanks to a three-hit, four-RBI afternoon against Pittsburgh's John Smiley. Clark had gone hitless in his first 15 career at-bats against Smiley and entered that July 15 game 2-for-24 against the left-hander. Clark played down the hoopla surrounding his best game against Smiley, saying, "I've put balls in play, but they just weren't falling. Today, they fell." Smiley took it out on the elements, ferociously cursing the Candlestick winds.

On July 23, after the Giants' first-place lead over Houston having dwindled from 4½ games to 1½ in just four days, Matt Williams was recalled from the minor leagues. After his miserable April with the Giants, Williams went down to Triple-A Phoenix and hit .320 with 26 homers in 76 games and earned yet another chance to shine at the big-league level. Ernest Riles, who saw most of the duty at third in Williams' absence, was mired in a 4-for-22 slump, and once again Williams arrived on the scene with great recommendations and greater potential. But this was a time the Giants could not afford any more disasters, and Williams agreed, saying, "I'm ready to help this team." And the Giants, who had been rumored to be discussing a deal for Wade Boggs earlier in the month, were in the market for an everyday third baseman. Although Williams needed 15 at-bats before his first hit in April, he needed just one at-bat for his first hit in July. He had one of only three Giants hits on July 24, but Mitchell's two-run homer beat Atlanta's John Smoltz 2-0 and gave Reuschel his 13th victory, his first in more than a month.

Although Reuschel's first three months were impressive, July was easily his most disappointing. The main reason was a pulled groin, but the Sports Illustrated Jinx and the All-Star Syndrome shouldn't be discounted. On July 14, in his first appearance since he made the cover of SI — which has a long and lurid history of seeing its cover athletes go into horrendous slumps after publication — Reuschel was knocked around by the Pirates for five runs and eight hits. It was also his first outing since his All-Star start, and Reuschel struggled much like he did against Bo and friends.

The whole scenario brought back uneasy comparisons with the 1983 All-Star Game at Comiskey Park, where the Giants' Atlee Hammaker suffered through the worst pitching performance in the game's history. Hammaker, then the National League ERA leader, coughed up seven runs, six hits and a walk — all in two-third of an one inning. Which put his All-Star ERA at 94.50. Both Jim Rice and Fred Lynn belted home runs, Lynn's a memorable grand slam, to lead the American League to a 13-3 win that snapped its 11-game losing streak. Some say Hammaker has never recovered from that evening in Chicago. For Reuschel, he had another bad outing on July 29 and lost 8-1 to the Astros. This was easily his worst time of the season. "I'm going to pitch until they physically drag me off the field," Reuschel said. "I've still got a World Series ring I'd like to be wearing." However, no dragging was necessary. It became evident that his injuries were too severe to allow him to continue to pitch, and Reuschel was placed on the disabled list July 30, the day the Giants closed out a 4-7 road trip and an 18-10 month.

Across the bay, the A's were not quite sure when their three missing links — Canseco, Dennis Eckersley and Walter Weiss — would return to the roster. La Russa couldn't even commit to any of the three for the first game after the break at Toronto's new SkyDome. It was obvious that Weiss would need another week or two to get his surgically repaired knee in shape. There was less doubt about Eckersley and Canseco, but La Russa waited until the A's July 13 workout in Toronto to make it official — Canseco and Eckersley would be activated simultaneously. Canseco started in right field, and Eckersley was available for duty in short relief. Few comebacks have been quite as dramatic as the ones Oakland saw that night.

"I have no idea what to expect," Eckersley said before the game. "It would be hard for me to believe that I will be all that sharp right now. I'm just hoping I can pitch without pain. Then we'll take it from there." Canseco issued an equally gloomy forecast, suggesting he was no better than 80 percent recovered. "For the next two weeks, it's the pitcher's turn. They'd better enjoy it while they can. After that, it will be my turn."

Despite their pessimism, both Canseco and Eckersley quickly made their mark. From the first, it was Canseco's turn to shine. And, to a lesser degree, Eckersley's. Canseco, who had been having trouble driving the ball in Huntsville, batted sixth — the lowest spot in the batting order La Russa had ever assigned him — and hit a sacrifice fly in the fifth inning, giving Oakland a 6-5 lead. Dave Parker hit a three-run homer later in the inning to give the A's a big cushion, and Canseco came back in an at-bat in the seventh inning with a two-out solo homer, his first in the big leagues since his grand slam in Game One of the '88 World Series. That was also only the second home run by an A's right fielder in '89; in the first 88 games, only Stan Javier had gone deep. And in the ninth inning of the A's 11-7 win, Canseco followed a Ron Hassey double with an RBI single. For the night, Canseco went 2-for-3 with three RBIs, far beyond Canseco's or anyone else's expectations. In addition, the right fielder combined with second baseman Glenn Hubbard to throw out Blue Jays speedster Tony Fernandez at third base in Fernandez's bid for a triple in the third inning. For his part, Eckersley pitched a 1-2-3 ninth inning to close out the win.

Parker searched out Canseco in the SkyDome clubhouse. "Man, pretty soon I'm going to be calling you the best player in baseball instead of just the best player in the American League," said Parker, who had long maintained that Eric Davis, his ex-team-mate in Cincinnati, was the best in baseball. Turning to the media, Parker said, "When a great player like Jose comes back, hits a homer, steals third base, drives in three runs, he's the whole story. But don't forget Eck." But even Eckersley was in awe of Canseco's debut. "Jose's an absolutely unique player," Eckersley said with a disbelieving shake of his head after the game. "He so good that nothing he does really can be a surprise."

Canseco, the King of the Road — he'd gotten another speeding ticket on the day of the All-Star Game — did his best to downplay his return but said his sudden success came as a surprise after his lackluster Huntsville performance. "I still think pitchers are going to abuse me for a while," he said. The difference between Canseco in Huntsville and Canseco in the big leagues was he went into Huntsville not having seen a breaking ball for three months. "I had no clue down there, absolutely none. but I worked hard to get ready." And he hadn't lost his Ruthian flair for the dramatic. "I couldn't believe it, but he called the home run on the bench," Rickey Henderson said. "They were pitching him down and away, and he told me he was going to go down and get one." Canseco also homered in the third game of the series. For the month of July, he hit just .233, but he had five homers and nine RBIs.

The best Oakland player in July was Mike Moore, who went 5-0 in six starts in addition to his All-Star relief stint. With a good bullpen behind him, Moore no longer had to be the "Iron Mike" who'd compiled the staggering total of 46 complete games his last four seasons with the Mariners. Just three of his first 14 wins in 1989 were complete games. "Here you don't have to feel like you have to go nine if you want to get a win," Moore said. If anything, Moore — or any other A's starter, for that matter — had a better chance to go nine innings if the A's were behind than if they were ahead. La Russa was determined to give his starters every chance to win, and in a game where his starter was strong and the A's were only a run or two down, the manager often stuck with the starter in hopes of getting him the win.

That certainly was the case on the last day of July, when Moore and the A's were facing Chicago in a Friday night home game. The A's came into the game 1½ games behind California, which was playing a series-opener at the same time in Seattle. Perhaps more than any time all year, it was the perfect night to be a scoreboard watcher in the Oakland Coliseum. As was his wont, Moore pitched nine strong innings, allowing just two sacrifice flies, one in the second inning to Carlton Fisk to tie the game at 1-1 and another in the eighth to Greg Walker to give the White Sox a 2-1 lead. At the same time in Seattle, the Angels built up an imposing 4-0 lead over the Mariners. The A's were just nine outs shy of falling 2½ games off the lead in the West when Chicago starter Eric King was replaced by ace reliever Bobby Thigpen. Terry Steinbach walked on four pitches, and Tony Phillips tied into a 0-1 pitch and drove it over the right-field fence for a 3-2 victory. Moments earlier in Seattle, Moore's ex-teammate, Jim Presley, homered to cap a dramatic rally as Seattle erupted in the eighth and beat the Angels 6-4. "I saw the score change on the scoreboard," Phillips said after just his third home run of the season. "But that doesn't help you hit a 90-mph fastball. We can't spend too much time worrying about what they (the Angels) do. All we control is our own destiny." But that home run would mark a turning point in the A's season. From that point on, Oakland would never be more than one game out of first place and three weeks later would take up permanent residence in first place.

What was perhaps the A's biggest series to date took place one week earlier against the Angels in Oakland. The Angels led Oakland by percentage points in the West when La Russa started Curt Young in the July 24 opener against Angels right-hander Kirk McCaskill. The A's picked up a run in the first inning, but in the third Young surrendered consecutive singles to Johnny Ray, Devon White, Wally Joyner and Brian Downing, the Angels scoring three runs. The A's hit McCaskill equally hard, but they didn't bunch their hits, and Oakland was going nowhere until a Tony Phillips walk and a Mike Gallego double set up back-to-back sacrifice flies by Rickey Henderson and Carney Lansford, tying the game. Reliever Gene Nelson put the A's in a hole when he gave up a solo home run to the Angels' Chili Davis with two out in the seventh. He then allowed another homer to Jack Howell to lead off the eighth. McGwire delivered an RBI single in the eighth, but the A's could go no further and lost 5-4 to fall a game out of first.

On July 25, Angels manager Doug Rader pitched left-hander Chuck Finley at Stewart and the A's. It appeared to be a mismatch on the surface because the A's had pounded out 16 hits in 8⅓ innings in those two April meetings with Finley, handing him his first two losses of the year. Those had been the continuation of a long stretch of frustration for Finley, who had never beaten Oakland. But since those losses, Finley had found himself and crept into the ERA race, which was becoming an All-West Coast battle among Moore, Finley and the Angels' Bert Blyleven. Finley, who had won 10 of 14 decisions since last seeing Oakland, made a pleasant Bay Area night anything but pleasant for the A's, limiting them to six hits as he and reliever Greg Minton combined to throw a 4-0 shutout. For the first time all year, Stewart was rocked by three home runs in a game, with Howell getting his second in two games, a two-run shot in the second. "It's about time I beat them," Finley said. "It took me three years, but I finally got it done." Chili Davis also homered for the second straight game, afterward saying, "This is the way we did it across the bay in '87," reflecting on the Giants' division title, of which he was a major part.

After that game, with Oakland now two games behind the Angels, the A's did their best to downplay the importance of the series' third game, set for July 26. "It's no more important than any other game on the schedule," La Russa said, dodging the tough question of how a sweep would affect his troops. Parker said, "Win or lose tomorrow, we still have two months more to play."

For all the success Moore enjoyed in July, this was to be his poorest start. He struggled from the outset, giving up a run on three straight hits in the first and two more runs in the third on a two-run double by A's killer Chili Davis. Rickey Henderson had begun the first inning with a home run, and Oakland took the lead in the fourth with four runs. Moore, despite missing his best stuff, threw perfect 1-2-3 innings in the fourth, fifth and sixth, leaving the game with a 5-3 lead in the seventh. Devon White looped an RBI single off Rick Honeycutt, who then walked Joyner to load the bases for designated hitter Brian Downing. Todd Burns replaced Honeycutt, and Downing launched a bullet to left-center. Dave Henderson, starting in dead center, broke back with the swing and kept his legs churning and his glove hand extending until he ran under the ball one step shy of the padded wall. With the ball in flight, the Angels believed they'd broken the game open, but Henderson shattered their moment with perhaps his best catch of the year.

Even after the catch, the Angels never quit. Burns surrendered a run-scoring single to Schofield in the eighth that tied the game at

5-all before Matt Young pitched out of a jam with runners on second and third by getting Ray to ground out. In the bottom of the inning, McGwire singled and Dave Henderson followed with his third hit of the day, another single to chase starter Mike Witt. One out later, Hassey singled against reliever Rich Monteleone, giving the A's the lead again. After Phillips walked, Gallego got a run home with an infield out before Rickey Henderson and Lansford put the Angels away with consecutive run-scoring singles. La Russa later called the A's 9-5 win one of the team's three or four biggest of the year. For as much as he downplayed the game's importance beforehand, he said later, "It was pivotal. The difference between being one game back in the standings and three games back is enormous. We played that game like it was the seventh game of the World Series."

Lansford gave a glimmer of what was to happen in August and September by finishing with a rush in July. On July 28, he delivered a bases-loaded single in the 11th inning to give the A's an 8-7 win over Seattle. Then he drove in three runs with a pair of doubles in a July 29 loss and knocked home the A's fifth run in a 5-3 win over the Mariners July 30. When Phillips' dramatic ninth-inning two-run homer off Chicago gave the A's a 3-2 victory July 31, Oakland exited the month with a 16-10 record, trailing California by just a half game and setting up a confrontation with the Angels in the first half of August.

THE COMEBACKS
How Dave Dravecky and the injured A's returned to form

Comebacks are an intriguing part of baseball lore. Stories of the underdog team that has the grit to rise to glory, of the has-been player who has the will to stage a last hurrah, are our modern-day allegories. They are the stories that are passed from generation to generation; for comebacks touch the hearts of fans and give soul to the sport.

Almost everyone involved with the 1914 Boston Braves is gone now, but the Braves, who went from last place on July 18 to win the National League title by a staggering 10½ games, live on as the "Miracle Braves." Fifty-five years later, the New York Mets earned the "Miracle Mets" title by going from last place in 1968 to the World Series title in 1969. And 1951 is the year that produced "The Shot Heard 'Round the World," when Bobby Thomson's homer in the playoffs capped a comeback of heroic proportions by the New York Giants.

On an individual level, Los Angeles left-hander Tommy John was the talk of the medical and baseball communities in the mid-1970s when he had a ligament from his right arm placed into his left arm, then resumed pitching — and winning — for the Dodgers. And all of Detroit rallied behind the 1978 and '79 comeback tries of the injured pitching marvel known as Mark "The Bird" Fidrych.

The August days — the dog days of August — are the days when comebacks are traditionally noted. In baseball parlance, these are the hot, hard days that set apart the good from the bad, the contenders from the pretenders, the better-thans from the also-rans. August is also the month for the flipside of comebacks. If a team is headed for the doghouse, August is usually the month it'll grow four legs and fetch the paper. August is the month when the Dodgers held a 13½-game lead over the Giants in 1951. It's the month when the Cubs held an 8½-game lead over those Miracle Mets in 1969. And it's the month when the '51 Giants and '69 Mets began their improbable comebacks, forcing the Dodgers and Cubs to roll over and play dead.

In August 1989, there were no teams charging from out of nowhere to win it all. But individual comebacks? Definitely. For both the Giants and A's, August was the comeback month. These were cases of athletes battling back from illness or injury to compete in peak form during the pennant race. Although they didn't all end in storybook fashion, they nevertheless captured the imagination of the Bay Area and, in at least one case, the baseball world.

For the A's, the comeback road had to be as wide as an interstate freeway to accommodate Oakland's entourage — Jose Canseco, Dennis Eckersley, Walter Weiss, Storm Davis and Bob Welch. For the Giants, the list was equally long and included all pitchers — Rick Reuschel, Scott Garrelts, Kelly Downs, Don Robinson and Dave Dravecky. Especially Dave Dravecky. In one way or another, they all battled back from adversity in the best tradition of baseball comebacks. In their own ways, they were all stubborn enough and willing enough to overcome the aches and pains to make August one of the more memorable months of the Bay Area season.

Easily the most memorable story of them all was Dave Dravecky. While Dravecky put in months of grueling work to savor the biggest comeback story of the year — the Grand Poobah of all 1989 baseball comebacks — he just as dramatically shifted to the other end of the emotional spectrum and suffered like a fine and decent man should never suffer.

To understand the Dravecky saga is to understand the events of October 7, 1988. That's when Dravecky underwent eight hours of surgery performed by Dr. George Muschler at the Cleveland Clinic in Ohio, not far from Dravecky's home in Youngstown. Muschler used a technique called cryosurgery, a type of operation that destroys tissues through a freezing process and, in this case, destroyed the malignant tumor attached to the upper part of Dravecky's humerus, the bone that joins the elbow to the shoulder. In addition to removing the tumor — estimated to be the size of a golf ball — Muschler also removed the lower half of Dravecky's deltoid, one of the muscles that controls the throwing motion of the arm.

The surgery was necessary to make sure no more cancer cells remained in the area. But at the same time, the process destroyed a section of the bone and weakened the arm. Muschler gave Dravecky no chance of pitching again and warned him that the humerus could fracture if it weren't allowed to heal for at least two years. But two years would keep Dravecky out of action until the 1991 season, by which time he would be 35 years old. What was worse was the knowledge that two years of rest wouldn't even guarantee full strength in the arm. In addition, there was a chance that a new tumor could develop. Although a majority of the baseball world pronounced Dravecky's career over, Dravecky himself never arranged any retirement plans. His only plan was to return to major-league form as quickly as possible.

Although Muschler had expected Dravecky to do no more than play catch with his kids in his back yard, Dravecky was targeting mid-season as his goal to pitch again in the majors.

Dravecky rested, relaxed and rehabilitated through October, November and December. Even though he needed help just to raise his arm in the early days of his recovery, he began throwing footballs and working with light weights in January and appeared at the Giants' spring training site in late March, complete with his 10-inch scar. "My God," Kevin Mitchell said. "It looks like Jaws took a bite out of you." On April 10, only two weeks later and only six months after his surgery, Dravecky was throwing for 10 minutes off the Candlestick Park mound. No 90 mph fastballs, no breaking pitches, just 10 minutes' worth of easy lobs from his patented pitching motion. He had nothing on his pitches, but at least his natural and smooth delivery was back. And that in itself signified tremendous progress.

Dravecky had endured an extensive workout program to get back to top shape, and his body appeared as solid as ever in the early season. But through every step of his comeback, he talked little about his own physical work and focused on his faith in Jesus Christ, to whom he gave full credit for his progress. Dravecky's opinions were never secret — he was controversially linked to the John Birch Society during his playing days in San Diego. On the subject of religion, Dravecky, a born-again Christian, spoke his mind as one of an increasing number of ballplayers going public with their religious beliefs. Others on the Giants included Atlee Hammaker, Scott Garrelts, Kelly Downs, Brett Butler and Bob Knepper, and all battled the notion that Christian athletes, because they claim their fate rests with Jesus, are not tough athletes. One question raised is: "Who does God favor when a Christian pitcher faces a Christian batter?" The answer, as Dravecky would say, is neither, that Jesus allows each athlete the ability to perform at his best in every such situation. And Dravecky described his battle with cancer as simply a test administered by Jesus, chalking it up to his belief that God works in mysterious ways.

The word "miracle" was tossed around a lot throughout Dravecky's comeback. It was mentioned even before he threw a pitch. The fact that Dravecky put on his uniform again was the real miracle, agreed Dravecky and everyone concerned with his comeback bid. Everything else would be gravy. But half of his deltoid muscle was lost forever. Teammates were constantly reminded by the long scar on his left arm as Dravecky hung around the Giants' locker room in April. It still seemed a comeback was only wishful thinking. No one had ever gone through such an operation and returned to the big leagues, especially someone whose position required such significant, wrenching arm movement. But Dravecky never paid attention to the low odds and never doubted he would return to help the Giants down the stretch in the pennant race.

Although pains in his arm early in the season postponed throwing for a month and put a dent in his comeback plans, Dravecky bounced back to throw several sessions of batting practice and simulated games. By mid-July, the Giants had seen enough progress to send him on rehabilitation assignment to the minor leagues, although they had no idea how Dravecky would fare.

Dravecky's first stop would be with the Single-A San Jose Giants, whose schedule took them to Stockton for a July 23 game with the Stockton Ports, an affiliate of the Milwaukee Brewers. The Ports' stadium, Billy Hebert Field, is probably best known as the site where poet Ernest Thayer had his legendary Casey At The Bat go down swinging. But on this uncomfortably hot July afternoon, little attention was paid to the men who swung the bat. The featured attraction, even though he played for the visiting team, was that old left-handed pitcher on the mound.

As Dravecky completed his hour-long southeast drive and parked outside Hebert Field, he realized he was a long way from Candlestick Park. By major-league standards, the park, the crowd and even the hitters were small. But as it turned out, there was nothing minor-league about Dravecky's performance. Having prepared for this day for the past nine months, Dravecky pitched a complete game, seven innings by California League standards. He finished with a five-hitter. He threw 78 pitches, one of which was clocked at 88 mph. He threw 51 strikes, 27 balls. He struck out two, walked none. He threw all the pitches in his repertoire, and even a new one. Because he didn't anticipate being able to throw as hard as before the operation, he had begun developing the split-fingered fastball for another off-speed weapon.

Just to pitch made him a remarkable success. And there he was, beating the pants off those Ports. He probably made a few of them think twice about considering a big-league career. The sellout crowd of 4,469 — the biggest since Hebert Field was modified two years earlier — came to cheer for Dravecky and honored the pitcher with standing ovations from start to finish. Each time he took the mound before an inning, he received a standing ovation. "In my career, that had never happened to me," he said.

Although he was in Stockton solely for rehabilitation duties, with the final score meaning very little, Dravecky gave every indication that winning was a priority. In the final inning, with relievers ready in the bullpen, the first two hitters roped singles off Dravecky, and the next batter lifted a bunt up the third-base line that should have landed for a single. But Dravecky went airborne, which was not really what the doctor ordered for the first game back after surgery. Although Dravecky dropped the ball, he still managed to force the runner at third and prove — if there was ever a doubt — that he was dead serious about this comeback business. As San Jose manager Duane Espy said afterward, "There's nothing wrong with his heart." After retiring the final two batters to secure the win, Dravecky walked off to the clubhouse beyond the outfield wall. The crowd went nuts during his entire journey. It was clear that a return to the majors was imminent — no longer a matter of if, but when.

"This is probably one of the most exciting experiences I've ever had in my life," Dravecky said moments after the game. "As far as I'm concerned, whether I come back to the big leagues or not, it's already a miracle. If today is the last performance I ever had on the mound, I'll still be thrilled about it."

The Stockton mound wasn't the last to be climbed by Dravecky. He also pitched the San Jose Giants to a 7-3 win at Reno on July 28. Moving up to Triple-A Phoenix on August 4, he beat Tucson 3-2 and looked so good (seven hits, no walks, three strikeouts) that the Giants canceled his last minor-league appearance and brought him up to the big club. With a 3-0 record and three complete games in the minors, why wait any longer?

Following a rehabilitation that appeared long but was truly short considering the circumstances, the Giants — not San Jose, but San Francisco this time — scheduled Dravecky to start against the Cincinnati Reds on August 10 at Candlestick Park. He was finally on the verge of completing his "miracle" and returning to the big leagues, 10 months after the cancer surgery and 15 months after his last major-league appearance. It was back on May 28, 1988, that Dravecky last started for the Giants. He shut out the Phillies through five innings but didn't receive a decision in the Giants' 4-3 loss in 10 innings. The following day, he was placed on the disabled list with "sprained posterior capsulitis," and two weeks later he underwent arthroscopic shoulder surgery. In August, he tried throwing for Phoenix but was shelled and didn't throw another pitch the rest of the season. In September, the cancerous tumor was detected and surgery was scheduled for October 7.

Ten months and millions of prayers later, Dravecky had emerged from the Candlestick clubhouse tunnel near the bullpen in right field, hearing the crowd cheer with his every warm-up pitch but not really knowing exactly what to expect of himself. He had mastered the minor-leaguers the past two weeks, but these were the Cincinnati Reds. And Eric Davis was a far cry from the Stockton Ports, just as the National League was a far cry from the California League. And don't forget the pennant race, although most people couldn't help forgetting something so seemingly irrelevant on this momentous day. The Giants had lost three of four and five of seven in a month that wasn't headed in a positive direction. They were just two games ahead of second-place Houston and eight ahead of the revamped Padres, so more was on the line in all of this than the concern for Dravecky's health and good will. The Giants, emotion aside, needed Dravecky to pitch well.

The day after Dravecky was named the starter, the Giants received an additional 40 media requests, and an extra 1,500 tickets were sold. A crowd of nearly 35,000, well above average for a Thursday afternoon game in mid-August, turned out to witness Dravecky culminate his celebrated and extraordinary comeback. The miracle talk was still rampant, and Dravecky said on the eve of his return that "anything after this is icing on the cake."

The fans stood and screamed when Dravecky's name was announced, and they did the same when he took the mound for the first time. At this stage and on this stage, Dravecky realized his prayers had been answered. He was away from the surgeons, away from the therapists, and he had discovered inner peace. Standing on a big-league mound ready to face big-league batters in a big-league park packed with big-league fans made for a big-league high. Dravecky was up to enjoying the feeling of the moment, and everyone — his family, his fans, his teammates, even his opponents — was trying to share that feeling, whether it was through cheering, meditating or crying. Dravecky took a moment to reflect on his fortunes and give thanks. Then he went to work.

First inning. One-two-three. Second inning. No runs. Same with the third, fourth, fifth, sixth and seventh. Dravecky was carrying a one-hitter into the eighth inning and receiving an average of one standing ovation per walk to the mound. He wasn't adequate, average or fair. He was dominant, aggressive and, yes, miraculous. Through seven innings, he walked just one batter and faced only two over the minimum. And he had four strikeouts. A few months earlier, he couldn't lift his arm. Now he had four strikeouts with two innings still to go.

Roger Craig had hoped Dravecky could manage just five innings, but with the Giants on top 4-0 through seven, thanks in part to Matt Williams' two-run home run, Dravecky walked out to begin the eighth. It was a long day for Dravecky — heck, it was a long year — and by the eighth inning, he had lost much of his strength and location. Todd Benzinger led off with a bloop single, and Joe Oliver hit a fly to the warning track that was caught. Scotti Madison doubled down the left-field line to put two runners on base with one out. But Dravecky made pinch-hitter Ron Oester his fifth strikeout victim, and he was one out from another scoreless inning. Luis Quinones, however, stepped to the plate and ruined Dravecky's shutout bid, blasting a three-run homer to left field and pulling the Reds closer at 4-3. Dravecky retired the next batter to finish the inning and his day's pitching chores.

Steve Bedrosian, in what he'd later call his most important save of the year, replaced Dravecky in the ninth and retired the side in order. Afterward, instead of following custom and shaking the reliever's hand for completing the game, everybody approached Dravecky to offer congratulations for his wonderful and successful comeback. Even a few of the Reds made it a point to give Dravecky a pat on the rear. The day, after all, belonged to Dravecky and all the people to whom his comeback sent messages of hope.

One was little Alex Vlahos, a 7-year-old leukemia patient from nearby Hillsborough who was in need of a bone marrow transplant. Dravecky was inspired by the boy during his comeback and raised thousands of dollars in pledges through a campaign run by KNBR radio, the Giants' flagship station. At the post-game press conference, attended by some 100 media members, Alex announced to the world that his hero "did good." Dravecky announced to the world that the goodness came from a higher source, his first words being, "I want to take this opportunity to give all the praise and glory to Jesus Christ, my Lord and savior." Writers who generally leave such religious quotes out of their notebooks scribbled each word coming from Dravecky, realizing that this story went far beyond the typical comebacks from knee or elbow surgeries. "It's a miracle," Roger Craig said for about the 62nd time.

When the exuberant Dravecky reported to work the next day, he claimed he felt minimal pain, maybe even less than the normal day-after stiffness. He joked that a man shouldn't feel pain in his deltoid muscle when more than half of it was missing. Dravecky was at ease in the wake of his success, and the mental high from the day before had carried over for the rest of the Giants. Craig played golf with Bob Lurie that morning and parred the first four holes. Someone asked him what gives, and he answered, "After yesterday, anything can happen." The feeling on the club was that Dravecky had conquered cancer and would be an instrumental force in the stretch drive.

Now it was time to take his comeback show on the road. His next start, following a four-day and three-game rest, was August 15 in Montreal. (He was moved up a day because Don Robinson, originally scheduled to pitch August 15, had been scratched after being used in relief on August 13.) The Giants were beginning a nine-game Eastern road swing with a three-game edge over Houston, and Dravecky would start against Bryn Smith. In the early innings, Dravecky pitched as well as he had in his debut, throwing shutout ball through five innings, the first 3⅓ hitless. But in the sixth, with a 3-0 lead, he allowed a leadoff home run to Damaso Garcia and nailed Andres Galarraga with an errant pitch. With Tim Raines up next, pitching coach Norm Sherry jogged out to the mound, and Dravecky insisted he was OK. Craig would have inserted Jeff Brantley to pitch if the next batter were anyone but Raines, but the manager chose to stick with Dravecky for another batter. When Sherry returned to the dugout, Dravecky set himself on the mound, looked back at Galarraga on first base, kicked up his right leg and fired his 67th pitch of the game. Then it happened. There was no follow-through.

Dravecky let out a cry. He tumbled to the mound. The ball was sailing off in the distance, some 15 feet from Raines' strike zone. Dravecky was alone and motionless, gripping his left shoulder, as the Giants on the field and in the dugout, and even some Expos players, rushed to the center of the diamond to tend to the fallen pitcher. En route, catcher Terry Kennedy slammed his mask to the turf in frustration. It was an image that was repeated hundreds of times on national news broadcasts. At first, Dravecky thought he had been struck by a sniper hidden somewhere in the stands or that someone had driven an axe into his body. But he quickly realized the cold truth. His left arm was broken. First baseman Will Clark was the first to reach Dravecky. "Will, I'm in a lot of pain," Dravecky said.

The pop was clearly heard. Clark had heard a similar sound

when he broke his elbow in 1986 and knew exactly what had happened this time. Olympic Stadium is usually a very quiet place to play baseball anyway, even if the crowd is as big as the 24,490 that witnessed Dravecky's fall. Earlier in the year, Mike Krukow disagreed with an umpire's call at Olympic Stadium and let out a curse word heard throughout the upper regions of the park. After the inning, the embarrassed Krukow approached the umpire to assure him he'd try not to show him up any more. When Dravecky took his fall, the crowd was even more silent, knowing that only five days earlier he had made a triumphant return from cancer surgery.

As Dravecky left the game, he told Sherry to make sure his teammates went on to beat the Expos. Then he was taken by ambulance to nearby Queen Elizabeth Hospital, where X-rays proved what everyone feared yet expected. He had suffered a fractured left humerus — in the same area where the malignant tumor had been removed 10 months earlier. It was clear Dravecky was finished for the season and maybe his career.

Back at Olympic Stadium, the stunned Giants tried to maintain Dravecky's lead over the Expos, but it wasn't easy. On Dravecky's wild pitch, which had flown past the Expos' on-deck circle and against a wall near Montreal's dugout, Galarraga advanced all the way from first to third, nobody paying him the slightest bit of attention. Jeff Brantley relieved Dravecky, and Raines hit a sacrifice fly to pull the Expos to within 3-2. Brantley preserved the lead until the ninth, when Bedrosian saved his second straight game for Dravecky.

In the clubhouse after the game, his teammates were choked up with emotion and holding back tears while discussing what had just unfolded. Kennedy recalled how he told everybody to "win one for Dave." Scott Garrelts said he noticed the pitch fly wildly, then looked back at Dravecky before "I started praying." Craig, saying his move to keep Dravecky in the game was a manager's decision that was warranted at the time, said, "It was a helpless feeling to see him lying on the ground. He's a courageous man. I've been in the sport a long time, but I've never seen anything like this." Dravecky's reaction: "It was the strangest experience I've ever felt."

During all the confusion, Dravecky asked his close friend Garrelts to call his wife, Jan Dravecky, and tell her what had happened. That evening, instead of resting in the hospital, Dravecky returned to the team hotel and held a Christian fellowship meeting with Garrelts, Brantley, Knepper and Greg Litton. Dravecky, his arm in a protective sling, was forced to sleep in a sitting position and managed only three hours of sleep. The next morning, he flew back to San Francisco to meet with Giants physician Dr. Gordon Campbell at the Palo Alto Medical Clinic. At Gate 75 of the United Airlines terminal, his wife at his immediate left and his future in immediate doubt, Dravecky was met by dozens of media representatives and answered several questions before driving to Palo Alto.

Dravecky spoke about the moments leading up to the break, he spoke about the break and he spoke about the moments after the break. He also emphasized he would return to pitch once again, leaving the crowd to believe Miracle II was already in the making. No surgery was needed, and the break would require only six to eight weeks to heal. In nine months, should everything go as scheduled, he would be able to pitch again. Dravecky had no apparent reservations about rehabilitating for another nine agonizing months, and like any stubborn athlete would do in his situation, he vowed he would come back, even though his return wouldn't be until May 1990 at the earliest.

It would have been understandable if Dravecky announced his retirement after the Montreal incident, but he insisted upon returning — even before meeting with his doctors. This prompted a string of questions that couldn't immediately be answered: Would he come back as strong? Would he come back at all? Would the Giants take him back? It also set off a debate among people in the medical world, some of whom wondered whether Dravecky's comeback had been rushed and whether a pitching career demanded too much of his vulnerable arm.

In the aftermath, Dravecky and Campbell disclosed that the bone hadn't fully healed from the October 1988 surgery and that they had been aware the weakened humerus could snap at any time. Dr. George Muschler, who had performed the surgery, again said the complete healing process required at least two years. In the surgery, healthy cells had been destroyed when the bone was frozen and the tumor removed. As a result, the bone still wasn't at full strength. "Obviously, the stress of throwing the baseball at this point in time was just too much for the bone to handle," Dravecky said when arriving at the airport. And it wasn't that Dravecky hadn't been warned. As Campbell said, "Our role is to explain what the risks are. After that, it's up to Dave to make the decision." So

Dravecky had decided to come back on his own, even though it wasn't what the doctor ordered.

Said Dr. Harry Jergesen of the UC Medical Center in San Francisco: "It's not uncommon for an athlete, with adrenaline flowing, to listen to a physician and, where others would hold back, the athlete would take the risk. If you win, you win. If something bad happens, you take the loss. The doctor must not mislead the patient. We don't know the percentages, just the possibilities. We treat, we advise and the individual goes from there. Many athletes don't like what they hear and shop around until they hear what they want to hear."

Said Dr. Ralph Gambardella, who works with noted sports injury specialist Dr. Frank Jobe in Inglewood: "One always has to apprise the person — athlete or non-athlete — of the increased risk of injury by continuing to perform. Most of the time, we can assess for them the increased risk. But it's up to the individual. He knows more than anyone else."

Rosen, who two weeks earlier chose to put Dravecky in a big-league uniform after only three minor-league appearances, wasn't about to speculate on whether Dravecky returned too soon. And he, too, didn't tell Dravecky not to pitch. "How can you do that?" Rosen asked. "Would you want someone to do that to you? He had pitched four games, including three in the minor leagues and a successful major-league game. Not being a doctor, I can't tell you if there's a relationship between the fracture and the operation. I can only deal in facts. He was in the doctor's care, he sought advice, he got in shape, he pitched successfully and then tragedy struck."

Through all the hardships, Dravecky never publicly criticized any of his doctors, trainers or employers. Rather, he praised them for their support, both physically and spiritually. And he never appeared worried, even about his health or future, always placing his destiny in God's hands. "If it's in God's plan for me to go back on the mound, I'll be there," he said.

Campbell viewed the episode as unprecedented. "You can always learn from this," the doctor said. "But you have to understand. This is a rare instance, and we don't have a series of these to make judgments on. In the future, we would probably want someone (making a similar comeback) to wait a little longer." There was additional concern over the possible recurrence of a malignant tumor. Doctors said that tumors of this type recur in 30 percent to 70 percent of cases. At the time Dravecky broke his arm, there was no evidence of a new tumor.

The loss of Dravecky was considered major in more ways than one. Emotions and friendships aside, Dravecky was an above-average pitcher and his loss delivered a blow to the Giants' chances of winning the West. He was, after all, 5-0 on the season — 3-0 in the minors and 2-0 in the majors — and had always been a money pitcher who excelled in clutch situations. After his acquisition from the Padres in '87, he tossed three shutouts in the second half of the season and allowed just one run in two playoff starts against St. Louis. In 25⅔ career post-season innings, he allowed just one run for a dynamic ERA of 0.35. His performance down the stretch in '87 earned him the Opening Day nod in '88, and he tossed a three-hit shutout at Fernando Valenzuela and the Dodgers in Los Angeles. But he was placed on the disabled list a month later and hadn't been the same since.

Shortly before Dravecky's first game with the '89 Giants, the team was missing seven pitchers. It was as if the plague had taken up residence on the Candlestick Park mound. There was Dravecky's absence. Krukow (rotator-cuff surgery) was out for the season. Hammaker (knee surgery) might come back, but he might not. Kelly Downs (shoulder stiffness) at best seemed two minor-league starts from being ready. Rick Reuschel (groin pull) was still in agony. Karl Best (elbow stiffness), although not expected to be a factor, had been on the disabled list since spring training. And on August 7, Garrelts was added to the wounded list after spraining his back during pre-game batting practice. Garrelts chased an outside pitch thrown by Candy Maldonado — Candy's problems weren't only at the plate. While lunging for the ball, Garrelts hurt his back, and the injury might have been serious enough for the disabled list. But the front office discovered that the Giants already had maxed out on the disabled list with two players on the 15-day list and three on the 21-day list. Although he was in no shape to pitch, Garrelts remained on the roster while missing two weeks.

"That's amazing, boy, the things that have happened to us," Craig said. "Pretty soon, we'll be down to the Rookie League. I wish I would've been throwing batting practice all year. I'd go out there. This is unbelievable here. The weirdest things have happened. We've even had more guys on the disabled list than last year." In 1988, eight Giants pitchers were disabled, although the injuries were generally more severe, including four surgeries. In '89, 10 pitchers were put on the disabled list.

Things looked bleak at Candlestick when the home team was forced to start the untested arms of Jeff Brantley and Russ Swan. By the time Dravecky came aboard, a staggering total of 15 pitchers had started a game for the Giants. Responding to the whole mess, Rosen signed Knepper while releasing Goose Gossage, adding a healthy starter to the injury-riddled rotation. Knepper broke into the majors with the Giants in 1976 but had played the previous eight seasons in Houston. However, his 4-10 record and 5.89 ERA prompted his release from the Astros days before he signed with the Giants. His agreement with the Giants marked the second time Rosen — the Astros' general manager in 1980 when the Giants traded the left-hander — had acquired Knepper. "It will be a good relationship in a situation where I'm involved," said Rosen, hoping Knepper would improve his numbers as a Giant.

As was the case in the Gossage signing, the Giants paid Knepper only the big-league minimum of $68,000, with the Astros obliged to pick up the rest of a $1 million contract. Ironically, Knepper's first start was against his former Houston pals during a crucial early August series between the West's top teams. Rosen thought it was a good move for the Giants to sign Knepper — and so did the Astros. They viewed Knepper as nothing more than an erratic and inadequate pitcher and were happy enough that their division rivals had picked him up. Following the news of the signing, one Houston writer said, "That puts the Astros over the hump."

But in his Giants debut, Knepper showed the Astros a side of him they hadn't seen all year: success and emotion. Knepper struck out the side (Rafael Ramirez, Craig Biggio and Glenn Davis) in the fifth inning, then paraded off the field as if he had just won the seventh game of the World Series, leaping off the mound and pounding his glove with his fist several times. Knepper is one to keep his emotions hidden, but on this day his veins were bulging and his mouth was rattling. And his former mates were seething. "I thought he was trying to win the triple jump at the Olympics," said Houston pitcher Jim Deshaies. "The next thing I thought I'd see is a little guy in a bow tie measuring how long he jumped." Manager Art Howe said, "I wonder where all that emotion was when he was with us." Second baseman Eric Yelding: "We saw that. He never did that with us. The guys got really hyped up after that."

Knepper's bid for victory was shelved when he left the game with a 2-2 tie after six innings. Craig Lefferts later allowed the deciding run in a 3-2 loss to hand Houston its only win of the three-game series. In the first two games, Will Clark hit a massive home run to highlight a 4-2 victory, and Mike LaCoss (with the help of two relievers) whipped Mike Scott 7-0.

It seems that every time the Giants faced Scott, the same "he's-a-cheater" stories surfaced. In this series, Craig was telling the stories. Craig, who boosted Scott's career by teaching him the split-fingered fastball, reminded everyone that he taught Scott the splitter but had nothing to do with "that other pitch." That's the one in which Scott allegedly rubs sand paper on the ball to make his pitches do all kinds of crazy things. Of course, no umpire had ever caught Scott in the act, and Scott always denied the charges, but Craig made it a point even after the 7-0 victory to discuss Scott's wrongdoings. Craig suggested Scott doesn't fare well at Candlestick (4-5 lifetime) because "the balls come out of our dugout and not theirs. We get a better chance to check them." Scott, as he does in every city, calmly brushed off the accusations with his company line: "I'm not a physics major, but balls fouled off in the dirt probably have marks in them, right? And that's why they threw them out of the game."

Incidentally, Craig's accusations of wrongdoing extended beyond Scott. He also placed '88 Cy Young champ Orel Hershiser in the same company. "I don't think he's all legal, either," Craig said. "He spits on his hand and goes to his face, and that's illegal."

On August 4, the day before the LaCoss-Scott game, Clark launched a Candlestick rarity — an upper-deck home run above the right-field football bleachers. It was his 17th homer of the season and his fourth off Houston pitching. Clark has always eaten up the Astros. Why? Here's his explanation: "For the four years I've been in the major leagues, the Astros have had basically the same pitching staff. Teams like the Braves and Reds, they bring up guys and send them down, and I don't know them as well. At least I know something about these guys." But that doesn't fully explain his success against Nolan Ryan. Clark knew absolutely nothing about Ryan when he faced him in his first major-league at-bat, which resulted in a home run at the Astrodome. Nor does Clark's statement explain why he hits the ball with such explosive force against the Astros. In '87 at Candlestick, Clark knocked Houston pitcher Dave Meads for an upper-deck homer that landed in the general vicinity of his August 1989 blow. For Clark, who doesn't make a habit of showing up opposing pitchers, that was the only home run that impressed him enough to remain in the batter's box and simply observe the flight of the ball, a la Reggie Jackson.

Clark's August 4 launch was just as impressive, although it might not have carried much weight with the folks who gauge such things. In this modern day of massive corporations purchasing advertising space in nearly every square foot of nearly every big-league stadium, it was only a matter of time before some outfit began making a buck off measuring home runs. Say hello to IBM, known in the real world as International Business Machines but known in the sports world as Inaccurate Baseball Measurements. When Clark hit the home run, IBM flashed this on the scoreboard: 397 feet. Considering the distance from the plate to the fence in right-center is 365 feet, and considering Clark hit the ball above the football bleachers, above the concrete slabs supporting the second level and into the fifth row, the measurement seemed brutal. "Ill-measured," Craig said. "That went at least 430. It was in the upper deck, if I'm not mistaken. I might be old, but I've got good eyes." Don Robinson said, "It didn't go 397. Probably 497." And Ken Oberkfell: "Let's just say this. I wouldn't buy an IBM computer." The Giants weren't the only team complaining about wrong measurements. After Jose Canseco blasted a home run over the 375-foot fence at the Coliseum, the "official" estimate was 364 feet. To which Tony La Russa responded, "Where'd they start measuring? Second base?"

After the Giants won two of three from Houston, they still led the division by just two games. Consecutive embarrassing losses (10-2 and 10-4) to the Reds lessened the lead to one game, but Don Robinson followed with his third straight complete-game victory, and Dravecky's impressive comeback win followed. Beginning with Dravecky's second win over Montreal, the Giants managed a successful 6-3 road trip that included a couple of bouts with old friends now residing in Philadelphia, Terry Mulholland and Dennis Cook, who had been sent off two months earlier in the Steve Bedrosian trade. On August 19, Mulholland pitched the best game of his career by two-hitting the Giants and winning 1-0. The next day, Cook allowed one run through 6⅔ innings and would have beaten his old club had Ernest Riles not delivered a grand slam off reliever Roger McDowell in the ninth inning to lift the Giants to a 5-2 victory.

Curiously, it was during that series in Philadelphia when Bedrosian, ignoring team policy with little fanfare, saw his beard all but reach full growth after two weeks of trying. "I missed it. I wish I'd never cut it," he said. "I thought about it and thought about it. It's not that big of a deal. I just feel comfortable with it. This might hurt me in the long run, but if I can pitch well with it, I should be able to keep it." Management was not too keen on the idea, especially after Bedrosian went out and blew a game against the Phils. In Mulholland's game, Bedrosian allowed the lone run when Ricky Jordan singled home Tommy Herr in the bottom of the ninth inning. But the Giants went on to New York and won two of three, both wins shutouts.

Just as important as the six wins on the trip was the fact that Downs, Garrelts and Reuschel all had rejoined the rotation. While the returns of Garrelts and Reuschel were routine, the case of Downs was a baffler. Before the season, Sport magazine had predicted a Cy Young season for Downs. And Rosen admitted, "We thought he'd be our biggest winner." But as the season wore on, Downs wore out. He spent most of the season on the disabled list, working on a new pitching motion to ease his bad shoulder. After winning 13 times in 1988, he started only 15 times in '89. With two losses in August, he extended his losing streak to a career-worst five games until he finally beat the Phils August 30.

Nevertheless, the same day Cincinnati manager Pete Rose was hitting a new low by being banned from baseball for life for his gambling habits, the Giants were sky high while flying home from their Eastern road trip. That state of euphoria dulled when the Giants lost four of their first five home games. But Bedrosian redeemed himself for losing the game in Philly a week earlier by closing the door on the Phils in a 3-2 Candlestick win. That game finished off August with the Giants posting their second .500 month of the season, finishing 14-14 to enter September with a four-game lead in the West.

Oakland's August was quite a bit more successful. But given the way the American League West competition was playing, the A's had to be at the top of their game. They went 18-11 during the month.

When Canseco returned from the disabled list July 13 with a

home run and three RBIs, it seemed too good to be true. It was. As he'd predicted before first testing his arthroscopically repaired left wrist, Canseco was at the mercy of American League pitchers. Moved from the number six to the number four spot in the Oakland batting order after that spectacular debut, the right fielder hit just .233 in the 2½ weeks that comprised his July. Despite the pessimists who thought the injury might have robbed him of his strength — a similar wrist injury a decade earlier had taken much of the punch from the bat of 1979 American League MVP Don Baylor — Canseco's power seemed intact. After hitting 36 homers and driving in 139 runs in 1979, Baylor hit only five home runs in 1980. Canseco dispelled thoughts of a parallel power failure when, despite his poor batting average, he hit five homers and drove in nine runs in July.

Still, he wasn't the Canseco of old. He suffered through a 1-for-15 slump in the early days of his comeback despite the fact that pitchers were daring him to hit the ball by throwing fastballs 90 percent of the time. Canseco, a dead fastball hitter, couldn't coax his injured wrist to whip the bat through the strike zone fast enough. "I probably asked Jose to do some things he wasn't capable of doing," La Russa said in retrospect. "The first day, he looked so good. I moved him up in the batting order. After that, he didn't look as good for a long time." Canseco complained not of wrist problems but of tired shoulders and arms. And of a tired — not sore — wrist. "I go up to the plate knowing what I want to do," Canseco said. "My mind says 'Do this,' but my body says 'No.' It's fatigue, lack of stamina. My timing's off on everything."

Reliever Dennis Eckersley continued to feel some nagging pain in his shoulder, but it was insignificant; he was much closer to form. "Hey, I can throw," he said. "A month ago, I wasn't sure I'd be back to do that." The first time Eckersley felt right was July 21, when he picked up his first post-injury save, a one-inning stint against American League East-leading Baltimore. And while Eckersley, who went on to save four games in the final 10 days of the month, was warming hearts with his performance, Canseco was merely adjusting. In the same July 21 game, he drove in a key run with an opposite-field single. Carney Lansford put it best, saying, "Tonight, for the first time all year, it felt like last year."

Canseco admitted he was finally beginning to make the necessary alterations to his swing after his return. "If my strength and quickness was right, I might have hit that ball in the air," he said. "But what I was trying to do was to move the runner over by hitting the ball to the right side. I did, and something good happened."

When Canseco returns to the spotlight, he returns in a style all his own. Not just on the field, but off the field as well. During the layoff, Canseco found a way to make a few extra bucks. With the help of his agent, Dennis Gilbert, Canseco became the first big-leaguer to own a pay-per-call 900 telephone number. For two dollars, a caller could dial 1-900-234-JOSE and receive Canseco's insights on baseball, cars, guns and other things in his life. It wasn't very enlightening, but at least it was original. And it was all Jose. The development caught Canseco's teammates by surprise, which is hard to do since they had become used to him doing the extraordinary. And he had a new nickname in the A's clubhouse. Mr. 40-40 became Mr. 900.

August was a great month for both Canseco and Eckersley. The reliever was back at the peak of his game. Used 11 times, Eckersley saved 10 of the club's 18 August wins, not allowing a run as the A's moved into first place to stay. And Canseco came alive, hitting .299 with five homers and a team-leading 25 RBIs. On top of that, shortstop Walter Weiss rejoined the A's on the last day of July, giving La Russa the option, after 104 games, of putting his best nine-man lineup on the field for the first time all year. Not that he always did, though. Weiss, who never showed his 1988 consistency at the plate, wound up splitting time at short with Mike Gallego after La Russa called Gallego "our MVP" for his play in Weiss' absence.

But it was the return of Eckersley that was the most critical for the A's. In the 40 games he missed, the A's were exactly .500 at 20-20. When Canseco was out, on the other hand, the A's were 16 games over .500 at 52-36. When Weiss was out, Oakland owned a 37-28 record, 11 over .500. "We don't have anyone who's not replaceable," La Russa said earlier in the year. "But of all the players we have, we'd have the most trouble replacing Eck." And so it proved. When the reliever finally came back, the pressure was on for Eckersley to prove himself on the field — even more than Canseco. "When I was hurt," Eckersley said, "I craved the pressure. I missed it."

Weiss, Canseco's best friend on the team, said almost exactly the same thing after being activated. If anything, the concurrent time the two spent on the disabled list brought the two men closer. The former Rookies of the Year both discovered they weren't invincible. But where Canseco, who returned two weeks earlier than Weiss, found himself back at the top in August, Weiss couldn't find himself at all.

The hangover from Weiss' injury lasted most of the rest of the year. In '88, Weiss made just 15 errors and had a rookie record string of 58 consecutive errorless games. But he was a different shortstop after his return from the disabled list. In a span of 16 games, he committed eight errors. He had a chance to win back his job, but with converted second baseman Gallego playing better defense and hitting upward of .250, Weiss suddenly found himself a platoon player for the first time in his career.

The platoon was bothersome, Weiss admitted, but not nearly as much as the errors. The day after making an error, Weiss was quite a sight. He'd come into the clubhouse bleary-eyed and looking troubled. "I can't sleep after I make an error," he said. "And to be making so many is definitely playing on my mind. I've had a lot of problems making plays that shouldn't be a problem. Since coming back from the injury, I've had some physical problems with the knee, but it's become a mental thing."

Storm Davis knew all about "physical problems." Most players go on the disabled list with one ailment. Davis, out of action for 21 days in May and June, was a three-time victim, needing the time off to mend a sore right shoulder, a weak right knee and a pulled left hamstring that had been acting up since spring training. At the time of his return, the starter was 3-3 with an ERA that bordered on the ludicrous — 6.14. Davis then ran off a four-game winning streak before hitting the skids again in July. He lasted just 3⅔ innings on July 13 against Toronto and just one-third of an inning on July 29 against Seattle.

A couple of days after that latter drubbing, Davis found a flaw in his pitching. He accompanied third-base coach Rene Lachemann to a clinic that was part of the A's annual outreach program to the youth of the East Bay. At one point during his talk, Lachemann mentioned that most kids find that if they throw a fastball with their fingers across the seams rather than parallel to the seams, they get more movement on the ball. Davis' eyes widened when he heard that. For his entire career, the muscular, 6-foot-4 pitcher had thrown a fastball that was quick enough but perhaps a little too flat.

Davis came out for his next start with fire in his eyes — as well as in his fastball. The White Sox could do nothing with the new-look Davis on August 2; he shut them out for five innings on five hits and a walk. In a rematch against the Mariners on August 6, Davis' metamorphosis continued with a seven-inning shutout that carried the A's to a 2-1 win, keeping Oakland within a half game of first place. "Storm's a battler," second baseman Tony Phillips said, with both respect and approval. "No matter how ugly it looks or how grim it gets, Storm's never going to quit. He won't run away and hide." Armed with a nastier pitch and a new inner desire not to nibble at the corners with pitches, Davis breezed through the American League in August, going 6-1 with a 2.36 ERA in seven starts.

For fellow starter Bob Welch, being on the disabled list for a couple of weeks in June was the least of his concerns. He and his wife, Mary Ellen, were expecting their first child sometime after the All-Star break, and, in the words of La Russa, "No one wanted to be a father more than Bob." The child, Dylan, was born July 28 with great celebrating all around. But just a few hours later came word from Kentucky that Welch's mother had died. Nine days earlier, Welch had left the team after the final day of a road trip in Detroit to see his mother for what he instinctively felt might be the last time. He'd returned to the team two days later to start against and beat Baltimore. A week later came birth. And death. In just hours, Bob and Mary Ellen had felt the high that new life can bring and the low of a tragic loss. The A's told the pitcher he could have as much time off as he wanted, but on the way to the airport, Welch had trouble catching the last flight of the night. He found himself stuck in traffic, so much so that he eventually turned his car around and headed to the Coliseum, where he had been scheduled to start against Seattle that night.

"I had one hell of a time getting out to the airport, so I just said, 'Forget it.' " Welch said. "The last thing my mother would have wanted me to do was to rush to her funeral. That was the kind of positive attitude she had." Welch left the game that night after seven innings with a 6-3 lead, but the Mariners tied the game against Eckersley in the eighth. Oakland ultimately won the game in the 11th inning when Stan Javier, himself a father for the first time just a week earlier, returned from the disabled list to start and trigger the win with an 11th-inning single and steal. Lansford's single brought Javier home with the game-winning run.

By that time, Welch was on a midnight flight to Kentucky, with Mary Ellen and their baby boy still in the hospital. Before leaving, though, Welch pitched perhaps the guttiest game of his life. "To go from being a new father to losing your mother like that, it's so difficult," La Russa said. "But that was still Bob out there." Welch's catcher, Ron Hassey, said, "I never thought Bobby would pitch after what happened. We all could have respected and understood, of course. And there were times when I could see that he was thinking about other things out there. But in those circumstances, he was outstanding, unbelievable." Said Lansford, "I never could have done it. But that's just the kind of competitor Bobby is."

"Pitching that night," Welch said later, "helped a little, but it was the first time in my life I ever rubbed up a baseball and wondered why my mother wasn't there instead of rubbing up a baseball and wondering how I'm going to get this guy out. I wasn't in very good shape out there. But then, it wasn't a very easy time. I went from having the most wonderful thing happen to me to having the saddest. Having Dylan is great, but I never imagined how hard losing your mother is."

Welch got only better in August; he put his personal tragedy behind him and concentrated on the job at hand. After a two-game August losing streak left him at 11-5, Welch went on a five-game winning streak. He had a club-high 24-inning scoreless streak, pitching eight shutout innings in three straight starts. He was named American League Player of the Week for August 21-27 after the second and third of those starts, wins in Texas and Kansas City. The win August 22 in Texas seemed to be especially therapeutic for Welch, who pitched against the Rangers' Nolan Ryan on the night the Ryan Express recorded his 5,000th career strikeout. If ever a pitcher needed to be focused to survive a festive, circus-like atmosphere, that was the night. And Welch responded, allowing five singles and tying his season-high with nine strikeouts in eight innings. Eckersley closed it out with a perfect ninth inning.

One of the A's who had followed Welch's career the closest was fellow pitcher Matt Young, who had come to the A's in the same trade that brought Welch from Los Angeles in the winter of 1987. Ironically, Young had come off the disabled list to make the starts Welch missed when injured in June. "Bobby is one of the most agreeable people in this game, and he can be hard to read some-times," Young said. "When you think about all he went through, I don't know how many guys could have put up with that sway in emotions. He and Mary Ellen waited a long time for their first child. And the day after it comes, his mother is gone. Hard to imagine."

But then, Welch's entire career had been hard to imagine. A product of Eastern Michigan University, he came to the major leagues for the first time in 1978 with the Dodgers in the heat of an August pennant race with the Giants. When the Dodgers needed a big win after the Giants had taken the first two games of a four-game August series at Candlestick Park, Welch stuffed the Giants' offense. The Dodgers came back to get a split of the series and used that momentum to win the West. Two months later, Welch was in the World Series, striking out New York's Reggie Jackson in a memorable Game Two confrontation. Jackson came back to burn Welch later in the series with a big home run, but the strikeout marked Welch as a fighter.

Four years later, he needed all of that fighting spirit to win a battle with alcohol that threatened to ruin his life. Welch's pitching didn't seem to have been affected much — he had winning records for five of his first six years with the Dodgers — but he came to realize that he was a captive of alcohol. Dave Stewart, then a teammate with the Dodgers, recalled one time walking into a restaurant where Welch was dining. "He was so drunk that I had to cut his steak for him so that he could eat," Stewart said. "The day after a binge, which for Bob was every day, he always had the same refrain: 'I have to stop.' "

Easy to say. Hard to do. But Welch did just that. In a time when athletes didn't go public with their drinking problems, Welch documented his struggle — including his 36 days in a detoxification clinic — in his 1982 book, "5 O'Clock Comes Early, A Young Man's Battle With Alcoholism." Said Welch, "I had become a wild animal. I had to get it out of my system. If I hadn't stopped drinking, I would have found myself close to the gates of heaven. Or somewhere else, trying to strike out Babe Ruth during batting practice. I have to give credit to Jesus for enlightening me and also to Alcoholics Anonymous, which I've belonged to since I gave up drinking. We're all fighting the same battle. I don't want to give a sermon to anyone, but if I can preach by example, I'll be satisfied. I'll deliver my message by staying sober. I see that as a question of life or death." And by the time questions of life and death arose again in 1989, Welch was experienced with such battles and found himself strong enough to see his way through.

By getting the lineup healthy, hearty and whole again, the A's could reasonably expect that many of the struggles of the non-injured holdovers would be over. But such was not the case. If anything, the troubles encountered by first baseman Mark McGwire increased after Canseco and Company returned. It had already been a tough year for McGwire, who'd seen his marriage break up during the off-season. That meant he saw much less of his son, Matthew, to whom he was extremely devoted and who remained in Southern California with his mother, Kathy. Throughout the season, McGwire's mother, Ginger, flew up from Southern California with Matthew in tow so that McGwire could participate in Matthew's formative years.

In April, when McGwire missed 14 games with a bad back, he hit .295 and tied for the team lead in RBIs with 13. After that, his average dived into previously unexplored depths. A .244 hitter at the All-Star break, the slugger saw his batting average — and his pride — plunge even deeper in the next six weeks. By the end of August, he was under .230 for the first time in his career. "I've been playing baseball since I was 8, and I've never had anything that compares with this," McGwire said as his sad August (.165, five homers, 11 RBIs) came to a conclusion. "This is supposed to be a learning experience, but it's a very severe learning experience. This is the toughest thing I've gone through at any level of baseball. When I'm hitting .230, that's simply not acceptable from where I stand." Canseco, lying on the floor of the A's Yankee Stadium clubhouse as McGwire talked, broke in by saying, "Mac, that's not even hitting your weight." McGwire took a deep breath by way of acknowledging the bitter truth — there was no way at this late stage to repair such a terrible average. "I know that .280 (his career average coming into the season was .271) is out of the question, but I would love to get back up to .250 by the end of the year. That would be big in my book."

Several times in the course of the season's final six weeks, McGwire and Canseco got together to talk about slumps. Canseco was something of an expert, having gone 0-for-40 during the middle of his rookie season. But even those talks didn't help all that much, as Canseco readily admitted. "It was different for me," Canseco said. "I was a rookie then, and I'd really struggled my first two or three years in the minor leagues. My first year, I hit .159. So when I was hitting .240 after going 0-for-40, I was thrilled. That was about as much as I could have hoped for anyway. But this is all new for Mac."

"It's the damnedest thing I've ever seen," La Russa said of McGwire's year. "If you pick apart each at-bat, he's one hell of a lot better than somebody whose average had dipped into the .220s. His at-bats are good, so we're not worried. It's just that nothing's falling, and nothing has fallen for a long time. What I want to do is give him a magic wand so those balls he hits well will fall in." Lansford, whose batting average was more than 100 points higher at the time, stopped by McGwire's locker to say, "Mac, whatever you stole from church, give it back. Nobody should be this unlucky." Maybe not, but McGwire's hoped-for return to the high side of .250 wouldn't happen.

Although McGwire had trouble knocking out the hits, his club continued to roll. The A's, after having lost two of three games to the division-leading Angels in the last week of July, spent the first 10 days of August spoiling for a rematch. Oakland, one-half game behind the Angels as the month started, won six of its first 10 to pull into a virtual tie. The Angels owned a lead of just .002 percentage points as the series started on August 11 in Anaheim. Unlike the earlier meeting, this time La Russa went so far as to set up his rotation to toss his top three starters — Stewart, Mike Moore and Welch — at California.

Moore pitched the first game against Mike Witt, who'd started the only game the A's had won in the July duel. Moore was overpowering; he ran his record to 15-6 by throwing an eight-hit shutout and striking out eight. The A's won 5-0, with Tony Phillips and Lansford providing home runs.

The August 12 game featured Welch and Angels rookie Jim Abbott. Terry Steinbach's two-run single gave the A's a lead in the third, but Welch gave those runs back in the bottom of the inning. Two walks by Abbott in the fourth led California manager Doug Rader to dip into his bullpen, only to find that Dan Petry was no sharper. Petry loaded the bases with a four-pitch walk to Dave Henderson, then forced home the tie-breaking run by walking McGwire. After the A's moved ahead 4-2 on Dave Parker's sacrifice fly, Johnny Ray hit his second straight double in the fifth inning to score the Angels' third run and chase Welch. But Todd Burns took over and pitched four one-hit innings of shutout relief, saving Welch's 12th win. Oakland blew the game open with a four-run eighth inning, Lansford driving in one run and McGwire the final three with his 21st home run.

As the third game on August 13 rolled around, it was Oakland (playing without Canseco, who was feeling pain after straining a leg muscle a week earlier) that had a two-game West lead and the Angels who were facing their most important game of the season. Southern California's Sunday newspapers suggested that the Angels had to either win or kiss off their pennant hopes. Oakland had its ace, Stewart, pitching, but the Angels also had their best in Bert Blyleven. The A's grabbed the lead on a first-inning homer by Parker, who called the blow "one of my most gratifying moments of the year because when I faced him (Blyleven) in April, I was going bad and he exposed a lot of weaknesses in my swing."

Former Athletic Tony Armas' solo shot in the second tied the game. In the sixth, with two outs and one on, Stewart walked Jack Howell. First base wasn't open, but the walk was semi-intentional on Stewart's part because next up was rookie Kent Anderson. Howell already owned a big July homer off Stewart. Anderson got the end of his bat on the ball, blooping a triple down the right-field line and scoring two runs. Washington followed with a single, giving the Angels a seemingly commanding 4-1 lead. But the A's fought back for two runs in the seventh on a run-scoring grounder by Stan Javier and an RBI single by Weiss. A blinding right-field sun gave Oakland an opportunity to win in the ninth. Center fielder Devon White and right fielder Armas avoided a collision, but White was charged with a three-base error. Reliever Bryan Harvey then had to face pinch-hitter Canseco with the tying run 90 feet away. Harvey got Canseco on a called third strike, then struck out pinch-hitter Dave Henderson to end a 4-3 California victory, moving the Angels back to just one game from first place.

The key stretch during Oakland's road to the playoffs began August 21 in Detroit. Privately, some of the A's called it "the road trip to hell" — 14 days and 13 games in five cities in what figured to be a humid late August and early September. August 21 originally had been scheduled as an off-day before the A's longest road trip of the year, but the A's were forced to go to Detroit to make up a July

19 rainout. After that, it was three games each at Texas, Kansas City, New York and Milwaukee. It was no secret that the A's division rivals were hoping this stretch would prove to be Oakland's downfall. The A's started the trip in a virtual tie with California, two percentage points behind the Angels with Kansas City lurking 4½ games out.

In Detroit, Oakland defused much of the pressure by scoring four times in the first inning. While the Angels were losing to Kansas City, Oakland's Curt Young had the honor of pitching the A's into first place to stay when he allowed just one run in six innings and Gene Nelson and Matt Young finished up in a 6-1 win. If this was hell, the A's didn't mind. The weather on the trip was relatively mild, and the most searing heat the A's felt was generated by their own bats. They won eight of the 13 games to assume a 2½-game lead over the Royals. Young's win in Detroit marked the start of one of the A's finest stretches of the year.

The A's played well even when other men were stealing the headlines. On the night Nolan Ryan vaulted the 5,000-strikeout barrier, Welch and Eckersley combined on a shutout and the A's defense turned three double plays in a 2-0 win. It didn't matter that a man who most likely will one day join Ryan in the Hall of Fame, Rickey Henderson, was victim number 5,000. True to form, not only did Henderson not seem to mind going into the record books with Ryan, he almost celebrated the moment, swinging through a 3-2 fastball in the fifth inning. "Rickey didn't seem to be bitter," Ryan said, somewhat relieved. "I told him, 'Somebody had to be 5,000. I'm sorry it had to be you.'" Henderson said he knew what Ryan was feeling, having broken Lou Brock's seemingly insurmountable record of 118 steals back in 1982. "I know that, deep inside, as much as it hurts him to lose, he's got to be happy to reach 5,000," Henderson said. "I know how it felt to get 119. You can't imagine how good it feels to get it out of the way. And to tell you the truth, I don't mind being in the record book, even if it isn't the way I'd like. He got his 5,000th. We got the win. We'll take that trade any day."

The backbone of the road warriors' performance was the pitching. Oakland threw three shutouts. Welch and Eckersley combined against both Texas and Kansas City, and Davis and Gene Nelson pitched a 5-0 win over the Brewers in Milwaukee in the trip's finale. In eight of the 13 games, Oakland pitching gave up three or fewer runs. The key game of the trip was the August 27 series finale in Kansas City. The A's had lost their last game in Texas, ending a five-game winning streak, then lost the first two games in Kansas City, cutting their lead over California to one game and bringing the Royals to within 2½ games. In winning his 15th and perhaps most important game of the season by a 6-0 score, Welch allowed just six hits and a walk in eight innings and stretched his shutout-inning streak to 24. Rickey Henderson added a three-run homer before Eckersley pitched a quiet ninth to preserve the win.

But the injury situation, which had become almost forgotten, came back in a big way during the stopover in Kansas City. Canseco came out of the finale after just two trips to the plate, both times his left wrist and shoulder giving out. He left for a pinch hitter after some horrid swings in the third inning. "I don't know if I can play tomorrow," Canseco said. "Right now, I'd guess that I can't, maybe not for a while. Every time I swing, the soreness really gets to me. It keeps on going like this. I'll rest and it will be OK. I'll play for a while and it gets sore. Right now, it's about as sore as it's been. You can't have healthy-looking swings when you're not healthy." The A's headed off for the second half of the trip, New York and Milwaukee, with their star slugger once more a concern.

Then things got weird. Canseco wanted to sit out of the first game in Yankee Stadium, until he took a pain-free batting practice, that is. Weiss, wearing a "Jose Canseco Baseball Camp" T-Shirt under his game jersey, slammed a two-run homer in the second inning and doubled and scored a run in the ninth as the A's beat the Yankees 7-3. Canseco ditched the massive bat he usually swings and opted for the smaller and lighter Weiss bat and drove the ball hard three times, getting a couple of singles and an RBI without any of the pain that had slowed him in Kansas City. "Face it, my bats needed the help," Weiss said. "Jose made those bats look good, didn't he?" Canseco, who generally swings a 35-inch, 36-ounce bat, found he generated better bat speed with his buddy's 33-inch, 31-ounce model. The next night, the Weiss model still in his hands, Canseco pounded out four hits, including a pair of home runs, and tied the club's season high with five RBIs in a 19-5 romp. Canseco was so impressive that the frequently hostile fans in Yankee Stadium gave him a standing ovation after his second homer, a three-run shot in the A's 10-run fifth inning.

Oakland's offense took off at that point, with Canseco enjoying a monster streak, thanks to Weiss. Canseco crushed five home runs in four games, three in two games in New York and two in two games in Milwaukee. Twice in Milwaukee, Canseco and McGwire homered in the same game in answer to a La Russa challenge. "This team hasn't scored as much as it could have for a lot of reasons," the manager said. "But I think from this point on, we should challenge ourselves to out-score everyone else in the league." They didn't, but after being in the middle of the pack in runs scored for most of the year, the A's would be among the top four from that point on.

The A's and Giants entered the final month of the regular season in first place, a position not expected of them months earlier, but a position neither team was willing to give up. Thank goodness for the dog days of August.

THE CLINCHINGS
How the A's and Giants won the West

September was a wild time in the wild Wests for the Giants and A's. As the magic numbers dropped, the attendance totals soared. There wasn't a better time in history to be a fan of Bay Area baseball. It was baseball heaven. The Giants were in first place. The A's were in first place. The fans soaked it up and poured into Candlestick Park and the Oakland Coliseum.

They were there to see history happening. And they were making history themselves, setting a new watermark for Bay Area attendance. Candlestick and the Coliseum were attracting everyone from die-hard loyalists to bandwagon jumpers. Entering September, the Giants had drawn 1.65 million fans through 64 dates, which averaged out to nearly 26,000 per game. The A's, who a season earlier had became the first Northern California franchise to reach the 2 million mark, had hit 2.16 million through 66 dates, averaging almost 33,000.

Set against this scene, it was difficult to imagine that both clubs were once about a suicide squeeze away from leaving town. Toronto. Or Vancouver. Or Denver. Or any one of several cities in Florida. In those dark days, rumors surfaced by the week. Anywhere seemed better than the Bay Area, where the Giants could barely break a half-million in attendance in both '74 and '75 and the A's brought in an embarrassingly low 306,763 in '79.

When times were toughest, a couple of local businessmen stepped forward to purchase the clubs and keep them in place. In 1976, Bob Lurie saved the Giants from moving to Toronto by buying the club from Horace Stoneham with the help of Arizona cattleman Bud Herseth. Twice in the late 1970s, Denver oil magnate Marvin Davis was close to buying the A's from Charlie Finley before Finley sold the club to the Walter A. Haas Jr. family. After the sales, attendance steadily improved for both clubs, but not enough to defuse the cries of critics who said the Bay Area could not support two baseball teams.

A decade later, the hubbub wasn't about drawing 1 million. Or even 2 million. In the final season of the '80s, the question was, how much more than 2 million is possible? It was clear entering September that the Giants would draw the most fans in their 32-year history in San Francisco. And the A's were on target to turn in a 22-year high in Oakland.

On September 8 in Oakland and September 21 in San Francisco, the ticket-taking books were officially rewritten when the clubs shattered their respective attendance records. Ultimately, the A's drew 2,667,225; the Giants 2,059,829. The total of 4,727,054 provided proof that 1989 was the cornerstone of a new age for baseball in the Bay Area. There was no longer any doubt that the Bay Area could support two baseball teams. The business groups from Colorado and Florida would have to look elsewhere for a team to lure.

Down the stretch, not just the eyes of Northern California but the eyes of an entire nation were focused on the Bay Area, although the Eastern divisions weren't without competition. The Orioles and Blue Jays were running in a dead heat for the American League East lead, each bringing a 72-62 record into September. In the National League East, the Cubs held a shaky 2½-game advantage over the Mets and Cardinals. But because the White Sox and Yankees were far removed from the division races, the only possibility of a metropolitan World Series existed in the Bay Area. There hadn't been such a clash since Don Larsen and the Yankees toppled the Dodgers in the 1956 New York Subway Series.

For several weeks, the Giants had figured that Houston would be their only competition in the final month. But another team silently began a run that carried over into September and presented a challenge to the Giants. The San Diego Padres, also-rans at the All-Star break, won seven of their final eight games in August to finish the month 18-11. But the Giants still maintained a seemingly secure 6½-game lead over Tony Gwynn and Company. It was Gwynn's consistent bat and his quest for a third straight batting crown that helped push the Padres back into contention. In the final weeks, Gwynn proved to be the only obstacle Will Clark needed to hurdle in his quest to become the first Giant to win a batting title since the franchise's move to San Francisco.

Ironically, the A's also featured a pair of similar races down the stretch. California, which had dogged the A's all season, was still just 2½ games back. Kansas City, which had fallen as many as seven games off the pace in early August, emulated San Diego and closed with a rush. On September 1, the Royals, too, were just 2½ back. In the hunt for the American League batting title was Carney Lansford, who was on the verge of becoming the first Athletic in Oakland history to lead the league in hitting. While Clark was battling Gwynn down to the season's final day, Lansford was facing off against Minnesota's Kirby Puckett in a similar battle. In the end, the battles were not won, but the wars were another story.

Lansford and Clark aside, there were other individual goals to be reached. Kevin Mitchell had a chance for 50 home runs. Pitchers Dave Stewart, Mike Moore, Storm Davis and Bob Welch of the A's and Rick Reuschel of the Giants each had a chance for 20 wins. And ERA titles were in the grasp of both Moore and the Giants' Scott Garrelts. Ultimately, only Stewart and Garrelts succeeded, but there were few complaints. These were individual races, mere side shows to the main attractions. The biggest events were the team-versus-team clashes for the division flags that climaxed on the memorable evening of September 27.

To get to that moment, the Giants and A's had to overcome

gutty challenges from their competition. And nothing overcomes the competition like a good old-fashioned winning streak of, say, five in a row. In this case, both the Giants and A's did just that. Wasting no time, the Giants struck first, opening the month with a five-game streak that culminated with a spectacular 9-8 comeback victory in Cincinnati — the Reds had led 8-0 — and boosted their lead to seven games. The A's waited until September 18 to begin a five-game streak that improved their lead to four games by September 22.

In San Francisco, the final month opened to rave reviews. On September 1, good ol' Bob Brenly put on a Giants uniform for the first time in nearly a year. After he hit .189 in 1988, the long-time San Francisco catcher discovered that the Giants didn't want to sign him to an '89 contract, at least not for the amount of money he wanted. The popular catcher — he had his own post-game radio show — was signed by Toronto, but Brenly never adjusted to Canada or the American League, and the Blue Jays dismissed him, and his .170 average, in July. Although they had let him stray during the off-season, the Giants still thought Brenly could provide leadership and maybe make a spot start here and there, so they signed him to a minor-league contract with the idea of promoting him to the big club for the final month. Brenly had caught every pitcher on the Giants' staff with the exception of Bob Knepper; he had even caught newcomer Steve Bedrosian in winter ball. Basically, Brenly was signed for insurance, and Lloyds of London couldn't have done better. The insurance policy paid off when catcher Kirt Manwaring suffered a hairline fracture of a bone in his left foot on August 30. The presence of Brenly now became a necessity instead of merely a luxury. If Brenly thought it was good news to hear that the Giants wanted him in uniform on September 1 (when rosters expand from 24 spots to 40), it became great news when he was activated August 31, an off-day. Under baseball rules, September call-ups are ineligible for post-season. Players active on August 31 or earlier, however, are eligible for the post-season, so now Brenly was in contention for a playoff roster spot, depending on Manwaring's injury status come the post-season.

Brenly's first game as a born-again Giant came and went peacefully — he spent his day playing catch in the bullpen — but he was summoned to start September 2 against Frank Viola and the Mets. In front of 31,000 Candlestick fans and a nationally televised audience, Brenly received a standing ovation and obliged by tipping his helmet and then lining a full-count changeup into left-center field to lift the Giants to a 6-2 victory. Although the Giants weren't expecting game-deciding hits from Brenly every day, they loved to see it. San Francisco did expect Brenly's presence to have an influence in the clubhouse on a daily basis. It was Brenly and Mike Krukow who kept the troops loose when the Giants won the division in '87, and the brass was hoping for a repeat performance, even though Krukow was on the disabled list and Brenly was now just a role player.

It helped the Giants' chances that Mitchell had opened September needing just 10 more homers to become only the 11th major-leaguer to reach 50 in a season. The road to 50 homers wasn't impossible for Mitchell to follow; he'd hit 10 homers in one month and nine in another. And he started off September on track, homering in a 7-1 win over New York in the month's first game. Mitchell had 27 more games to get the final nine homers, an average of one every three games, to reach a pinnacle not climbed by the likes of Joe DiMaggio, Lou Gehrig, Harmon Killebrew, Reggie Jackson, Carl Yastrzemski or Mike Schmidt. Even the all-time power king himself, Hank Aaron, never hit the half-century mark in a single season. But 69 years after Babe Ruth became the charter member of the 50-1 Club (50 homers, one season), an unlikely guy in a Giants uniform was knocking on the door.

"Getting 50 would be a great honor," Mitchell said. "I'm not going to try for 50 because the main thing to concentrate on is winning a team championship. I'm fatigued right now, but I'm going to play. And 50 home runs might just happen."

Willie Mays was the last Giant to sock 50 homers (51 in '55 and 52 in '65), but he wasn't about to apply any pressure on his protege, the man he tutored in spring training and kept in constant contact with during the season. "If he hits 50, he'd be one of the very few guys who could hit 20 one year and 50 the next," Mays said. "I don't think there's much pressure to hit 50. The real pressure is hitting 40. He shouldn't even worry about it. He's had a tremendous year already."

Indeed, Mitchell was in only his fourth season and had almost doubled his previous career high, 22 in 1987. But Mitchell realized he would have to overcome huge odds to hit nine more. First of all, he was tired; he had played all but five games. Second, he was hurt;

he had felt aches and pains in his ribs, knees, wrist, thumb and finger. Third, he would be facing pitchers he had never seen before as teams out of contention looked toward the future by using minor-leaguers in starting assignments. Finally, he couldn't count on seeing many good pitches; he was among the league leaders in walks (74) and figured to get a lot more if fifth hitter Matt Williams didn't have a strong September.

Yet there were things that could work in Mitchell's favor. There was the need to excel in a pennant race. Also, the Giants would play the Braves and Reds four more times apiece, and Mitchell had homered seven times against Atlanta and six against Cincinnati. On the other hand, Houston also was on the schedule six more times, and the Astros were the only team Mitchell hadn't victimized with the long ball.

"I don't see why he can't hit 50," Giants hitting coach Dusty Baker said. "People asked if he could hit 40 after he hit 30. A lot of people will say no to this. But a lot of people said Willie Mays couldn't hit a changeup, Bobby Bonds a breaking ball or Hank Aaron a slider. But when you hit that many home runs, you learn to adjust. Pitchers will do everything in their power not to let him hit 50. In April, May and June, no one knew for sure if he was for real. But now he's like a gunfighter with a reputation. Other teams talk about him heavily in meetings before a series."

Mitchell was the second Bay Area ballplayer in three years to flirt with a 50-homer season. In 1987, the year of juiced-up baseballs, Oakland's Mark McGwire had 49 home runs with one game remaining on the schedule, but the rookie cut short his bid for 50 to be at the side of his then-wife, Kathy, who was giving birth to their son, Matthew. Two years later, McGwire wasn't regretting his decision, but he was pulling for his buddy across the bay. "He needs nine. He could do that," McGwire said. "The only pressure he'll feel comes when he's close. The constant answering of questions. 'Can you do it?' 'Will you do it?' 'How soon will you do it?' Kevin knows that if it's going to happen, it's going to happen. The longer you can keep it out of your mind, the better you are. If they switched him with Clark in the lineup, so he'd hit in front of Clark, he'd have a much better chance." Jose Canseco had finished eight homers short of 50 in his 40-40 season of 1988, and he was also keeping an eye on Mitchell's stretch run. "The question is, are they going to pitch to him?" Canseco said. "If they pitch to him, I think he has the ability to do it." Then Canseco got off the subject of Mitchell and onto the subject of himself. "I'd like to get 50. Heck, it would be nice to get 60. A new bionic club. The 60-60 Club."

Mitchell began September willing to challenge the 50 barrier, but not able to swing properly. His sprained left wrist altered his stroke. And, typically, controversy caught up with him. News surfaced on September 7 that Mitchell was facing a civil complaint accusing him of beating his former girlfriend and threatening her with a gun. The allegations against Mitchell stemmed from a September 1988 incident in Foster City. Mitchell denied the charges. Coincidentally, it was on September 7, the same day the allegations surfaced, that he hit his next homer, his 42nd of the year. Another five days elapsed before he hit his 43rd. And despite exploding for two home runs on September 17 — his sixth twin killing of the season — he still needed five homers with only 12 games remaining. He hit his 46th on September 20 but concluded his power barrage on September 24 by smacking his 47th and final home run of the season. As it was, Mitchell hit the most home runs by a Giant since Mays' 52 in '62. He did that despite being intentionally walked 32 times — the major-league record for a right-handed hitter.

Despite the lack of a consistent number five hitter behind him, Mitchell had hit six home runs in a month once (April), seven twice (August and September), eight once (July), nine once (May) and 10 once (June). The only month in which he enjoyed the presence of a legitimate power threat behind him was September, when Williams collected five homers and 22 RBIs. "I want to be the guy who hits behind those guys and protects them and makes the other teams have to pitch to them," Williams said. "I want other teams to say, 'Hey, you can't pitch around Clark because then you face Mitchell.' And 'You can't pitch around Mitchell because then you face Williams.' That's what I want them to think." And they did think that every so often. But not always. Despite the burst of power in September, Williams hit only .173 in the month.

As Mitchell was eyeing 50 homers, Oakland was without anyone chasing a home-run milestone for the first time in three years. McGwire made his 50-homer bid in '87, and Canseco was pursuing his 40-40 quest in '88. But in '89, aside from Lansford's contention in the batting race, the big major statistical push involved the A's starting pitchers. Entering the month, the A's hoped to become the second team in big-league history (the '71 Orioles were the first) to boast four 20-game winners. Stewart got his, hitting the 20-win mark for the third straight year. And both Moore and Davis were in position to win 20 in the final week of the season, but they had to settle for 19. Only Welch failed to come close, betrayed too often by the Oakland offense. Entering his final 10 starts of the year, Welch had only a dozen wins. But in those 10 starts, he allowed one or no runs seven times, so winning eight of his final 10 certainly should have been possible. However, he won only five more to finish with 17, tying his career high.

The A's, despite surviving their monster 13-day road trip in late August and early September, were finding it much more difficult to run away from the competition in '89 than in '88, when they brought a nine-game lead into September. But Stewart's 19th win on September 2 — his 10th win following an A's loss — increased the lead to 2½ games, a margin that would only grow. The beginning of the end for the rest of the pack came on September 5 at the Coliseum, where the A's threw their fifth starter, Curt Young, at former Cy Young Award winner Roger Clemens of Boston. It had been a tough year for Young, a consistent loser for two reasons — he either didn't pitch well or, more frequently, didn't receive enough offensive support. At one point in July, after he'd been asked about getting such little support, he stopped talking to the press. That lasted briefly, but Young's bad luck lasted most of the year. He was shuttled in and out of the rotation, never confident in knowing when his next start would be. Because Tony La Russa was dedicated to keeping as many of his top four starters on an every-fifth-day schedule whenever possible, Young was often the odd man out. "It's not fair to Curt," La Russa acknowledged. But that's the way it was, nevertheless. Young went into the Clemens game without having made a start in 10 days.

Fortunately for the A's, something curious happens when they face Clemens. Clemens suffers the ultimate curse — the curse of looking ordinary. Boston scored an unearned run off Young in the first inning, but Terry Steinbach homered — he hit four of his seven homers off Red Sox pitching — in the second inning to tie the game. Oakland got just one hit in the third inning but turned it into four runs to blow the game open. An error, a misplayed sacrifice bunt and a walk loaded the bases for Lansford, who slammed the first pitch down the right-field line for a double, good for two runs.

An infield out and sacrifice fly brought home two more runs. Clemens left the game after seven innings trailing 5-1, although he gave up just three hits. The A's went on to slaughter the Boston bullpen for eight more runs in a 13-1 win. Clemens fell to 1-6 lifetime against Oakland, his only win coming in his Cy Young Award-winning '86 season. Young earned his fifth and final win of the year. As the season wound down, La Russa went with his big four, and Young made just one more start the rest of the season. But the win over Boston was good enough for an entire month's salary.

The night Young outdueled Clemens, the Royals lost their second straight to the Tigers. Kansas City eventually was swept in the three-game Detroit series, and it was the crippling blow to the Royals' pennant hopes. Oakland won two of three to begin its final road trip of the year with leads of 3½ games over Kansas City and four over California.

On September 15, in the first game of an A's-Red Sox series in Boston, in Boston, Clemens finally broke his jinx with a 7-2 victory. But the Royals lost, the Angels were off, and the A's lead remained at 3½ games. The Red Sox won the second and third games to hand Oakland its second three-game sweep of the season, but both the Royals, who were in Baltimore, and the Angels, who were in Chicago, were having troubles of their own. Both lost two out of three, blowing a great chance to pick up ground, and the A's escaped Boston having lost only one game off their lead.

The debacle in Boston was ugly. The A's hitters struck out 25 times in three games and went 1-for-19 with men in scoring position. The pitchers walked 20 men, and the starters didn't even last an average of five innings. The first time the A's had been swept, by Minnesota, they turned around and swept three games from Cleveland. And guess what? The A's were going to Cleveland next. In the first game, Stewart pitched through what he termed "normal, end-of-a-long-season pain" to help beat the Tribe 4-2. The win was a milestone, considering the A's had lost the first game of their previous five series. The A's held a 2-1 lead in the ninth, but Stewart didn't get credit for the win because Dennis Eckersley gave up a homer to Brook Jacoby. It was the second consecutive time in September that Eckersley had denied Stewart a win; Greg Vaughn homered for Milwaukee off Eckersley on September 13. Eck was devastated both times. After the first, a game in which he got the win, he said, "I feel as bad as you can feel after a win." But Stewart dismissed it both times, saying, "I feel that Eck's saved me 1,000 times in the last three years. It's no big deal. He'll save me again." After Jacoby's homer off Eckersley denied Stewart the victory, the A's retained enough composure to snap back. Dave Henderson and Tony Phillips singled in runs in the 10th inning. The next two nights, Moore and Davis took turns collecting their 18th victories to clinch Oakland's sweep of the Indians.

The week was a perfect example of the club's unique off-field harmony. "The Oakland teams of the 1970s fought with Charlie Finley and they fought with themselves," La Russa said. "There's none of that here, though. I've never been around a team that gets along as well as this one does. There are no fights, no short tempers, no shouting matches." There was a lot of good-natured verbal abuse — much of it coming from the corner of the locker room that contained Dave Parker, Dave Henderson and Phillips — that kept players sharp. McGwire said, "We have our fights. We call them 'love matches.' We wrestle, but it's all in good fun. That's how we get our aggressions out."

While the A's were keeping their composure, some of their opponents were having trouble doing the same. On September 24, Twins reliever Roy Smith saved a 5-3 win over the A's for starter Allan Anderson. It was a game in which McGwire homered twice to become only the second player to hit 30 or more home runs in each of his first three full seasons in the major leagues. The other was Canseco. But McGwire's fireworks couldn't compare to those in the Twins' clubhouse. After the game, Smith said he'd like to be traded if he couldn't start for Minnesota. Smith had been a starter before being passed over in the Twins' youth movement, and a reporter asked Twins manager Tom Kelly if Smith would get another chance to start. Kelly didn't like the question. He stormed out of his office, screaming obscenities and marched through the clubhouse knocking over chairs. It had been a tough year for Kelly, just two years removed from managing the World Series champion. With the Twins struggling, he'd waved goodbye to 1988 Cy Young Award winner Frank Viola in a trade. The Twins had gotten plenty of young starting pitching from the New York Mets in return, and, despite strong performances from veterans such as Smith, Kelly found himself under obligation to use the newcomers, resulting in an absurd seven-man rotation. The comic potential of the Twins' unwieldy rotation aside, Kelly's outburst seemed to be directed more at the front office for putting him in an obviously unsavory situation than at the writers involved.

Welch's final win of the season came in the first game of that Minneapolis series after Oakland had swept Cleveland. He allowed six hits and one walk in 7⅔ innings of a 2-1 decision. Oakland won three of four in Minnesota — Smith's win prevented a sweep — including Stewart's 20th. Having won six of 10 games — and six of their last seven — on the trip, the A's returned to the Coliseum for the final seven games of the season holding a commanding 5½-game lead over both the Angels and Royals. A pennant clinching party was just days, maybe hours away.

In Giantsville, the road to the playoffs was not easy. Exciting, yes. Easy, no. It was becoming the Year of the Comeback, and not just because of Dave Dravecky. Forty times the Giants came from behind to win. More impressive was the size of some of the deficits in question. Take September 4 in Cincinnati, when the Giants were down 8-0 after six innings. It looked for all the world like a routine blowout, but the Giants came back to win 9-8. And then there was the September 20 game against the Dodgers. The Giants trailed 7-0 after five innings and roared back to win 8-7. If there were any doubters among the faithful, these two games made them believe.

The Cincinnati game was the most shocking. Roger Craig pulled his starters when the score got to 8-0. The skipper had given up on winning and had gone to the end of his bench, not for the second string, but for the third string, a group he called his Killer C's — Bill Bathe, Chris Speier, Ernie Camacho and Mike Laga. For goodness sakes, Mike Laga. This was the same Mike Laga who had hit .199 over bits of seven seasons with Detroit and St. Louis. Laga was a September 1 callup and did a lot of damage in a little time. He concluded the Giants' big comeback by driving in the ninth run with a single to right field. "The biggest game I've ever won as a manager," Craig said. "I'll never forget that game. The Killer B's did a hell of a job, but it's the Killer C's that won it." The Giants, employing 25 players including 11 who had played in Triple-A during the year, had scored two runs in the seventh, two in the eighth and five in the ninth. The dramatic win increased their lead in the West to seven games and reduced their magic number to 19. The chants in the clubhouse afterward went "Lags! Lags! Lags!" The next day, the jollity continued as third-base coach Bill Fahey for some reason agreed to have his head shaved. Terry Kennedy and

Steve Bedrosian raised $5,000 from the troops as incentive.

Three days after coming back to beat Cincinnati, the Giants were at it again in Atlanta. They spotted the Braves a 4-1 lead before charging back and scoring three in the seventh, two in the eighth and one in the ninth to prevail 7-5. Laga also had a hand in this one, igniting the game-tying rally in the seventh inning with a pinch-hit RBI single. Mitchell's 45th homer in the ninth concluded the winners' scoring.

Six days later came another startling comeback. After the Reds scored two runs in the top of the 13th at Candlestick, the Giants rallied for three in the bottom of the inning to pull out an 8-7 win. After Greg Litton's two-run double tied it, Brett Butler slapped an opposite-field single to drive home the winning run.

On September 20 at Candlestick, the Giants put together perhaps their most important comeback of all. They trailed the Dodgers 7-0 through five innings. And 7-3 through eight innings. Most remarkable about this particular surge was the fact that the Giants scored all five of their ninth-inning runs without making an out. Seven up, seven safe. It was like spring training against the A's, only now it was the Giants who were on the march. Mitchell opened the rally with a solo home run, his 46th. As Ken Oberkfell said, "And it all started with a harmless leadoff homer." Then came an Ernest Riles single. And a Williams double. And a Kennedy single. And a Speier double. And a Litton single. And then Butler faced new reliever John Tudor. When Butler pulled a grounder up the right-field line to score Speier with the deciding run, the Giants acted as if they had won the pennant. Almost.

Rrrring. (It's Roger Craig's office phone.)

"That must be the president," he said.

"Hello. . . . Yes, and there are still no outs. We're still hitting." Click.

"That was the president."

It just might have been.

Earlier in the day, both the Padres and Astros had won, and a Giants loss would have narrowed the first-place gap to four games for the first time since September 1. But instead, the cushion remained at a comfortable five games with 10 left. "The Padres are probably cussing us out right now," Mitchell said.

The Padres probably did a lot of cussing in the final weeks. San Diego was playing incredible baseball but couldn't get anywhere. In their streak of winning 14 of 17, the Padres gained only three games on the Giants, who were winning 11 and losing six. Nevertheless, the Padres were accepting applications for playoff tickets, hoping the Giants would eventually turn in one of the all-time collapses. And sure enough, the Giants gave their fans reason to be concerned once or twice.

The first came when the Padres visited rain-soaked Candlestick in mid-September for a three-game series. Although the Padres were the hotter team, they were the ones feeling the pressure. "It ain't on us," assured Will Clark. Realistically, at six games back with only 15 to play, the Padres had to sweep the series for any hope of overtaking the Giants. And they took the first step with a 5-3 win in the first game. Bob Knepper allowed all five runs in his six innings, and the Giants squandered several scoring opportunities.

The next day's game was rained out, only the 22nd in the Giants' Candlestick Park history. A double-header was scheduled for the next day, September 17, with Garrelts facing Calvin Schiraldi in the opener. The Giants wanted at least a split, knowing that would retain their five-game lead and get two more games out of the way. The Giants quickly accomplished their mission with a 5-3 win in the opener. Garrelts, Craig Lefferts and Bedrosian limited the Padres to three runs, and Mitchell slugged two home runs. Bruce Hurst beat the Giants 6-1 on a five-hitter in the nightcap, but the Giants had already chalked up the entire day as a success. "That first game kind of meant the whole year for us," Craig said. "It's going to be tough for anybody to catch us now."

The Giants put some pressure on the Padres by sweeping the Dodgers and taking two of three from the Astros. Included in the Dodgers series was that game in which the Giants overcame a 7-0 deficit. Another memorable moment came when Laga smacked a three-run double off the right-field fence to beat the Dodgers 3-2 and hand Orel Hershiser his career-worst sixth straight loss. However, the Giants didn't put any distance between themselves and the just-as-hot Padres, and they left San Francisco for a season-concluding six-game road trip still leading by five games.

It appeared the Giants were a cinch to clinch the pennant, but they didn't necessarily think so. What else could explain their interest in a Braves-Astros series being played 3,000 miles away? While the Astros (still mathematically alive) were in Atlanta,

Braves manager Russ Nixon, who had long since given up on his pathetic club and was only looking toward the future, took his top starters out of the rotation and replaced them with the likes of rookies Gary Eave and Rusty Richards. An unwritten baseball rule, however, prohibits managers from severely altering their lineups against contending teams, and Al Rosen found the practice so disturbing that he complained to Bill White, the National League president. Nixon received a phone call from White a half-hour before the second Astros game and then promptly called the Giants "paranoid" and refused to change his pitching plans. As it was, Eave went out and allowed just two hits in 7⅔ innings. "Maybe Russ Nixon knows something," Craig said.

By the final week of the season, a Giants division championship seemed a whole lot more secure than a Clark batting championship. Clark and Tony Gwynn were neck and neck for most of the month. But whatever the outcome, Clark had already secured a spectacular season for several reasons. If Mitchell wasn't helped much by the Giants' fifth hitters, he certainly was helped by the presence of the number three hitter. Clark hit in front of Mitchell all season, and if success is contagious, then plenty of Clark rubbed off on Mitchell. Clark had had a wonderful '88 season, as his 29 homers and 109 RBIs would attest, but he wasn't keen on his .282 average. So Clark went into 1989 trying to follow turn-of-the-century batting whiz Wee Willie Keeler's philosophy of "hitting 'em where they ain't." Clark became a patient batter who waited on pitches before blasting balls to the power alley in left-center. He became so successful hitting to all fields that his average would soar 51 points in a year. His home-run output fell by six, but Clark finished with 111 RBIs to become the first Giant to produce back-to-back 100-RBI seasons since Willie McCovey in '69- 70. But in the final week, the power figures were almost cast aside as Clark found himself smack in the middle of the batting race. With Mitchell assured of the home-run and RBI titles, Clark was attempting to provide San Francisco with its first two-man Triple Crown.

Clark topped .300 each month — .375 in April, .351 in May, .303 in June, .307 in July, .352 in August and .330 in September — and opened the final month with an overall .337 average. Gwynn began the month seven points better than Clark at .344, but Clark hit in each of his first seven games to stretch his hitting streak to nine. On September 6 in Atlanta, although the witnesses numbered just 1,528 — the Braves' smallest home crowd in 10 years — Clark went the other way with an outside slider by left-hander Derek Lilliquist, peppering the pitch over the left-field fence for his 22nd home run and 100th RBI to help beat the Braves 7-2. "If you're a left-handed hitter and take a left-handed pitcher the other way, that's a pretty decent bit of hitting," Clark said. Will collected two hits that day and two more the next to improve his average to .342 and move ahead of Gwynn by two points in the batting race.

Beating Gwynn at his own game would have been no easy feat for Clark, a .292 career hitter. Gwynn had won three batting titles, his first coming in 1984 in his first full year in the majors. After taking a couple of years off — if .317 and .329 can be considered years off — Gwynn came back to win the batting crown in '87 and '88. His .370 mark in '87 was the highest in the National League since 1948 when Stan "The Man" Musial batted .376. In '88, in a down year for averages, Gwynn played with nagging injuries all season but still emerged as the best hitter at .313. Through it all, it's refreshing that Gwynn — the Padres' answer to Dave Stewart because of his willingness to talk to the media through bad times as well as good — can compare to the all-time greats yet remain one of the most sincere and genuinely nice guys who ever put on a jock strap. And another championship in '89 would give Gwynn three straight, which hadn't been accomplished since Musial did it in '50, '51 and '52.

History favored Gwynn to beat Clark, but history hasn't always been known to get in the way of a guy like Clark. No one from San Francisco had ever led baseball in All-Star votes. Until Clark. No one from San Francisco had ever played in as many as 320 straight games. Until Clark. And talk abouts firsts — Clark's first swing in the majors was a home run off Nolan Ryan. In his first game at Candlestick, he homered off Knepper, then with the Astros. Clark was the first Giant in 19 years to join the 100-100-100 Club (100 runs, 100 walks, 100 RBIs). He was the first Giant in 19 years to lead the league in RBIs. First Giant in 19 years to hit .300 with 30 homers in the same season. First Giant in 18 years to get an RBI in nine straight games. First Giant in 15 years to be selected as an All-Star starter. And maybe even the first Giant in who-knows-how-many years not to complain about Candlestick Park.

Clark was certainly a pleasant sight, what with his patented sweet swing that makes old-timers remember Ted Williams and

Stan The Man. Clark stands in the box, never appearing afraid, always waving his bat back and forth. It's amazing how Clark can always wiggle the bat in perfect time, moving it forward but always pulling it back in sync with the pitch, rarely being caught off balance. And his upward swing, often toward the upper deck in right field, pushes his entire body in that direction. All the while, a zoom lens will reveal his just-as-amazing jaw movements. Easily a member of the All-Jaw Team with George Foster and The Wicked Witch of the West, Clark can move his jaw like no one else in the game today. Left, right, up, down, in, out. Even Clark admits, "I didn't know one man's jaw could go through that many contortions." Coupled with those fixed and focused eyes, Clark's game face is one of a kind. It's such a piece of art that his teammates just had to find a name for it. Nuschler is his middle name, so "The Nuschler" it was. "The Nuschler Look." It fits, just as Will fits.

Clark was just 25 years old in the '89 season, hardly an age for a team leader. But if every team has a leader, who on the '89 Giants would be better qualified? The A's had a horde of leaders, including Dave Parker, Carney Lansford and Dave Stewart. And there had been no lack of leadership on the '87 Giants. In Clark's first full season, he could look up to Mike Krukow, Brenly, Chili Davis and Jeffrey Leonard, all known as leaders, although Clark spent more time feuding with Leonard than looking up to him. But the presence of those four wasn't felt in '89. Davis and Leonard were long gone, Krukow was injured most of the season and Brenly didn't show up until the final month. So Clark, more than anyone, had to be the leader of the Giants. Mitchell didn't want the label. Neither did Reuschel. Butler, maybe, but he's not the fierce type around which a team would rally.

That left Clark, who in spring training gave his first indication that he was interested in the vacancy. "I wouldn't mind having that role," Clark said. "But you can't be self-appointed. You have to gain the respect of your teammates." He had shown the signs. He hustled to first base on routine ground balls. He was not afraid to console a veteran pitcher on the mound when times are tough. He'd even put up his dukes when summoned. In the summer of '88, Clark slid hard into St. Louis second baseman Jose Oquendo and prevented Oquendo from pivoting and throwing to first base. Oquendo responded by kneeing and swinging at Clark, and shortstop Ozzie Smith came over to take a swing. Clark got to his feet and proceeded to take on four Cardinals at once, taking a swipe or two at Smith until receiving assistance from his teammates. Clark not only sent a message to Oquendo and Ozzie, but to his teammates as well, that he would not be intimidated.

"He's going to be a team leader here for a long, long time," said Krukow, the pitcher who was a big reason Clark had matured both on and off the field since his brash rookie days. Krukow counseled Clark and even took him under his roof and, as Clark said, "told me what you can do and what you can't do." Clark, just a couple of years later, tried to do with Matt Williams what Krukow had done with him. When Williams stayed at Clark's off-season New Orleans home the winter before the '89 season, Clark acted as Williams' mentor, teaching him the do's and don'ts of big-league baseball while emphasizing the mental aspects of the game. As it turned out, Williams lasted only a month with the Giants before being shipped back to Phoenix, but at least Clark had made the effort that only a team leader would make. And throughout the season, Clark became a team spokesman, constantly using the "we" word and referring to his teammates as "the troops," as if he were the commanding officer.

Clark had no problem talking about his teammates or talking about himself. But he tightened up slightly when asked about the batting race. He had never been close to a batting championship and all but refused to discuss the matter in early September. But there was a sense that he would love to hang a Silver Bat above his mantle. For Gwynn, well, his mantle was awfully crowded, and he spoke freely of the batting race, although the words weren't what you would have expected from a three-time batting champ challenging for a fourth. "Let him win it," Gwynn said. "I'd rather get to the World Series and let him have it. The shine of it is unbelievable for the first one. But I've won it three times, so it doesn't have the same effect any more. You can be sure I'll be moving the runner over, whether it's a bunt or a ground ball. I want to win a pennant. Everybody thinks the batting title is on my mind, but it isn't. It's just fun helping this team win and putting heat on the Giants."

Clark, in a rare batting-race interview, pointed out that the competition featured "two different types of hitters. I'll have a lot more outs in the air than Tony, but Tony is a consistent line-drive hitter." Another difference was RBIs. Although both were hitting third in their lineups, Clark had 108 RBIs by mid-September while

Gwynn had just 52. But until the final weeks, Clark was generally mum about the prospect of leading the league in hitting. "I'm too busy worrying about a pennant," Clark said. "I'll worry about a batting race when the season's over."

Oakland's Carney Lansford was also mum, but for another reason. Lansford not only refused to talk to the media about the batting race; he refused to talk to the media about anything. His "Quiet Man" status stemmed from a late August bout with Minnesota relief ace Jeff Reardon. In the 10th inning of a 4-4 game, Lansford ripped a Reardon pitch off the wall on two hops to drive home the winning run. Shortly afterward, he discussed the sequence.

"Normally in that situation, you don't like to see a stopper like Reardon," Lansford said. "In this case, though, I wanted to see him. I know what pitches he has and what he likes to do with them. And I know that right now his fastball isn't comparable to the one he's had in the past. It's probably tougher for him about now. The ball isn't jumping for him like it has."

Lansford was voicing his sympathy for Reardon's predicament, something that is rare in professional sports. He might have suggested luck was on his side, but at least Lansford acknowledged that Reardon wasn't throwing well and that the story might have been different if the pitcher had been able to throw his best stuff. But compassion didn't come into play 24 hours later, when Lansford found he had cause to regret those words. Reardon learned of Lansford's quotes through a story by Frank Blackman in the San Francisco Examiner. Through intermediaries, Reardon let Lansford know that he wasn't hurting, that he was mad as hell, and that Lansford had better be on guard the next time the two faced. Lansford considered his options briefly, apologized to Reardon and said he'd been quoted out of context by the Bay Area media. Had that been the end of it, Reardon might have been mollified.

However, Lansford went an extra step, also telling Reardon that he wouldn't talk to the Bay Area media for the rest of the year in retribution for having been misquoted. In telling the Bay Area beat writers that he was now The Quiet Man, Lansford said, "This way, there will be no more confusion, no more garbage." There was just one slight problem. He hadn't been misquoted. Lansford is usually one of the most affable of men and can be gregarious when the mood hits him. Now he'd drawn an invisible wall between himself and the print media — radio and television interviewers were exempt from the ban. It wasn't a particularly good idea for the team captain and player representative to be tight-lipped, and friends on the team indicated that Lansford had come to regret his rash decision.

Lansford would still talk off-the-record to the writers but would hush up whenever a notebook and pen came into view. He softened his stance twice after his original proclamation. His first modification came when he said he'd talk in the post-season, if the A's got that far. Then he went further a few weeks later, saying that he'd talk once the A's clinched the pennant. He did that, putting to rest an uneasy relationship between himself and the writers. And he made an exception after the early September death of Commissioner Bart Giamatti, acknowledging that the team captain should speak for the club at such a time, no matter what differences might exist.

It was becoming obvious that there was a two-in-three chance that a right-handed batter would win the American League batting title. The last time a right-handed hitter had won the award was in '81, when Lansford, then with the Red Sox, hit .336 during the strike-shortened season. Since then, thanks primarily to Lansford's replacement in Boston, Wade Boggs, left-handers had dominated the batting charts. Boggs won five titles in the 1980s, the last four in succession. And since the unpredictable star known as Alex Johnson hit .329 for the Angels in 1970, Lansford had been the only right-hander to break two decades' worth of left-handed dominance. Even in '81, two of Lansford's primary threats for the title were left-handed — Cecil Cooper of Milwaukee and Kirk Gibson of Detroit.

"This is a left-hander's game," A's hitting coach Merv Rettenmund said. "Left-handers are a step closer to first base. And while that doesn't help Boggs all that much, it helps some. And the other big difference is that pitchers have to hold runners on first base. They don't hold them on third base. So when there are men on base, left-handers have a much bigger hole to pull the ball through." Canseco, in his usual off-handed way, blamed the spacious Coliseum for keeping Lansford's average down. "Carney should be hitting .360, at least," said Canseco, adding that the preponderance of right-handed pitching also swung the balance in favor of the left-handers. "It's hard for a right-hander like Carney to hit for as high an average when most of what he sees is pitches breaking away from him from right-handed pitchers," Canseco said. "Carney doesn't have the left-hander's luxury of seeing all those right-handers throwing pitches breaking in toward him. That's what makes what he's done extra special."

And what had Lansford done? June had been something of a wash for him. He'd hit a respectable .292 but drove in just five runs, scored just five and missed a week after blowing out his left hamstring on a steal of second base on June 2. Still, it was a vast improvement over June 1988, which he began as the league's hottest hitter. He had a 17-game May hitting streak during which he hit .486 to push his overall average close to .400. He was Player of the Month and, in the process, passed Dave Winfield to become the league's top batter. His hitting streak ended when he went 0-for-2 June 1 against New York, but he started the A's subsequent road trip in Minnesota with back-to-back 3-for-5 games to push his average over .400. After taking a day off, he had two more hits in the first game of a series in Kansas City, at which time he had hit in 20 of 21 games and was leading the league with a .402 batting average. Not only was Lansford smoking the ball, but he was on a pace to shatter the all-time single-season hit record of 257, held by Hall of Famer George Sisler. He was so hot that even if he had gone 0-for-66, his average would still be above .300. In recognition of what he had accomplished by June 2, Sandy Alderson extended and upgraded Lansford's contract, tying him to the A's through the 1992 season.

And then the merry-go-round suddenly stopped. Only once during the rest of the month did Lansford get as many as two hits in a game, after having done it 29 times in his first 53 starts. He wound up hitting a horrendous .160 for June and never recovered his batting stroke. After reaching .402 for the last time on June 6, Lansford hit .196 the rest of the way, sinking ever deeper into an offensive morass. The man who "couldn't" fall under .300 not only did that, his average fell all the way to .279, the third-lowest mark of his career.

Lansford's May 1989 was a virtual twin of his May 1988. He hit .444 in May '88 and came back with .404 a year later. But Lansford was not willing to fall into the same June traps that had ruined his batting average 12 months earlier. He did his best to put talk of batting titles, of a possible All-Star Game selection, even talk of the slump of 1988 out of his system. And he succeeded, hitting an acceptable .292. Still, June was not an easy time for Lansford. He read newspaper reports that cast doubt on his ability as a hitter with men on base. At the end of the month, despite his batting average, he had driven in just 17 runs. Part-timers Stan Javier (20), Ron Hassey (18), Phillips (21) and Mike Gallego (23) all had more RBIs despite lower batting averages and fewer at-bats. "I'm not sure what it is," Lansford said. "For whatever reason, I just haven't gotten the job done. But for whatever reason, I just haven't gotten the hits with men on. After 12 years in this game, I've stopped trying to figure it out. But it does make for a quiet batting average."

Lansford found that the best way to counteract that kind of depressing thought was not with his mouth, but with his bat. July, the month that Canseco and Dennis Eckersley came back from the disabled list, saw Lansford get off to a 0-for-17 start. From that point on, though, he hit .359 with 11 RBIs, picking up in three weeks two-thirds as many RBIs as he had in his first two months. He managed a 10-game hitting streak in mid-July but bettered that in August when he hit safely in 19 straight games. Over the course of the streak, he hit .354 to climb back into the batting race.

Through all of that, Lansford's concentration on his on-field job never wavered. At the beginning of September, Boggs and another right-hander, Puckett, had separated themselves from the pack. Puckett entered the final month hitting a league-leading .340 with Boggs at .338 and Lansford at a rather distant .326. But unlike the other two, Lansford could use the heat generated by the A's pennant chance as a motivator.

And while both Puckett and Boggs tailed off slightly in the final month, Lansford came on strong. In the first four days of September, Lansford hit his way into the race by going 8-for-19. By September 7, there were just three points separating Boggs, Puckett and Lansford. By the middle of the month, Lansford had moved into a three-point lead over Puckett and a six-point lead over Boggs. So many times before, Boggs had buried the opposition with a big September finish, but this time he was the first man to drop. By September 24, he conceded that he was too far back, that his streak of batting titles was over, and that Puckett and Lansford would have to battle it out without him.

The batting races were big news for the fans and the media, but Tony La Russa and Roger Craig had more important matters on their minds. There was a little matter of pennants yet to be clinched. While the A's were slowly pulling further ahead of Kansas City and California by producing an 18-9 record in the final month, the Giants were not far behind at 17-12. Yet San Francisco was still losing ground to the Padres.

The A's had opened their final homestand on September 25 with a 3-2 loss to Texas' Charlie Hough. Welch allowed one run in seven innings only to have Todd Burns allow a game-losing two-run homer to Fred Manrique in the eighth inning. The next night, Oakland closed to within one win of repeating as division champions when Dave Henderson's two-run homer in the eighth inning snapped a 2-all tie and carried the A's to a 4-3 win over the Rangers. But it was another rough night for Dennis Eckersley, who blew a 2-1 win for again luckless Curt Young by allowing the Rangers to tie the game in the top of the eighth on a Manrique single. Henderson's homer gave Oakland back the lead in the bottom of the inning, and Eckersley, despite allowing a run in the ninth, closed out the game to reduce Oakland's magic number to one, sewing up at least a tie for the West title. Kansas City, by virtue of having beaten California on the 25th and 26th, was now the only team standing between the A's and another crown. The Royals were hoping for a miracle, praying that the Rangers would win twice more in Oakland, thereby giving the Royals a chance to catch the A's in their scheduled three-game season finale on the weekend. But as soon as the A's saw success, they jumped at it.

Moore allowed the Rangers just one hit in seven innings on September 27, and Canseco hit his 17th homer, a two-run shot in a three-run first inning off Rangers starter Jaime Moyer. The A's went on to win 5-0, Gene Nelson getting the final out when Rafael Palmeiro grounded out to McGwire at first base. McGwire scooped up the ball, pointed his glove at the heavens and raced to the bag, tapping it lightly as the players and their 32,280 Coliseum fans shared the joy of a special moment, closing out Oakland's season-long pursuit of a second straight divisional flag.

In typical form, it was the A's hidden Most Valuable Player, infielder Mike Gallego, who starred in the clincher. Gallego did what he'd done all year, turning in three simply spectacular defensive plays to help Moore win his 19th. Moore, who had never tasted champagne in his 6½ years in Seattle, used his first bottle of Wente Brut to douse Gallego. "Gags was outstanding," Moore said. "He did what he'd done all year. After that, all I had to do was to keep throwing zeroes." All year long, La Russa pointed to Gallego as the A's secret weapon. Gallego started the season in a second base platoon with Tony Phillips and Glenn Hubbard. When Walter Weiss went on the disabled list for 10 weeks, Gallego made a career change and became a shortstop with surprising range and an awesome glove. Wherever they asked him to play, he did, and well. In the clincher, with Gallego playing second base, he made a nice play to begin a double play in the third inning and soared high to spear a looping line drive in the fourth inning. He started off the fifth by making a perfect mid-air throw from behind second base to gun down fleet Ruben Sierra. Each time, Gallego wowed not only the crowd, but his teammates. "Gags probably is our MVP," Dave Henderson said. "When you look at all he's done, and all he's meant to us, he's been spectacular when we needed him to be." La Russa had earlier admitted as much by naming Gallego his starting shortstop for the playoffs.

In the middle of the champagne-sprayed clubhouse, two men who had meant much to the development of the A's had very different thoughts in celebration. Owner Walter A. Haas Jr., who'd become more involved with the club in the previous three years, was a little in awe of what had happened. "When you think of all that we had to go through to get here, it's amazing. There's no doubt in my mind that after what we've overcome, this one is that much sweeter." But for Lansford, one of the team leaders, the thought was not so much about what the A's had overcome to make it back into the post-season, but that so many people, especially in the media, doubted Oakland's ability and resolve. Even in clinching the pennant, the A's were less than whole. Lansford couldn't start the clincher because of sore ribs, but La Russa, who wanted his captain on the field when the clinching happened, snuck Lansford into the game on defense in the ninth inning so that he'd be part of the first wave of celebrants. Later, in a happy Oakland clubhouse, Lansford thought back to April in Anaheim, when the A's were incensed after hearing a Southern California radio broadcaster who, in Lansford's words, said "without Canseco and McGwire, we were a less-than-mediocre team. I've kept that thought in the back of my mind all year. I wonder what that guy's thinking now."

There was only one thing to think. The A's had played without Canseco. Without McGwire. Without Davis. Without Welch. Without Eckersley. Without Weiss. And yet, at the end, they were again the champions of the American League West and again the winningest team in baseball, with 99 W's.

Coincidentally — or magically — the A's clinched their division title in Oakland minutes before the Giants clinched theirs in Los Angeles.

But the Giants had to survive a harrowing three days to do so. It had appeared the Giants' National League West title would be clinched well before the final week. However, the Padres put on a spectacular second-half show for the second straight season. In '88, when the Padres fired manager Larry Bowa after his 16-30 start, they brought Jack McKeon downstairs to manage in the majors for the first time since he guided Charlie Finley's A's in '77 and '78. Those Oakland clubs finished fifth and sixth, respectively, so Jack had some experience with bad clubs. But '88 was different. He took a fifth-place team and finished third, thanks to a 67-48 post-Bowa record. Those Padres won 10 of their final 12 in '88, and the addition of Jack Clark, Bruce Hurst and Walt Terrell made the Padres division favorites in '89. But they found themselves 60-63 and 10 games back on August 19.

Then something crazy happened again to the San Diegans; they actually thought they could win the thing and began posting wins in frenzied fashion. They won eight of nine, 14 of 16 and 20 of 25. The fans began believing. And on September 12, after the Padres beat the Astros 9-0, some 2,500 fans remained in San Diego Jack Murphy Stadium to catch the end of the Giants-Braves game on the right-field scoreboard screen. This was a bigger crowd than the one a week earlier that watched the Braves-Giants game live in Atlanta, and the Padres' organist made the folks feel a part of it all by staying in his seat and providing some background entertainment. Scoreboard operators hung out to count balls and strikes on the big board. And down in the clubhouse, the Padres were catching the game on TV. They all cheered in unison when the Braves beat the Giants on Dale Murphy's eighth-inning home run off Bedrosian.

The Giants went into the final week with a five-game lead, and the season's last road trip included three games in Los Angeles and, appropriately, three in San Diego. The trip to Dodger Stadium was a three-game disaster. Pitchers John Wetteland, Ramon Martinez and Tim Belcher did great imitations of Sandy Koufax, Don Drysdale and Johnny Podres, and the Giants scored only three runs the entire series. After a 5-2 loss in the opener, a television reporter had the audacity to ask Craig if he liked his chances. Five games in front, five to play. But Mr. Craig, sir, "Do you like your chances?" Craig's first reply was a sharp "Whuuut?" Then Craig, as he always does, softened. "Yeah, I like my chances." The quick response drew laughter in Craig's overcrowded Dodger Stadium office because everyone knew the magic number had shrunk to one. Despite the Giants' loss, the division title was closer because the Padres had dropped a 5-3 decision to the Reds. But anyone who knew baseball history knew that there was still a chance for failure. Craig was on the '64 St. Louis team that overcame a 6½-game deficit to the Phillies with 12 to play. A Padres comeback would have to be even more dramatic, but there was still that mathematical possibility, not to mention Yogi Berra's "it ain't over 'til it's over" philosophy.

"I feel it's going to happen tomorrow," said Craig, referring to the champagne celebration. "I don't want it to happen the next day. I have to drive to San Diego after the game, and I don't want to get a chauffeur." But Craig's prediction was off. While Martinez was beating the Giants 2-1, the Padres were blanking the Reds 3-0. It was now a four-game lead with four to play, and it appeared the Giants would need to wait until the San Diego series for uncorking ceremonies. "Let them celebrate somewhere else," Dodgers manager Tommy Lasorda said. "I don't want to see them do it here." According to history, the Giants should have been destined to celebrate in San Diego anyway. The town had become the unofficial clinching grounds for division champions. The Braves of '82, the Padres of '84, the Dodgers of '85, the Giants of '87 and the Dodgers of '88 all clinched titles in San Diego.

The morning of the series' third game, a conference call involving Rosen, Bill White and Padres Vice President Tony Siegle was conducted to determine where a one-game playoff would be situated in the case of a 162-game tie between the Giants and Padres. Rosen called tails. White's coin showed heads, so the game would be played in San Diego. Fortunately for the slumping Giants, the magic number was still just one. A Giants win or a Padres loss would give San Francisco the title.

But the Giants-Dodgers series finale was more of the same, with Belcher winning 1-0 on a four-hitter to hand the Giants their only three-game series sweep of the season. But what followed was one of the most bizarre episodes in pennant-race lore. In Giants annals, nothing but perhaps the 1962 season could be considered comparable. It was in '62 that the Giants had to win their season finale and the Dodgers had to lose theirs in order for San Francisco to clinch a first-place tie with Los Angeles. The Giants did their part, beating the Houston Colts 2-1. One long hour later, they learned that the Dodgers had also done theirs: Down in Chavez Ravine, Gene Oliver's solo home run stood up as the lone score in a 1-0 St. Louis victory. The Giants went on to beat the Dodgers in a three-game playoff for their first pennant since moving to San Francisco.

Now fast forward back to the future to the '89 Giants, who had just lost 1-0 to the '89 Dodgers. Just as Belcher was completing the ninth inning, the Giants were preparing to party anyway, because the Padres were trailing in San Diego. Partying had to wait, however, when with one out in Los Angeles, the Padres tied the Reds 1-1 in San Diego. And after Ernest Riles flied to right for the final out in Los Angeles, the Padres were loading the bases with two outs in San Diego. One more run in the ninth would have prolonged the party one more day. But Benito Santiago struck out, sending the game into extra innings.

While the Dodgers' players packed and left, the Giants sat and waited, their two team buses parked in front of their dugout, not even warming up for the trip two hours south to San Diego. The 10th inning came and went with no score. Craig sat in his office chair, surrounded by coaches and beat writers and listening to updates provided by the San Diego Tribune's Barry Bloom, who was on the phone with Padres writer Chris DeLuca of the Escondido Times-Advocate in the San Diego press box. The 11th inning came and went, no score. The players swarmed the busy clubhouse searching for either privacy or a good position to pick up the Padres game over the radio — there was no chance to get both. The 12th inning came and went, no score.

Then came the 13th. With two outs and Herm Winningham on second base, Eric Davis stepped to the plate. Todd Benzinger was in the on-deck circle, so it seemed a perfect time to intentionally walk Davis, one of the most feared hitters in the league. But Jack McKeon surprised an entire ballpark and allowed Calvin Schiraldi to pitch to Davis. Whoops! Davis smacked a double to score Winningham. The Padres failed to score in their half of the inning, giving the Reds the win and the Giants the division title.

An hour and a half after losing their third straight game, the Giants finally let loose with their first championship celebration since they won the West in '87. "This is better than '87," said Al Rosen, in a clubhouse corner safe from the champagne shower. "There was something special about tonight. In '87, they went out and won it. There wasn't the type of pressure that San Diego has put on us."

And so the Giants lost the battle but won the war. Simple mathematics told the story. Sure, the Giants had backed into the title, but no one in their clubhouse seemed to care. Except maybe catcher Terry Kennedy. "Hey, we didn't back into this," he said, popping the cork on a bottle of Domaine Montreaux, which was among the six cases that had been on ice and untouched for three days. Steve Bedrosian said, "It doesn't matter how you do it, as long as you do it." Will Clark, who had cussed over live television during the '87 division-winning celebration, was just as wild in the '89 celebration, although he made it a point not to scream the (bleep) word this time.

The Giants' celebration went on for another hour, and it wasn't until late in the evening that they finally boarded their buses and headed for San Diego, for their final series of the regular season on the Padres' home turf. It was a bitter pill for the Padres, who were the league's best team down the stretch for two straight years but had nothing to show for it. "They gave it their best shot," said Giants reliever Craig Lefferts. "Unfortunately for them, the first half hurt them. It's our championship, and it's theirs to wish for next year."

Hours after Oakland's clinching, many of the A's players and their wives gathered at Rickey's Sports Bar in suburban San Leandro, about 10 minutes from the Coliseum. But Dave Stewart wasn't there. He had joined the celebration in the clubhouse, then had gone home to put his game face on; he was pitching the wrap-up game the next afternoon in the A's series finale against Texas. The A's had the pennant locked up, but they still had four games to go in the regular season. Now was no time to let up. Stewart won his 21st.

On September 30, Oakland beat Kansas City 4-3. But Storm Davis, who left the game with a 3-2 lead, saw his chance for his 20th win of the season die when George Brett's single off Rick Honeycutt tied the game in the eighth. The A's won in the ninth on the strength of the surging bat of Dave Henderson, who singled home Lansford with the game-winner. And on October 1, the final day of the regular season, Moore was scheduled to get his last chance at his 20th win. But minutes before the game, Moore was scratched and replaced by rookie Dave Otto. Moore, who had every right to be miffed about not getting a shot at the magic 20-win mark, took the news that he was now going to pitch in Game Two of the playoffs in his usual bullet-proof style. "The playoffs are more important than winning 20. They asked me to think about the switch, but I didn't have to think about it. The playoffs come first."

The A's wouldn't make any predictions about the playoffs. But others were willing to make them for them. Bret Saberhagen, after beating Oakland on the next-to-last day of the season, said the A's would win everything. "They have great starting pitching, a great bullpen, a good, explosive offense that's hard to pitch to, and good defense. What more do they need? They're the best team in baseball again this year."

Before the question of which was the "best team in baseball" could be answered, though, both leagues' batting races had to be settled. After the A's won the division, Carney Lansford could concentrate on beating Kirby Puckett, but Lansford's swing was still slowed by his rib injury. Four days before the end of the season, Puckett went back on top by four points. Lansford made a final surge with two hits on September 29 and went 1-for-3 on September 30, moving into an almost flat-footed tie with Puckett entering the season's final day. The Twins, with Puckett sitting at .33809, were at Seattle while the A's, with Lansford fractionally in second place at .33759, hosted Kansas City. Lansford hit a bullet in his first at-bat — right into the glove of second baseman Brad Wellman. Minutes later, Puckett doubled in his first at-bat. He went on to get another double as well, going 2-for-5 to finish as the American League champion at .339. Lansford went 0-for-3 before leaving the A's 4-3 season-ending, 11-inning win after nine innings. Lansford had ended with the same .336 average that had been his previous career best.

Even in finishing second, Lansford's season was an exceptional piece of work. No Oakland batter had ever hit above .308 for a full season. With its deep fences and largest-in-baseball foul territory, the Coliseum depresses batting averages more than any park in baseball. And while Puckett's home games came on the hit-happy turf of the Metrodome, Lansford wouldn't allow that to take away from Puckett's accomplishment. "I respect Kirby that he can play every game on turf, going out there day after day," Lansford said. "You get extra hits, but it takes a real toll on your body." For his part, Puckett was slightly defensive about his first batting title, which came with diminished home run and RBI totals. "I know some people are going to say my homers are down and I didn't drive in as many runs as last year," he said before calling it a season. "But it's hard to do the same thing, year after year."

The National League batting championship was determined on the same day, culminating a three-game series in San Diego that featured only one race — Clark vs. Gwynn. The night of the clincher, while busing from Los Angeles to San Diego to begin the Padres series, the fatigued Giants were thankful they were off the next day. Weeks earlier, Craig had planned a team barbecue on his 40-acre ranch in San Diego County's tiny northeast village of Warner Springs. It was a marvelous coincidence that the Giants had won the division the previous night, and it was only natural to continue the victory party. Aside from their recent inability to score runs, the only remaining concerns were health and the batting crown.

For Craig, the team's health was a tremendous concern. Don Robinson (right knee), Jose Uribe (left shoulder), Lefferts (left shoulder), Manwaring (left foot) and Clark (right shinbone) were all weakened by injuries. Robinson, Uribe and Lefferts could afford to rest for the playoffs, but Clark wasn't about to call it a season. He was still trying to steal a batting title from Gwynn. Like most of his teammates, Clark hadn't hit well in Los Angeles. His 2-for-12 series lowered his average to .333, but Gwynn was only at .332 after breaking out of a 0-for-11 slump in his previous game. And while Clark wasn't at 100 percent, Gwynn was also handicapped over the final month with a sore Achilles' tendon.

The Giants' second string (plus Clark) beat the Padres' second string (plus Gwynn) in the first game 7-2, and Clark took a three-point edge with a 2-for-4 showing. Gwynn was 1-for-5. The next day, on September 30 (an 11-5 Padres win), Clark was 1-for-4. Gwynn was 3-for-4, all three hits going for singles on pitches over the heart of the plate by Rick Reuschel. But Gwynn still trailed Clark — .334 (actually, .333904) to .333. With his three-hit day, Gwynn reached 200 hits on the season, a plateau he claimed he'd treasure more than the batting title. Clark, meanwhile, had heard all of Gwynn's talk, how another Silver Bat wouldn't matter to Gwynn and how a batting crown was secondary to the 200 hits. But Clark wasn't buying any of that talk. "Tony's a man with a lot of pride," said Clark, who wouldn't speak freely of his race with Gwynn until after the division was clinched. "Deep down inside, he wants this batting title just as much as I want it. He's just like me, always striving for perfection, striving to be better." The third game of the series and 162nd of the season would thus go down as the Strive Bowl.

Craig was considering batting Clark leadoff to give him as many at-bats as possible, but Clark wanted no part of that and remained the third hitter in the regular season finale. In front of a crowd whose primary interest was to see Gwynn outduel Clark, Gwynn proved to be the master once again. Clark managed only one hit in four tries, while Gwynn singled in the first, fifth and eighth innings, although his fifth-inning single didn't lack for controversy. Gwynn chopped a high bouncer over the mound, and Chris Speier at short made a nice short-hop stab and fired quickly to Clark at first. Umpire Ed Montague began to raise his fist to call Gwynn out, but he quickly changed his arm movements to signal safe. The Giants argued the call. Even bench coach Bob Lillis, usually mild-mannered, showed emotion, and he was rewarded with only his third career ejection. This batting race stuff was serious. Afterward, Clark wasn't disputing the call, but down the hall Gwynn was reporting that Clark had told him, "If it had meant something in the regular season, I'd have to argue." All that was at stake was individual honor, with Gwynn prevailing, .336 to .333.

When Gwynn singled for the third time to emerge as the league's best hitter for the fourth time in six years, Clark removed the glove from his right hand and offered a handshake. The two best hitters in the league stood on the bag for a moment, the crowd standing and cheering.

Gwynn tipped his cap. Clark remained still.

For Tony and Kirby, this was the final day. Will, like Carney, would play again.

Dino Vournas

The Giants open spring picked to finish fourth in the National League West.

Dino Vournas

The A's, stretching before a workout, battle the no-repeat syndrome.

2

Dino Vournas

Kevin Mitchell has tremendous spring.

Dino Vournas

Roger Craig talking up his Giants.

Dino Vournas

Scott Garrelts' problems in relief prompt his "demotion" to the starting rotation.

Dino Vournas

Mark McGwire acknowledges fans on way to A's spring training locker room.

Dino Vournas

Writers seek Canseco's story.

Dino Vournas

Mike Moore, Storm Davis team up.

Martin Klimek
Walt Weiss homers twice in 2nd game.

Frankie Frost
Tony La Russa greets Jim Lefebvre.

Robert Tong

Life isn't easy for Dave Parker in April.

Matt Williams never finds April swing.

Robert Tong

Scott Henry
Mike LaCoss has troubles in relief.

Martin Klimek
Will Clark hits .375 in April.

Scott Henry

Kevin Mitchell makes a smooth transition from third base to left field.

Scott Henry

Mitchell has 15 homers through May.

Martin Klimek

Times aren't always easy for Mitch.

Canseco is coming off a 40-40 year.

He's better suited on the field than off.

Jose Canseco spends first half of season on disabled list with bad left wrist.

Robert Tong

Rickey Henderson proves to be an excellent addition to the A's in June.

Dino Vournas
Luis Polonia is dealt to New York.

Martin Klimek
Rickey's first return to the Coliseum.

Dino Vournas

Tracy Jones never hits with Giants.

Scott Henry

Pat Sheridan doesn't hit much, either.

Scott Anger

The June acquisition of closer Steve Bedrosian solidifies Giants' bullpen.

Martin Klimek

Martin Klimek

Rick Reuschel is bombed as All-Star.　Will Clark is baseball's top vote-getter.

Robert Tong

Kevin Mitchell has 31 home runs at the All-Star break and starts for the NL.

Robert Tong
Dave Stewart is easy choice to start on mound for American League All-Stars.

Scott Henry
Mike Moore pitches perfect inning.

Scott Henry
Mark McGwire hits 8th for All-Stars.

Dino Vournas
Terry Steinbach, '88 MVP, returns.

Marian Little Utley
Dave Dravecky acknowledges cheers after successful August 10 comeback.

Marian Little Utley
Dravecky dramatically beats Reds 4-3.

Frankie Frost
After breaking his arm in Montreal.

Scott Henry
Even after disheartening injury, Dravecky fully intends to resume his career.

Scott Henry

Mike Gallego fills in for injured Walter Weiss and is dubbed the A's MVP.

Robert Tong   Dino Vournas

Jose Canseco returns after surgery.   Dennis Eckersley is "Mr. August."

Scott Henry

Rick Reuschel pulls groin in August.

Marian Little Utley

Kelly Downs is on DL most of season.

Scott Henry

Atlee Hammaker, one of many wounded Giants pitchers, holds his sore arm.

Martin Klimek

Carney Lansford loses American League batting race on season's final day.

Robert Tong

Bob Welch still shows his determination during his trying personal times.

Dino Vournas
Chris Speier finally calls it quits.

Martin Klimek
Bob Brenly returns for final month.

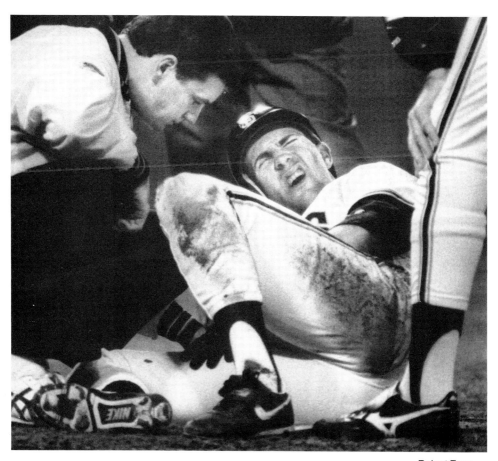

Robert Tong
Will Clark collides with Dodgers catcher Mike Scioscia in middle of batting race.

Scott Henry

On eve of NL playoffs, status of Don Robinson and other Giants is uncertain.

Scott Henry

Will Clark goes 4-for-4 with grand slam and six RBIs to blast Cubs in opener.

Scott Henry

Matt Williams, hitting the dirt, enjoys superb defensive series at third base.

Martin Klimek

Will Clark and Kevin Mitchell embrace after five-game playoff win over Cubs.

Robert Tong
Tony La Russa meets Toronto manager Cito Gaston before AL playoff opener.

Robert Tong
Rickey Henderson steals the show by breaking Lou Brock's playoff record.

Robert Tong
Fan grabs Canseco's long home run.

Scott Henry
George Bell and Jays lose in five.

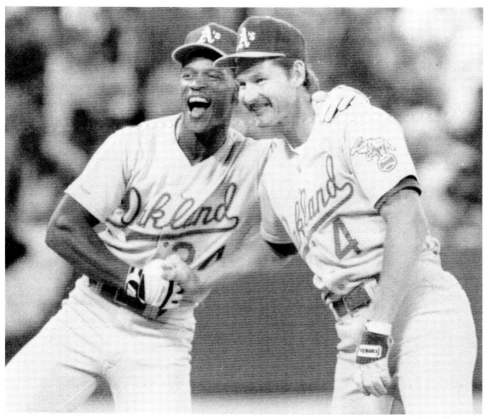

Scott Henry
Rickey and Carney Lansford savor the moment of beating Jays in five games.

Scott Henry

Mark McGwire collects three singles, one on a broken bat, in Game One.

Robert Tong

Terry Steinbach scores on catcher Terry Kennedy's error in second inning.

H. Darr Beiser
Will Clark gets two of Giants' four hits.

Martin Klimek
Oakland fans emulate Bash Brothers.

Martin Klimek
Roger Craig gathers with his infield and makes another pitching change.

Scott Henry

Dave Dravecky grants autograph requests before Game Two at the Coliseum.

Scott Henry

Candy Maldonado: 0-for-7, two K's.

Scott Henry

Terry Steinbach bashes Giants.

Scott Henry

Walter Weiss pivots and skies over sliding Terry Kennedy in the third inning.

Martin Klimek

Mike Moore's forkball is virtually impossible to hit in Oakland's 5-1 victory.

Robert Tong
Fans follow reports of Oct. 17 quake.

Dino Vournas
A's wait for news from TV and radio.

Robert Tong
Jose Canseco comforts wife, Esther.

Scott Henry
Terry and Mary Steinbach leave field.

Candlestick fans' moment of silence before rescheduled Game Three Oct. 27.

H. Darr Beiser
Dave Henderson's home-run trot.

Scott Henry
Terry Kennedy slows Jose Canseco.

Scott Henry
Kevin Mitchell slides across the plate to score a Giants run in Game Three.

Robert Tong

Rickey Henderson continues bothering Giants pitchers in A's 13-7 victory.

Martin Klimek

Henderson easily steals third base after his double in the third inning.

Scott Henry

Brett Butler shows his frustration after being gunned down trying to steal.

Martin Klimek
Candy Maldonado's last Giants game.

Scott Henry
Steve Bedrosian in the final inning.

Scott Henry

Dennis Eckersley punches the air after registering final out of '89 season.

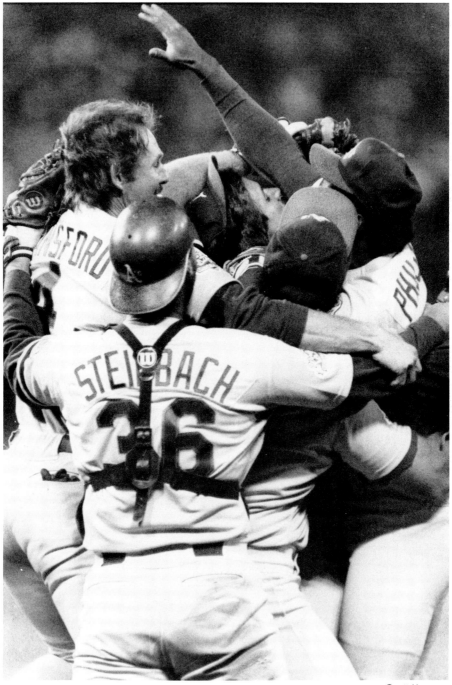

Scott Henry
A's circle around Dennis Eckersley to celebrate their world championship.

THE PLAYOFFS

How the A's and Giants won the pennant

Long before the A's and Giants clinched their respective divisions, talk in Northern California focused on a possible Bay Area World Series. But even with the contenders narrowed down to four teams, it was unwise to look that far ahead. Even as fans argued the pros and cons of having the Bay Area hog baseball's primo party, the A's and Giants were preparing for East-versus-West wars in the playoffs.

The only teams on the planet that could dash hopes for a Bay Area World Series were the Chicago Cubs and Toronto Blue Jays, who were starved for an appearance in the World Series. Toronto, Oakland's opponent in the American League playoffs, had never advanced to the finals in its 13-year existence. The Cubs had been in the World Series 10 times since the series' inception in 1903. Their last appearance was in 1945. They'd won only twice, the last time in 1908.

The '89 World Series entries would soon be decided by a pair of best-of-seven playoffs, but the chances weren't necessarily good that both Bay Area teams would meet for the first time in the grand finale. Mathematically, considering the possible combinations, it was a one-in-four chance. Historically, considering the 1971 playoffs, it was a one-in-none chance. The '71 season marked the first time the A's and Giants simultaneously won their divisions. Then, too, talk of a Bay Area World Series ran high. The '71 Giants were a blend of aging stars (Willie Mays, Juan Marichal) and promising youth (Bobby Bonds, Chris Speier) who captured the franchise's first National League West championship under manager Charlie Fox by outlasting the Dodgers on the final day of the season. In Oakland, the beginning of a dynasty got under way when manager Dick Williams guided a bunch of newcomers (Joe Rudi, Reggie Jackson, Sal Bando, Vida Blue) to their first of five straight American League West flags.

But the dream of a Bay Area World Series was ruined when the Giants and A's ran into playoff road blocks in the forms of the Pittsburgh Pirates and Baltimore Orioles. Bob Robertson homered four times to lead Pittsburgh to a 3-1 series rout of the Giants, and pitching-heavy Baltimore swept the A's in three games. Seven games later, Roberto Clemente's Pirates were champions of the world.

Although the A's lived up to their promise by playing in (and winning) the next three World Series, the Giants regressed after 1971, struggling just to break .500. Over those next three seasons, San Francisco finished 26½ games, 11 games and 30 games out of first place, respectively. It wasn't until 1989 that both the Giants and A's were able to take another shot at fulfilling the dream that had begun 18 years earlier.

The '89 A's post-season roster and post-season goal had long been set. Oakland was in the exact spot it had been one year earlier, only this time they had Rickey Henderson and Mike Moore on the payroll. The A's hadn't needed those guys when they cruised through the '88 playoffs in four straight over Boston, but they sure could have used them against the Dodgers in the World Series when Oakland managed only one victory in five games. In '89, their mission was simple, and anything less than winning in the playoffs and World Series would be disappointing.

The A's figured their chances'were much better in '89. They had post-season experience, they had Rickey, and Rickey wanted it all. For 10 years, Henderson had been baseball's premier leadoff hitter, but he'd never had the opportunity to test his expertise in the World Series. Only once had he been as far as the playoffs, and that was with the '81 Oakland team during the strike-shortened season. They beat the Royals in the divisional playoffs but were swept by the Yankees in the American League Championship Series. Henderson and the A's eventually parted company, and Rickey joined forces in 1984 with the then-powerful Yankees. He nevertheless found himself sitting at home in the Bay Area in front of his big-screen TV during the playoffs, munching out with Lloyd Moseby, the Toronto outfielder who'd been his buddy since childhood. As far as the post-season went, Moseby's career strangely paralleled Henderson's. He'd also made the post-season just once, in 1985, when his Blue Jays outlasted Henderson's Yankees by two games in a furious pennant race.

Since rejoining the A's in June 1989, Henderson not only kept Oakland afloat but added new dimensions to a versatile offensive attack. Come the playoffs, however, there was no need to keep the A's afloat. They'd won 11 of their final 14 games in the regular season. All that was required of Henderson now was to play well enough to allow Oakland to beat Toronto four times.

"I don't think any player can say he's done what he's wanted to in baseball until he can say he's at least played in the World Series," Henderson said. "I've done a lot, I know, but I haven't got a World Series ring, not even the chance to play for one. The playoffs mean a lot to everybody in this clubhouse, but I doubt if they mean more to anyone than they do to me."

Moseby begged to differ. Henderson, he said, wasn't the only player in the playoffs who hadn't been to the show of shows. "Rickey and I have talked about this for as long as we've been in baseball," Moseby said. "Every year, it seems we're at home eating popcorn and watching the World Series. Now at least we know one of us won't be watching. The question is, which one? I'll be very happy to buy the popcorn this year — for him."

Toronto certainly wasn't convinced that the A's were vastly

improved with the addition of Henderson. Henderson's first full series for the '89 A's came against the Blue Jays in Oakland. The Jays watched Henderson go 7-for-16 with five walks, three steals and six runs scored. It had been a stunning debut, but the best the A's could do was split the four-game series with the Jays. And immediately after the All-Star break, the A's played in Toronto's SkyDome for the first time and dropped two of four games. Both of those series fueled the Jays' hopes that he could be contained in the post-season. "It's always a mistake to divulge too much of your strategy before a big series," said Dave Stieb, the Toronto pitcher who was scheduled to start Game One of the playoffs."But this much I will say, and it's the most obvious thing: Rickey Henderson. You want to beat Oakland? You've got to keep him off the base paths." It was simple and sound advice but tough to follow, even for the champions of the American League East.

Of all of the teams in baseball's Final Four, none had a tougher road to the playoffs than the Blue Jays. They were buried deep in the division on May 15 when Jimy Williams was fired as manager and replaced by soft-spoken, unassuming hitting coach Cito Gaston. Gaston, close to Jays moody slugger George Bell and a great favorite of the players in general, took a club that was a dozen games under .500 and lit a fire that smoked out the rest of the competition in the East. Under Gaston, the Jays went 77-49 — the best record in baseball from May 15 on. Still, the Jays had to survive a harrowing series against second-place Baltimore on the final weekend of the regular season in the SkyDome to win the East title. The Orioles, 1989's miracle team after having lost 21 straight to open the '88 season, came into the series just one game behind the Jays. Toronto had moved into first place on the first day of September, but the Orioles never fell more than 2½ games off the pace. The lead had stood at one game for a tense, pressure-packed week before the final showdown. The Jays clinched at least a tie for the title when Moseby ended a long streak of frustration with a game-winning 11th-inning single to score pinch-runner Nelson Liriano for a 2-1 victory in the first game. And 24 hours later, the Jays became the East champs when Frank Wills pitched four sharp innings of one-hit relief and the offense scraped together three runs in the bottom of the eighth to claw from behind for a 4-3 victory.

Oakland, on the other hand, had the better part of a week to prepare, giving manager Tony La Russa the opportunity to set up his pitching rotation, rest his regulars and study the reports compiled by advance scouts Ron Schueler and Jeff Scott. The A's needed the time, because the team they were preparing to face was not quite the one they'd seen during the regular season. On August 1, still looking for a final piece to the puzzle, the then-third-place Jays traded pitcher Jeff Musselman to the Mets for Mookie Wilson, who'd been floundering as his heavily favored team crumbled in the National League East. Wilson struggled for the first week in his new environment, then caught fire. He averaged .462 during a 14-game hitting streak that lasted the second half of August. While starting in each of the outfield positions, Wilson became the firebrand who led the Jays. Outfielder-designated hitter George Bell heaped much of the credit for the Jays' overtaking Baltimore on Wilson, saying, "He came over and showed us what you had to do to win." Wilson was no Rickey Henderson, but he brought many of the same qualities to his new team. While batting either first or second, he stole 12 bases in 13 attempts, hit .298 and scored 32 runs in 54 games.

"There's no secret that Wilson has made them a better club," said Dave Stewart, Oakland's Game One starting pitcher. "And it's no secret that if we're going to beat them, we've got to keep Lloyd Moseby and Mookie Wilson off the bases."

The Giants were tougher to figure than the A's. They had won the West in '87, but that club's roster was a far cry from the '89 division-winner's. In two short years, Al Rosen had given his club a new identity, replacing a power-laden team with a more well-rounded group, which included a type of player the Giants desperately lacked in '87: a leadoff hitter. In the playoffs two seasons earlier against the Cardinals, the Giants held a 3-2 lead in the best-of-seven series only to drop the final two games in St. Louis. The reason was simple. The Giants had failed to score in the final 22 innings of the series. They had the hitters, but not enough people on base for those hitters to drive in. The Giants tried Robby Thompson, Eddie Milner and Mike Aldrete in the leadoff spot during the '87 playoffs, but the number one hitters were a combined 1-for-23. During the '87 season, manager Roger Craig had tried several players in the top spot, even Will Clark, but he couldn't settle on anyone. So Rosen went out and signed free agent Brett Butler, and two years later the Giants were back in the playoffs.

Butler scored 100 runs in each of his first two seasons as a

Giant. He also played solid defense in center field, another Giants weak spot in '87. In '88, he collected 43 stolen bases and 20 bunt singles. In '89, he had 31 stolen bases and 23 bunt singles. With the addition of another speedster, Donell Nixon, the Giants sported one of the quickest one-two punches in the game. Two years after the Silence in St. Louis, Craig was offering this warning: "It'll be hard to shut us out like that now."

Although the Giants had added a legitimate leadoff hitter in Butler — and a legitimate bullpen closer in Steve Bedrosian — they had lost a significant amount of punch. The '87 team set a San Francisco record with 205 home runs. And though the total might have been inflated by juiced-up baseballs, the lineup clearly packed more punch man-for-man than the '89 bunch. The '89 lineup produced 141 home runs, but exactly one-third were supplied by one person, the majors' long-ball champion Kevin Mitchell.

While the Giants were winning the 1987 division crown, Jeffrey Leonard hit 19 homers during the regular season, and he knocked four more in the first four playoff games against St. Louis. Leonard became the first player to win Most Valuable Player honors while playing for a losing playoff team. Two years later, Mitchell appeared ready to follow in Hac Man's footsteps. "Mitchell is not a bad replacement," Craig said. "Hac was a leader. He was tough, which was good in the clubhouse." Craig, mulling over his club's dismal right-field situation throughout '89, added, "If I only had him (Leonard) now in right field, or in left and Mitch in right . . ." Indeed, on a team that had changed significantly (of the 26 position players who saw action for the Giants in '87, 17 were gone; of the 20 pitchers, 11 were gone), the outfield had gone through the most dramatic changes. Leonard, Aldrete and Chili Davis were all former Giants, and Candy Maldonado was just as good as gone. Mitchell moved from third base to left field, Butler took over center and Pat Sheridan and Donell Nixon spelled the slumping Maldonado in right.

The catching corps also had a new look, with Terry Kennedy and Kirt Manwaring splitting time, and Bob Brenly and Bob Melvin out of the limelight. The infield was similar, with Will Clark, Robby Thompson and Jose Uribe still manning their positions. The only difference was Matt Williams replacing Mitchell at third base. The pitching staff had remained constant, with the exception of Steve Bedrosian and rookie Jeff Brantley. The lone missing link from the '87 playoffs was Joe Price, who was released in May and signed by the Red Sox.

Another major difference, of course, was the opponent. The Cardinals blew their chance for another showdown with the Giants when they bowed out of the National League East race in September. Manager Don Zimmer's Cubs finished ahead of the Mets by six games and the Cards by seven — 1989's largest winning margin behind Oakland's. And for the Giants, facing the Cubs would be no easy task. It wasn't so much the faces in the other dugout — Andre Dawson, Mark Grace and Mitch Williams. It was facing perhaps the most-loved team in the country. Thanks to cable superstation WGN and pitchman Harry Caray, the Cubs were America's Team. Not only did they have an entire nation of well-wishers supporting them, but the Cubs were due. Boy, were they due.

It had become fashionable to appreciate the Cubs because of their long association with failure. The Cubs hadn't won a World Series in 81 years and were 2-8 lifetime in the Fall Classic — or in Chicago's case, the Classic Fall. The Cubs lost the World Series in '06, '10, '18, '29, '32, '35, '38 and '45. Chicago's only wins had come in 1907 and 1908, and it had been 44 years since the Cubs advanced to the series, although they had come awfully close a couple of times. They blew a 9½-game August lead in 1969 to the Miracle Mets. And they blew a 2-0 lead in the 1984 best-of-five playoffs with the Padres. Now it was 1989, and a new group of Caray's "Cubbies" would take its turn.

This Cubs team was well-rounded, and not just in the form of its manager. There were clutch performers up and down the roster, with a new hero emerging with almost every victory. No other team in baseball produced nine different players with at least 40 RBIs. (The Giants had five, the A's eight.) The Cubs' heroics were especially visible in the second half. In their final 68 games, the Boys of Zimmer won 11 times in their last at-bat. The most memorable win of that genre equaled any comeback the Giants had made. On August 29 at Wrigley Field, the Cubs spotted Houston a 9-0 lead and came back to win 10-9 in 10 innings. Chicago even had a comeback history against the Giants. On July 20, Steve Bedrosian led 3-0 with two outs in the ninth, but the Cubs rebounded to win in the 11th on a double by, of all people, pitcher Les Lancaster.

Orchestrating these late-game heroics was the man who had coached third base for the Giants in '87. Don Zimmer was known as a perennial loser. He was the manager of the '78 Red Sox team that had owned a 14½-game lead in August, only to end in a tie with the Yankees and lose in a one-game playoff featuring Bucky Dent's home run over Fenway Park's fabled left-field wall, the Green Monster. In 10 years as a big-league manager, Zimmer had never won anything, and his 1989 Cubs came out of spring training seemingly destined for 100 losses and the National League East cellar after having finished 24 games out of first place in 1988. Despite his unexpected and against-the-book moves — or perhaps because of them — Zimmer was mysteriously successful and pulled out wins in the most unlikely ways. If the book called for a left-handed pitcher, he would often throw a right-hander. If the book called for a bunt, he'd hit away. With two strikes, Zimmer wouldn't hesitate to put on a squeeze bunt. When the other side least expected it, Zimmer would hit-and-run. And down the stretch, Zimmer played another hunch, going with a four-man pitching rotation that all but exhausted veteran Rick Sutcliffe. But it worked.

But ZimBall, as crazy as it was, prevailed over and over at Wrigley with guys like Steve Wilson, Lloyd McClendon, Rick Wrona and Domingo Ramos. This was a team that supposedly had made a fool of itself the previous winter by trading a .300-hitter, Rafael Palmeiro, to the Rangers. But the trade didn't take long to make Cubs general manager Jim Frey look good. Wild but effective reliever Mitch Williams came over from Texas to re-popularize the tune "Wild Thing" while anchoring a previously beaten-up bullpen with 36 saves.

Now that Zimmer was making his first post-season appearance as a manager, what could be better than a reunion with his longtime buddy, Roger Craig? Zimmer and Craig had been teammates. They had coached together. Craig once hired Zimmer. Zimmer once fired Craig. Hey, these two were made for each other. But now it was manager versus manager, winner versus winner. Never before had these old pals competed in anything so important, and a couple of episodes suggest the pressure might have briefly taken its toll on their friendship.

Zimmer tells a story about a radio interview he heard after that September game in which the Giants overcame an 8-0 deficit to beat the Reds. According to Zimmer's account, Craig said, "I know we're going to win this thing. And not only win (the division), we're going to win the pennant." To which Zim responded, "I thought to myself, if someone asks me about this, I'll say, 'If we do meet, we won't lose a game by forfeit. We will show up.' " When Craig was asked about Zim's reaction, he said, "I must've just meant the division. . . . But what am I going to say? We're going to lose?"

Another touchy subject for Zimmer was pitchouts. Some believe Zimmer learned from Craig — acknowledged as the master at calling pitchouts at the right time — when he served as Craig's third-base coach in '87. Baloney, he says. "Hey, I was doing it 14 years ago."

The two men's relationship survived perhaps its toughest professional test when Zimmer was forced to fire Craig. When Zimmer replaced Preston Gomez as San Diego's manager in 1972, Craig was the Padres' pitching coach, but Zimmer already had promised another old friend, Johnny Podres, that Podres would be his pitching coach at Zimmer's next managerial stop. So it was a case of, "See ya later, Roger." Nevertheless, Craig hired Zimmer to coach third in San Francisco in 1987 and once or twice reminded Zim of that earlier dismissal. "Why the heck did I hire you? You're the SOB who fired me."

Perhaps their closeness was a reason their managing styles were similar. And neither Craig nor Zimmer was about to shelve his gambling instincts just because of the playoffs. As Craig said, "We have no set pattern. The game dictates what we do. We both try to catch the other guy off guard with the hit-and-run and squeeze or whatever. I'm not going to change." Agreed Zimmer: "I ain't gonna act no different."

Entering the playoffs, the Giants' biggest problem was health. They used the disabled list 14 times for nine players during the season. By October, San Francisco had lost the services of Dave Dravecky and Mike Krukow and wasn't too sure about the health of several others, including pitchers Don Robinson, Craig Lefferts, Atlee Hammaker and Kelly Downs and position players Terry Kennedy, Jose Uribe, Kirt Manwaring, Kevin Mitchell and Will Clark. The injured list read like a telephone directory. The day before Game One, Craig was still uncertain about his playoff roster, let alone his starting lineup. During the final practice session on the eve of the playoffs, Craig staged no fewer than four meetings with the media — not to comment on the series, but to update his injury report.

Considering that the Giants clinched the National League

West exactly a week before Game One, they seemed to have enough time to regain their health. But, in fact, the injury list didn't diminish through the week. It grew. While Lefferts (shoulder), Hammaker (knee), Downs (shoulder), Uribe (shoulder) and Manwaring (foot) appeared close to full strength, others were destined to visit the trainer's room. "It's not a good situation," Craig said. "We're trying to bit and piece this thing together and then see who we can throw on the field tomorrow."

The most baffling of injuries was Terry Kennedy's. Originally slated as the Game One starting catcher, Kennedy felt a sharp muscle tightness in his right shoulder two nights before the opener, and it only worsened on the workout day. Team doctor Will Straw called the injury a "mystery" and administered a cortisone shot into Kennedy's his rear end. The Giants were considering omitting Kennedy from the playoffs; no use keeping a catcher with a bum shoulder — and now a bum bum. But something funny happened on the way to the midnight deadline for submitting rosters. Kennedy healed. "Maybe the deadline mentally made me better," he said.

Another strange case was Don Robinson's. The starter had pitched just once since mid-September and used the workout session to decide whether his right knee could hold up for the playoffs. After 70 pitches, Robinson was deemed fit to start Game Three by both himself and Craig. But later in the day, Craig backtracked and threatened to start Mike LaCoss.

Then there were the injuries to Kevin Mitchell and Will Clark. Clark's sore shinbone was little more that a side show, given the scope of the Giants' injuries. Typically, Mitchell's injury emerged as one of the peculiar ones. He complained about his sore right elbow and insisted he hadn't been able to fully extend his arm since the season-ending Padres series, yet he'd never said word in the San Diego series.

While the Giants were picking the wrong time to experience one of their patented injury binges, the Cubs were relatively healthy. They knew their exact roster. Their exact lineup. Even their exact game plan. The Cubbies were eager to start the playoffs. As Jim Frey said after clinching, "I wish we could play in 20 minutes." The Giants would have preferred 20 days.

But as the midnight deadline — as well as his dinner reservations — were nearing, Craig was forced to make decisions. Craig chose to keep just nine pitchers, retaining Robinson and dumping

Bob Knepper, who had been hit hard down the stretch. Although he had planned to start Pat Sheridan in right field, Craig kept the still slumping Candy Maldonado.

Earlier, Craig had told a couple of popular old-timers that they wouldn't be needed in the post-season, but Bob Brenly and Chris Speier made the trip to Chicago anyway. The Brenly news (he was hitting .182) wasn't a surprise because Bill Bathe figured to get the job as the third catcher and right-handed pinch hitter. But the Speier news brought an emotional response or two from Giants fans, new and old. He was their local hero. Literally. He was born and raised in Alameda, just across the Bay Bridge from San Francisco. In addition, Speier was the only Giant who had played for all three of the division-winning teams, and he had already indicated that the '89 season would be his last. His final goal was to play in the World Series, but the numbers game, not to mention a back injury that had sidelined him much of the year, ended his season prematurely.

Aside from a World Series appearance, the only thing missing for Speier was a proper sendoff, a going-away party, a retirement bash. Speier informed the Giants in spring training that he would retire at the end of the season, but the club never set aside any sort of Chris Speier Day to honor the longtime infielder. The only plan was for Speier to throw out the first pitch before Game Five, but the seven-game playoff format didn't even guarantee a fifth game. Speier found himself playing his career finale on the last day of the regular season in San Diego, with many good memories but little fanfare. The same weekend in which Speier finished his 19-year career in peace, the Padres were honoring their own popular infielder, Tim Flannery, who also was retiring. During the so-called "Flan Appreciation Night," Flannery was removed from the game after four innings so he could receive a standing ovation from the sellout crowd. The next night, the Padres held a 20-minute pregame ceremony for Flannery to treat him to several presents, including a pair of $25,000 checks for his kids' college educations. They even gave out commemorative pins for the occasion.

Speier simply sat in the visitors' dugout and watched, knowing his final home game a week earlier hadn't been quite like Flannery's. Speier entered in the ninth inning of a 10-2 Candlestick Park victory — as a defensive replacement. Of course, the Giants were still in a pennant race at the time and weren't about to get all sentimental about a player's retirement. But for many fans, Speier wasn't just another player. Back in '71, the shortstop emerged after only one year in the minors and was a key ingredient in the Giants' first division-winning season. To gauge the scope of Speier's career, consider that his rookie year was Willie Mays' last full season in San Francisco. Sixteen years later, after Speier had made the rounds with four other clubs, he returned to the Giants in 1987 and played for another division-winner. And another two years later saw Speier score the only San Francisco hat trick. But this time, Speier was beaten out for a playoff roster spot by a kid named Greg Litton.

The Giants and A's both finished their regular seasons on October 1. The American League Championship Series was scheduled to open first, with Game One on October 3 in Oakland. The A's, who had closed their season in Oakland, awaited Toronto's arrival. The Giants got an extra day of rest before the National League Championship Series, which was to start October 4 in Chicago. The Giants flew from San Diego (the site of their season finale) to San Francisco and finally to Chicago.

In the hiatus before the playoffs, there was time to read the mail. The A's clubhouse was stuffed with congratulatory telegrams from fans such as Mick Jagger, California Governor George Deukmejian and Tigers manager Sparky Anderson. Roger Craig received telegrams from several well-wishers, including A's general manager Sandy Alderson, National League President Bill White, Sparky Anderson, Cubs general manager Jim Frey and the Grateful Dead. That last telegram was a puzzler to Craig. "I didn't know who they were," he said. "I thought they were a funeral home." Enough of the pre-game fun. Let's play ball.

On a pleasant evening at the Coliseum, the A's Dave Stewart was matched with Toronto's Dave Stieb in the first post-season clash of '89. By the third inning, Toronto manager Cito Gaston was already trying to cross up the A's infield by calling for a hit-and-run, and Tony Fernandez delivered perfectly, slapping a single through the area vacated by A's shortstop Mike Gallego. With runners on the corners, catcher Ernie Whitt, who had been with the Blue Jays since the club's inception in 1977, delivered a sacrifice fly. Fernandez then stole second base and number nine hitter Nelson Liriano delivered an RBI single. It wasn't a great start for Stewart, but it was somewhat typical considering his legendary troubles in the opening innings.

Dave Henderson led off the bottom of the second by driving Stieb's second pitch into the left-field stands. It wasn't an unfamiliar scene for Henderson, who had homered off Stieb on July 14, the last time he'd seen him. It was his fifth post-season homer since 1986, and his teammates immediately dubbed Henderson "The New Mr. October." But when Whitt homered off Stewart to open the Blue Jays' fourth, Oakland was staring at a 3-1 deficit. "That's just the way Stew is," reliever Dennis Eckersley said. "He was down 3-1 early, but you almost never see him give up the hit that will put us out of the game. He just bounces back and keeps us close." Stewart admitted that the game "was a bit of a struggle early. I have three pitches, and none of them was working in the first few innings. But I knew that if I stuck with it, they'd come around." They did. Stewart pitched through the eighth inning, and only two more Blue Jays reached base, both on walks.

Meanwhile, Oakland was putting men on base every inning against Stieb, who was pitching on six days' rest but was struggling. But it wasn't until the fifth inning that Oakland struck big. Carney Lansford singled and stole second, bringing up Dave Parker, who didn't drive in one run in the '88 post-season. His prospects didn't look much better when he fell behind 0-2 to Stieb, but Parker fouled off a couple of pitches and worked the count to 2-2. He then looped a single to left to bring the A's to within one run at 3-2. Mark McGwire tied the game in the sixth with a home run, the surging third baseman's 10th since September 1. Stieb never recovered, and Gaston called on reliever Jim Acker later in the inning. But Acker also had trouble, hitting Rickey Henderson with a pitch to load the bases. Lansford hit a possible double-play ball to shortstop Tony Fernandez, but a charging and determined Henderson caused second baseman Nelson Liriano to jerk his body toward the third-base side of the bag before releasing the relay. The ball went flying up the right-field line and hit the photographers' box in front of the main stands. Two runs scored, and the A's took the lead for good.

Fernandez didn't blame Liriano for running for cover. He blamed Henderson for running wild. "I never thought that wouldn't be a double play," Fernandez said. "I don't know how anybody could get from first base to second base so fast. I even moved in toward the plate before the pitch to get the ball off early.

Rickey just beat it." Clearly, Oakland's 7-3 win belonged to Henderson. "This one is Rickey's," Parker said. "When he decides to turn his game up a notch, there is nobody who can play with him."

Such would be the case 18 hours later, when the A's and Jays closed the Oakland portion of their series with a noon game October 4 that pitted Mike Moore against Toronto right-hander Todd Stottlemyre. Stottlemyre had pitched well for the Jays down the stretch, but Gaston couldn't have been looking at his history books when he made the choice. He had left-hander Mike Flanagan ready, and Flanagan had two of his eight 1989 wins — including his only complete game and only shutout — against Oakland. And in a 12-year career, Flanagan was almost unbeatable in Oakland. "The Coliseum is almost a perfect park for a pitcher to pitch in," Flanagan said. And so it was — for him, at least. He was 9-1 lifetime in Oakland, and his 18 career wins over the A's were his most against any one club. Furthermore, Flanagan was one of the pitchers who gave Rickey Henderson the most trouble as a base stealer. Flanagan's tricky move is especially tough to decipher. For his part, Stottlemyre had a five-game winning streak in August and September. He had given up more than two runs just once in his previous five starts, including a five-inning, no-decision stint in the Jays' crucial September 29 11-inning win over Baltimore. But he'd gone the entire year without seeing Oakland, a flaw that would prove to be decisive.

Toronto again led first when the top of its batting order singed Moore for a run in the third. But it wasn't time for Lloyd Moseby to pay for the popcorn quite yet. Rickey Henderson, who had singled earlier, worked Stottlemyre to a full count to open the fourth, and then earned a walk. Henderson then proceeded to work Stottlemyre over. He stole second base with Carney Lansford batting, then stole third on a 1-2 pitch. By this time, knowing that Stottlemyre was rattled, Lansford saw his opportunity and grabbed it, knocking a single to tie the game. A grounder by number three hitter Dave Parker (Jose Canseco was out with a migraine headache and didn't start) moved Lansford up a base. Mark McGwire drove home.

Stottlemyre hung around until the sixth, when Parker greeted him with a solo homer into right-center. Parker had played for the '79 "We Are Family" Pirates when they rallied from a 3-1 deficit to beat Baltimore in the World Series, but he had never hit a post-season home run until this one. When McGwire followed with his third straight hit, a searing single off the left-field wall, Jim Acker again took the mound. And the A's again worked him over, scoring two more runs on Ron Hassey's sacrifice fly and Tony Phillips' single, and Moore was left with a 5-1 lead.

Moore, making his first career post-season start, pitched seven innings, settling down toward the end much as Stewart had done the previous night. Between the fourth and seventh, Moore retired 12 of 13 batters, walking only Liriano with one out in the fifth. The Jays were able to hit only two balls out of the infield, but even Moore had to take a back seat to Rickey Henderson. Everybody had to take a back seat to Henderson. In the seventh inning, he ran the A's into their final run by drawing a walk, stealing second, stealing third and tip-toeing home on a Toronto pickoff attempt. Pitcher David Wells had caught Lansford off first base, and Lansford broke for second on Wells' throw to first baseman Fred McGriff. But McGriff's throw to second drilled Lansford in the back, allowing Henderson to trot home.

For the day, Henderson had two hits, two walks, four steals and two runs scored. His exploits gave the A's a 6-3 victory and a 2-0 lead in the series. "I'd like to think that I started us going with my homer," Parker said. "But nobody does that like Rickey does." But Parker was wrong. In fact, he had started something. He and Henderson both. Together, they had broken the Blue Jays' concentration. Parker had done his patented around-the-world-tour trot after his homer, the same trot that had annoyed National League pitchers for 15 years. That was hard enough for the Blue Jays to swallow, but it got harder still. In the seventh, Henderson stole second base without even drawing a throw. Seeing that, he slowed to a crawl before finally, deliberately, tapping the bag lightly. Jays third baseman Kelly Gruber was the most incensed of the Jays at such cavalier play, saying, "If I was the pitcher, I'd have some guys decked. I mean Parker. I mean Henderson. And I don't care if they know it."

Two American League games concluded before the first pitch was thrown in Game One of the National League playoffs. The Cubs-Giants opener in Candlestick Park, played on the evening of October 4, was to pit 19-game-winner Greg Maddux against Scott Garrelts, the once disturbing reliever who was now the Giants' most durable starter. In 1988, Garrelts' big stat was blown saves; he was among the league leaders. In '89, he led the league in two very different departments: ERA and winning percentage. His 14-5 record and 2.28 ERA made this the best season of his career. By September, thanks to an eight-game winning streak, he had surpassed Rick Reuschel as the staff ace, and the starting nod for the playoff opener was his reward. Now it was Wrigley Field. The grass. The ivy. The millions watching on TV. The pressure. Uh-oh. The pressure. For all his 1989 success, Garrelts hadn't been known as a guy who could handle pressure well. The ninth inning of a 2-1 game was pressure. By comparison, a 0-0 game in the first inning was no pressure, and the latter is what Garrelts encountered all year. But in the playoffs, every inning is more important than any ninth inning he might have entered in the past. And if he didn't win Game One, the Giants were in trouble. Reuschel would go Game Two, but Reuschel was only 5-5 since the All-Star break. Don Robinson would go Game Three, but Robinson was pitching on a tender knee. Mike LaCoss would go Game Four, but LaCoss had a 5.68 ERA and 0-1 record against the Cubs. The pressure was on Garrelts.

As it turned out, Garrelts' teammates eased the pressure. He never had to pitch in a 0-0 game. By the time he took the mound, the Giants were leading 3-0. Will Clark doubled home one run and Matt Williams, who later made several tremendous plays at third base, doubled home two more. After failing to score in their final 22 innings in the '87 playoffs, the Giants struck on their first try of '89. But in just moments, Garrelts was again feeling the pressure. Chicago's Mark Grace slugged a two-run homer in the first inning to make the score 3-2. Garrelts, despite allowing only one more run through his seven innings, would soon be an overlooked man. For Game One of the playoffs was about to be taken over by Clark.

Viewers soon realized why they called Will "The Thrill" or "The Natural" or any other god-like nickname. Clark, who hit just .271 against the Cubs during the season but .304 at Wrigley, finished the game a remarkable 4-for-4 with four runs and a playoff-record six RBIs in an 11-3 whipping. He delivered a run-scoring double in the first, a solo homer in the third, a grand slam in the fourth, a single to center in the sixth and drew a walk in the eighth that preceded Kevin Mitchell's home run. "This is the game you always dream about as a kid," Clark said. "You don't want a night like tonight to end." And to think, Clark had been concerned about his bruised right shinbone, the shinbone that slowed him in his final six games when he went just 6-for-24 and lost the batting title to Tony Gwynn. But . . . "What he wanted to do was take it out on the Cubs," Brett Butler said.

Clark's grand slam was obviously the game's biggest blow, making a 4-3 lead 8-3. Even as Clark turned on a Greg Maddux first-pitch fastball, Cubs fans were wondering why Maddux was still in the game. Don Zimmer, in what proved to be the first of many moves that backfired, put the odds in Clark's favor with a mismanaged fourth inning. With one away and runners on second and third, Zimmer chose to intentionally walk Butler, loading the bases. Unless Robby Thompson hit into a double play, the move ensured Clark of a plate appearance in the inning. Thompson, who had hit into just six double plays in 547 at-bats (1.09 percent), popped up for the second out. That brought up Clark with the bases still loaded, and most everyone expected Zimmer to replace the right-handed Maddux with the left-handed Paul Assenmacher. But no go. Maddux's first pitch to Clark was a fastball knee-high. Booom! Sheffield Avenue. "It didn't turn out too good," Zimmer later acknowledged. The Giants weren't about to publicly second-guess Zimmer, but that's OK. There were plenty of other people — the fans and the media — who did the second-guessing for them.

The Cubs players weren't in a second-guessing mood, either. Their mood was one of disgust. They didn't necessarily appreciate the way Clark and the Giants celebrated after each of the 11 runs, especially the home runs. The Giants, in their answer to Oakland's forearm bash, congratulated each other by throwing both hands to the sky, grasping another teammate's set of hands and constructing a complete circle top to bottom. It's the windmill. Or the air traffic controller. Or, as Cubs catcher Rick Wrona says, "the circus high-five." In fact, Wrona said, he became ill watching all those wild gestures at the plate. "It was disgusting to watch those guys cross home plate, high-fiving and everything. (Clark) is doing these circus high-fives and pointing to someone in the crowd. I don't know, his wife or something. It just gave me a stomach ache." Clark might have been performing the "circus high-fives," but he wasn't pointing to his wife. Clark was a bachelor. He had been waving to his father, Bill, sitting 15 rows behind the plate. Will's mother, Letty, home in New Orleans with Will's kid brother, was celebrating her birthday that day. "This is the first part of the present,"

Will promised. And after all he had just done, it was difficult not to believe him.

It was clear that Clark and his teammates were subscribing to a different philosophy than in '87. During the '87 playoffs, Chili Davis referred to St. Louis as a "cow town," and Jeffrey Leonard rubbed it in with his one-flap-down home-run trots. When the Giants went back to St. Louis for the final two games, they were welcomed by a loud, rowdy crowd at Busch Stadium. And lost both games. So before the '89 playoffs, Roger Craig held a team meeting to warn his players to keep such emotions to themselves. "I was hoping we could stand up to (Davis' and Leonard's) words and win, but we didn't score another run," Craig said. "I think a lot of guys learned a lesson. I talked to them a couple of weeks ago and said, 'When we do win this (division), let's be careful what we say. If you've got something to say, say something nice.' I'm not saying that's what beat us in '87. But a lot of people think that's what beat us."

Craig cited the American League playoffs as a potential motivational tool, suggesting Rickey Henderson's and Dave Parker's irritating ways could come back to haunt the A's. "Oakland is playing good, but Toronto could go up there (to the SkyDome) and win two or three," Craig said. "You've got to be careful with what you say. You could wake people up and make them try harder." Asked about Rick Wrona's comment, Clark said, "I don't care. My job is to beat him. My job is not to please him. End of discussion."

With at least a split in the two games at Wrigley guaranteed, it was Rick Reuschel's turn to start Game Two for the Giants on October 5. Reuschel was 12-3 at the All-Star break but 5-5 afterward, including two terrible games in September. Ever since the Bo Jackson All-Stars ate him up in July, Reuschel hadn't shown the same Big Daddy consistency. Perhaps he had been shaken by that All-Star Game, when Jackson and Wade Boggs blasted that off-speed stuff into Anaheim oblivion. But to Reuschel's credit, none of his second-half games was as bad as his one-inning stint in the All-Star Game. That is, until Game Two of the playoffs. Reuschel threw just 16 pitches in the All-Star Game. And he threw just 18 at the Cubs, who used a six-run first inning as a springboard to a 9-5 victory that evened the series at a win apiece.

Reuschel always had had trouble in the post-season. Dating back to the '87 playoffs with the Giants and '81 World Series with the Yankees, Reuschel had fashioned a 0-3 playoff record and 7.08 ERA. Against the Cubs, Reuschel allowed five hits — all crushed — through seven batters to earn the quickest post-season hook since Los Angeles' Doug Rau lasted two-thirds of an inning in the '74 World Series.

A string of five Giants pitchers were blitzed by the Cubs. Carrying out most of the blitzing was Mark Grace, who closed in on Clark in the race for the Most Valuable Player award. Grace produced his second straight 3-for-4 game and sported a .750 average to Clark's .625. Both had six RBIs through two games, and Clark had a home run. Although some were calling the playoffs the Will and Mark Show, Grace wanted none of that. "I'd be crazy to think about competing with Will Clark," Grace said. "He was right there for the batting title. He drove in 115 runs. If you look at our stats and compare them over the year, I'd be an idiot to try to outdo Will Clark. It's ludicrous."

If there was a positive to come out of the game for the Giants, it was their continued offense. They supplied three more home runs, including Mitchell's second in two games, putting him on Jeffrey Leonard's '87 playoff pace.

The A's enjoyed the day off on October 5, and Kelly Gruber had a night to think about his earlier comments regarding Dave Parker and Rickey Henderson. On the off-day, Gruber recanted slightly, saying, "To some extent, it's true that you don't recognize it as much on your own team. You seem to notice it more when they are on the other team." Later still, Gruber backed away from predicting an all-out beanball war, saying, "I'm a firm believer that you settle it then and there. Settle it and let bygones be bygones. It's over, now." Through it all, Henderson refused to let Gruber get under his skin. "This is fun," Henderson said. "I'm not going to stop having fun." Parker recalled the time he had been warned by then-Commissioner Peter Ueberroth after spouting off in a similar manner. "What I want to know is, where is the call from the commissioner? Where is the call from the president of the league? He can't be making those kinds of statements."

Dennis Eckersley, for one, could understand Gruber's point of view, even if he did not subscribe to it. As early as 1980, Eckersley, who because of a big windup was particularly susceptible to Henderson's speed on the basepaths, was calling Henderson "the biggest hot dog in baseball." Henderson had answered in kind, and the two spent most of the decade taking particular delight in beating each other. But when the June 21 trade made them teammates, it was time for Eckersley to do some re-evaluating. By the time of Gruber's outburst, Eckersley and Henderson had a good working relationship. "Rickey is a player who likes his own style of play," Eckersley said. "He's emotional, especially in a series like this. He may seem like he gets a little too high. But that's his style of play."

Other than following up Gruber's complaints, the major story of the October 5 off-day was whether the SkyDome, hosting its first playoffs, would be shown to a dual-national television audience with its roof open or closed. The Jays were 34-20 when calling the Dome home, winning 20 of their last 26. And with the roof closed, Toronto was a perfect 10-0. The days in Toronto immediately preceding Game Three were sunny and pleasant, and the nights went from cool to downright cold. Playing with the roof open would have been possible, but American League President Bobby Brown decreed that the dome would remain closed for the duration, which left the Blue Jays, looking for any edge they could get, elated.

That elation carried over into Game Three on October 6. Oakland, which had rallied from deficits in winning twice in Oakland, made the mistake of jumping out in front in this one. Rickey Henderson, as usual, led the charge. He drew a walk from lefty Jimmy Key, who then walked Carney Lansford. Two long flies sent Henderson to third and home. Henderson's onslaught continued in the third inning when he doubled, stole third and scored on Lansford's single. In the fourth, the other guy on Kelly Gruber's hit parade, Dave Parker, did it again, crashing a solo homer to deep right-center.

But if another long, slow Parker trot seemed to be telling the Blue Jays the party was over, they weren't turning out the lights. Oakland starter Storm Davis had retired the first nine men he'd faced and had made it look easy. But Davis, now owning a 3-0 lead, suddenly became a different pitcher. He couldn't get anyone out in the fourth. A walk and two singles were followed by a sacrifice fly. Tony Fernandez cracked a double that Jose Canseco misplayed in right field, pushing home two runs to tie the game. Ernie Whitt followed with a soft looper in front of on-racing Dave Henderson in center to give the Jays the lead. Oakland got just four hits off Key and relievers Jim Acker and Tom Henke in the 5⅓ innings that followed Parker's homer. And Davis left the game in the seventh as the Jays scored three more runs to roll to a 7-3 win in a game they could not afford to lose.

Now the pressure had shifted ever so slightly back toward Oakland. The A's had come roaring into the SkyDome, confident if not cocky. And when they were holding a 3-0 lead one-third of the way through the game and a 19-game winner on the mound, it would figure that the A's would have Game Three — and the play-offs — in the bag. "Not true, not true at all," Terry Steinbach said. "If we had that lead in the seventh or eighth innings, you might be able to say that. But there was too much of the game left to play. Just like there's too much of the series left to play." Unfortunately for the A's, not only had they lost the game, but they lost the services of the league's number two hitter when Lansford, who'd gone 5-for-11 to that point, left with a hamstring injury.

Lansford was on the bench for Game Four the morning of October 7, but what the Blue Jays really needed was to find a way to put Rickey Henderson on the bench. Rickey came up in the third inning of a scoreless game, picked out a 2-1 pitch from Mike Flanagan and launched a 430-foot homer to dead center that gave Oakland a 2-0 lead, silencing a boisterous SkyDome crowd. Two batters later, Jose Canseco hit a ball that changed time zones before it landed. Canseco's blast carried where none other had gone before — five rows deep into the fifth deck of the left-field stands.

The homer was such a monster that the media conducted a talent hunt to find the fan who had caught it. Up to a dozen photographers and writers surrounded a surprised Jake Neely, a 26-year-old part-time classical singer from Toronto. "It was sort of unbelievable," Neely said. "It was just sort of disbelief when it hit my hands."

Disbelief was everywhere after that. "If I die and I'm reborn, I might be able to hit one like that — one," said the awestruck George Bell. "I can't believe he hit it there." The tale of the tape flashed 480 feet, a far cry from reality and another indication that scoreboard measurements sponsored by huge corporations should never be trusted. "Four-eighty? They've got to be kidding," Terry Steinbach said. "That's way over 500 feet." A press box consensus had the ball carrying at least 520 feet, but even conceding it to be 480, it was a blast of gut-wrenching majesty. "Four-eighty? Let me tell you about 480," Fred McGriff said. "I can't even see 480 feet." For his part, Canseco put on his best ho-hum stance, saying he hit the ball well, "but I could have hit it better. That wasn't my best swing." Maybe not, but it might have been better than anything else any of the participants had ever seen. "In anybody's top 10, that has to be the top one," Dave Henderson said.

As mammoth as Canseco's homer was, it accounted for only one run and didn't put the Blue Jays away. That feat was left for Rickey, of course, when he faced Flanagan in the fifth inning. The Jays had pitched around Henderson whenever possible in the first three games, walking him five times. But all that had done was help set up seven stolen bases, so Cito Gaston decided to change tactics. The order: Don't walk him. Pitch to the guy. See if you can get him out. Flanagan tried. But Rickey hit the two-run homer in the third that put the A's in command. And again in the fifth, Henderson was up with a chance to do some damage. First base was open, but Flanagan had his orders. Henderson saw one strike. He swung at the next and launched a liner that faded toward the left-field corner, prompting two questions: "Would it stay fair?" And, "Would it clear the fence?" The answer to both was yes, and Oakland had a 5-1 lead.

Reliever Rick Honeycutt, shaky throughout the series, gave up three runs in 1⅔ innings before Dennis Eckersley came out of the bullpen to close out the final 1⅔ innings and preserve a 6-5 win. In the first few moments after Eckersley induced Lee Mazzilli to pop out to end the game, Tony La Russa, his gut still churning, took aside Gaston, at that time unsigned for the next season, and said, "Are you sure you want to do this for a living?" Later, La Russa expanded, saying, "This was as tough a game as we've had since I've been here. I'm drained. We're all exhausted. We had to play great to win because the Blue Jays played great today."

Later in the day, the Giants played Game Three, the Candlestick opener. Their original starter was Don Robinson, but Roger Craig didn't want to risk Robinson's troubled knee and decided to let Mike LaCoss pitch. LaCoss had nearly matched Candy Maldonado in boos from Giants' crowds because of his wildness and lack of success in the bullpen. "Hey, they boo me when the count goes to 3 and 2," LaCoss said. Since he had become a starter, the boos had lessened but hadn't disappeared. And LaCoss was hoping a lot of his hecklers would do their booing at home in front of the TV. "The guys who own the season tickets will be there instead of having their buddies and neighbors there," LaCoss said. "You expect to hear boos on the road, not at home. When you're on the road and the home team is being booed, it puts something in your mind that something's bad. It shouldn't be like that." One of the reasons the boobirds were out in force at home was that LaCoss had walked 29 batters in 68 innings at Candlestick. By comparison, Craig Lefferts had just five walks in 55 innings.

It wasn't just the fans who had problems with LaCoss. It was the umpires, the media, even his teammates at times. "Back when I first met him in spring training (in '86), my first impression was I didn't like him," Kelly Downs said. "A lot of guys couldn't stand him. But when you get to know the guy, he's not at all like you'd think. He's a very giving person. He'd do anything for you. He keeps the team loose, practical jokes, stuff like that." Some media types might disagree. Let Buffy explain. "I'm not the kind of person that you can stick a microphone in my face and turn lights and a camera on me and then ask me a stupid question and expect me to stand there and answer it. I'm not that kind of person, and some of these guys know it and get intimidated. I feel like they're probably incompetent, and the hell with them." And then there are umpires, some of whom would prefer a day off to calling a LaCoss game. Before one start in which Frank Pulli had the plate assignment, Pulli approached Craig and said, "Thanks for giving me Buffy."

As the Giants flew out of Chicago, it was easy to assess the magnitude of their pitching woes. A team that had prevailed all season despite numerous pitching injuries found itself in its biggest series of the year with the same problems. Scott Garrelts had been shaky for the first three innings of Game One and settled down only after Will Clark's grand slam. And after Rick Reuschel couldn't complete the first inning of Game Two, Craig said he had planned to ask the 40-year-old if he was tired, if six months of stress on his arm had finally caught up to him. If Reuschel wasn't able to return for Game Five, Craig would have to go to Robinson or even Kelly Downs, who also had been rocked in Game Two. And Craig Lefferts, the left-handed bullpen ace who replaced Downs and allowed a three-run double to Mark Grace, hadn't been sharp after his return from the disabled list with shoulder troubles. The Giants touched down at San Francisco International Airport knowing they'd have to win two of three at Candlestick to regain the momentum, although the '87 playoffs was a reminder that winning two of three might not even be good enough. In the Giants' favor was the fact that the Cubs' starting pitcher, Rick Sutcliffe, was 0-2 against the Giants during the season and 6-9 lifetime. And Sutcliffe, too, was battling a bum shoulder.

It wasn't the shoulder that knocked Sutcliffe from the game in the seventh inning. It was a bad leg. He fell while fielding a ball in the second and again while running the bases in the seventh. After pulling into third base, Sutcliffe was replaced by a pinch runner, and the Cubs went on to score in the inning to move ahead 4-3. Sutcliffe insisted he was healthy enough to pitch, but Don Zimmer, who had been feuding with the veteran all season, got out the hook. Paul Assenmacher began the bottom of the seventh and allowed a one-out single to Brett Butler. That brought up Robby Thompson, 6-for-6 lifetime off Assenmacher. Zimmer left Assenmacher in the game for all of one pitch. With a 1-0 count, Zimmer motioned to the bullpen for right-handed Les Lancaster.

What transpired thereafter was a rare piece of baseball that either seldom happens or is so embarrasing that nobody ever admits it happens. Lancaster inherited a 1-0 count and threw an off-speed pitch for a ball. Then, as Lancaster recounted the story, he looked at the scoreboard and noticed a 3-0 count, not 2-0. Three balls, no strikes, he thought. He didn't want to walk Thompson because Will Clark was up next, and he figured Thompson would be taking the next pitch. So Lancaster, like any pitcher with a 3-0 count in that situation, grooved a fastball down the heart of the plate. Thompson's eyes widened, and his grip on the bat tightened. The next thing Lancaster knew, he was watching Thompson's two-run homer sail over the left-field fence.

The Giants held onto the 5-4 lead to win it. Lancaster stood at his clubhouse cubicle wondering why Thompson would ever swing at a 3-0 pitch with Clark on deck. Nearly an hour had passed, and Lancaster still didn't realize the count had been only 2-0. Zimmer hadn't told him; neither had any of his teammates. Not until a sportswriter brought up the subject did Lancaster finally realize his oversight. "I wish I had known that," Lancaster said. "I looked at the scoreboard and saw it was a 3-0 count. I just misread the scoreboard." Lancaster was a third-year big-leaguer who had pitched in just one other post-season game, that coming in Game Two when he tossed four innings and was touched for a meaningless solo home run by the same Robby Thompson. This latest Thompson homer was not quite so meaningless. All it did was give the Giants a two-games-to-one advantage.

As for LaCoss, he allowed three of the Cubs' four runs before spraining his left knee while fielding a bunt in the fourth inning. He then limped off the field and called it a day.

The A's final game in the SkyDome was slated for October 8. It also proved to be the final game of the series. "I'm on a mission; we're on a mission," Rickey Henderson said. "Our mission now is to win. We're one step away." Henderson, the 190-pound keg of dynamite, exploded again in the first inning of Game Five. This was a rematch of Game One pitchers Dave Stewart and Dave Stieb, and Henderson got Oakland off to a quick lead, drawing a walk off Stieb, stealing second and scoring on Canseco's single. Three runs in the third gave Stewart a 4-0 lead, but Stewart lost the shutout when Lloyd Moseby homered in the eighth. And he lost the chance to finish the game when George Bell homered to open the ninth. That left Dennis Eckersley on familiar turf, in position for a routine save, when all hell broke loose.

Cito Gaston waited for Eckersley to complete his warmups before asking plate ump Rick Reed to check the reliever for something — anything — with which Eckersley could deface baseballs. Gouged baseballs perform aerodynamic oddities that greatly favor the pitcher. As such, they are illegal. But because they can work devilishly well, they also are not unheard of. Illegal, too, is any object — a nail, a thumbtack, a key, a nail file, even a wedding ring — that can be used to mar the ball's smooth surface and make it hop, skip, jump or sing the Hallelujah Chorus. Texas manager Bobby Valentine had accused Eckersley of doctoring the ball in the past, but nothing had come of it. This time, Eckersley seemed amazed he was being accused before even throwing a pitch. Tony Phillips, playing third base, got into a shouting match with Gaston. And Tony La Russa became furious. On his way to the mound, he threw down his lineup card with such velocity that the attached pen bounced high off the SkyDome turf.

As soon as Gaston was within earshot, Eckersley let fly with a string of profanities that would blister the most jaded ears. Ignoring the fact that Reed was in the immediate vicinity, Gaston challenged Eckersley on the spot. "I didn't like what he said to me. I told him he should say that to me on the street. He wouldn't do that. He had to do it out there where he has protection." Eckersley countered by saying, "He provoked me with all that (bleep). What was I supposed to say to him? Can I let him get away with that? No. I'm sorry I said it, but I'm still ticked off about it."

A popular assumption after the game was that Valentine, who has had a rocky relationship with La Russa, had tipped off Gaston. Gaston denied it. Valentine, working the series as a television analyst, also denied it. La Russa didn't care where it came from. He was livid even after Eckersley, victimized by a bloop single, got out of the inning by allowing just one more run, giving the A's a 4-3 win and a return ticket to the World Series. "It gives me a little problem, because I respect (Gaston)," Tony said. "I didn't appreciate it. There was never one ball turned in this season. To me, you go out, and whoever plays the best wins. Not like this."

For all of that, the series remained the private domain of Rickey Henderson, who had all but retitled the anthem of the north "Woe, Canada" with his devastating display. He was a unanimous choice as the series' Most Valuable Player. "This is the ultimate dream of any ballplayer," Rickey said, echoing words that could be heard time and again in the A's clubhouse. "I've always wanted this moment to arrive. You only dream that you can peak at a time like this." Rickey might have had the finest offensive playoff series in history. By the time it all ended, Henderson had gone 6-for-15 with two homers, seven walks and a playoff-record eight steals. He was responsible for half of Oakland's 26-run offensive output, scoring eight times and driving in five more. But the A's were far from a one-man show. Dave Stewart won Game One and Game Five, but he had no doubt that the MVP award went to the right player. "That had to be the best," he said. "Rickey Henderson is the premier player in baseball today."

The Cubs had reason to dispute Stewart's claim, considering they were being victimized by the Giants' Will Clark, who collected another three hits that evening in Game Four of the National League playoffs. Despite Clark's fine game, his performance didn't match the memorable effort turned in by Matt Williams.

This game followed much the same course of earlier games — another questionable move by Don Zimmer and another Giants victory. The deciding factor was a magnificent at-bat by Williams, but Williams had to wait to become a star until after Zimmer came through with an assist. The score in the fifth inning was 4-4 with one out and Clark on second base. First base was open, which would normally be the cue for a manager to intentionally walk Williams, setting up a force and the potential for a double play. But Zimmer, as he had proven throughout the season, wasn't a by-the-book manager. He allowed left-handed Steve Wilson to go after Williams, who despite an anemic average had hit the second-most homers in pro ball in '89 — 44, 18 for the Giants and 26 for Triple-A Phoenix. Wilson went after Williams, all right, in an at-bat that seemed to last a half-hour. The at-bat required a total of 12 pitches, with Williams barely staying alive by fouling off pitch after pitch.

Wilson worked Williams to a 2-2 count before Williams fouled off two straight fastballs and watched the next go by for a ball. The count was full, and there was no Les Lancaster misinterpretation here. Wilson threw his first changeup. Foul. Two more changeups. Foul, foul. And another changeup. Foul. Finally, pitch number 12, a fastball on the inside corner. Williams pulled the pitch down the left-field line and several yards above the 335-foot marker posted at the corner of the fence. This one wasn't foul. This one was a two-run home run that pushed the Giants ahead 6-4, which stood as the final score.

Clark, who scored ahead of Williams, awaited his teammate at the plate. "I didn't say anything like 'nice homer.' I said, 'That's a great at-bat,' " Clark said. Roger Craig took the praise to another level. "That's one of the greatest at-bats I've ever seen," he said. Williams was naturally stoked: "The best at-bat of my life." The best, the most lengthy, the most exciting and the most important. Especially the most important because, after Kelly Downs and Steve Bedrosian blanked the Cubs the rest of the way, the Giants moved to within one victory of their first National League pennant in 27 years.

In the losers' clubhouse, Wilson was holding back tears. He had been pitching in Double-A the year before, and this was no doubt the biggest letdown of his short career. "It cost us the game," he said. While Wilson was grieving, Zimmer was defending himself once again. He said he didn't walk Williams because he figured Craig would pinch hit for the two left-handed batters due up next, Terry Kennedy and Pat Sheridan, and he wanted to leave Wilson in the game. Craig later admitted he would have hit Bill Bathe and Candy Maldonado for Kennedy and Sheridan. So, in short, Zimmer chose to have Wilson pitch to Williams instead of Scott Sanderson to Bathe. "It's not his fault," Wilson said. "It's my fault. I just made a bad pitch." Williams finished the game with four RBIs to increase his series total to nine, a National League playoff record.

The Giants took turns knocking game-clinching home runs in the first three victories. Will Clark's grand slam ended Chicago's hopes in Game One, Robby Thompson's homer beat the Cubs in Game Three, and Matt Williams' long ball was the crusher in Game Four. Who would rise to the occasion in Game Five? Brett Butler? Terry Kennedy? Candy Maldonado, finally? No, no, no. Let there be Will. Let there be a way. And so it went.

Will Clark versus Mitch Williams. It was the culmination of a wild week of scintillating showdowns. Clark versus Greg Maddux. Thompson versus Les Lancaster. Williams versus Steve Wilson. The best of all would come in Game Five. Although Thompson and Williams and even Kevin Mitchell had their moments of glory, it was Clark who enjoyed an entire series of glory. He introduced himself with a 4-for-4 night and a grand slam in Game One, and he bid adieu with one of the best pieces of clutch hitting ever witnessed in this game.

Despite Mark Grace's playoff numbers, Clark's name was already inscribed onto the Most Valuable Player trophy when he stepped to the plate with the bases loaded and two outs in the eighth inning of a 1-1 ballgame. Clark had watched both Rick Reuschel and Mike Bielecki pitch into the fateful inning, and he calmly observed Bielecki walk three straight batters in the eighth, all with two away. He had watched Don Zimmer go to the mound after the second walk, only to leave Bielecki in the game despite the fact that Mitch Williams was warm and ready in the bullpen. "I didn't think he was losing anything," Zimmer said of yet another move that went sour. Finally, after Bielecki walked Thompson on four pitches, Zimmer summoned Williams.

Clark realized the Cubs couldn't afford another walk and took Williams' first pitch for a strike. He fouled off the next and took the third for a ball. Then he fouled off two straight. This was Wild Thing against The Thrill. This was power (Williams had 67 strikeouts in 81 innings) against power (Clark had 23 homers and two more in the playoffs). But this was also Will Clark at his best. And don't talk about pressure. Clark never does. Claims he never feels pressure. Even on a 1-2 pitch with the bags juiced in the eighth inning of a tie game in the playoffs. Hey, no pressure. So here comes that 1-2 delivery. No surprise. A fastball. A heater. A hit-it-if-you-can heater. A can-you-top-this heater. Clark saw, Clark swung, Clark conquered. If Williams' fastball came in at 95 mph, Clark's line drive went out at 950 mph. Just as Williams was completing his follow-through, Clark's liner was sizzling past his ear and well on its way into center field. It was a fabulous two-run single that had the biggest crowd in Candlestick history, 63,084, going absolutely wild. These fans had experienced a moment that may be treasured for as long as baseball is America's pastime.

"It was probably the proudest moment I've had," Clark said.

"You have Wayne Gretzky and Michael Jordan. And you've got Will Clark," Brett Butler said.

The eighth-inning single was Clark's 13th hit — a playoff record — in 20 at-bats. He also set records in runs (eight), extra-base hits (six), total bases (24), batting average (.650) and slugging percentage (1.200). What made the performance even more incredible was the fact that he played with a bruised shin which weakened his leg and caused an obvious limp.

Steve Bedrosian retired the first two batters in the ninth before the never-say-die Cubs bunched three singles, Jerome Walton scoring Curt Wilkerson on the third. But moments later, Ryne Sandberg was grounding out to Thompson at second base. Game, series and pennant. As his teammates piled up on the mound, Clark raised his fists, the game ball still clutched in his glove. It was his ball, his moment.

The Cubs had accomplished something no other team in baseball could match. They dropped a National League Championship Series to the Giants. The Pirates in '71 couldn't do it, and neither could the Cardinals in '87. They both defeated the Giants. But the '89 Cubs will always be popular conversation pieces among Giants fans. Long live the Cubs' tradition.

Chris Speier, the only Giant to have played for all three division winners, was in a reflective mood after the clincher. He was remembering the '71 gang of Willie Mays, Willie McCovey and Juan Marichal and how they bowed out against Pittsburgh. Eighteen years later, Speier wasn't on the active post-season roster, but he was in uniform and enjoyed the celebration as much as anybody. "I feel for a lot of guys who never got here," he said. "It takes so much to get here, but most people never do. You'd prefer to be in the World Series as an active player, but at least I'll be in uniform. A lot of guys don't even get that far." For the first time since 1962, the Giants got that far. And it was sweet.

The only drawback of the celebration involved Dave Dravecky, who had watched the series from the dugout while resting his broken left arm in a sling. Dravecky was one of the first Giants onto the field, but he was also the first off the field. Trainer Mark Letendre escorted Dravecky away after the pitcher suffered another bone fracture in his left arm in the celebratory pushing and shoving. Dravecky rushed out to the field quickly so he wouldn't get bumped from the front, but he didn't anticipate any collision from the rear, and that's exactly what happened. "A freak thing," said Dravecky, who would officially retire from the game less than a month later.

Despite more bad news on the Dravecky front, San Francisco had earned the chance to play in the World Series. And best of all, for Bay Area fans, Oakland was the opponent.

The Giants and A's could play the entire series without boarding one airplane or checking into one hotel. There was no place like home.

THE WORLD SERIES
How the Fall Classic
became unlike any other

One of the enduring, and frequently endearing, qualities of the World Series is how each molds a unique view of baseball onto the national consciousness. Each of the first 85 World Series brought to the forefront one lasting memory to those who saw it:

Willie Mays' over-the-shoulder catch of Vic Wertz's Polo Grounds drive in 1954.

Don Larsen's perfect game in 1956.

Bill Mazeroski's series-winning homer in 1960.

Willie McCovey's wicked line drive that died in the glove of Bobby Richardson in 1962.

Baltimore's three straight shutouts in a sweep of the Dodgers in 1966.

The Miracle Mets' unbelievable saga in 1969.

Carlton Fisk's waving arms that telepathically willed a ball to stay fair for a 12th-inning home run in 1975.

Reggie Jackson's three-homer day in 1977.

Rookie reliever Bob Welch's dramatic strikeout of Jackson in 1978.

The Pirates' we-are-family unit of Willie Stargell and Dave Parker coming from a three-games-to-one deficit and allowing Baltimore just two runs in the last three games in 1979.

Mookie Wilson's grounder through Bill Buckner's legs that dashed Boston's hopes for a world title in 1986.

Kirk Gibson's game-winning, pinch-hit home run in Game One of the 1988 series.

The one thread they all share is the human element, mortal men snatching a piece of baseball immortality. Baseball in autumn has been an unbroken tapestry, a weave of Americana depicting common men doing uncommon things under the intense scrutiny of the national eye. But the thread snapped in 1989, the weave broke and the eye refocused as Mother Nature shook the Boys of October, wresting the series and the story out of their grasp.

Just 31 minutes before the scheduled start of Game Three, the perception of baseball forever changed for the players, for the 62,000 fans crammed into Candlestick Park and for a national television audience that had tuned in for a World Series but instead spent hours witnessing a horror story unfold. Seismic movement on the San Andreas Fault shook loose a section of the Bay Bridge, the lifeline that links San Francisco with Oakland, collapsed a freeway in Oakland only five miles from the A's home field, and jerked buildings off their foundations in San Francisco's Marina District. The Bay Bridge World Series would take on another meaning after 5:04 p.m. on October 17. Nature, in the form of a 7.1 earthquake, gripped Northern California and baseball for 15 interminable seconds. Neither would be quite the same again.

A massive shock wave rippled through Candlestick's field and parking lot, sharply jolting the second-oldest ballpark in the National League and whipping the stands back and forth like trees on a windy day. But luck was with Candlestick Park, where no one was killed and no one was seriously injured. Structural damage was slight. The most critical problem seemed to be the loss of electrical power. In the initial moments following the quake, some fans thought there would still be a game that evening. Eventually, however, through reports coming over the battery-operated radios and TVs a few spectators had brought to the game, word spread about the severity of the quake. An hour passed before Commissioner Fay Vincent postponed the game, and a police officer announced the news over the loud speaker in his car, which he had driven onto the field. The fans, players and officials remaining in the ballpark slowly evacuated Candlestick by the light of the setting sun. It took six hours for the stadium parking lots to clear. The World Series had to be put on the back burner while the Bay Area began its recovery from nature's twitch.

Ten days would pass before baseball returned to Candlestick Park. Ten long days. Ten days in which the A's and Giants saw their momentum and focus trickle away and their World Series strategies dashed.

On the Oakland A's six-hour flight back from Toronto after the playoff clincher, celebration was the order of the night. But through the toasts and the tippling, a curious migration took place. Manager Tony La Russa, occupying his customary bulkhead seat on the A's chartered Continental A300 Airbus, sat next to the window, the seat next to him open. In his lap was a SkyDome souvenir notebook, a commemorative gift that had been given out to the media. La Russa had seen it lying around his office in the visitors' clubhouse and put it in his briefcase. It would later become more than just another souvenir. La Russa, who generally relaxes with paperback fiction during long airplane rides, this time got out a pen and started making notes. The A's were at the top of their game and had beaten a Toronto club that was one of the hottest teams in baseball. But there was still the problem of putting together a game plan to take on the National League champions. The Giants, leading three games to one in the National League playoffs at the time, seemed the likely competition. So La Russa started filling up notebook pages. Players and coaches, one and two at a time, came by to talk. Some came because they wished to. Others were asked. But by the time the flight had landed at Oakland International Airport, the notebook had become a working outline for the way the A's would approach the World Series.

"I remember that flight as vividly as I remember anything about the season," La Russa said. "I remember feeling good but wanting the one more piece. Then I finally started drawing on my memory of last year." The memory of the final week of 1988 was, if not bitter, at the very least distasteful. Winners of 104 games in the regular season and a four-game sweep in the playoffs, the A's had fallen on their collective face in the World Series. Overconfident and underprepared, the A's paid for not being able to solve Los Angeles' pitching. Oakland batters hit .177 and scored just 11 runs. Only three times in 45 innings had the A's put together back-to-back hits. The A's were frustrated because, as third baseman Carney Lansford said, they "didn't play the way we did the rest of the year." But the final impression the '88 A's left with the baseball world was a lasting one, a portrait of a team that looked nowhere as good as its credentials. Despite that failure, La Russa predicted at the time that Oakland would win a World Series title "some time before I'm fired. You can bet your ass on it."

From the first aching muscles of spring training to the third strike Dennis Eckersley blew past Junior Felix for the final out of the American League playoffs, Oakland's entire 1989 season had been a crusade to erase that picture. Making it to the World Series again was a great accomplishment because no team had made back-to-back World Series appearances in over a decade. But making it back wasn't the goal. Winning it was.

La Russa spent the early part of the flight reliving the two major losses of his career. His '83 division-winning White Sox won the opener of a best-of-five playoff series against Baltimore only to lose three straight. And after thrashing Boston, his '88 A's failed against the Dodgers. "I told myself both times that if I ever got in those kinds of situations again, there were a lot of things I would do differently," La Russa said. "The thing is, you don't know at the time that you'll ever get another chance. Now it was here. I couldn't blow it. So before I talked to anybody, really, I started making notes about how I could make the workouts before Game One better. I said to myself, 'We've got this week to try and do something better than we did last year.' And I planted a seed in the players and coaches that we had to do better."

The next day, October 9, the A's went through an informal workout after watching on television as Will Clark propelled the Giants into the World Series with his game-winning single off Chicago Cubs' reliever Mitch Williams. San Francisco's inclusion in the series came as no surprise to La Russa, who predicted publicly in June that San Francisco would win the pennant. If being in the World Series wasn't enough of an emotional high for the A's, learning they'd be playing the Giants elevated the feeling. They could live almost normal lives through the biggest series of their careers because they wouldn't have to deal with the miseries of traveling. They would need only to commute.

A major bone of contention among the Oakland players was whether to accept the club's offer of staying in a downtown San Francisco hotel during the Candlestick Park portion of the series. Dave Parker was the player leading cheers for heading to San Francisco, for treating the road games as if they were a trip to Milwaukee or Cleveland. Dave Stewart led the opposition, which wanted to take advantage of the rare opportunity to stay at home. Although management was willing to let some stay home and others head for the hotel, the players weren't having any of that. It would be every man on the road — or none. A vote was taken the day after the Giants clinched, and the A's, the American League's best road team, elected to remain in their own homes throughout the series.

La Russa, convinced that the A's had been unnecessarily flat in the '88 World Series after a six-day layoff, brought in more than a dozen players from Oakland's instructional league team in Scottsdale, Arizona, to change the flavor and pace of the '89 workouts. Another change came right out of the first pages of that precious notebook. Instead of separating his pitchers and hitters, La Russa made them mini-adversaries. Instead of throwing on the sidelines, pitchers threw their best stuff in competitive, if simulated, games. By forcing the A's hitters to face live pitching — Mike Moore and Curt Young started one day, Bob Welch and Dennis Eckersley the next — instead of the lame stuff batting practice pitchers offer, La Russa hoped to be able to keep his hitters' timing intact. The pages of the notebook bore ample evidence that Oakland's timing had gone sour in 1988 after six days of seeing nothing more challenging than lukewarm fastballs from coaches Jim Lefebvre and Dave McKay.

On October 11, the A's were greeted by a story clipped from the pages of USA Today in which Yankees scout Charlie Fox, a one-time Giants manager, dissected the Oakland roster, piece by piece. To say it was flattering is to say Antarctica is Earth's garden spot. Fox found plenty of fault with baseball's winningest team, and the sections the A's would find most objectionable had been circled in purple ink. Fox's criticism included this about Rickey Henderson, who had started the season with Fox's Yankees: "When Rickey was with us, he didn't run. When Rickey doesn't run, he's a dull ballplayer." Fox said of starter Bob Welch, "He isn't the power pitcher he was as a kid." Of the A's designated hitter, Fox said, "Dave Parker is a cripple hitter. He wants the pitcher to get behind and have to come into him." And he said, "the Giants are better equipped to beat the A's than the Cubs. The Giants can offset the A's power with Clark and Mitchell. The A's have an edge in depth, but Roger handles a pitching staff better than La Russa." The clipping, put up on the bulletin board by the A's resident purple pen owner, third base coach Rene Lachemann, was more than adequate to get a rise out of the team. Lansford had been lauded by Fox, who said "he's my kind of player," but the A's captain found it necessary to speak out: "How did he get to be an expert on us? It doesn't make sense."

Jose Canseco laughed off Fox's commentary. "The Giants have great players in Clark, Mitchell and Thompson," Canseco said. "But I don't think they have as many quality players as we do. If we play the way we should, we will win." Canseco, burned by the miserable experiences of the 1988 World Series both personally — he was 0-for-18 after a Game One grand slam — and as part of the A's overall collapse, wouldn't say that the A's would play great baseball. But neither would he dodge behind a veil of false humility. Oakland, he said, was the better club. And, as an aside, he said something curious, something that would, under vastly different circumstances, be repeated later in the series, although in slightly different forms. "When you look at what we do here in relation to death or in relation to starvation, baseball doesn't compare at all," Canseco said. "It's just a game."

While the World Series was Oakland's focal point, some bad feelings left over from the playoffs were still being aired. Three days after the Game Five debacle in which Toronto manager Cito Gaston insisted that Eckersley was cheating and throwing a scuffed ball, the Blue Jays sent a video tape to league President Bobby Brown and Commissioner Fay Vincent that apparently showed Eckersley trying to hide something down his pants. La Russa was asked about his reaction should the Giants ask the umpires to check Eckersley for contraband. La Russa said he would not stand still for any kind of "gamesmanship" from the Giants and suggested Roger Craig had too much "class" for such shenanigans. To which Craig responded, "He must not know me too well. If I think someone is cheating, I don't care if it's a spring training game. If someone is cheating, I'm going to try to stop them."

For his part, Eckersley received a telegram from Rangers manager Bobby Valentine in which Valentine said he hadn't, like several of the A's suggested, taken time from his duties as a television analyst to tip off Gaston about scuffed balls. And Valentine, who had a lengthy history of complaining about the nature of the balls that Eckersley throws, demanded an apology. Eckersley was backed into a corner and couldn't help but agree. "He told me he didn't do it, and I have to believe him," Eckersley said. "I said some stuff before, but there's no doubt in my mind now that Valentine had nothing to do with what happened." There was just one problem. "I just don't remember what I said, exactly. I don't know what to apologize for."

There's nothing like an off-day or two to upset the rhythm of a charging ballclub. While it seemed the Eckersley controversy wouldn't die quickly in the A's camp, it paled in comparison to what transpired in the Giants' first workout of October 11. Giants fans had been sky high. Their team, after finishing off the Cubs on October 9, was as positive and encouraged as a pennant winner could be. The good news carried over to October 10, when San Francisco unveiled a proposal for a downtown, waterfront baseball stadium. Giants owner Bob Lurie wanted to move his team out of Candlestick, and this was an option he was giving the city's voters. The stadium proposition was on the November ballot, and it was favored to pass. It seemed that the pennant-winning Giants would be San Francisco's team for a long, long time. Life couldn't have been better.

Life changed, however, when the Giants held their first World Series workout the next day. Roger Craig had earned a reputation as a motivator, able to generate the maximum out of a roster often depleted by injuries. But he had no control over what his two best players did on the first day of workouts. None of his inspirational team meetings could possibly have erased the actions of Kevin Mitchell and Will Clark. It will never be known exactly how much that day's side shows affected the continuity and attitude of the Giants' most successful club in 27 years, but it was certain that the

Giants' brass was not pleased with the day's developments.

Mitchell was the first to make news. He didn't do much. He just didn't show up. He said he had decided to stay in San Diego for the day, to close escrow on a home. Of course, his manager and teammates were infuriated that the man most responsible for San Francisco's fabulous season was threatening team morale by his unsanctioned absence. By making it to the World Series, the Giants were already in the big money. But much more money could be made with a World Series victory, and Mitchell was messing with the momentum that could make it happen. Craig was also upset that Mitchell didn't ask permission to leave the Bay Area in the first place. "If I let one guy get away with this, everyone will think they could do it," Craig said. "I'm not very strict. I overlook a lot of things, but I have two rules I strictly enforce. No drinking on the plane, and be on time." The story, in typical Mitchell fashion, was confusing. Craig said Mitchell was unaware of the practice, but Giants hitting coach Dusty Baker said he had informed Mitchell. Mitchell's roommate, Donell Nixon, didn't want to comment. "There's no use in having three stories," he said.

Later in the day, Clark took his turn at controversy. In front of a tiny group of writers, he harshly criticized former Giant Jeffrey Leonard, calling him a "tumor" despite the Hac Man's four-homer performance in the '87 playoffs. Two days after Clark won the '89 playoff MVP trophy, he surprisingly ripped into the '87 playoff MVP. "We got rid of him. Now look where we are." Although Clark had privately criticized Leonard after Leonard's June 1988 trade to Milwaukee, he waited until World Series week to go public with his feelings. He said Leonard's brash personality and mannerisms had hurt the team's chemistry. "The way he rode me had nothing to do with baseball," said Clark, describing their relationship as "slim and none." Leonard was one of the team leaders when Clark arrived on the scene after only 65 minor-league games. A college All-American, U.S. Olympian and first-round draft choice, Clark described Leonard as a "jealous ballplayer. He couldn't understand why a guy just called up could get all the attention and not him."

For the second time in the same day, Craig was asked to defend one of his superstars. But he found himself defending Leonard more than Clark. "The years he played for me, he and I had our problems. But we always ironed them out. I do think he helped Will in a lot of ways, though maybe Will won't admit that. But that's my feeling."

The next day, October 12, Leonard told his side of the story to Lowell Cohn of the San Francisco Chronicle. "It's about time Will Clark came out of the closet. Talk about my personality! He's a talented hitter, but he's a prejudiced bastard," began Leonard, referring to an incident involving another former Giant, Chris Brown. "He actually called Chris Brown a nigger to his face. Roger and Al Rosen asked me, 'What should we do?' I took batting practice and thought about it. By the batting cage, I said, 'Make Will hold a meeting to apologize to all the Latins and brothers on the team.' Roger said, 'Good idea.' We held a meeting after batting practice, but they closed that, too, like Will was Clark Kent or something and they had to protect his true identity. They wanted a white hero, so they had to close it up. I can understand that. Will stood at the opposite end of the clubhouse from Roger's office. I was about three feet away from him. He said, 'I said some words I shouldn't have said. I want to apologize to all the Latins and blacks on the team, even you, Hac.' He was trying to put some humor in it, I guess. I said, 'What word was that?' Roger said, 'He doesn't need to repeat it. We all know what the word was.' Those are personality flaws in Will's character. I hope by now he's cleared them up."

Leonard also responded to Clark's implication that the Giants were in the World Series in part because Leonard was gone. "I did what I had to do, and I did it well. I was the MVP. If he did what he's doing now, we would have gone to the World Series. He didn't hit. . . . I don't agree with what he said about me making his life miserable. His life wasn't more miserable than other rookies. It happened to me and every other son of a bitch who came up since the beginning of baseball time. I got rode so hard by Reggie Smith and Enos Cabell. . . . Will is a great hitter, but I'm not jealous. I was there with Joe Morgan, Reggie Smith, Jack Clark, Darrell Evans and Vida Blue. I'm going to be jealous of Will Clark! I still love the Giants' organization. I have nothing against Bob Lurie. I hope they complete what we started in 1987 and, who knows, like Will Clark said, without me, maybe they'll win it. I expect Will Clark to have a big World Series."

Naturally, Clark was asked to comment on Leonard's response to Clark's original statements. But Clark ended the public bickering when he brushed off questions on the matter put to him October 13, the day before the World Series opener. "He had an opinion.

I had an opinion. That was it." Asked if he regretted going public with his opinion, Clark said, "If I would, I wouldn't have said it."

By the time October 14 came around, players on both sides of the bay were ready for the biggest baseball event of their lives. The A's went into their second straight World Series as the favorites. Looking at the position-by-position matchups, there were only two significant differences separating the two teams — right field and starting pitching — but the A's held the big edge on both fronts. There were edges in the other matchups, but most were slight. Terry Kennedy and Terry Steinbach behind the plate. Will Clark and Mark McGwire at first base. Robby Thompson and Tony Phillips at second base. Jose Uribe and Walter Weiss or Mike Gallego at shortstop. Matt Williams and Carney Lansford at third base. Kevin Mitchell and Rickey Henderson in left field. Brett Butler and Dave Henderson in center field. (Give Dave Parker the nod over Ernest Riles in the matchup of designated hitters, but the DH would be used only in the Oakland games.) One clear advantage was right field, where Jose Canseco towered well above anyone the Giants could throw out there. The bullpens were moderately close, with the Giants' righty-lefty combo of Steve Bedrosian and Craig Lefferts not far below Oakland's Dennis Eckersley and Rick Honeycutt. But the difference in starting pitchers was not close at all. The A's rotation of Dave Stewart, Mike Moore, Bob Welch and Storm Davis was noteworthy because each had had a chance to win 20 games. The Giants' rotation of Scott Garrelts, Rick Reuschel, Don Robinson and Mike LaCoss was noteworthy because they each had had a chance to spend time on the disabled list.

The home-field advantages didn't figure to be too significant, even though four of the seven games were scheduled at the Coliseum. Oakland would no doubt host a good many Giants fans, and Candlestick would surely accommodate a few A's fans. The home fields, although partisan, were not nearly as one-sided as in the most recent one-area World Series in 1956. That one featured the Brooklyn Dodgers and New York Yankees. Roger Craig, then a pitcher with the Dodgers, remembered the home team owning a distinct advantage. "When you went to Yankee Stadium, your only fan there was your wife," he said.

Deciding which manager had the edge was close to impossible because each was perfectly suited to his team. Craig was from the old school and blended well with the Giants' aging pitching staff.

Tony La Russa was a new-school graduate and meshed nicely with the A's divergent personalities. Craig had 15 years on La Russa and was entering his sixth World Series, although it was his first as a manager. La Russa was managing his second World Series team in two years. This would be the first official meeting between the managers, who had met previously only in spring training. And as everyone from the avid fan to the bandwagon jumper knew by then, the A's had obliterated the Giants in eight of nine spring meetings. But, hey, that was the spring. This was the fall. Big difference, right?

Dave Stewart, the A's starting pitcher, got out of bed at 11 a.m. the day of Game One, spent a couple of hours on the phone, then threw on a dirty shirt, a pair of jeans and some sneakers with no socks and drove around. As it happened, he drove past the Coliseum about 2 p.m., at which time cars were already filling up the parking lots. If the Bay Area's baseball fans were intent on getting to the park early, it didn't rub off on the A's starting pitcher. He went back home, took a short nap followed by a hot shower and reported to the park just after 4 p.m. It wasn't until 5:37 p.m. that all the hype, the talk and the speculation was put to rest when Stewart delivered the first pitch of the World Series to Giants lead-off batter Brett Butler.

While Stewart was consummately playing the role of the laid-back Californian, Will Clark took exactly the opposite approach to the opener. He stayed up late, well past midnight, intensely studying a video of Stewart. It worked. Clark had two hits off Stewart. But the rest of the lineup had just three — two by Mitchell and an infield bleeder by Uribe — and Stewart had the first complete-game World Series shutout in seven years to lift the A's past the Giants 5-0. Clark said the Giants "just ran into a buzz saw in Dave Stewart. I tell it like I see it, and they just kicked our ass. The man's a great pitcher."

Stewart brought a three-hit shutout into the ninth inning when Clark and Mitchell singled. La Russa came to the mound, but he didn't tell Stewart anything he didn't know. When La Russa left the dugout, he did so at a trot, the tipoff that the Oakland manager wasn't going to lift his pitcher. He just wanted "to break their momentum." That done, La Russa retreated to the dugout. Stewart blew a vicious 1-2 slider past Williams, and after a passed ball moved the two runners up a base, he struck out Ernest Riles, slip-

ping a fastball by him for the second out. Candy Maldonado was
the Giants' final hope in Game One, but the best he could do was a
routine grounder to third base.

The tail end of the A's lineup was responsible in one way or
another for four of the A's runs. Number nine hitter Walter Weiss,
a surprise choice to start at shortstop over Mike Gallego, hit a
home run. Number eight hitter Tony Phillips drove in the first run
with a single that triggered a three-run second inning, later scoring
on a Rickey Henderson single. And number seven hitter Terry
Steinbach scored after kicking a ball out of Terry Kennedy's glove
in a second-inning collision at the plate.

Scott Garrelts, the Giants' starter, seemed to give evidence in
the first inning that he would be overpowering, allowing no runs
and striking out Jose Canseco. That show of mastery, however,
would prove to be transitory in nature. By the second inning, the
A's began to strike. Garrelts opened the second with a big mistake,
a walk to Dave Henderson. Mark McGwire, who would finish the
night with three hits, lined out, but Steinbach laced a single to center. Phillips then roped a grounder between first and second to
score Henderson for the first run. Steinbach, who had taken third
on Phillips' hit, attempted to score when Weiss tapped a ball to
Clark at first base. Clark bobbled the ball slightly before throwing
to Kennedy at the plate. "I was having problems chewing gum and
walking at the same time right there," Clark said. Although Clark's
throw beat Steinbach to the plate, Steinbach smashed into Kennedy and jarred the ball loose. As the ball trickled away in front of the
plate, Steinbach touched home. "I've been on the other end of
those collisions," Steinbach said. "I thought I was out, way out, so I
just tried to make a good slide and hope for the best. Nobody was
more surprised than me when (umpire) Richie Garcia signaled that
I was safe." Rickey Henderson lined a run-scoring single to right to
increase the lead to 3-0.

An inning later, Dave Parker made it 4-0 with a drive into the
right-field seats, his first World Series homer. Another inning later, Weiss also went deep after hitting only three homers during the
regular season. Garrelts was gone after four innings. While the Giants seemed to have left their bats in the playoffs, the A's had carried their playoff momentum into the World Series. Someone
asked Giants pitching coach Norm Sherry about the A's explosive
offense: "In all your time as a pitcher and pitching coach, have you

ever faced such a lineup of big hitters as Oakland's?" To which
Norm calmly responded: "Well, first of all, I never pitched an inning. I was a catcher." On that note, Game Two awaited.

It was Mike Moore's turn at the game ball, and the Giants
found themselves haunted by the the split-fingered fastball for the
second straight night. Roger Craig was supposed to be the guru of
the so-called pitch of the '80s, but the A's were beating his team
with his own trick. "Their pitching can't get any better than it's
been the last two nights," Craig said after watching Moore allow
just four hits in seven innings before Rick Honeycutt and Dennis
Eckersley closed out a 5-1 win. "I thought the guy last night had a
dominating split-finger. But this guy tonight was even better."
Back in spring training, Moore had been encouraged to try the
split-finger by A's pitching coach Dave Duncan, and the pitch
turned into one of Moore's best. In Game Two, Moore threw 114
pitches, including 42 split-fingers, 29 of which were strikes. "It's a
pretty good pitch," conceded Moore.

Rickey Henderson again ignited Oakland, working Rick Reuschel for a first-inning walk, then stealing second before Carney
Lansford scored him with a double to left. By the third inning, the
Giants had pulled into a tie. Terry Kennedy opened the inning with
a single and Jose Uribe forced him at second base. Brett Butler
singled Uribe to third, and Robby Thompson tied the game with a
fly ball.

Reuschel worked 1-2-3 innings in the second and third before
he lost control in the fourth. He walked Jose Canseco and got too
much of the plate on a pitch to Dave Parker, who drilled the ball
into the right-field corner. Candy Maldonado played the carom off
the top of the wall perfectly, but when he turned to throw back to
the infield, he couldn't immediately spot Thompson. Canseco ran
through a stop sign put up by third-base coach Rene Lachemann
but scored when Maldonado's throw went into second base. "My
mistake," Lachemann said. Trailing 2-1, Reuschel committed another crime by walking Dave Henderson, and one out later he was
facing Terry Steinbach. Before the game, Tony La Russa had
looked at the Steinbach-Reuschel matchup and predicted that
Steinbach would hit a home run. Sure enough, Steinbach teed off
on a 2-0 pitch, homering deep into the left-field bleachers. It took
Parker, standing on second base before the homer, almost as long
to come around to score as it took Steinbach to complete the circuit

on the homer, which gave Oakland a 5-1 lead. "I figured this was my last game of the series," Parker said of his long lope home. Steinbach sprinted around the bases. "I'm no showboat," he said. "I knew it was out, but so what? To each his own. I hit it and go."

When Ken Oberkfell singled to open the eighth, La Russa summoned Rick Honeycutt, who had struggled in the playoffs. The left-hander was back in form now, however, striking out Butler and getting Thompson to hit into an inning-ending double play. In the ninth, Clark was robbed by Phillips at second base, and Eckersley took over for the final two outs, never letting the ball get out of the infield. The A's had a 2-0 lead heading to Candlestick, but they weren't of a mind to get carried away. "I've been surprised," Eckersley said. "Everything has gone so smoothly. But I've trained myself not to get carried away. When I was with the Cubs (in the 1984 playoffs against San Diego), we were up 2-0 and we lost it. Anything can happen."

Roger Craig naturally was disappointed in his lineup and promised to make changes for Game Three, the Candlestick opener. The most obvious casualty of Craig's change of heart was Candy Maldonado, who had gone 0-for-7 with two strikeouts. Before the series, Craig said he'd start Maldonado because he had a "hunch" Candy would shine in this forum. "I think he'll come through," Craig said. So much for hunches. On the so-called travel day of October 16, Craig announced that Pat Sheridan would start in right field for Maldonado, and Candy realized the end of his Giants career was near. "I had four good years of memories," said Maldonado, already giving his farewell speech. "Unfortunately, in the last two, things didn't go as expected. I had a year that I wouldn't wish anyone who plays this game would have." Another of Craig's offensive-minded moves was to bench Jose Uribe, move Matt Williams to shortstop and insert Ken Oberkfell at third base. Ernest Riles, 0-for-7 as the designated hitter in Oakland, would also be benched.

Game Three starters Don Robinson and Bob Welch were making their final preparations at 5:04 p.m. . . .

. . . when the field began rolling. Light standards swayed. Power flickered, then went out. Fans in the stands were riding an unwelcome roller coaster, the upper deck shaking every which way. Fans in the parking lot were caught up in a wave of concrete. Players from both sides were caught in ghastly pitch-black clubhouses where the walls were still moving and dust was seeping through air vents. Telephone lines went dead. On the field, players not caught in the clubhouse reacted with nervous good humor, waiting for the power to come back on so they could start the game. But as it became increasingly evident that there would be no game on October 17, players from both sides started scanning the stands looking for families and friends. They bunched up near the seats, trying to get a glimpse of the few battery-operated televisions owned by fans. When that didn't work, they asked for portable radios to be turned up.

They began removing their families from the stands. Wives and girlfriends were given escorts down to the field. A baby was handed down over the railing to an open-armed Storm Davis. Most players and coaches began leaving the field hand-in-hand with their families. A few had moments of anxiety when they couldn't immediately find their loved ones. A's reliever Gene Nelson knew his wife, Ceilia, hadn't yet arrived at the park, and he had calculated that she might have been near the Bay Bridge at the time of the quake. "It was the scariest moment of my life," Nelson said. "But a few minutes later, I spotted her."

Without power, there was no direct way for fans to hear about the game's status. Commissioner Fay Vincent's decision to postpone the series for at least the night was made within one hour of the quake, and at 6:01 p.m., a police officer announced over his vehicle's public-address system for all remaining fans to clear the stadium. At 6:03 p.m., some of the power from scoreboard and light poles had been restored and fans began to cheer, but it had been clear for a long while that there would be no game.

The Giants, most of whom had driven on their own to Candlestick, were left to get home as best they could. It wouldn't be any easier a drive for the players than for the fans, many of whom required six hours to get to Richmond, San Jose, Fremont, Concord and Marin. The A's packed players, families and staff members on three buses and made the long drive back to Oakland. With the San Mateo and Dumbarton bridges temporarily closed for safety inspections, the A's caravan drove all the way to San Jose before backtracking to Oakland. Even as the Candlestick parking lots slowly — very slowly — emptied onto packed freeways, engineers and architects began studying the stadium and searching for structural damage.

If Candlestick had been shaken, much of the rest of Northern

California had been brought to its knees. It became apparent that restoring power wasn't the primary concern. It was lives and livelihoods. Power and even property were secondary. When first word came that the Bay Bridge — the very symbol of this World Series — had collapsed, it seemed beyond belief. It was. Most of the bridge was intact, but one section of the top deck had fallen onto the bottom, effectively severing the main artery between the two cities.

The Goodyear blimp, which had been in the Bay Area to provide overhead camera shots of the World Series for ABC, transmitted the first pictures to a stunned national television audience of a thoroughly disabled, if still upright, Bay Bridge. The collapse of the double-decked sections of Interstate 880 during what should have been the peak of rush hour, killed, according to early estimates, as many as 250 persons. In San Francisco's exclusive Marina District, gas, water and power lines were broken and homes were knocked off their foundations. A huge fire engulfed one full block of the Marina, and residents trying to return to their homes after the game were turned away, forced into makeshift emergency shelters until safety officials could pronounce judgment on the livability of their homes, most of which were built on land fill and therefore particularly susceptible to earthquake damage. Some would never return to homes and apartment buildings burnt or shaken beyond saving.

As was the case for virtually everyone in Northern California, the next 24 hours seemed like a week. There was little enough time to enumerate sorrows, much less to begin reconstruction. The best that could be hoped for was to begin a catalog of the damages. The Coliseum and Candlestick were declared safe, pending some work. At Candlestick, which had been built partially on landfill, the most visible damage appeared in upper-deck sections 51 and 53, where separations were several inches wide and big enough to see from the lower deck. But structural engineers said that Candlestick had endured just as it was supposed to in a 7.1 earthquake. Because the stands rest on expansion joints, they withstood the quake by shifting without collapsing.

On October 18, just 25 hours after the quake hit, Commissioner Vincent held a press conference to discuss the World Series' future. In a candle-lit ballroom of the St. Francis Hotel in downtown San Francisco, Vincent said the series would tentatively resume exactly one week after the quake, on October 24. "There is substantial disarray in this community, and baseball is not a top priority," he said. The announcement had come following a meeting involving the two teams, the political hierarchies of the two cities, Major League Baseball, the players' association and ABC, the network televising the games.

Vincent said he couldn't offer anything more than a target date for resumption of the World Series, as the city of San Francisco could not hope to promise sufficient numbers of police to monitor the game. Vincent could promise that rumors of the World Series moving to a neutral site were nothing but speculation. Seattle, Los Angeles, San Diego and even Houston's Astrodome had been named as possible sites, but an absentee World Series was not something anyone wanted to consider. There were many questions that couldn't yet be answered. Would the games all be moved back to the Coliseum? If so, could fans enjoy a baseball game knowing officials would be sifting through the debris of a collapsed freeway and the Bay Bridge only a few miles away? And if the series were to return to Candlestick, would the fans return? What would happen if the Giants were rallying in the seventh inning? Would the fans root loudly and stomp their feet? Or would they be afraid to shake the place? Would they simply sit back and smile if Will Clark went deep, treating the event like a golf match? And what if the lights went out again, say, two hours later in the evening? Would the crowd be as orderly if the electricity were knocked out after dark?

Vincent, in only his second month on the job, replacing A. Bartlett Giamatti after his untimely death due to heart failure, was thrust into a position of deciding the fate of one of the most highly publicized events in the world. He listened to all sides and was forced to weigh each issue. He had to consider the lost lives and destruction in the community. He had to consider the tens of millions of dollars baseball would have to return to ABC in the event the series was canceled. And he had to consider that players wouldn't receive full financial shares until at least four games were played. Through it all, Vincent realized the World Series was relatively insignificant and received praise for the manner in which he temporarily kept his sport out of the limelight.

The NFL's San Francisco 49ers were scheduled to play New England that Sunday at Candlestick, but the game was moved down to Stanford Stadium in Palo Alto while Candlestick underwent some cosmetic repairs. The Giants didn't plan to go elsewhere, however, scheduling an afternoon workout for the next day,

October 19. The A's settled on a mid-day practice in the Coliseum, where Dave Parker emerged from a 90-minute meeting to announce the club had decided to withdraw from the traditional champagne-bathing celebration should the A's go on to win. Champagne didn't seem appropriate. What did? Both teams decided to donate a portion of their World Series checks to earthquake relief.

When the players arrived at their first post-quake workouts, few seemed eager to continue the games. Some favored Vincent's timetable to resume, but others wondered aloud at the wisdom of playing a game in the midst of such tragedy. One was Dave Stewart, who had spent part of the night talking with rescue workers at the collapsed Cypress structure of Interstate 880, just a couple of miles from his home.

"We're not in the mood for baseball," Stewart said. "I don't know if it's in good taste to play. But I do know that if we don't play it in the Bay Area, then we shouldn't play it at all."

Dave Henderson: "It's a personal decision each man has to make. Baseball is baseball; life and death go way beyond that. But we've all lost parents. Some players here have lost children. Each of us has a personal side and a professional side. You've got to divide the two."

Carney Lansford: "I lost a 2-year-old son and had to be back playing two weeks later. You have to overcome tragedy. The Bay Area has to get back on its feet and get back to a normal routine. It's going to take time. Maybe having something positive to look forward to like the World Series instead of all the negatives will divert all those negative vibes."

Tony Phillips: "We may not want to be here. I don't think being in California right now is the best thing for me, personally. But people have to put themselves in our position. Should we play? I don't know."

Mark McGwire: "Nobody wants to play right now. I know that I wouldn't play if they asked us to do it today."

Over at the Giants' camp, where sounds of baseballs meeting bats blended oddly with sounds of hammers meeting concrete, the feelings were similar.

Brett Butler: "With all that's gone on, I could take it or leave it."

Mike Krukow: "What's happened overshadows the World Series. It's not even close."

At that first post-quake workout, the most popular question to the players was: "Would you bring your family back to Candlestick if the series resumed?" Many A's said no.

Lansford: "My family will not go to Candlestick Park. There's no way."

Parker: "I don't want to risk it. It's just my wife and I that are out here. I'm going to be putting myself on the line. I'm not going to be putting her on the line."

Phillips: "My family is not going back there. No way."

Walter Weiss: "My family already left."

The Giants, although it wasn't easy, tried to remain upbeat.

Roger Craig: "Everything I hear is the stadium is perfectly safe. . . . But I'm gonna manage from second base."

Just one player missed the October 19 workouts — Rickey Henderson, who said his phone system at his Hillsborough residence was still out and hadn't received the message that there would be a practice. The one player who would have been forgiven for skipping out, however, did show up. Just two weeks earlier, Bob and Mary Ellen Welch had bought a condo in San Francisco's Marina District, a home that was nearly destroyed by the earthquake. They had not moved into their new place, and they were fortunate that their temporary apartment, also in the Marina, escaped damage as well. Their infant son Dylan, at home in the Marina with a babysitter, was unscathed. For safety's sake, the Welches spent the night of the quake with friends in Daly City.

By October 20, Welch and Storm Davis were told that they would be bypassed in favor of Dave Stewart and Mike Moore in Games Three and Four. Welch, whose season had already encompassed the death of his mother, the birth of his son and the battering of his new house by the earthquake, seemed to take the news in stride. "I don't worry about the World Series. Anyone who thinks I do is crazy. . . . Hopefully, it works out so I don't have to pitch again," Welch said, looking toward a sweep.

Davis wasn't as upbeat about losing a World Series start. "I'm trying to understand Tony's position. This tells me maybe they have too much pitching here. Maybe they don't need me," said Davis, eligible for free agency after the season. "One way I don't want to be perceived is as being an athlete with a big humongous ego. I don't want people to think, 'Well, listen to this crybaby.' I'm not crying. But I'd like to say what I feel. Things have been strange, hectic, but I'd like to pitch, too."

When he heard that Davis had vented his spleen to the media, Tony La Russa erupted. He took Davis onto the outfield grass for a long talk. Davis heard it from La Russa that if he had any gripes, he should see the manager. "It doesn't take much to set me off right now," La Russa said. "And that was the 'much.' That's just not the way we do things around here. It's as tough for Bob as it is for Storm. Especially when those guys have earned their points the way they have this year. But this club relies on the manager to make the decisions based on what's best for the club. They have to realize that."

After the Giants ended practice October 20, they loaded a bus and took a good-will trip to downtown San Francisco. Bob Lurie, Al Rosen, Roger Craig and 15 other members of the club bused over to an earthquake relief shelter at the Moscone Center, where 1,100 people were on hand. The Giants' contingent stayed on the site for 20 minutes, signing autographs and handing out balls, caps and posters. "We spread some good cheer," Will Clark said. It wasn't easy, though. Said Terry Kennedy, "It's just another in a long line of reality checks. Those Red Cross people are the real heroes. They won't be on TV like we will."

If any rush of adrenaline surfaced as the week progressed, it was dashed on October 22 when Vincent and San Francisco Mayor Art Agnos announced that the series would undergo an additional delay. The series wouldn't resume now until October 27. If the series went seven games, it wouldn't be concluded until November, which would be a World Series first. The further extension was necessary because community leaders agreed the Bay Area would be closer to normal on October 27 than October 24. Realistically, however, it would be a long while before life returned to normal in the Bay Area. Without access to the Bay Bridge, traffic was a mess every day, and rain was only worsening the situation. Commuters were rediscovering travel via public transportation, and ferry boats and the Bay Area Rapid Transit system were carrying almost three times their normal daily loads.

The second delay meant 11 days would elapse between Game Two and Game Three, marking the longest pause in World Series history. There had been 17 World Series delays, with rain or cold generally the cause. The 1989 series provided the very first earthquake delay.

The latest delay wasn't the first to involve the Giants and A's. In 1911, rain caused a six-day delay between Games Three and Four of a Giants-A's clash —New York Giants and Philadelphia A's, that is. That series resumed October 24, and the A's won in six games. In 1962, the last time the Giants had played in the World Series, there was another delay. Game Six was rained out three times before it was finally played at Candlestick Park, and the Giants eventually bowed out to the Yankees.

When news of the second delay surfaced at the respective ballparks, there were the expected groans. But there was humor, too.

Terry Steinbach: "At this rate, we're going to have a Mr. November."

Don Robinson: "There's nothing we can do about it. . . . But if we keep waiting, Dravecky's going to start."

Kevin Mitchell: "Let's just play. I don't care if we play two or three in one day."

After hearing of the second postponement, Tony La Russa gave his troops a day off on October 23. Two days earlier, both teams' workouts had been abbreviated by rain, and La Russa was searching for a way to guarantee competitive workouts. Concerned about continued forecasts of rainy weather in the Bay Area, La Russa told the team to pack up. The A's were heading to their spring training home in Phoenix to work out under clearer skies. Getting the players, coaches, front office personnel and media shuttled from Oakland to Phoenix was a tremendous headache for A's traveling secretary Mickey Morabito, but by chartering a plane at the last minute and then splitting the traveling corps into two different hotels, he managed to put the package together in less than 24 hours.

When the Giants heard about the A's plans to return to their spring training site, they wondered why — especially when the sun had been creeping through the Bay Area skies. While the A's went to Phoenix, the Giants stayed at Candlestick. "This is a gorgeous day," Al Rosen said. "I don't know why you'd want to leave. This is a beautiful California day." Will Clark said, "It's a little tough to leave here. It's 80 degrees with no clouds in the sky. Anyway, it's October whatever, and I'm tired of traveling. The next bit of travel I'm going to do is when I go home."

The first inkling that Oakland's October 25 workout in Phoenix would be very unusual came when the chartered airplane was

20 minutes from Phoenix's Sky Harbor when the pilot announced, "I think you'll be surprised at the reception you get. I've heard that there will be 2,000 people at the practice." La Russa leaned across the aisle to catch the ear of team owner Walter A. Haas Jr. "Two thousand?" La Russa whispered. "No way. They've got to be joking." The joke was on the A's. Phoenix-area television and radio stations had built the two-day workouts into an extravaganza. And they asked for a voluntary admission to be donated to the Northern California earthquake relief, with a local TV station matching the pot. The two-hour workout, which was followed by a one-hour simulated game, drew some 6,000 Valley of the Sun fans, who contributed more than $10,000, into Phoenix Municipal Stadium,

"We heard 2,000, and there was no way we could believe that," Mark McGwire said. "We've been practicing in the Coliseum with maybe a dozen fans and the media. Then this. When I came out here and the fans were cheering, the adrenaline kicked in. My legs were sore, but I can't feel any of the pain now."

"This is just what we needed to give us a boost," Stewart said. "To be playing where everyone is excited is getting us excited, too."

While Oakland's momentum picked up in Arizona, things threatened to stall back in California. The rock concert production company Bill Graham Presents was fuming over the rescheduling of the World Series. If the series stretched to Game Six or Seven at the Coliseum, it would cut into time the Graham company had been guaranteed to set up for another major Northern California event. The Rolling Stones were scheduled to perform November 4 and 5, and Graham's contract with the Coliseum called for five days' setup time beginning October 30. After three days of negotiations, the Graham company agreed to settle for three days of preparation time, meaning there would only be a conflict if the series lasted seven games.

While Tony La Russa, a 90-minute plane ride away, was successfully firing up his troops for the Game Three, Part II, Roger Craig was planning his own motivational strategy. Craig received an assist via the U.S. Postal Service when he found on his desk a letter from a 38-year-old fan from Concord named Glenn Smith. Craig had never met, nor heard of, Glenn Smith, but the letter was strong enough even to pump up Craig. He read the letter aloud to a few sportswriters in his Candlestick office and said he planned to read it to his players in the minutes before Game Three. The letter:

"Whether you like it or not, you gentlemen have a large cross to bear. Your home has just been devastated by a natural disaster, and you are being asked to entertain the victims. Please, don't just go through the motions. You have been soundly defeated in the only two games played. You are facing the almighty and supposedly invincible Oakland A's, who have better pitching, more speed, equal power and equal defense. Your home park almost came crashing down around you last week. Don't cave in when faced with such adversity! Set an example. Show the Humm-Baby spirit that has characterized the Giants all year long. You haven't necessarily been the best team in terms of talent. You've been the most determined team, the team that won't quit, the team that can't die. All you know how to do is win! . . . You represent the earthquake capital of the world at its most downtrodden moment. You know that out there will be injured people, homeless people, rescue workers and just plainly depressed sympathizers temporarily focused on your activities. . . . Show your city, the Bay Area, the nation and the whole world what the Humm-Baby spirit is all about. You will never have another opportunity to contribute so much."

After reading the letter to the writers, Craig said, "I might memorize it and have my players think it's coming from me."

On October 27, the Giants and A's met at Candlestick Park for Game Three of the 1989 World Series. An eternity — 10 days — had elapsed since the last time they had tried to play the game. Despite some lingering fears about returning to Candlestick, the players were ready. "We're still hungry," Rickey Henderson said. "We still want to be number one and go out a winner." The fans were ready, too. The stadium was packed; fewer than 100 tickets had been returned to the Giants ticket office. The fans had been through an earthquake together, and as they took their seats, they greeted one another like old friends. The stadium announcer called for a moment of silence in honor of the quake victims, and at exactly 5:04 p.m. a hush fell over Candlestick. It was perhaps the quietest any crowd of 62,000 has been. Then the exotically costumed cast of "Beach Blanket Babylon," a popular, long-running cabaret show in San Francisco, took the field and led the fans in song. Reading from lyric sheets that had been handed to them as they entered the ballpark, the fans lustily sang "San Francisco." It's the song Jeanette MacDonald sang in the 1936 movie of the same name about the city's comeback after the 1906 earthquake and fire. Hun-

dreds of fans blinked on flashlights they had brought, just in case of another power outage. Originally, Willie Mays was supposed to throw out the first pitch of Game Three, but he stepped aside for 12 public safety workers and volunteers who had helped pull things together after the quake. Then the sun set over Candlestick, the field lights came up and home plate umpire Vic Voltaggio hollered, "Play ball!" Baseball was back.

If there was any doubt about that, three batters into the game, Giants starter Scott Garrelts threw a pitch that came in at Jose Canseco's head. Before that, Garrelts had forced Carney Lansford off the plate with a chest-high inside pitch. Lansford retaliated with a single before Canseco, seeing a ball at his eyes, backed out of the box, then took two threatening steps toward Garrelts and yelled at him. Giants catcher Terry Kennedy tried to restrain Canseco, but the slugger wasn't deterred until Voltaggio and La Russa combined to get between Canseco and the mound. "I don't think he was trying to hit me," Canseco said. "But I've seen it happen too many times. You're hit in the face and end up in the hospital with a broken jaw or a broken face. You're eating out of a straw. You lose 20, 30, 40, 50 pounds. And all you're going to get from the pitcher is, 'I'm sorry.' That's why power hitters have to establish that (pitchers) do not come up and in at the face. And I will establish it." Canseco stepped back in the box, singled and set up a two-run A's first inning.

Dave Henderson came up with two out and Lansford and Canseco on base and mauled a Garrelts pitch, lining it off the top of the right-field fence. He had to settle for a double and two RBIs, but he wouldn't be homerless for long. In the fourth inning, with Oakland holding a 2-1 lead, he hit a home run to right-center. When Tony Phillips homered later in the inning, Oakland led 4-1. With Will Clark and Kevin Mitchell getting back-to-back hits and Kennedy delivering a two-run single to center, San Francisco climbed back to within a run in the bottom of the fourth against Dave Stewart, but Garrelts walked two men in the fifth before Canseco snapped the Giants' spine with a three-run homer. Dave Henderson followed with his second homer of the game, finally pulling the ball and driving it into the left-field seats. With Oakland tying a World Series record with five homers, the A's crushed the Giants 13-7.

Henderson, who'd had three doubles and a homer in the A's playoff win over Toronto, said "I've always prided myself on being a good eighth- and ninth-inning hitter. And every at-bat in the post-season is like being in the eighth or ninth. The pressure's on. You have to perform. And I take pride in that."

This was the third time in four years that Dave Henderson found himself playing in the World Series. And if he had distinguished himself in the post-season hitting .400 in the 1986 series and .333 in the 1988 post-season, his teams had not. The '86 Red Sox kicked away a win over the Mets, and the A's had fallen flat in 1988. He'd even been on a playoff team in '87 — with the Giants. Concerned about the durability of Jeffrey Leonard's legs, the Giants acquired Henderson for the stretch drive. But Leonard was OK, and Henderson didn't make the post-season roster. After the season, the Giants released Henderson, at which time he jumped across the bay and revived his career.

Henderson's history had been one of big post-season hits. In 1986, his 12th-inning homer in Game Six of the World Series would have given the Red Sox the title had the Boston bullpen been able to hold the lead. In the 1988 playoffs against Boston, he had the game-winning hit in Game One and homered in Game Three. But, as he said, "When you don't win it, what you do gets swept under the rug."

For a while, it seemed that Mother Nature would sweep him away in 1989, again denying him a World Series ring. But once the games resumed, Henderson was back at the top of his game.

Before Game Four on October 28, Roger Craig went to great lengths to make sure that the Giants had not given up on themselves. He went as far as to make sure that none of his guys came to the park with bags packed for a possible trip home. "I checked, and if I saw one piece of luggage out there (in the clubhouse), I was going to release that guy before the game," he said, only half-jokingly. "I checked their cars and everything." Craig found nothing, but staving off elimination was going to take more than the resolve to stay in town.

Game Four saw the Giants' Don Robinson try to do what prior starters Scott Garrelts and Rick Reuschel had been unable to do — restrain the Oakland offense. But Robinson didn't make it out of the second inning. Rickey Henderson set the tone for the game with a leadoff homer in the first. Oakland added three more runs in the second with Mike Moore, who hadn't gotten a hit since his college days at Oral Roberts University, whacking a line drive beyond the desperate lunge of the back-racing Brett Butler for a two-run double and Rickey Henderson adding an RBI single. Back-to-back doubles by Terry Steinbach and Tony Phillips in the fifth chased home three more runs, and a Rickey Henderson triple and a Carney Lansford single in the sixth gave Moore an 8-0 lead.

Kevin Mitchell finally broke the shutout when he unloaded with a two-run homer in the sixth, and the Giants scored four more runs off the A's bullpen in the seventh. But San Francisco was spent after that spirited comeback, and Rick Honeycutt, Todd Burns and Dennis Eckersley put down the final eight Giants in order. With the 9-6 victory, the A's captured their first world championship in 15 years.

Oakland didn't trail at any point in the four games, the first team to do that since Baltimore swept Los Angeles in 1966. Oakland won the four games by a total of 18 runs (32-14), tying the all-time record of domination established by the Yankees over the Cubs in 1932. And the Giants only made it that close with late-inning rallies in Games Three and Four after they'd already been blown out. "They kicked our butts from start to finish, from beginning to end," Brett Butler assessed. "They're the better ballclub. They've got great pitching and hitting, and they just steamrolled us. Actually, that makes it easier to accept, because by beating us four games, we know they're the better club."

True to the A's post-earthquake promise, there were no cases of champagne open and ready for spraying when the players returned to the clubhouse; just an occasional bottle for, as Dave Stewart put it, "after everybody else clears out of the clubhouse." But if the A's believed that the earthquake would rob them of a season's worth of celebrating, they were very much mistaken. From the second that Eckersley crossed the first base bag, taking in a throw from Phillips at second base to cut down Butler, their celebration rang true with every bit as much joy as the 1969 Mets or 1927 Yankees could have mustered. Candlestick's visitors' clubhouse isn't small, but it quickly became cramped and soon evolved into little more than a maze of bear-hugging ballplayers, television cameras wrapped in protective plastic, and a forest of microphones that seemed to go on for ever, swaying slightly like some sort of metallic Kansas wheatfield. Shortly after the clinching, the wives and children of the players, coaches, manager and the executive officers became part of the celebration.

"This makes up for everything," said Dave Henderson. "This year we were on a mission. This year we weren't letting it slip away."

In a corner of the clubhouse, Bill Rigney, an assistant to A's general manager Sandy Alderson, embraced Alderson and La Russa. Then he stunned La Russa by telling him that in his 51 years in baseball as player, coach, manager (he was the first manager the Giants ever had in San Francisco) and adviser, this was his first world championship.

La Russa eventually escaped the mad crush. "I went to to the umpires' room, after they'd left, to take a shower," he said. "While I was there, I had 15 or 20 minutes of solitude that I'll never forget. It was the first time I'd really been able to pay attention to feelings and memories that were significant to me. That little break got me off the merry-go-round."

Dave Stewart's wins in Games One and Three earned him the Most Valuable Player trophy over the two Hendersons — Rickey hit .474 with four extra-base hits, scoring nine of Oakland's 32 runs, and Dave hit .308 with two homers, two doubles and six runs scored. But Stewart couldn't get his mind off the earthquake and the resultant tragedy. "I wasn't sure at first what was the right thing to do," he said. "But life did go on, and I'm sure playing the World Series was the right thing to do." Stewart said he would have understood if either of the Hendersons had earned the MVP, but Dave Henderson said, "Stew set the tone for this team from day one, when he shut the Giants out at the Coliseum. The night he did that, he all but told the Giants that the A's were going to win this thing."

"If anything, winning is sweeter this year than it would have been last year," Tony Phillips said. "It was worth the wait. This is all we ever wanted."

"This is what you play the game for," Mike Moore said. "This was my first chance to win, and we won it all. What could be better?"

Perhaps in no other World Series were two teams asked to do the things demanded of the A's and Giants. After having persevered throughout the baseball season, both clubs were emotionally shaken by the October 17 earthquake. They came back to play through a most trying and tragic World Series, and in that sense, both teams were winners. But it is the nature of baseball that one team wins and one team loses. The A's won, and victory was sweet. The Giants lost and were left to comfort themselves with baseball's healing words, "Wait 'til next year." But there will never be another year like 1989.

Epilogue

The key to the A's and Giants' success in 1989 was their depth; they used every man on their rosters, and every man had something to give. The two teams personified the 24-man concept. In neither case was it a one-man, two-man or three-man performance. Given the number of roster moves the two clubs made, they weren't even 24-man efforts. More like 30, plus coaches, managers and front offices, each filling vital roles.

Indicative of their all-around showings was the fact neither team dominated the post-season award ceremonies, as did both the Dodgers and A's of 1988. There were no Cy Young Award winners in the Bay Area. No Rookies of the Year. No Managers of the Year. San Francisco's Kevin Mitchell did walk away with a Most Valuable Player trophy, and Oakland's Dave Parker was named baseball's best designated hitter, but otherwise the awards were distributed elsewhere.

As teams, though, the Giants and A's couldn't be outdone statistically. The Giants ranked in the top three in the National League in both pitching — Scott Garrelts won the ERA title — and runs scored. Oakland was fourth in the American League in runs scored and, for the second straight year, posted the lowest ERA. Of course, the biggest team award of all was participating in the World Series and collecting the hefty playoff shares.

As was the case in the winter of '88-89, the winter of '89-90 was packed with news. And not all good. In fact, the Giants might have suffered a more serious setback than the one handed to them in the World Series. San Franciscans voted down Proposition W, which would have authorized the construction of a downtown baseball stadium. Giants owner Bob Lurie was miffed with the outcome and announced he was still planning to move his team out of Candlestick Park. Like 1987's similar Proposition P, the issue brought out heavy lobbying efforts on both sides. But with San Francisco still in the midst of rebuilding after the earthquake, a new stadium didn't seem to be much of a priority. San Francisco Mayor Art Agnos accused Sacramento sports interests of pouring large amounts of money to the anti-stadium forces and said any impropriety might necessitate putting another stadium measure back in front of San Francisco voters in the near future. Lurie, however, said he wasn't interested in a third San Francisco vote.

Not surprisingly, both teams saw their championship rosters begin breaking up shortly after the World Series. The A's were especially hard hit by free agency. Dave Parker (Milwaukee), Storm Davis (Kansas City) and Tony Phillips (Detroit) all signed with other teams. In an effort to counteract the losses, Oakland signed longtime Cubs pitcher Scott Sanderson, himself a free agent, and Ken Phelps, the left-handed slugger who had played a minor role in the A's 1989 season after coming over from the Yankees on August 31.

San Francisco felt the same kind of free agency swing. Craig Lefferts signed with San Diego, Candy Maldonado with Cleveland and Ken Oberkfell with Houston. But the Giants also used the market to their benefit, signing outfielder Kevin Bass, infielder Dave Anderson, catcher Gary Carter and pitcher Dan Quisenberry.

On a sadder note, another lump was detected in Dave Dravecky's left arm. He underwent surgery and formally announced his retirement. He said he planned to write a book to document his story.

Through the years, the A's and Giants' rosters will continue to change and their successes and failures will continue to be experienced. But will there ever be another season in the Bay Area like 1989? Probably not. The simultaneous success the A's and Giants enjoyed comes about as often as the killer earthquake that helped set the '89 season apart. On the other hand, a repeat performance can't be ruled out. The A's and Giants proved that anything can happen in the game of baseball.

In 1989, they produced magic by the bay.

APPENDIX

Giants' day-by-day log

Gm	Day	H/R	Score	Winner/Loser	Save	Record	Pos.	GA/B
1	4-3	R	SF 5, SD 3	Reuschel/Show	LaCoss	1-0	T1	—
2	4-4	R	SF 8, SD 3	Downs/Hurst		2-0	1	+½
3	4-5	R	SD 4, SF 3	Whitson/Robinson	Davis	2-1	T1	—
	4-6		Off				T1	—
4	4-7	R	Cin 4, SF 3 (16)	Birtsas/Price		2-2	2	-1
	4-8		Rain				2	-1
5	4-9	R	SF 9, Cin 1	Reuschel/Jackson		3-2	2	+½
6	4-10	H	LA 7, SF 4	Hershiser/LaCoss	Pena	3-3	T2	-1
7	4-11	H	SF 8, LA 3	Downs/Leary	Lefferts	4-3	T2	-½
8	4-12	H	SF 3, LA 1	Garrelts/Valenzuela	LaCoss	5-3	T1	+½
	4-13		Off				T1	+½
9	4-14	H	SF 7, Atl 5	Reuschel/Z. Smith	Lefferts	6-3	T1	+1
10	4-15	H	SF 1, Atl 0	Hammaker/P. SMITH		7-3	1	+1
11	4-16 (1)	H	Atl 7, SF 2	Smoltz/Downs	Alvarez	7-4	1	+1
12	4-16 (2)	H	SF 6, Atl 1	Price/ Puleo		8-4	1	+½
13	4-17	H	SF 9, SD 0	GARRELTS/Rasmussen		9-4	1	+½
14	4-18	H	SD 4, SF 2	Terrell/Reuschel	Davis	9-5	1	+½
15	4-19	H	SD 4, SF 3	Show/Hammaker	Davis	9-6	1	+½
	4-20		Off				1	+½
16	4-21	R	LA 8, SF 2	Hershiser/Downs		9-7	1	+½
17	4-22	R	SF 5, LA 4	Lefferts/Howell		10-7	1	+½
18	4-23	R	LA 7, SF 6 (10)	Howell/Hammaker		10-8	1	+½
	4-24		Off				1	+½
19	4-25	R	SF 4, StL 0	Robinson/Hill	Lefferts	11-8	1	+½
20	4-26	R	StL 3, SF 1	DeLeon/Downs	Dayley	11-9	T2	-½
21	4-27	R	StL 10, SF 1	Terry/Garrelts		11-10	T3	-1
22	4-28	R	Pitt 1, SF 0	SMILEY/Reuschel		11-11	3	-2
23	4-29	R	SF 4, Pitt 3	LaCoss/J. Robinson		12-11	3	-1
24	4-30	R	Pitt 11, SF 1	WALK/Robinson		12-12	3	-2
25	5-1	H	Chi 4, SF 3 (12)	Pico/LaCoss	Schiraldi	12-13	3	-2½
26	5-2	H	SF 4, Chi 0	Reuschel/Maddux	Gossage	13-13	T3	-2
27	5-3	H	Pitt 5, SF 3	Smiley/Robinson	Easley	13-14	4	-3
28	5-4	H	SF 6, Pitt 3	Krukow/Kramer	Lefferts	14-14	T2	-2
29	5-5	H	StL 3, SF 1	DiPino/LaCoss	Worrell	14-15	T2	-2
30	5-6	H	SF 9, StL 0	Reuschel/DeLeon	LaCoss	15-15	T2	-2
31	5-7	H	SF 5, StL 1	ROBINSON/Terry		16-15	2	-1
	5-8		Off				2	-1
32	5-9	R	SF 4, Chi 2	Krukow/Kilgus	Lefferts	17-15	2	-½
33	5-10	R	SF 4, Chi 3	LaCoss/Williams	Lefferts	18-15	1	+½
	5-11		Off				1	+½
34	5-12	R	SF 2, Mon 1	Reuschel/Perez	Gossage	19-15	1	+½
35	5-13	R	Mon 5, SF 4	Burke/Hammaker		19-16	2	-½
36	5-14	R	Mon 4, SF 3	Martinez/Krukow	Burke	19-17	2	-1½
37	5-15	R	Phill 3, SF 2 (12)	Bedrosian/Lefferts		19-18	2	-2½
38	5-16	R	SF 13, Phil 5	Hammaker/Maddux		20-18	2	-1½
39	5-17	R	SF 6, Phil 0	Reuschel/Howell		21-18	2	-1½
	5-18		Off				2	-1½
40	5-19	R	NY 3, SF (10)	Myers/Lefferts		21-19	2	-1½
41	5-20	R	SF 3, NY 0	Krukow/Ojeda	LaCoss	22-19	2	-½
42	5-21	R	SF 10, NY 6	Hammaker/McDowell	Lefferts	23-19	2	-½
	5-22		Off				2	-½
43	5-23	H	SF 4, Mon 2	Reuschel/Holman	LaCoss	24-19	2	-½
44	5-24	H	Mon 1, SF 0	GROSS/Robinson		24-20	2	-1½
45	5-25	H	Mon 2, SF 0	Martinez/Krukow	Burke	24-21	2	-2
46	5-26	H	SF 6, Phil 1	Garrelts/Sebra		25-21	2	-2
47	5-27	H	SF 6, Phil 2	Hammaker/Madrid	Lefferts	26-21	2	-1
48	5-28	H	SF 8, Phil 5	Reuschel/Howell	LaCoss	27-21	T1	—
49	5-29	H	SF 3, NY 2	Robinson/Darling	Lefferts	28-21	1	+1
50	5-30	H	SF 10, NY 3	Krukow/Cone		29-21	1	+2

Gm	Day	H/R	Score	Winner/Loser	Save	Record	Pos.	GA/B
51	5-31	H	NY 3, SF 1 (10)	Myers/Lefferts	Aguilera	29-22	1	+1
	6-1		Off				1	+1
52	6-2	R	SF 7, Atl 6	Reuschel/Glavine	Gossage	30-22	1	+1
53	6-3	R	SF 4, Atl 0	Hammaker/Z. Smith		31-22	1	+1
54	6-4	R	Atl 6, SF 3	Lilliquist/Krukow	Boever	31-23	T1	1 ½
55	6-5	R	SF 11, Cin 8	Garrelts/Rijo		32-23	1	+1
56	6-6 (1)	R	Cin 4, SF 3	Franco/LaCoss		32-24	T1	+½
57	6-6 (2)	R	SF 3, Cin 2	Reuschel/Dibble	Lefferts	33-24	1	+1
58	6-7	R	Cin 12, SF 5	MAHLER/Hammaker		33-25	T1	—
59	6-8	R	Cin 3, SF 2	Dibble/LaCoss	Franco	33-26	3	-1
60	6-9	H	SF 12, SD 2	Robinson/Hurst		34-26	3	-1
61	6-10	H	SF 1, SD 0	Garrelts/Whitson	Lefferts	35-26	3	-1
62	6-11	H	SF 3, SD 1 (12)	Gossage/Davis		36-26	T2	-1
	6-12		Off				2	-1
63	6-13	H	SF 3, Atl 2	Hammaker/Z. Smith	Lefferts	37-26	T1	+½
64	6-14	H	SF 10, Atl 1	Robinson/Lilliquist		38-26	1	+1
65	6-15	H	Atl 2, SF 1	Smoltz/Garrelts		38-27	1	+1
66	6-16	H	Cin 5, SF 4	Charlton/Gossage	Franco	38-28	T1	+½
67	6-17	H	SF 8, Cin 1	COOK/Jackson		39-28	1	+1
68	6-18	H	SF 2, Cin 1	LaCoss/Rijo	• Lefferts	40-28	1	+1
69	6-19	H	SF 3, Hou 2	Robinson/Knepper	Bedrosian	41-28	1	+2
70	6-20	H	SF 4, Hou 0	Garrelts/Forsch	Lefferts	42-28	1	+3
71	6-21	H	SF 2, Hou 0	Reuschel/Clancy	Bedrosian	43-28	1	+4
	6-22		Off				1	+4
72	6-23	R	SF 8, SD 7	Gossage/Harris	Bedrosian	44-28	1	+4
73	6-24	R	SF 3, SD 1	Robinson/Terrell	Bedrosian	45-28	1	+4
74	6-25	R	SD 10, SF 7	Grant/Garrelts		45-29	1	+3
75	6-26	R	SF 4, Hou 3	Lefferts/Agosto	Bedrosian	46-29	1	+3
76	6-27	R	Hou 7, SF 5	Darwin/Bedrosian		46-30	1	+3
77	6-28	R	Hou 7, SF 3	Deshaies/Robinson		46-31	1	+2
78	6-29	H	SF 12, Chi 2	Brantley/Kilgus		47-31	1	+2
79	6-30	H	Chi 6, SF 4	Sanderson/Wilson	Williams	47-32	1	+2
80	7-1	H	Chi 3, SF 2	Maddux/REUSCHEL	Williams	47-33	1	+1
81	7-2	H	SF 4, Chi 3	Brantley/SUTCLIFFE	Bedrosian	48-33	1	+2
	7-3		Off				1	+2
82	7-4	R	Pitt 5, SF 3	Kramer/Robinson	Landrum	48-34	1	+1½
83	7-5	R	SF 6, Pitt 4	Wilson/Walk		49-34	1	+2
84	7-6	R	SF 2, Pitt 1 (10)	Brantley/SMILEY	Lefferts	50-34	1	+2
85	7-7	R	StL 6, SF 4	DiPino/LaCoss	Dayley	50-35	1	+2
86	7-8	R	SF 8, StL 5	Brantley/Power		51-35	1	+2
87	7-9	R	StL 6, SF 4	Magrane/Wilson	Dayley	51-36	1	+2
88	7-13	H	SF 3, Pitt 2 (13)	Brantley/Garcia		52-36	1	+2½
89	7-14	H	Pitt 7, SF 4	Drabek/Reuschel	Landrum	52-37	1	+2½
90	7-15	H	SF 8, Pitt 3	LaCoss/Smiley		53-37	1	+2½
91	7-16	H	SF 3, Pitt 1	Garrelts/J. Robinson	Bedrosian	54-37	1	+3
92	7-17	H	SF 8, StL 4	McCament/Power	Gossage	55-37	1	+2½
93	7-18	H	SF 7, StL 3	Robinson/Hill		56-37	1	+3½
94	7-19	H	SF 7, StL 5	Brantley/Terry	Lefferts	57-37	1	+4½
95	7-20	R	Chi 4, SF 3 (11)	Lancaster/McCament		57-38	1	+4
96	7-21	R	SF 4, Chi 3	Garrelts/Sutcliffe	Lefferts	57-38	1	+4
97	7-22	R	Chi 5, SF 2	Sanderson/Hammaker	Lancaster	58-39	1	+2½
98	7-23	R	Chi 9, SF 5	Maddux/Robinson		58-40	1	+1½
99	7-24	R	SF 2, Atl 0	Reuschel/SMOLTZ	Bedrosian	59-40	1	+2
100	7-25	R	SF 5, Atl 4	LaCoss/Lilliquist	Lefferts	60-40	1	+3
101	7-26	R	Atl 5, SF 4	Boever/Bedrosian		60-41	1	+2
102	7-27	R	Atl 10, SF 1	Glavine/Hammaker		60-42	1	+2
103	7-28	R	SF 3, Hou 2	ROBINSON/Clancey		61-42	1	+3
104	7-29	R	Hou 8, SF 1	PORTUGAL/Reuschel		61-43	1	+2
105	7-30	R	Hou 6, SF 2	Scott/LaCoss		61-44	1	+1
	7-31		Off				1	+1
106	8-1	R	SF 5, LA 2	Garrelts/Valenzuela	Lefferts	62-44	1	+1
107	8-2	R	LA 7, SF 4	Martinez/Wilson	Howell	62-45	1	+1
108	8-3	R	LA 6, SF 3	Hershiser/Swan	Howell	62-46	1	+1
109	8-4	H	SF 4, Hou 2	ROBINSON/Darwin		63-46	1	+2
110	8-5	H	SF 7, Hou 0	LaCoss/Scoitt		64-46	1	+3
111	8-6	H	Hou 3, SF 2	Agosto/Lefferts	Smith	64-47	1	+2
112	8-7	H	Cin 10, SF 2	Robinson/Brantley	Birtsas	64-48	1	+2
113	8-8	H	Cin 10, SF 4	BROWNING/Swan		64-49	1	+1
114	8-9	H	SF 10, Cin 1	ROBINSON/Mahler		65-49	1	+2
115	8-10	H	SF 4, Cin 3	Dravecky/Scudder	Bedrosian	66-49	1	+3
116	8-11	H	SF 10, LA 2	LaCoss/Belcher		67-49	1	+4
117	8-12	H	LA 5, SF 1	VALENZUELA/Knepper		67-50	1	+2

Gm	Day	H/R	Score	Winner/Loser	Save	Record	Pos.	GA/B
118	8-13	H	LA 3, SF 2 (12)	Howell/Robinson	Pena	67-51	1	+3
	8-14		Off				1	+3
119	8-15	R	SF 3, Mon 2	Dravecky/B. Smith	Bedrosian	68-51	1	+3
120	8-16	R	Mon 4, SF 2	Burke/Bedrosian		68-52	1	+2
121	8-17	R	SF 10, Mon 5	Knepper/Hesketh		69-52	1	+2
122	8-18	R	SF 5, Phil 2	Reuschel/Ruffin	Bedrosian	70-52	1	+2
123	8-19	R	Phil 1, SF 0	MULHOLLAND/Downs		70-53	1	+2
124	8-20	R	SF 5, Phil 2	Brantley/McDowell		71-53	1	+2
125	8-21	R	NY 4, SF 1	Darling/LaCoss	Myers	71-54	1	+1½
126	8-22	R	SF 5, NY 0	KNEPPER/Viola		72-54	1	+2½
127	8-23	R	SF 5, NY 0	Reuschel/Cohn		73-54	1 ·	+3½
	8-24		Off				1	+4
128	8-25	H	Mon 12, SF 2	Martinez/Downs		73-55	1	+4
129	8-26	H	SF 8, Mon 3	Garrelts/Langston		74-55	1	+5
130	8-27	H	Mon 6, SF 3	B. Smith/LaCoss	Burke	74-56	•1	+4
131	8-28	H	Phil 9, SF 1	Howell/Reuschel		74-57	1	+4
132	8-29	H	Phil 6, SF 1	Ruffin/Robinson	McDowell	74-58	1	+4
133	8-30	H	SF 3, Phil 2	Downs/Mulholland	Bedrosian	75-58	1	+4
	8-31		Off				1	+4
134	9-1	H	SF 7, NY 1	Garrelts/Darling		76-58	1	+4
135	9-2	H	SF 6, NY 2	Reuschel/Viola		77-58	1	+5
136	9-3	H	SF 4, NY 0	ROBINSON/Ojeda		78-58	1	+6
137	9-4	R	SF 9, Cin 8	Camacho/Franco	Bedrosian	79-58	1	+7
138	9-5	R	Cin 6, SF 5	Armstrong/LaCoss	Franco	79-59	1	+6
139	9-6	R	SF 7, Atl 2	GARRELTS/Lilliquist		80-59	1	+6
140	9-7	R	SF 7, Atl 5	Bedrosian/Stanton		81-59	1	+7
141	9-8	R	Hou 5, SF 2	Portugal/Robinson	Darwin	81-60	1	+6
142	9-9	R	Hou 4, SF 1	SCOTT/Downs		81-61	1	+5
143	9-10	R	SF 5, Hou 3	Knepper/Rhoden	Lefferts	82-61	1	+6
144	9-11	H	SF 3, Atl 2	Garrelts/Castillo	Bedrosian	83-61	1	+6
145	9-12	H	Atl 6, SF 5	Aldrich/Bedrosian	Stanton	83-62	1	+5
146	9-13	H	SF 8, Cin 7 (13)	Camacho/Rodriguez		84-62	1	+5
147	9-14	H	SF 4, Cin 1 (12)	Camacho/Charlton		85-62	1	+6
148	9-15	H	SD 5, SF	Rasmussen/Knepper	Harris	85-63	1	+5
	9-16		Rain				1	+5
149	9-17 (1)	H	SF 5, SD	Garrelts/Harris	Bedrosian	86-63	1	+6
150	9-17 (2)	H	SD 6, SF 1	HURST/Reuschel		86-64	1	+5
	9-18		Off				1	+5
151	9-19	H	SF 3, LA 2	LaCoss/Hershiser	Bedrosian	87-64	1	+5
152	9-20	H	SF 8, LA 1	Wilson/Hartley		88-64	1	+5
153·	9-21	H	SF 4, LA 3	Downs/Martinez	Bedrosian	89-64	1	+5
154	9-22	H	Hou 3, SF 1	Portugal/Garrelts	Schatzeder	89-65	1	+5
155	9-23	H	SF 3, Hou 1	REUSCHEL/Scott		90-65	1	+5
156	9-24	H	SF 10, Hou 2	LaCOSS/Clancy		91-65	1	+5
157	9-25	R	LA 5, SF 2	Wetteland/Robinson	Pena	91-66	1	+5
158	9-26	R	LA 2, SF 1	Martinez/Downs	Howell	91-67	1	+4
159	9-27	R	LA 1, SF 0	BELCHER/Garrelts		91-68	1	+4
	9-28		Off				1	+4
160	9-29	R	SF 7, SD 2	LaCoss/Benes		92-68	1	+5
161	9-30	R	SD 11, SF 5	Grant/Reuschel		92-69	1	+4
162	10-1	R	SD 3, SF 0	Harris/Downs	Davis	92-70	1	+3

A's day-by-day log

Gm	Day	H/R	Score	Winner/Loser	Save	Record	Pos.	GA/B
I	4-3	H	A's 3, Sea 2	Stewart/LANGSTON	Eckersley	1-0	T1	—
	4-4		Off				T1	—
2	4-5	H	A's 11, Sea 1	Welch/Bankhead		2-0	1	+½
3	4-6	H	A's 11, Sea 3	Davis/Campbell	Burns	3-0	1	+½
4	4-7	H	Chi 7, A's 1	Long/C. Young	Jones	3-1	T1	—
5	4-8	H	Chi 7, A's 4	Perez/Moore	Thigpen	3-2	5	-1
6	4-9	H	A's 4, Chi 2	Stewart/Reuss	Eckersley	4-2	T2	-½
7	4-10	R	A's 4, Cal 0	Welch/Finley		5-2	T2	-½
8	4-11	R	Cal 7, A's 1	BLYLEVEN/Davis		5-3	T4	-1
9	4-12	R	Cal 5, A's 0	McCaskill/C.Young		5-4	T4	-2
10	4-13	R	A's 5, Cal 0	Moore/Abbott		6-4	T4	-2
11	4-14	R	A's 7, Chi 4	Stewart/Perez		7-4	2	-2
12	4-15	R	Chi 7, A's 4	Reuss/Welch	Thigpen	7-5	3	-3
13	4-16	R	A's 3, Chi 2	Eckersley/King		8-5	3	-3
14	4-17	R	Sea 7, A's 2	Hanson/C. Young		8-6	T2	-2
15	4-18	R	A's 5, Sea 3	Plunk/Reed	Eckersley	9-6	T2	-3
16	4-19	R	A's 7, Sea 5	Stewart/Langston	Eckersley	10-6	2	-3
	4-20		Off				2	-3
17	4-21	H	A's 10, Cal 6	Welch/Finley	Honeycutt	11-6	2	-2
18	4-22	H	A's 4, Cal 3	C. Young/BLYLEVEN	Eckersley	12-6	2	-1
19	4-23	H	A's 2, Cal 0	Moore/McCaskill	Eckersley	13-6	2	-1
20	4-24	H	A's 5, Tor 4	Nelson/Henke		14-6	2	-½
21	4-25	H	A's 3, Tor 1	Davis/Cerutti	Eckersley	15-6	2	-½
22	4-26	H	Balt 2, A's 1	Bautista/Welch	Olson	15-7	2	-1½
23	4-27	H	A's 9, Balt 4	Burns/Thurmond		16-7	2	-1
24	4-28	H	A's 2, Det 1	Moore/Gibson	Eckersley	17-7	2	-½
25	4-29	H	A's 3, Det 2	STEWART/ALEXANDER		18-7	T1	—
26	4-30	H	Det 7, A's 2	Tanana/Davis	Hernandez	18-8	2	-1
	5-1		Off				2	-½
27	5-2	R	A's 8, Tor 5	Honeycutt/Ward	Plunk	19-8	1	+½
28	5-3	R	Tor 2, A's 0	FLANAGAN/Moore		19-9	2	-½
	5-4		Off				T1	—
29	5-5	R	A's 5, Det 3	Stewart/Tanana	Eckersley	20-9	1	+1
30	5-6	R	Det 5, A's 3	Morris/Davis	Hernandez	20-10	1	+1
31	5-7	R	A's 5, Det 4	Welch/Hudson	Eckersley	21-10	1	+1½
32	5-8	R	A's 6, Balt 1	Moore/Milacki		22-10	1	+1½
	5-9		Rain				1	+1
	5-10		Rain				1	+1
33	5-11	R	Balt 6, A's 2	Ballard/Stewart		22-11	1	+1
34	5-12	H	A's 5, Mil 4	Burns/Plesac		23-11	1	+2
35	5-13	H	A's 4, Mil 3	Welch/Bosio	Eckersley	24-11	1	+2
36	5-14	H	Mil 2, A's 1	Crim/Moore	Plesac	24-12	1	+1
37	5-15	H	A's 12, Mil 2	Stewart/August		25-12	1	+1
38	5-16	H	NY 3, A's 2	Parker/C. Young	Righetti	25-13	T1	—
39	5-17	H	A's 8, NY 3	Davis/Dobson	Eckersley	26-13	1	—
40	5-18	H	A's 6, NY 2	Welch/John	Burns	27-13	1	+1
41	5-19	H	Bos 7, A's 4 (10)	Stanley/Nelson		27-14	T1	—
42	5-20	H	A's 6, Bos 3	Stewart/Gardner	Eckersley	28-14	1	+1
43	5-21	H	A's 5, Bos 4	Burns/Clemens	Eckersley	29-14	1	+1
	5-22		Off				1	+1
44	5-23	R	Mil 9, A's 1	Bosio/Welch		29-15	1	+½
45	5-24	R	A's 6, Mil 2	Moore/Birkbeck		30-15	1	+½
46	5-25	R	Mil 4, A's 1	Clutterbuck/Stewart	Plesac	30-16	1	+½
47	5-26	R	A's 4, NY 0	Burns/Hawkins		31-16	1	+½
48	5-27	R	A's 3, NY 0	C. Young/LaPoint	Honeycutt	32-16	1	+1
49	5-28	R	A's 4, NY 3	Moore/Parker	Honeycutt	33-16	1	+1
50	5-29	R	Bos 3, A's 2 (10)	Smith/WELCH		33-17	T1	—
51	5-30	R	A's 4, Bos 2	Stewart/Smithson	Honeycutt	34-17	T1	—
52	5-31	R	Bos 4, A's 3 (10)	Smith/Plunk		34-18	T1	—
	6-1		Off				T1	—
53	6-2	H	Cle 5, A's 3	Swindell/Moore		34-19	T1	—
54	6-3	H	A's 7, Cle 0	Welch/Candiotti		35-19	T1	—
55	6-4	H	A's 4, Cle 0	Stewart/Farrell		36-19	T1	—
56	6-5	H	Min 1, A's 0	Oliveras/C. Young	Reardon	36-20	T1	—
57	6-6	H	A's 1, Min 0	MOORE/ANDERSON		37-20	T1	—
58	6-7	H	A's 3, Min 2	Welch/Viola	Burns	38-20	1	+1
	6-8		Off				1	+1
59	6-9	R	Tex 11, A's 8	Guante/Nelson	Russell	38-21	1	+1
60	6-10	R	A's 5, Tex 1	Davis/Witt		39-21	1	+2
61	6-11	R	A's 5, Tex 1	Moore/Brown	Nelson	40-21	1	+3

Gm	Day	H/R	Score	Winner/Loser	Save	Record	Pos.	GA/B
62	6-12	R	KC 2, Oak 1	Gordon/Burns		40-22	1	+2½
63	6-13	R	KC 5, Oak 3	Appier/C. Young	Farr	40-23	1	+1½
64	6-14	R	A's 2, KC 1	Stewart/Leibrandt	Honeycutt	41-23	1	+2½
	6-15		Off				1	+2
65	6-16 (1)	R	A's 7, Balt 5	Davis/Holton	Honeycutt	42-23		
66	6-16 (2)	R	Balt 5, A's 1	Tibbs/Moore		42-24	1	+2½
67	6-17	R	Balt 4, A's 2	Bautista/M. Young	Olson	42-25	1	+2½
68	6-18	R	Balt 4, A's 2	Schmidt/C. Young	Weston	42-26	1	+1½
69	6-19	H	Det 6, A's 4	Tanana/Stewart	Henneman	42-27	1	+1½
70	6-20	H	A's 6, Det 4	Nelson/Havens	Burns	42-37	1	+2
71	6-21	H	A's 6, Det 3	Moore/Schwabe	Honeycutt	44-27	1	+2
72	6-22	H	Tor 4, A's 2 (13)	Hernandez/Corsi	Wells	44-28	1	+2
73	6-23	H	Tor 10, A's 8	Buice/C. Young	Henke	44-29	1	+1
74	6-24	H	A's 7, Tor 1	STEWART/Stieb		45-29	1	+2
75	6-25	H	A's 6, Tor 3	Davis/Key	Honeycutt	46-29	1	+2½
76	6-26	R	Min 4, A's 3 (10)	Reardon/Burns		46-30	1	+2
77	6-27	R	Min 11, A's 5	Wayne/Nelson	Berenguer	46-31	1	+1
78	6-28	R	Min 2, A's 0	VIOLA/STEWART		46-32	1	+1
	6-29		Off				1	+½
79	6-30	R	A's 5, Cle 0	Welch/Swindell	Honeycutt	47-32	1	+½
80	7-1	R	A's 6, Cle 4	Moore/Yett	Burns	48-32	1	+½
81	7-2	R	A's 11, Cle 3	Davis/Farrell		49-32	1	+1½
82	7-3	H	A's 1, KC 0	Stewart/Gubicza	Honeycutt	50-32	1	+1½
83	7-4	H	KC 10, A's 1	Saberhagen/M. Young		50-33	1	+½
84	7-5	H	KC 12, Oak 9 (11)	Crawford/Honeycutt		50-34	2	-½
85	7-6	H	A's 3, KC 1	Moore/Aquino	Burns	51-34	1	+½
86	7-7	H	Tex 6, A's 3	Witt/Davis		51-35	2	-½
87	7-8	H	Tex 5, A's 4 (10)	Russell/M. Young		51-36	2	-1½
88	7-9	H	A's 7, Tex 1	Welch/Hough	Honeycutt	52-36	2	-1½
89	7-13	R	A's 11, Tor 7	Burns/Key		53-36	2	-1½
90	7-14	R	Tor 4, A's 1	Stieb/Welch	Ward	53-37	2	-1½
91	7-15	R	Tor 6, A's 1	Flanagan/Stewart		53-38	2	-1½
92	7-16	R	A's 6, Tor 2	Moore/Cerutti	Burns	54-38	2	-½
93	7-17	R	Det 2, A's 1	Henneman/Nelson		54-39	T1	—
94	7-18	R	A's 7, Det 2	Davis/Beard		55-39	T1	—
	7-19		Rain				T1	—
95	7-20	H	A's 5, Balt 2	Stewart/Schmidt	Eckersley	56-39	T1	—
96	7-21	H	A's 3, Balt 2	MOORE/Olson		57-39	T1	—
97	7-22	H	A's 3, Balt 1	Welch/Harnisch	Eckersley	58-39	T1	—
98	7-23	H	A's 3, Balt 2	Davis/Ballard	Eckersley	59-39	T1	—
99	7-24	H	Cal 5, A's 4	Fraser/Nelson	Harvey	59-40	2	-1
100	7-25	H	Cal 4, A's 0	Finley/STEWART	Minton	59-41	2	-2
101	7-26	H	A's 9, Cal 5	M. Young/Witt		60-41	2	-1
	7-27		Off				2	-1½
102	7-28	H	A's 8, Sea 7 (11)	Burns/Harris		61-41	2	-1½
103	7-29	H	Sea 14, A's 6	Johnson/Davis	Swift	61-42	2	-2½
104	7-30	H	A's 5, Sea 3	Stewart/Holman	Eckersley	62-42	2	-1½
105	7-31	H	A's 3, Chi 2	MOORE/Thigpen		63-42	2	-½
106	8-1	H	A's 2, Chi 0	C. Young/Hibbard	Eckersley	64-42	1	+½
107	8-2	H	A's 2, Chi 0	Davis/Perez	Honeycutt	65-42	1	+½
108	8-3	H	Chi 6, A's 4	Pall/Welch	Thigpen	65-43	2	-½
109	8-4	R	A's 5, Sea 3	Stewart/Holman	Eckersley	66-43	2	-½
110	8-5	R	Sea 11, A's 5	Bankhead/Moore	Jackson	66-44	2	-½
111	8-6	R	A's 2, Sea 1	Davis/Dunne	Eckersley	67-44	2	-½
112	8-7	R	Sea 5, A's 1	Zavaras/Welch		67-45	2	-1
113	8-8	R	A's 3, Chi 2	Honeycutt/Pall	Eckersley	68-45	T1	—
114	8-9	R	Chi 3, A's 2 (11)	McCarthy/Corsi		68-46	2	-1
115	8-10	R	A's 4, Chi 1	Davis/Rosenberg	Eckersley	69-46	T1	—
116	8-11	R	A's 5, Cal 0	MOORE/Witt		70-46	1	+1
117	8-12	R	A's 8, Cal 3	Welch/Abbott	Burns	71-46	1	+2
118	8-13	R	Cal 4, A's 3	Blyleven/STEWART	Harvey	71-46	1	+1
	8-14		Off				1	+1½
119	8-15	H	A's 5, Cle 2	Davis/Nichols	Eckersley	72-47	1	+1½
120	8-16	H	Cle 6, A's 4	Olin/Honeycutt	Jones	72-48	1	+1½
121	8-17	H	A's 1, Cle 0	Welch/Farrell	Eckersley	73-48	1	+1
122	8-18	H	Min 4, A's 3	Smith/Stewart	Reardon	73-49	T1	—
123	8-19	H	A's 5, Min 4 (10)	DAVIS/Wayne		74-49	T1	—
124	8-20	H	A's 5, Min 0	Moore/Anderson		75-49	T1	—
125	8-21	R	A's 6, Det 1	C. Young/Tanana		76-49	1	+1
126	8-22	R	A's 2, Tex 0	Welch/Ryan	Eckersley	77-49	1	+2
127	8-23	R	A's 5, Tex 4	Stewart/Brown	Eckersley	78-49	1	+3
128	8-24	R	Tex 6, A's 2	Jeffcoat/Davis	Mielke	78-50	1	+2
129	8-25	R	KC 3, A's 1	Gubicza/Moore	Montgomery	78-51	1	+1

Gm	Day	H/R	Score	Winner/Loser	Save	Record	Pos.	GA/B
130	8-26	R	KC 2, A's 0	SABERHAGEN/C. Young		78-52	1	+1
131	8-27	R	A's 5, KC 0	Welch/Gordon		79-52	1	+1
132	8-28	R	A's 7, NY 3	Stewart/Hawkins	Eckersley	80-52	1	+1½
133	8-29	R	A's 19, NY 5	Davis/Cary		81-52	1	+3
134	8-30	R	NY 8, A's 5	Plunk/Moore	McCullers	81-53	1	+2
	8-31		Off				1	2½
135	9-1	R	Mil 6, A's 5	Crim/ Burns		81-54	1	1½
136	9-2	R	A's 7, Mil 2	STEWART/Filer		82-54	1	2½
137	9-3	R	A's 5, Mil 0	Davis/Navarro	Nelson	83-54	1	2½
138	9-4	H	Bos 8, A's 5	Dopson/Moore	Smith	83-55	1	2½
139	9-5	H	A's 13, Bos 1	C. Young/Clemens		84-55	1	3½
140	9-6	H	A's 7, Bos 5	Welch/Smithson	Eckersley	85-55	1	4½
	9-7		Off				1	4½
141	9-8	H	NY 5, A's 1	Mohorcic/STEWART		85-56	1	3½
142	9-9	H	A's 7, NY 5	MOORE/Parker		86-56	1	3½
143	9-10	H	A's 6, NY 2	Davis/Plunk		87-56	1	4½
	9-11		Off				1	4
144	9-12	H	Mil 7, A's 6	August/M. Young		87-57	1	3
145	9-13	H	A's 7, Mil 6	Eckersley/Crim		88-57	1	3
	9-14		Off				1	3½
146	9-15	R	Bos 7, A's 2	Clemens/Moore		88-58	1	3½
147	9-16	R	Bos 5, A's 2	Dopson/Davis	Lamp	88-59	1	3½
148	9-17	R	Bos 7, A's 6	Harris/Welch	Smith	88-60	1	2½
149	9-18	R	A's 4, Cle 2	Eckersley/Olin		89-60	1	2½
150	9-19	R	A's 5, Cle 1	Moore/Nichols		90-60	1	2½
151	9-20	R	A's 8, Cle 5	Davis/Swindell	Eckersley	91-60	1	2½
152	9-21	R	A's 2, Min 1	Welch/AGUILERA	Eckersley	92-60	1	3½
153	9-22	R	A's 5, Min 2	Stewart/Dyer	Nelson	93-60	1	4
154	9-23	R	Min 5, A's 3	Anderson/Moore	Smith	93-61	1	4½
155	9-24	R	A's 9, Min 3	Davis Tapani	Eckersley	94-61	1	5½
156	9-25	H	Tex 3, A's 2	Hall/Burns	Russell	94-62	1	5
157	9-26	H	A's 4, Tex 3	Eckersley/Jeffcoat		95-62	1	5
158	9-27	H	A's 5, Tex 0	Moore/Moyer		96-62	1	5
159	9-28	H	A's 5, Tex 3	Stewart/Arnsberg	Eckersley	97-62	1	6
160	9-29	H	A's 4, KC 3	Nelson/Luecken		98-62	1	7
161	9-30	H	KC 6, A's 1	Saberhagen/Burns		98-63	1	6
162	10-1	H	A's 4, KC 3 (11)	Corsi/Leach		99-63	1	7

Pitchers in capital letters indicate complete games.

Month-by-month standings

End of April

A.L. West

	W	L	Pct.	GB
Texas	17	5	.773	—
Oakland	18	8	.692	1
Kansas City	16	8	.667	2
California	15	10	.600	3½
Minnesota	10	12	.455	7
Seattle	11	15	.423	8
Chicago	8	16	.333	10

N.L. West

	W	L	Pct.	GB
Cincinnati	13	9	.591	—
San Diego	14	12	.538	1
San Francisco	12	12	.500	2
Los Angeles	11	13	.458	3
Houston	11	14	.440	3½
Atlanta	10	15	.400	4½

End of May

A.L. West

	W	L	Pct.	GB
California	33	17	.660	—
Oakland	34	18	.654	—
Kansas City	30	21	.588	3½
Texas	27	22	.551	5½
Seattle	25	28	.472	9½
Minnesota	23	27	.460	10
Chicago	18	33	.353	15½

N.L. West

	W	L	Pct.	GB
San Francisco	29	22	.569	—
Cincinnati	27	22	.551	1
San Diego	29	25	.537	1½
Houston	27	24	.529	2
Los Angeles	25	24	.510	3
Atlanta	22	29	.431	7

End of June

A.L. West

	W	L	Pct.	GB
Oakland	47	32	.595	—
California	45	31	.592	½
Kansas City	44	33	.571	2
Texas	43	35	.551	3½
Minnesota	40	39	.506	7
Seattle	37	42	.468	10
Chicago	30	50	.375	17½

N.L. West

	W	L	Pct.	GB
San Francisco	47	32	.595	—
Houston	45	34	.570	2
Cincinnati	41	37	.536	5½
San Diego	39	41	.488	8½
Los Angeles	37	41	.474	9½
Atlanta	32	46	.410	14½

End of July

A.L. West

	W	L	Pct.	GB
California	63	41	.606	—
Oakland	63	42	.600	½
Kansas City	57	47	.548	6
Texas	56	47	.544	6½
Minnesota	51	53	.490	12
Seattle	50	54	.481	13
Chicago	44	61	.419	19½

N.L. West

	W	L	Pct.	GB
San Francisco	61	44	.581	—
Houston	60	45	.571	1
San Diego	51	54	.486	10
Cincinnati	48	56	.462	12½
Los Angeles	49	57	.462	12½
Atlanta	43	62	.410	18

End of August

A.L. West

	W	L	Pct.	GB
Oakland	81	53	.604	—
Kansas City	78	55	.586	2½
California	78	55	.586	2½
Texas	68	63	.519	11½
Minnesota	68	65	.511	12½
Seattle	59	74	.444	21½
Chicago	56	77	.412	24½

N.L. West

	W	L	Pct.	GB
San Francisco	75	58	.564	—
Houston	71	62	.534	4
San Diego	69	65	.515	6½
Cincinnati	64	69	.481	11
Los Angeles	62	71	.466	13
Atlanta	53	80	.398	22

End of Season

American League

A.L. West

	W	L	Pct.	GB
Oakland	99	63	.611	—
Kansas City	92	70	.568	7
California	91	71	.562	8
Texas	83	79	.512	16
Minnesota	80	82	.494	19
Seattle	73	89	.451	26
Chicago	69	92	.429	29½

A.L. East

	W	L	Pct.	GB
Toronto	89	73	.549	—
Baltimore	87	75	.537	2
Boston	83	79	.512	6
Milwaukee	81	81	.500	8
New York	74	87	.460	14½
Cleveland	73	89	.451	16
Detroit	59	103	.364	30

National League

N.L. West

	W	L	Pct.	GB
San Francisco	92	70	.568	—
San Diego	89	73	.549	3
Houston	86	76	.531	6
Los Angeles	77	83	.481	14
Cincinnati	75	87	.463	17
Atlanta	63	97	.394	28

N.L. East

	W	L	Pct.	GB
Chicago	93	69	.574	—
New York	87	75	.537	6
St. Louis	86	76	.531	7
Montreal	81	81	.500	12
Pittsburgh	74	88	.457	19
Philadelphia	67	95	.414	26

Giants' season statistics

BATTING

	ab	r	h	rbi	2b	3b	hr	sb	avg.
Will Clark	588	104	196	111	38	9	23	8	.333
Ken Oberkfell	116	17	37	15	5	1	2	0	.319
Kevin Mitchell	543	100	158	125	34	6	47	3	.291
Brett Butler	594	100	168	36	22	4	4	31	.283
Bill Bathe	32	3	9	6	1	0	0	0	.281
Ernest Riles	302	43	84	40	13	2	7	0	.278
Donell Nixon	166	23	44	15	2	0	1	10	.265
Greg Litton	143	12	36	17	5	3	4	0	.252
Chris Speier	37	7	9	2	4	0	0	0	.243
Robby Thompson	547	91	132	50	26	11	13	12	.241
Terry Kennedy	355	19	85	34	15	0	5	1	.239
Jose Uribe	453	34	100	30	12	6	1	6	.221
Candy Maldonado	345	39	75	41	23	0	9	4	.217
Kirt Manwaring	200	14	42	18	4	2	0	2	.210
Pat Sheridan	161	20	33	14	3	4	3	4	.205
Matt Williams	292	31	59	50	18	1	18	1	.202
Mike Laga	20	1	4	7	1	0	1	0	.200
Jim Weaver	20	2	4	2	3	0	0	1	.200
Bob Brenly	22	2	4	3	2	0	0	0	.182
Mike Benjamin	6	6	1	0	0	0	0	0	.167
Pitchers	347	20	51	16	6	2	3	1	.147
Ed Jurak*	42	2	10	1	0	0	0	0	.238
Charlie Hayes*	5	0	1	0	0	0	0	0	.200
Tracy Jones*	97	5	18	12	4	0	0	2	.186
James Steels*	12	0	1	0	0	0	0	0	.083
Totals	**5469**	**699**	**1365**	**647**	**241**	**52**	**141**	**87**	**.250**

PITCHING

	w-l	ip	h	er	bb	so	sv	era
Scott Garrelts	14-5	193⅓	149	49	46	119	0	2.28
Steve Bedrosian	1-4	51	35	15	22	34	17	2.65
Craig Lefferts	2-4	107	93	32	22	71	20	2.69
Ernie Camacho	3-0	16⅓	10	5	11	14	0	2.76
Rick Reuschel	17-8	208⅓	195	68	54	111	0	2.94
Mike LaCoss	10-10	150⅓	143	53	65	78	6	3.17
Stu Tate	0-0	2	3	1	0	4	0	3.38
Don Robinson	12-11	197	184	75	37	96	0	3.43
Bob Knepper	3-2	52	55	20	15	19	0	3.46
Dave Dravecky	2-0	13	8	5	4	5	0	3.46
Atlee Hammaker	6-6	76⅔	78	32	23	30	0	3.76
Randy McCament	1-1	36⅔	32	16	23	12	0	3.93
Mike Krukow	4-3	43	37	19	18	18	0	3.98
Jeff Brantley	7-1	97⅓	101	44	37	69	0	4.07
Trevor Wilson	2-3	39⅓	28	19	24	22	0	4.35
Kelly Downs	4-8	82⅔	82	44	26	49	0	4.79
Dennis Cook*	1-0	15	13	3	5	9	0	1.80
Rich Gossage*	2-1	43⅔	32	13	27	24	4	2.68
Terry Mulholland*	0-0	11	15	5	4	6	0	4.09
Joe Price*	1-1	14	16	9	4	10	0	5.79
Russ Swan*	0-2	6⅔	11	8	4	2	0	10.80
Totals	**92-70**	**1457**	**1320**	**535**	**471**	**802**	**47**	**3.30**

*—Not on roster in September.

A's season statistics

BATTING

	ab	r	h	rbi	2b	3b	hr	sb	avg.
Chris Bando	2	0	1	1	0	0	0	0	.500
Carney Lansford	551	81	185	52	28	2	2	37	.336
Rickey Henderson	306	72	90	35	13	2	9	52	.294
Terry Steinbach	454	37	124	42	13	1	7	1	.273
Dave Parker	553	56	146	97	27	1	22	0	.264
Jose Canseco	227	40	61	57	9	1	17	6	.269
Tony Phillips	451	48	118	47	15	6	4	2	.262
Mike Gallego	357	45	90	30	14	2	3	7	.252
Dave Henderson	579	77	145	80	24	3	15	8	.250
Stan Javier	310	42	77	28	12	3	1	12	.248
Billy Beane	79	8	19	11	5	0	0	3	.241
Walt Weiss	236	30	55	21	11	0	3	6	.233
Lance Blankenship	125	22	29	4	5	1	1	5	.232
Mark McGwire	490	74	113	95	17	0	33	1	.231
Ron Hassey	268	29	61	23	12	0	5	1	.228
Felix Jose	57	3	11	5	2	0	0	0	.193
Ken Phelps	9	0	1	0	1	0	0	0	.111
Doug Jennings	4	0	0	0	0	0	0	0	.000
Dann Howitt	3	0	0	0	0	0	0	0	.000
Scott Hemond	0	2	0	0	0	0	0	0	.000
Glenn Hubbard*	131	12	26	12	6	0	3	2	.198
Jamie Quirk*	10	1	2	1	0	0	1	0	.200
Luis Polonia*	206	31	59	17	6	4	1	13	.286
Larry Arndt*	6	1	1	0	0	0	0	0	.167
Dick Scott*	2	0	0	1	0	0	0	0	.000
Totals	**5416**	**712**	**1414**	**659**	**220**	**25**	**127**	**157**	**.261**

PITCHING

	w-l	ip	h	er	bb	so	sv	era
Dennis Eckersley	4-0	57⅔	32	10	3	54	33	1.56
Jim Corsi	1-2	38⅓	26	8	10	21	0	1.88
Todd Burns	6-5	96⅓	66	24	28	49	8	2.24
Rick Honeycutt	2-2	76⅔	56	20	26	52	12	2.35
Mike Moore	19-11	241⅓	193	70	83	172	0	2.61
Dave Otto	0-0	6⅔	6	2	2	4	0	2.70
Bob Woloh	17-8	209⅔	191	70	78	137	0	3.00
Gene Nelson	3-5	80	62	29	30	70	3	3.26
Dave Stewart	21-9	257⅔	260	95	69	155	0	3.32
Curt Young	5-9	111	117	46	47	55	0	3.73
Storm Davis	19-7	169⅓	187	82	68	91	0	4.36
Matt Young	1-4	37⅓	42	28	31	27	0	6.75
Eric Plunk*	1-1	28⅔	17	7	12	24	1	2.20
Greg Cadaret*	0-0	27⅔	21	7	19	14	0	2.28
Bill Dawley*	0-0	9	11	4	2	3	0	4.00
Brian Snyder*	0-0	⅔	2	2	2	1	0	27.00
Totals	**99-63**	**1448⅓**	**1287**	**497**	**510**	**930**	**57**	**3.09**

*—Not on roster in September.

Giants' transactions

Date	Player	Transaction
1-24-89	Terry Kennedy	Acquired from Baltimore Orioles for Bob Melvin
3-21-89	Dave Dravecky	Placed on 60-day DL (left shoulder)
	Karl Best	Placed on 21-day DL (right elbow)
3-23-89	Mike Krukow	Placed on 21-day DL, retroactive to 3-19 (right shoulder)
3-24-89	Ken Gerhart	Acquired from Baltimore Orioles for Francisco Melendez
3-25-89	Keith Comstock	Released
4-14-89	Rich Gossage	Signed as free agent
	James Steels	Optioned to Phoenix
4-28-89	Mike Krukow	Reinstated from DL
	Chris Speier	Placed on 15-day DL (back), retroactive to 4-27
5-1-89	Matt Williams	Optioned to Phoenix
	Joe Price	Released
	James Steels	Recalled from Phoenix
	Greg Litton	Purchased from Phoenix
5-2-89	Karl Best	Transferred to 60-day DL
5-5-89	Kelly Downs	Placed on 15-day DL (right shoulder), retroactive to 5-2
	Charlie Hayes	Recalled from Phoenix
5-10-89	Ken Oberkfell	Acquired from Pittsburgh Pirates for Roger Samuels
	Charlie Hayes	Optioned to Phoenix
5-12-89	Chris Speier	Reinstated from DL
	Greg Litton	Optioned to Phoenix
5-17-89	Kelly Downs	Assigned to Phoenix for injury rehabilitation
	Chris Speier	Placed on 15-day DL (back), retroactive to 5-13
	Greg Litton	Recalled from Phoenix
5-23-89	Kelly Downs	Placed on 21-day DL (right shoulder)
	James Steels	Optioned to Phoenix
	Terry Mulholland	Recalled from Phoenix
5-29-89	Chris Speier	Activated from DL
	Greg Litton	Optioned to Phoenix
6-5-89	Mike Krukow	Placed on 15-day DL (right shoulder)
	Chris Speier	Placed on 15-day DL (back)
	Dennis Cook	Recalled from Phoenix
	Greg Litton	Recalled from Phoenix
6-9-89	Jeff Brantley	Optioned to Phoenix
	Ed Jurak	Optioned to Phoenix
	Ernie Camacho	Purchased from Phoenix
	Bill Bathe	Purchased from Phoenix
6-16-89	Pat Sheridan	Acuired from Tigers for Tracy Jones
6-18-89	Steve Bedrosian	Acquired from Philadelphia Phillies with player to be named later for Dennis Cook, Terry Mulholland and Charlie Hayes
6-21-89	Atlee Hammaker	Placed on 15-day DL (left biceps), retroactive to 6-21
6-22-89	Ed Jurak	Recalled from Phoenix
6-26-89	Randy McCament	Purchased from Phoenix
	Ed Jurak	Optioned to Phoenix
6-30-89	Atlee Hammaker	Moved to 21-day DL
	Mike Krukow	Moved to 60-day DL
7-1-89	Scott Garrelts	Placed on 15-day DL (left hamstring, retroactive to 6-30)
	Mike Benjamin	Purchased from Phoenix
7-15-89	Scott Garrelts	Reinstated from DL
	Mike Benjamin	Optioned to Phoenix
7-16-89	Atlee Hammaker	Reinstated from DL
	Bill Bathe	Optioned to Phoenix
7-23-89	Dave Dravecky	Assigned to San Jose for injury rehabilitation
7-24-89	Matt Williams	Recalled from Phoenix
	Randy McCament	Optioned to Phoenix

8-3-89	Rick Reuschel	Placed on 15-day DL (right groin)
	Atlee Hammaker	Placed on 21-day DL (left knee)
	Trevor Wilson	Optioned to Phoenix
	Randy McCament	Recalled from Phoenix
	Ernie Camacho	Recalled from Phoenix
	Russ Swan	Purchased from Phoenix
	Kelly Downs	Assigned to Phoenix
8-4-89	Dave Dravecky	Transferred to Phoenix for injury rehabilitation
	Kelly Downs	Transferred to San Jose for injury rehabilitation
8-5-89	Bob Knepper	Signed as free agent
	Rich Gossage	Released
8-7-89	Bruce Parker	Acquired from Reading (Philadelphia) to complete 6-18 trade
8-10-89	Dave Dravecky	Reinstated from DL
	Ernie Camacho	Optioned to Phoenix
8-13-89	Kelly Downs	Reinstated from DL
	Russ Swan	Optioned to Phoenix
8-16-89	Dave Dravecky	Placed on 21-day DL (left arm)
	Rick Reuschel	Reinstated from DL
	Chris Speier	Assigned to Phoenix for injury rehabilitation
8-31-89	Bob Brenly	Purchased from Phoenix
	Kirt Manwaring	Placed on 15-day DL (left foot)
	Bill Bathe	Recalled from Phoenix
	Randy McCament	Optioned to Everett
9-1-89	Trevor Wilson	Recalled from Phoenix
	Stu Tate	Recalled from Phoenix
	Ernie Camacho	Recalled from Phoenix
	Mike Benjamin	Recalled from Phoenix
	Mike Laga	Purchased from Phoenix
	Jim Weaver	Purchased from Phoenix
	Chris Speier	Reinstated from DL
9-2-89	Randy McCament	Recalled from Everett
9-15-89	Kirt Manwaring	Reinstated from DL
9-21-89	Atlee Hammaker	Reinstated from DL

A's transactions

Date	Player	Transaction
12-22-88	Mike Moore	Signed as free agent
3-18-89	Matt Young	21-day DL, strained left elbow
	Ozzie Canseco	21-day DL, broken bone in left hand
3-23-89	Jose Canseco	21-day DL, broken bone in left hand
4-8-89	Gene Nelson	15-day DL, right rib cage pull
4-12-89	Mark McGwire	15-day DL, herniated disk
	Billy Beane	Selected from Tacoma
4-15-89	Lance Blankenship	Recalled from Tacoma
4-23-89	Gene Nelson	Reinstated from 15-day DL
	Felix Jose	Optioned to Tacoma
4-26-89	Mark McGwire	Reinstated from 15-day DL
	Lance Blankenship	optioned to Tacoma
4-27-89	Ozzie Canseco	Reinstated from 21-day DL, optioned to Huntsville
5-16-89	Glenn Hubbard	15-day DL, strained right hamstring
5-18-89	Walt Weiss	15-day DL, torn cartilage in right knee
	Lance Blankenship	Recalled from Tacoma
	Jose Canseco	Transferred from 21-day DL to 60-day DL
	Storm Davis	21-day DL, strained left hamstring
5-25-89	Jim Corsi	Recalled from Tacoma
5-29-89	Matt Young	Transferred from 21-day DL to 60-day DL
	Walt Weiss	Transfered from 15-day DL to 21-day DL
5-31-89	Glenn Hubbard	Reinstated from 15-day DL

6-6-89	Dennis Eckersley	placed on 15-day DL (retroactive to 5-29), strained right shoulder
	Larry Arndt	Selected from Tacoma
6-10-89	Storm Davis	Reinstated from 21-day DL
	Larry Arndt	Optioned to Tacoma
6-13-89	Dennis Eckersley	Transferred from 15-day DL to 21-day DL
	Bob Welch	15-day DL, pulled groin
	Matt Young	Reinstated from 60-day DL
	Billy Beane	15-day DL, sore right wrist
6-16-89	Jamie Quirk	Selected from Tacoma
6-21-89	Rickey Henderson	Acquired from New York Yankees in exchange for Eric Plunk, Greg Cadaret and Luis Polonia
	Brian Snyder	Selected from Tacoma
	Bill Dawley	Selected from Tacoma
6-26-89	Billy Beane	transferred from 15-day DL to 21-day DL
6-30-89	Bob Welch	Reinstated from 15-day DL
	Brian Snyder	Outrighted to Tacoma
7-4-89	Billy Beane	Reinstated from 21-day DL, outrighted to Tacoma
7-13-89	Jose Canseco	Activated from 60-day DL
	Bill Dawley	Designated for assignment
	Dennis Eckersley	Activated from 21-day disabled list
	Stan Javier	15-day DL, sore right elbow, retroactive to July 9
7-24-89	Stan Javier	Reinstated from 21-day DL
	Jamie Quirk	Designated for assignment
7-27-89	Bill Dawley	Unconditionally released
7-28-89	Jamie Quirk	Unconditionally released
7-30-89	Felix Jose	Recalled from Tacoma
	Lance Blankenship	Optioned to Tacoma
7-31-89	Walt Weiss	Reinstated from 21-day DL
	Glenn Hubbard	Unconditionally released
8-16-89	Bill Beane	Selected from Tacoma
	Felix Jose	Optioned to Tacoma
8-22-89	Lance Blankenship	Recalled from Tacoma
	Jim Corsi	Optioned to Tacoma
8-31-89	Ken Phelps	Acquired from New York Yankees in exchange for Scott Holcomb
	Billy Beane	Outrighted to Tacoma
9-1-89	Jim Corsi	Recalled from Tacoma
	Felix Jose	Recalled from Tacoma
	Dave Otto	Recalled from Tacoma
	Chris Bando	Recalled from Tacoma
	Doug Jennings	Recalled from Tacoma
9-10-89	Billy Beane	Recalled from Tacoma

All-Star voting

(Top three, plus A's and Giants)
American League

Position	Place	Player	Team	Votes
Catcher	1	Terry Steinbach	A's	1,078,902
	2	Bob Boone	Royals	591,604
	3	Mickey Tettleton	Orioles	570,607
First base	1	Mark McGwire	A's	1,263,476
	2	Don Mattingly	Yankees	808,502
	3	Rafael Palmeiro	Rangers	666,375
Second base	1	Julio Franco	Rangers	974,373
	2	Steve Sax	Yankees	847,511
	3	Glenn Hubbard	A's	463,394
	15	Mike Gallego	A's	6,821
Third base	1	Wade Boggs	Red Sox	1,295,355
	2	Carney Lansford	A's	907,124
	3	Gary Gaetti	Twins	546,927
Shortstop	1	Cal Ripken	Orioles	1,172,506
	2	Walter Weiss	A's	674,235
	3	Kurt Stillwell	Royals	414,013
Outfield	1	Bo Jackson	Royals	1,748,696
	2	Kirby Puckett	Twins	1,555,881
	3	Jose Canseco	A's	932,329
	4	Mike Greenwell	Red Sox	826,577
	5	Rickey Henderson	A's	784,890
	6	Ruben Sierra	Rangers	729,775
	7	Dave Henderson	A's	576,467
	8	Dave Parker	A's	429,719
	9	Devon White	Angels	363,052

National League

Position	Place	Player	Team	Votes
Catcher	1	Benito Santiago	Padres	1,307,368
	2	Tony Pena	Cardinals	741,696
	3	Mike Scioscia	Dodgers	621,436
	18	Terry Kennedy	Giants	19,325
First base	1	Will Clark	Giants	1,833,329
	2	Pedro Guerrero	Cardinals	516,842
	3	Eddie Murray	Dodgers	411,801
Second base	1	Ryne Sandberg	Cubs	1,150,064
	2	Robby Thompson	Giants	608,641
	3	Willie Randolph	Dodgers	598,542
Third base	1	Mike Schmidt	Phillies	729,249
	2	Chris Sabo	Reds	713,113
	3	Bobby Bonilla	Pirates	649,659
	11	Matt Williams	Giants	179,646
	13	Ernest Riles	Giants	4,206
Shortstop	1	Ozzie Smith	Cardinals	1,756,038
	2	Barry Larkin	Reds	798,496
	3	Jose Uribe	Giants	493,784
Outfield	1	Kevin Mitchell	Giants	1,814,118
	2	Darryl Strawberry	Mets	1,464,605
	3	Tony Gwynn	Padres	977,574
	4	Eric Davis	Reds	810,744
	5	Vince Coleman	Cardinals	770,397
	6	Kirk Gibson	Dodgers	755,756
	7	Andre Dawson	Cubs	691,693
	8	Andy Van Slyke	Pirates	632,379
	9	Brett Butler	Giants	588,564
	20	Candy Maldonado	Giants	235,431

World Series box scores

Game 1

Saturday, Oct. 14, 1989
Oakland Coliseum
Oakland 5, San Francisco 0

San Francisco	ab	r	h	bi	Oakland	ab	r	h	bi
Butler cf	4	0	0	0	RHenderson lf	5	0	2	1
Thompson 2b	4	0	0	0	Lansford 3b	5	0	1	0
Clark 1b	4	0	2	0	Gallego 2b	0	0	0	0
Mitchell lf	4	0	2	0	Canseco rf	3	0	0	0
Williams 3b	4	0	0	0	Parker dh	4	1	1	1
Riles dh	4	0	0	0	DHenderson cf	3	1	0	0
Maldonado rf	4	0	0	0	McGwire 1b	4	0	3	0
Kennedy c	3	0	0	0	Steinbach c	4	1	1	0
Uribe ss	2	0	1	0	Phillips 2b	4	1	2	1
Oberkfell 3b	0	0	0	0	Weiss ss	4	1	1	1
Totals	33	0	5	0	Totals	36	5	11	4

San Francisco	000 000 000	— 0
Oakland	031 100 00x	— 5

E—Stewart, Kennedy. LOB—San Francisco 7, Oakland 9. 2B—Clark. HR—Parker (1), Weiss (1).

San Francisco	IP	H	R	ER	BB	SO
Garrelts (L, 0-1)	4	7	5	4	1	5
Hammaker	1⅔	3	0	0	0	2
Brantley	1⅓	1	0	0	1	0
LaCoss	1	0	0	0	0	1
Oakland						
Stewart (W, 1-0)	9	5	0	0	1	6

PB—Steinbach.

Umpires—Home, Garcia; First, Runge; Second, Voltaggio; Third, Rennert; Left, Clark; Right, Gregg.

Time—2:45. Attendance—49,385.

Game 2

Sunday, Oct. 15, 1989
Oakland Coliseum
Oakland 5, San Francisco 1

San Francisco	ab	r	h	bi	Oakland	ab	r	h	bi
Butler cf	2	0	1	0	RHenderson lf	3	1	3	0
Thompson 2b	3	0	0	1	Lansford 3b	3	0	1	1
Clark 1b	4	0	0	0	Canseco rf	2	1	0	0
Mitchell lf	4	0	1	0	Parker dh	4	1	1	1
Williams 3b	4	0	0	0	DHenderson cf	3	1	0	0
Riles dh	3	0	0	0	McGwire 1b	4	0	1	0
Maldonado rf	3	0	0	0	Steinbach c	4	1	1	3
Kennedy c	3	0	1	0	Phillips 2b	3	0	0	0
Uribe ss	2	1	0	0	Weiss ss	3	0	0	0
Oberkfell 3b	1	0	1	0					
Totals	29	1	4	1	Totals	29	5	7	5

San Francisco	001 000 000	— 1
Oakland	100 400 00x	— 5

DP—San Francisco 2, Oakland 1. LOB—San Francisco 4, Oakland 5. 2B—Lansford, Parker, McGwire. 3B—R. Henderson. HR—Steinbach (1). SB—R. Henderson (1), Butler 2 (2). SF—Thompson.

San Francisco	IP	H	R	ER	BB	SO
Reuschel (L, 0-1)	4	5	5	5	4	2
Downs	2	1	0	0	0	2
Lefferts	1	1	0	0	1	1
Bedrosian	1	0	0	0	0	2
Oakland						
Moore (W, 1-0)	7	4	1	1	2	7
Honeycutt	1⅓	0	0	0	0	1
Eckersley	⅔	0	0	0	0	0

Reuschel pitched to two batters in the 5th; Moore pitched to one batter in the eighth.

WP—Moore 2.

Umpires—Home, Runge; First, Voltaggio; Second, Rennert; Third, Clark; Left, Gregg; Right, Garcia.

Time—2:47. Attendance—49,388.

Game 3

Friday, Oct. 27, 1989
Candlestick Park
Oakland 13, San Francisco 7

Oakland	ab	r	h	bi	San Francisco	ab	r	h	bi
RHenderson lf	5	1	1	0	Butler cf	3	0	0	0
Nelson p	0	0	0	0	Nixon cf	2	1	1	0
Burns p	0	0	0	0	Thompson 2b	3	0	0	0
Lansford 3b	4	4	3	2	Litton 2b	2	0	2	1
Honeycutt p	0	0	0	0	Clark 1b	4	1	1	0
Gallego 3b	1	0	0	0	Mitchell lf	5	1	1	0
Canseco rf	5	3	3	3	Oberkfell 3b	2	1	1	0
Javier rf	0	0	0	0	Williams ss	4	1	1	1
McGwire 1b	4	0	1	0	Kennedy c	3	0	1	2
DHenderson cf	4	2	3	4	Manwaring c	1	1	1	0
Steinbach c	4	0	1	1	Sheridan rf	2	0	0	0
Phillips 2b	5	1	1	1	Brantley p	0	0	0	0
Weiss ss	5	1	1	0	Riles ph	1	0	0	0
Stewart p	3	0	0	0	Hammaker p	0	0	0	0
Blankenship 2b	2	1	1	0	Lefferts p	0	0	0	0
					Bathe ph	1	1	1	3
					Garrelts p	1	0	0	0
					Downs p	0	0	0	0
					Maldonado rf	3	0	0	0
Totals	**42**	**13**	**14**	**12**	**Totals**	**37**	**7**	**10**	**7**

Oakland	200 241 040 — 13
San Francisco	010 200 040 — 7

E—Oberkfell, Mitchell, Lefferts. DP—San Francisco 1. LOB—Oakland 7, San Francisco 6. 2B—D. Henderson, R. Henderson, Manwaring, Litton. HR—Williams (1), D. Henderson 2 (2), Phillips (1), Canseco (1), Lansford (1), Bathe (1). SB—R. Henderson 2 (3).

	IP	H	R	ER	BB	SO
Oakland						
Stewart (W, 2-0)	7	5	3	3	1	8
Honeycutt	1	1	0	0	0	1
Nelson	⅔	3	4	4	1	1
Burns	⅓	1	0	0	1	0
San Francisco						
Garrelts (L, 0-2)	3⅓	6	4	4	0	3
Downs	1	2	4	4	2	1
Brantley	2⅔	1	1	1	2	1
Hammaker	⅔	5	4	4	0	0
Lefferts	1⅓	0	0	0	0	0

Balk—Brantley. HBP—by Hammaker (D. Henderson).
Umpires—Home, Voltaggio; First, Rennert; Second, Clark; Third, Gregg; Left, Garcia; Right, Runge.
Time—3:03. Attendance—62,038.

Game 4

Saturday, Oct. 28, 1989
Candlestick Park
Oakland 9, San Francisco 6

Oakland	ab	r	h	bi	San Francisco	ab	r	h	bi
RHenderson lf	6	2	3	2	Butler cf	5	1	3	1
Lansford 3b	4	1	2	1	Oberkfell 3b	3	0	0	0
Canseco rf	4	1	2	0	Thompson 2b	1	0	1	1
McGwire 1b	5	0	1	0	Bedrosian p	0	0	0	0
DHenderson cf	3	2	1	0	Clark 1b	4	1	1	0
Steinbach c	4	1	1	3	Mitchell lf	4	1	1	2
Phillips 2b	5	0	1	1	Williams ss	4	0	1	0
Weiss ss	3	1	0	0	Kennedy c	3	1	0	0
Moore p	3	1	1	2	Litton 2b	4	1	2	2
Phelps ph	1	0	0	0	Nixon rf	3	0	0	0
Nelson p	0	0	0	0	Robinson p	0	0	0	0
Honeycutt p	0	0	0	0	LaCoss p	1	0	0	0
Burns p	0	0	0	0	Bathe ph	1	0	0	0
Parker ph	1	0	0	0	Brantley p	0	0	0	0
Eckersley p	0	0	0	0	Downs p	0	0	0	0
					Riles ph	0	0	0	0
					Maldonad ph	1	1	1	0
					Lefferts p	0	0	0	0
					Uribe ss	1	0	0	0
Totals	**39**	**9**	**12**	**9**	**Totals**	**35**	**6**	**9**	**6**

Oakland	130 031 010 — 9
San Francisco	000 002 400 — 6

LOB—Oakland 10, San Francisco 4. 2B—D. Henderson, Moore, Phillips, Butler. 3B—Steinbach, R. Henderson, Litton (1). HR—R. Henderson (1), Mitchell (1), Litton (1). SB—Canseco (1).

	IP	H	R	ER	BB	SO
Oakland						
Moore (W, 2-0)	6	5	2	2	1	3
Nelson	⅓	1	2	2	1	0
Honeycutt	⅓	3	2	2	0	0
Burns	1⅓	0	0	0	0	0
Eckersley (S, 1)	1	0	0	0	0	0
San Francisco						
Robinson (L, 0-1)	1⅔	4	4	4	1	0
LaCoss	3⅓	4	3	3	3	1
Brantley	⅓	3	1	1	0	0
Downs	1⅔	0	0	0	0	1
Lefferts	⅓	1	1	1	1	0
Bedrosian	1⅓	0	0	0	2	0

Umpires—Home, Rennert; First, Clark; Second, Gregg; Third, Garcia; Left, Runge; Right, Voltaggio.
Time—3:07. Attendance—62,032.

World Series statistics

Oakland	AB	R	H	2B	3B	HR	RBI	SB	AVG.
Lance Blankenship	2	1	1	0	0	0	0	0	.500
Rickey Henderson	19	4	9	1	2	1	3	3	.474
Carney Lansford	16	5	7	1	0	1	4	0	.438
Jose Canseco	14	5	5	0	0	1	3	1	.357
Mike Moore	3	1	1	1	0	0	2	0	.333
Dave Henderson	13	6	4	2	0	2	4	0	.308
Mark McGwire	17	0	5	1	0	0	1	0	.294
Terry Steinbach	16	3	4	0	1	1	7	0	.250
Tony Phillips	17	2	4	1	0	1	3	0	.235
Dave Parker	9	2	2	1	0	1	2	0	.222
Walt Weiss	15	3	2	0	0	1	1	0	.133
Mike Gallego	1	0	0	0	0	0	0	0	.000
Ken Phelps	1	0	0	0	0	0	0	0	.000
Dave Stewart	3	0	0	0	0	0	0	0	.000
Totals offense	**146**	**32**	**44**	**8**	**3**	**9**	**30**	**4**	**.301**

Oakland	G	W-L-S	IP	H	R	ER	BB	SO	ERA
Todd Burns	2	0-0-0	1⅔	1	0	0	1	0	0.00
Dennis Eckersley	2	0-0-1	1⅔	0	0	0	0	0	0.00
Dave Stewart	2	2-0-0	16	10	3	3	2	14	1.69
Mike Moore	2	2-0-0	13	9	3	3	3	10	2.08
Rick Honeycutt	3	0-0-0	2⅔	4	2	2	0	2	6.75
Gene Nelson	2	0-0-0	1	4	6	6	2	1	54.00
Totals pitching	**4**	**4-0-1**	**36**	**28**	**14**	**14**	**8**	**27**	**3.50**

San Francisco	AB	R	H	2B	3B	HR	RBI	SB	AVG.
Kirt Manwaring	1	1	1	1	0	0	0	0	1.000
Greg Litton	6	1	3	1	0	1	3	0	.500
Bill Bathe	2	1	1	0	0	1	3	0	.500
Ken Oberkfell	6	1	2	0	0	0	0	0	.333
Kevin Mitchell	17	2	5	0	0	1	2	0	.294
Brett Butler	14	1	4	1	0	0	1	2	.286
Will Clark	16	2	4	1	0	0	0	0	.250
Donell Nixon	5	1	1	0	0	0	0	0	.200
Jose Uribe	5	1	1	0	0	0	0	0	.200
Terry Kennedy	12	1	2	0	0	0	2	0	.167
Matt Williams	16	1	2	0	0	1	1	0	.125
Candy Maldonado	11	1	1	0	1	0	0	0	.091
Robby Thompson	11	0	1	0	0	0	2	0	.091
Scott Garrelts	1	0	0	0	0	0	0	0	.000
Mike LaCoss	1	0	0	0	0	0	0	0	.000
Pat Sheridan	2	0	0	0	0	0	0	0	.000
Ernest Riles	8	0	0	0	0	0	0	0	.000
Totals offense	**134**	**14**	**28**	**4**	**1**	**4**	**14**	**2**	**.209**

San Francisco	G	W-L-S	IP	H	R	ER	BB	SO	ERA
Steve Bedrosian	2	0-0-0	2⅔	0	0	0	2	2	0.00
Craig Lefferts	3	0-0-0	2⅔	2	1	1	2	1	3.38
Jeff Brantley	3	0-0-0	4⅓	5	2	2	3	1	4.15
Mike LaCoss	2	0-0-0	4⅓	4	3	3	3	2	6.23
Kelly Downs	3	0-0-0	4⅔	3	4	4	2	4	7.71
Scott Garrelts	2	0-2-0	7⅓	13	9	8	1	8	9.82
Rick Reuschel	1	0-1-0	4	5	5	5	4	2	11.25
Atlee Hammaker	2	0-0-0	2⅓	8	4	4	0	2	15.43
Don Robinson	1	0-1-0	1⅔	4	4	4	1	0	21.60
Totals pitching	**4**	**0-4-0**	**34**	**44**	**32**	**31**	**18**	**22**	**8.21**

The metropolitan World Series

Year	Winner	Loser	Outcome
1906	Chicago (AL)	Chicago (NL)	4-2
1921	New York (NL)	New York (AL)	5-3
1922	New York (NL)	New York (AL)	4-0-1
1923	New York (AL)	New York (AL)	4-2
1936	New York (AL)	New York (NL)	4-2
1937	New York (AL)	New York (NL)	4-1
1941	New York (AL)	Brooklyn (NL)	4-1
1944	St. Louis (NL)	St. Louis (AL)	4-2
1947	New York (AL)	Brooklyn (NL)	4-3
1949	New York (AL)	Brooklyn (NL)	4-1
1951	New York (AL)	New York (NL)	4-2
1952	New York (AL)	Brooklyn (NL)	4-3
1953	New York (AL)	Brooklyn (NL)	4-2
1955	Brooklyn (NL)	New York (AL)	4-3
1956	New York (AL)	Brooklyn (NL)	4-3
1989	Oakland (AL)	San Francisco (NL)	4-0

A's and Giants' salaries

Athletics	1989 Salary	Giants	1989 Salary
Rickey Henderson	$2,120,000	Steve Bedrosian	$1,650,000
Jose Canseco	1,600,000	Will Clark	1,125,000
Carney Lansford	1,375,000	Rick Reuschel	987,500
Mike Moore	1,241,667	Brett Butler	900,000
Bob Welch	1,133,333	Candy Maldonado	900,000
Dave Stewart	1,075,000	Don Robinson	900,000
Dave Parker	975,000	Atlee Hammaker	879,167
Dennis Eckersley	937,500	Mike Krukow	875,000
Dave Henderson	850,000	Terry Kennedy	850,000
Ken Phelps	655,000	Mike LaCoss	800,000
Rick Honeycutt	650,000	Dave Dravecky	750,000
Gene Nelson	607,500	Ken Oberkfell	725,000
Ron Hassey	600,000	Scott Garrelts	705,000
Storm Davis	587,500	Jose Uribo	687,500
Curt Young	572,500	Craig Lefferts	600,000
Mark McGwire	455,000	Kevin Mitchell	560,000
Tony Phillips	375,000	Robby Thompson	535,000
Terry Steinbach	280,000	Ernest Riles	470,000
Matt Young	250,000	Pat Sheridan	430,000
Mike Gallego	207,500	Chris Speier	425,000
Walt Weiss	190,000	Kelly Downs	315,000
Stan Javier	167,500	Karl Best	105,000
Todd Burns	100,000	Donell Nixon	102,500
Lance Blankenship	68,000	Matt Williams	95,000
		Jeff Brantley	78,000
		Kirt Manwaring	78,000
		Bill Bathe	75,500
		Bob Brenly	68,000
		Bob Knepper	68,000
		Greg Litton	68,000

Kevin Mitchell's home runs

No.	Date	Team	Where	Count	Inning	Pitcher	Score	Men on
1.	4-3	SD	SD	2-1	1	Show	0-0	1
2.	4-4	SD	SD	1-1	3	Hurst*	4-0	0
3.	4-12	LA	SF	3-0	1	Valenzuela*	0-1	2
4.	4-14	Atl	SF	1-0	3	Z. Smith*	3-4	0
5.	4-16(1)	Atl	SF	0-0	1	Smoltz	0-1	1
6.	4-29	Pit	Pit	0-0	9	J. Robinson	2-3	0
7.	5-2	Chi	SF	0-0	6	Maddux	2-0	1
8.	5-3	Pit	SF	0-0	4	Smiley*	0-4	1
9.	5-3	Pit	SF	1-1	9	Smiley*	2-5	0
10.	5-4	Pit	SF	2-1	3	Kramer	1-1	1
11.	5-7	StL	SF	0-1	8	Worrell	3-1	0
12.	5-15	Phi	Phi	0-0	12	Bedrosian	1-0	0
13.	5-20	NY	NY	2-2	4	Ojeda*	1-0	0
14.	5-21	NY	NY	0-0	2	Fernandez*	0-3	2
15.	5-30	NY	SF	1-0	3	Cone	0-1	1
16.	6-2	Atl	Atl	3-1	3	Glavine*	1-2	0
17.	6-2	Atl	Atl	3-1	5	Glavine*	5-2	1
18.	6-3	Atl	Atl	2-2	4	Z.Smith*	0-0	0
19.	6-4	Atl	Atl	0-1	7	Acker	0-5	2
20.	6-6(1)	Cin	Cin	2-1	1	Scudder	0-0	0
21.	6-6(2)	Cin	Cin	1-1	2	Browning*	0-0	0
22.	6-6(2)	Cin	Cin	1-1	9	Dibble	2-2	0
23.	6-9	SD	SF	1-1	2	Hurst*	0-0	0
24.	6-17	Cin	SF	1-1	3	Jackson*	3-1	1
25.	6-25	SD	SD	2-1	3	Show	2-3	1
26.	7-2	Chi	SF	0-0	8	Sutcliffe	2-3	1
27.	7-4	Pit	Pit	0-2	5	Kramer	1-1	0
28.	7-5	Pit	Pit	3-1	3	Walk	1-1	0
29.	7-7	StL	StL	1-1	2	DeLeon	0-1	0
30.	7-8	StL	StL	1-0	3	Power	2-0	0
31.	7-8	StL	StL	3-2	6	DiPino*	4-3	0
32.	7-14	Pit	SF	0-0	5	Drabek	2-5	1
33.	7-24	Atl	Atl	0-2	4	Smoltz	0-0	1
34.	8-3	LA	LA	2-2	1	Hershiser	0-0	2
35.	8-9	Cin	SF	1-1	1	Mahler	0-0	2
36.	8-9	Cin	SF	1-1	6	Charlton*	7-1	1
37.	8-11	LA	SF	3-2	4	Crews	8-1	1
38.	8-16	Mon	Mon	1-0	4	Langston*	0-0	0
39.	8-17	Mon	Mon	1-0	6	Hesketh*	9-5	0
40.	8-22	NY	NY	2-1	6	Viola*	1-0	2
41.	9-1	NY	SF	0-0	7	Darling	2-0	2
42.	9-7	Atl	Atl	3-2	9	Henry	6-5	0
43.	9-12	Atl	SF	0-0	3	Clary	3-1	0
44.	9-17(1)	SD	SF	2-0	4	Grant	0-2	0
45.	9-17(1)	SD	SF	0-0	7	Clemens*	4-3	3
46.	9-20	LA	SF	2-1	9	Howell	3-7	0
47.	9-24	Hou	SF	1-0	4	Clancy	0-2	0

* —Left-handers

Mark McGwire's home runs

No.	Date	Park	Opponent	Pitcher	Inning	Score	Men on
1.	4-3	Coliseum	Seattle	Langston	3rd	1-0	1
2.	4-5	Coliseum	Seattle	Bankhead	5th	2-0	0
3.	4-7	Coliseum	Chicago	Jones	8th	0-7	0
4.	4-27	Coliseum	Baltimore	Harnisch	3rd	0-3	0
5.	4-27	Coliseum	Baltimore	Williamson	7th	4-3	1
6.	5-2	Exhibition Stadium	Toronto	Henke	9th	4-5	3
7.	5-6	Tiger Stadium	Detroit	Morris	2nd	0-1	0
8.	5-6	Tiger Stadium	Detroit	Hudson	7th	3-3	0
9.	5-17	Coliseum	New York	McCullers	8th	5-3	1
10.	5-28	Yankee Stadium	New York	Parker	4th	1-1	0
11.	6-9	Arlington Stadium	Texas	Hough	1st	0-0	3
12.	6-11	Arlington Stadium	Texas	Brown	6th	3-1	0
13.	6-16 (1)	Memorial Stadium	Baltimore	Holton	4th	0-2	0
14.	6-17	Memorial Stadium	Baltimore	Bautista	1st	0-0	1
15.	6-21	Coliseum	Detroit	Hudson	3rd	1-4	2
16.	7-5	Coliseum	Kansas City	Leibrandt	3rd	2-5	2
17.	7-9	Coliseum	Texas	Hough	6th	3-1	0
18.	7-13	SkyDome	Toronto	Key	1st	1-0	2
19.	7-16	SkyDome	Toronto	Hernandez	8th	5-2	0
20.	8-9	Comiskey Park	Chicago	Dotson	4th	0-0	0
21.	8-12	Anaheim Stadium	California	Minton	8th	6-3	1
22.	8-19	Coliseum	Minnesota	Aguilera	5th	0-4	0
23.	8-21	Tiger Stadium	Detroit	Tanana	1st	2-0	1
24.	8-24	Arlington Stadium	Texas	Jeffcoat	4th	0-1	1
25.	9-1	County Stadium	Milwaukee	Bosio	6th	2-3	0
26.	9-2	County Stadium	Milwaukee	Filer	1st	2-0	1
27.	9-17	Fenway Park	Boston	Hetzel	5th	2-3	0
28.	9-17	Fenway Park	Boston	Murphy	8th	4-7	0
29.	9-21	Metrodome	Minnesota	Aguilera	5th	1-0	0
30.	9-24	Metrodome	Minnesota	Tapani	2nd	0-0	0
31.	9-24	Metrodome	Minnesota	Cook	9th	6-3	2
32.	9-29	Coliseum	Kansas City	Farr	6th	1-2	0
33.	10-1	Coliseum	Kansas City	DeJesus	2nd	0-1	1

Brett Butler's bunt hits

No.	Date	Team	Inning	Pitcher	Fielded	Scored
1.	4-5	SD	1	Whitson	Ready	No
2.	4-7	Cin	11	Tekulve	Sabo	No
3.	4-12	LA	1	Valenzuela	Hamilton	Yes
4.	4-12	LA	7	Searage	Hamilton	No
5.	4-15	Atl	3	P. Smith	Gant	No
6.	4-16(2)	Atl	3	Puleo	Gant	Yes
7.	5-3	Pit	5	Smiley	Smiley	No
8.	5-10	Chi	8	Williams	Grace	Yes
9.	5-17	Phi	5	Howell	Howell	Yes
10.	5-25	Mon	6	Martinez	Wallach	No
11.	5-30	NY	6	Fernandez	Jefferies	Yes
12.	6-2	Atl	9	Assenmacher	Gant	Yes
13.	6-18	Cin	5	Rijo	Harris	No
14.	6-21	Hou	6	Clancy	Davis	Yes
15.	7-9	StL	7	Magrane	Pendleton	Yes
16.	7-15	Pit	5	Smiley	Bonilla	Yes
17.	8-22	NY	3	Viola	Johnson	Yes
18.	9-2	NY	1	Viola	Johnson	No
19.	9-5	Cin	5	Armstrong	Sabo	No
20.	9-6	Atl	7	Lilliquist	Blauser	Yes
21.	9-13	Cin	6	Mahler	Quinones	No
22.	9-18	LA	5	Hershiser	Hershiser	No
23.	9-20	LA	6	Martinez	Hamilton	No

Rickey Henderson's stolen bases

No.	Date	Opposition	Pitcher	Base	Inning	Other
1.	6-25	Toronto	Key	2nd	5th	scored
2.	6-25	Toronto	Ward	3rd	7th	scored
3.	6-25	Toronto	Wells	2nd	8th	
4.	6-27	Minnesota	Wayne	2nd	4th	
5.	6-30	Cleveland	Swindell	3rd	5th	scored
6.	7-1	Cleveland	Bailes	3rd	6th	scored
7.	7-2	Cleveland	Farrell	2nd	3rd	scored
8.	7-5	Kansas City	Gordon	2nd	4th	
9.	7-6	Kansas City	Aquino	2nd	8th	scored
10.	7-7	Texas	Mielke	2nd	8th	scored
11.	7-9	Texas	Hough	3rd	3rd	scored
12.	7-15	Toronto	Flanagan	2nd	7th	
13.	7-17	Detroit	Gibson	3rd	1st	scored
14.	7-18	Detroit	Williams	2nd	6th	scored
15.	7-23	Baltimore	Ballard	3rd	6th	scored
16.	7-26	California	McClure	3rd	8th	
17.	7-28	Seattle	Dunne	3rd	1st	
18.	7-29	Seattle	Johnson	2nd	1st	scored
19.	7-29	Seattle	Johnson	3rd	1st	lead/double steal
20.	7-29	Seattle	Johnson	2nd	3rd	scored
21.	7-29	Seattle	Johnson	2nd	5th	scored
22.	7-29	Seattle	Johnson	2nd	6th	scored
23.	8-2	Chicago	Perez	3rd	1st	scored
24.	8-2	Chicago	Long	2nd	8th	
25.	8-3	Chicago	Dotson	2nd	5th	scored
26.	8-8	Chicago	Perez	3rd	3rd	scored
27.	8-12	California	Petry	3rd	4th	scored
28.	8-12	California	Minton	3rd	8th	scored
29.	8-15	Cleveland	Nichols	2nd	3rd	
30.	8-16	Cleveland	Black	2nd	3rd	
31.	8-18	Minnesota	Smith	2nd	8th	scored
32.	8-19	Minnesota	Berenguer	2nd	8th	
33.	8-19	Minnesota	Berenguer	3rd	8th	scored
34.	8-20	Minnesota	Anderson	2nd	1st	scored
35.	8-21	Detroit	Tanana	3rd	1st	scored
36.	8-26	Kansas City	Leach	2nd	8th	
37.	8-29	New York	Cary	2nd	5th	scored
38.	8-30	New York	Plunk	2nd	1st	
39.	9-4	Boston	Dopson	2nd	3rd	scored
40.	9-6	Boston	Lamp	2nd	4th	
41.	9-16	Boston	Dopson	2nd	1st	scored
42.	9-16	Boston	Dopson	3rd	1st	lead/double steal
43.	9-17	Boston	Harris	2nd	7th	
44.	9-18	Cleveland	Olin	2nd	9th	
45.	9-20	Cleveland	Swindell	2nd	6th	
46.	9-20	Cleveland	Swindell	3rd	6th	scored
47.	9-20	Cleveland	Seanez	2nd	7th	
48.	9-20	Cleveland	Seanez	3rd	7th	scored
49.	9-22	Minnesota	Berenguer	2nd	6th	
50.	9-23	Minnesota	Anderson	2nd	1st	scored
51.	9-25	Texas	Mielke	2nd	7th	
52.	10-1	Kansas City	Leibrandt	2nd	7th	scored

Rick Reuschel's pitching log

Gm.	Day	Opponent	W-L	IP	H	R-ER	BB	SO	ERA
1	4-3	at San Diego	1-0	6	6	3-3	4	4	4.50
5	4-9	at Cincinnati	2-0	6	4	1-1	2	3	3.00
9	4-14	Atlanta	3-0	6⅔	8	5-5	2	4	4.34
14	4-18	San Diego	3-1	6	4	3-3	2	6	4.38
18	4-23	at Los Angeles	3-1	5	8	4-2	3	2	4.25
22	4-28	at Pittsburgh	3-2	7	5	1-1	3	4	3.68
26	5-2	Chicago	4-2	7⅓	10	0-0	1	5	3.07
30	5-6	St. Louis	5-2	6	5	0-0	2	3	2.70
34	5-12	at Montreal	6-2	8⅔	6	1-1	1	3	2.45
39	5-17	at Philadelphia	7-2	8	1	0-0	1	6	2.16
43	5-23	Montreal	8-2	7⅔	6	2-1	0	1	2.06
48	5-28	Philadelphia	9-2	5⅓	7	4-2	2	4	2.15
52	6-2	at Atlanta	10-2	6⅓	9	4-4	2	3	2.41
57	6-6	at Cincinnati	11-2	8⅔	6	2-1	2	6	2.28
62	6-11	San Diego	11-2	9	8	1-1	1	7	2.17
66	6-16	Cincinnati	11-2	8	5	2-2	0	2	2.18
71	6-21	Houston	12-2	7⅓	4	0-0	1	2	2.04
75	6-26	at Houston	12-2	5	7	2-2	2	1	2.10
80	7-1	Chicago	12-3	9	9	3-3	0	9	2.17
84	7-6	atPittsburgh	12-3	7	7	1-1	1	3	2.12
89	7-14	Pittsburgh	12-4	5	8	5-5	5	1	2.36
99	7-24	at Atlanta	13-4	5	5	0-0	2	0	2.28
104	7-29	at Houston	13-5	4	6	4-4	1	1	2.45
122	8-18	at Philadelphia	14-5	6	8	2-2	1	0	2.48
127	8-23	at New York	15-5	6	3	0-0	1	2	2.39
131	8-28	Philadelphia	15-6	2⅓	7	7-6	7	1	2.67
135	9-2	New York	16-6	8	4	1-1	1	5	2.60
140	9-7	at Atlanta	16-6	6	4	4-4	1	4	2.71
145	9-12	Atlanta	16-6	6	4	1-1	0	5	2.68
150	9-17	San Diego	16-7	7	6	3-3	6	5	2.72
155	9-22	Houston	17-7	9	7	1-1	2	7	2.64
161	9-30	at San Diego	17-8	4	8	8-8	1	3	2.94

Dave Stewart's pitching log

Gm.	Day	Opponent	W-L	IP	H	R-ER	BB	SO	ERA
1.	4-3	Seattle	1-0	5⅓	4	2-1	2	2	1.69
6.	4-9	Chicago	2-0	8⅓	8	2-2	1	9	1.98
11.	4-14	at Chicago	3-0	6⅓	6	3-1	1	3	1.80
16.	4-19	at Seattle	4-0	6	8	4-4	2	1	2.77
20.	4-24	Toronto		7	7	4-3	5	4	3.00
25.	4-29	Detroit*	5-0	9	6	2-2	3	1	2.79
29.	5-5	at Detroit	6-0	6⅔	7	3-2	1	2	2.77
33.	5-11	at Baltimore	6-1	6⅔	12	6-6	2	3	3.42
37.	5-15	Milwaukee	7-1	7	6	2-2	1	4	3.32
42.	5-20	Boston	8-1	7⅔	6	3-3	5	3	3.34
46.	5-25	at Milwaukee	8-2	7⅓	9	4-4	3	6	3.49
51.	5-30	at Boston	9-2	7	10	3-3	0	2	3.42
55.	6-4	Cleveland	10-2	7	3	0-0	2	2	3.15
59.	6-9	at Texas		3⅓	9	7-7	1	2	3.71
64.	6-14	at Kansas City	11-2	7⅔	7	1-1	3	7	3.52
69.	6-19	Detroit	11-3	3⅔	9	6-6	4	1	3.91
74.	6-24	Toronto*	12-3	9	4	1-0	0	6	3.60
78.	6-28	at Minnesota*	12-4	8	6	2-2	1	3	3.51
82.	7-3	Kansas City	13-4	8	4	0-0	1	7	3.30
87.	7-8	Texas		8	8	2-2	1	5	3.24
91.	7-15	at Toronto	13-5	4	9	6-6	2	4	3.52
95.	7-20	Baltimore	14-5	7	7	2-2	2	6	3.48
100.	7-25	California*	14-6	9	11	4-4	3	9	3.51
104.	7-30	Seattle	15-6	7⅓	5	3-3	1	6	3.52
109.	8-4	at Seattle	16-6	8	8	3-3	1	6	3.51
113.	8-8	at Chicago		8	9	2-1	1	4	3.41
118.	8-13	at California*	16-7	8	7	4-4	4	9	3.45
122.	8-18	Minnesota*	16-8	9	10	4-3	0	5	3.43
127.	8-23	at Texas	17-8	7	8	4-3	0	7	3.45
132.	8-28	at New York	18-8	6⅓	9	3-3	2	3	3.47
136.	9-2	at Milwaukee*	19-8	9	5	2-2	1	8	3.41
141.	9-8	New York*	19-9	9	10	5-4	1	1	3.43
145.	9-13	Milwaukee		7	8	4-4	0	3	3.48
149.	9-18	at Cleveland		8	4	1-1	5	6	3.41
153.	9-22	at Minnesota	20-9	7	6	2-2	4	0	3.48
159.	9-28	Texas	21-9	5	4	0-0	3	6	3.32

*—Complete game

Steve Bedrosian's pitching log

Gm.	Day	Opponent	W-L-S	IP	H	R-ER	BB	SO	ERA
69	6-19	Atlanta	2-3-7	1	1	0-0	0	0	3.12
71	6-21	Houston	2-3-8	1⅓	1	0-0	1	2	2.97
72	6-23	at San Diego	2-3-9	1⅓	0	0-0	0	1	2.87
73	6-24	at San Diego	2-3-10	⅓	0	0-0	0	0	2.84
75	6-26	at Houston	2-3-11	2	2	0-0	0	1	2.70
76	6-27	at Houston	2-4-11	⅓	1	2-2	1	0	3.12
81	7-2	Chicago	2-4-12	1	0	0-0	0	2	2.98
83	7-5	at Pittsburgh		1	3	3-3	1	1	3.53
86	7-8	at St. Louis		2	1	1-1	1	1	3.65
87	7-9	at St. Louis		1	0	0-0	0	1	3.57
88	7-13	Pittsburgh		2	1	0-0	3	2	3.42
91	7-16	Pittsburgh	2-4-13	1	0	0-0	0	0	3.35
93	7-18	St. Louis		1	0	0-0	0	0	3.28
95	7-20	at Chicago		2	5	3-2	0	2	3.51
99	7-24	at Atlanta	2-4-14	⅔	0	0-0	0	0	3.46
101	7-26	at Atlanta		1	2	2-2	2	0	3.74
105	7-30	at Houston	2-5-14	1	1	0-0	0	1	3.67
107	8-2	at Los Angeles		2	2	2-2	1	0	3.96
110	8-5	Houston		1	1	0-0	1	0	3.79
113	8-8	Cincinnati		1	0	0-0	0	1	3.72
115	8-10	Cincinnati	2-5-15	1	0	0-0	0	2	3.66
118	8-13	Los Angeles		1⅓	2	0-0	1	2	3.56
119	8-15	at Montreal	2-5-16	1	1	0-0	0	0	3.50
120	8-16	at Montreal	2-6-16	0	0	2-0	4	0	3.50
122	8-18	at Philadelphia	2-6-17	1	0	0-0	0	0	3.45
123	8-19	at Philadelphia		0	1	0-0	0	0	3.45
125	8-21	at New York		1	0	0-0	0	0	3.39
127	8-23	at New York		1	0	0-0	0	1	3.34
129	8-26	Montreal		1⅓	1	0-0	0	2	3.26
133	8-30	Philadelphia	2-6-18	1	1	0-0	0	0	3.21
137	9-4	at Cincinnati	2-6-19	1	1	0-0	2	0	3.16
140	9-7	at Atlanta	3-6-19	3	1	1-1	0	1	3.15
144	9-11	Atlanta	3-6-20	1	0	0-0	0	2	3.11
145	9-12	Atlanta	3-7-20	1⅓	1	1-1	1	1	3.16
146	9-13	Cincinnati		2⅓	1	0-0	1	1	3.05
149	9-17	San Diego	3-7-21	2	1	0-0	1	2	2.97
151	9-19	Los Angeles	3-7-22	2	2	0-0	0	0	2.91
153	9-21	Los Angeles	3-7-23	2	1	1-1	1	2	2.94
159	9-26	at Los Angeles		1	1	0-0	0	2	2.90
162	10-1	at San Diego		1	0	0-0	0	1	2.87

Dennis Eckersley's pitching log

Gm.	Day	Opponent	W-L-S	IP	H	R-ER	BB	SO	ERA
1	4-3	Seattle	0-0-1	1⅓	0	0-0	0	1	0.00
5	4-8	Chicago		1	2	0-0	0	0	0.00
6	4-9	Chicago	0-0-2	⅔	2	0-0	0	1	0.00
10	4-13	at California		1	1	0-0	0	1	0.00
13	4-16	at Chicago	1-0-2	1⅔	0	0-0	0	0	0.00
15	4-18	at Seattle	1-0-3	1⅓	0	0-0	0	0	0.00
16	4-19	at Seattle	1-0-4	⅓	0	0-0	0	1	0.00
18	4-22	California	1-0-5	1	0	0-0	0	3	0.00
19	4-23	California	1-0-6	⅓	0	0-0	0	0	0.00
21	4-25	Toronto	1-0-7	1⅔	1	0-0	0	3	0.00
24	4-28	Detroit	1-0-8	1	0	0-0	1	1	0.00
29	5-5	at Detroit	1-0-9	1	0	0-0	0	1	0.00
31	5-7	at Detroit	1-0-10	1	1	1-1	1	1	0.68
35	5-13	Milwaukee	1-0-11	⅔	2	1-1	0	0	1.29
39	5-17	New York	1-0-12	2	0	0-0	0	2	1.13
41	5-19	Boston		0	1	1-1	0	0	1.69
42	5-20	Boston	1-0-13	1⅓	1	0-0	0	1	1.56
43	5-21	Boston	1-0-14	1	0	0-0	0	1	1.47
48	5-27	at New York		⅓	1	0-0	0	0	1.45
89	7-13	at Toronto		1	0	0-0	0	0	1.37
94	7-18	at Detroit		1	0	0-0	0	1	1.31
95	7-20	Baltimore	1-0-15	1	0	0-0	0	2	1.25
97	7-22	Baltimore	1-0-16	1	0	0-0	0	2	1.19
98	7-23	Baltimore	1-0-17	1	0	0-0	0	1	1.14
101	7-26	California		1	1	0-0	0	0	1.09
102	7-28	Seattle		1⅔	1	1-1	0	3	1.37
104	7-30	Seattle	1-0-18	1⅓	0	0-0	0	2	1.30
106	8-1	Chicago	1-0-19	1⅔	0	0-0	0	2	1.23
109	8-4	at Seattle	1-0-20	1	0	0-0	0	1	1.19
111	8-6	at Seattle	1-0-21	1	2	0-0	0	2	1.15
113	8-8	at Chicago	1-0-22	⅔	0	0-0	0	0	1.13
115	8-10	at Chicago	1-0-23	1⅔	2	0-0	0	1	1.07
119	8-15	Cleveland	1-0-24	1⅓	2	0-0	1	0	1.03
121	8-17	Cleveland	1-0-25	1	0	0-0	0	0	1.00
126	8-22	at Texas	1-0-26	1	0	0-0	0	2	0.97
127	8-23	at Texas	1-0-27	1	0	0-0	0	1	0.95
131	8-27	at Kansas City		1	1	0-0	0	1	0.92
132	8-28	at New York	1-0-28	2	2	0-0	0	2	0.88
135	9-1	at Milwaukee		2	2	1-1	0	3	1.05
139	9-5	Boston		1	1	0-0	0	1	1.02
140	9-6	Boston	1-0-29	1	2	1-1	0	0	1.20
143	9-10	New York		⅔	0	0-0	0	0	1.18
145	9-13	Milwaukee	2-0-29	2	2	2-2	0	1	1.51
148	9-17	at Boston		1	0	0-0	0	0	1.48
149	9-18	at Cleveland	3-0-29	2	1	1-1	0	3	1.60
151	9-20	at Cleveland	3-0-30	1	0	0-0	0	1	1.57
152	9-21	at Minnesota	3-0-31	1	0	0-0	0	0	1.54
155	9-25	at Minnesota	3-0-32	1⅓	0	0-0	0	0	1.50
157	9-26	Texas	4-0-32	1⅔	1	1-1	0	1	1.62
159	9-28	Texas	4-0-33	1	0	0-0	0	0	1.59
162	10-1	Kansas City		1	0	0-0	0	1	1.56

About the Authors

John Shea has been covering baseball since chronicling the San Diego Padres' path to the World Series in 1984. He continued with the Padres until the 1988 season, when he assumed the unique role of covering both Bay Area teams at home and on the road for the Marin Independent Journal and Gannett News Service. His works are also published regularly in Baseball America and USA Today.

He won an award from the Associated Press Sports Editors Association when his description of Game One of the 1988 World Series was selected first in the country under the category of sports event coverage.

Before becoming a full-time baseball writer, he served as a sports editor for two San Diego County newspapers. He was born in Chicago (30 minutes from Wrigley Field) and raised in the Bay Area (30 minutes from both Candlestick Park and the Oakland Coliseum). He holds journalism and speech communication degrees from San Diego State University.

John Hickey, born in San Francisco and raised on the Peninsula, is a 12-year veteran of Bay Area baseball beats, covering both the San Francisco Giants and Oakland Athletics for The Daily Review in Hayward, California. He has been exclusively the A's beat writer for the Review since 1983.

He received his first newspaper job at the age of 16, continuing to work at various Bay Area newspapers while attending the University of California-Berkeley. Despite spending most spring and summer days at the Oakland Coliseum and Candlestick Park, he managed to earn degrees in history and English.

Through it all, he has never won a Pulitzer Prize and has been consistently overlooked by the Nobel awards committee. He does, however, make a mushroom soup to die for, has a hippo collection that is the talk of Zaire and considers himself, somewhat fancifully, a cutthroat poker player.

About the Artist

Thom Ross, a longtime Giants fan — he once spent two hours talking with Bobby Thomson about Ralph Branca's famous pitch — is represented by the R. Talbott Gallery in Cupertino, California; the Barbara McDonald Gallery in Sacramento; Gallery on the Green in Lexington, Massachusetts; L.A. Arts in Sherman Oaks, California; and Gallery 53 in Cooperstown, New York, where his works are included in the annual baseball art show held in conjunction with the Hall of Fame induction ceremonies.

He's also displaying his work in the traveling baseball art show, Diamonds Are Forever, which will tour until the spring of 1992 in, among other cities, New York, Boston, Buffalo, La Jolla, California, and Winston, North Carolina.

Articles on his work have appeared in Sports Illustrated and Southwest Art magazine. He's been published in books by Random House Books, Ten Speed Books and North Atlantic Books.

Born in San Francisco, he was raised in Sausalito and graduated from Chico State University. He now lives in Palm Springs with his wife, Sarah, and daughter, Rachel.